Procurement Principles and Management

We work with leading authors to develop the
strongest educational materials in management,
bringing cutting-edge thinking and best learning
practice to a global market.

Under a range of well-known imprints, including
Financial Times Prentice Hall, we craft high quality print and
electronic publications which help readers to understand
and apply their content, whether studying or at work.

To find out more about the complete range of our
publishing, please visit us on the World Wide Web at:
www.pearsoned.co.uk

Procurement Principles and Management

Tenth Edition

Peter Baily
David Farmer
Barry Crocker
David Jessop
and
David Jones

 Prentice Hall
FINANCIAL TIMES

An imprint of **Pearson Education**
Harlow, England • London • New York • Boston • San Francisco • Toronto • Sydney • Singapore • Hong Kong
Tokyo • Seoul • Taipei • New Delhi • Cape Town • Madrid • Mexico City • Amsterdam • Munich • Paris • Milan

Pearson Education Limited

Edinburgh Gate
Harlow
Essex CM20 2JE
England

and Associated Companies throughout the world

Visit us on the World Wide Web at:
www.pearsoned.co.uk

First published 1968
Ninth edition 2005
Tenth edition 2008

ISBN: 978-0-273-71379-1

British Library Cataloguing-in-Publication Data
A catalogue record for this book is available from the British Library

Library of Congress Cataloging-in-Publication Data
Procurement principles and management / Peter Baily . . . [et al.]. – 10th ed.
    p. cm
  Rev. ed. of: Purchasing principles and management / Peter Baily . . . [et al.]. 9th ed. Harlow : Financial
Times Prentice Hall, 2002.
  Includes bibliographical references and index.
  ISBN 978-0-273-71379-1 (alk. paper)
 1. Purchasing–Management. 2. Industrial procurement–Management. I. Baily, Peter J. H.
II. Purchasing principles and management.
  HF5437.P7995 2008
  658.7′2–dc22

                         2008002874

10 9 8 7 6 5 4 3 2 1
12 11 10 09 08

Typeset in 9.5/13pt Stone by 35
Printed and bound in Great Britain by Ashford Colour Press, Hampshire

The publisher's policy is to use paper manufactured from sustainable forests.

Contents

Preface   xiii

Acknowledgements   xv

Part 1 PURCHASING OBJECTIVES AND DEVELOPMENT   1

1 Purchasing scope and development   3

Introduction	3
Objectives of this chapter	3
The scope of purchasing	4
The changing role of purchasing and supply	8
Proactive purchasing	12
Procurement positioning	16
Total acquisition cost and total cost of ownership	17
Non-manufacturing organisations	22
The supply chain concept	23
Purchasing development	24
Best practice in strategic supply management	32
Summary	32
References and further reading	33

2 Strategic procurement and supply chain management   35

Introduction	35
Objectives of this chapter	35
Strategic procurement	36
The concept of strategy	38
The mission statement	39
Levels of strategy	40
Category management	41
Strategic management	42
Strategic analysis	42
Strategic development	48
Strategy implementation	50
Objectives for purchasing	51
Strategies and their scope	51
Selecting a strategy	52

Effective supply market strategies   54
Purchasing and supply in different types of organisation   56
Organisation of the activity   58
Purchasing in the organisation structure   63
Purchasing devolution   65
The supply chain   66
Improving the efficiency of the supply chain   71
Types of supply chain   73
Strategic development of purchasing   73
Summary   80
References and further reading   81

3 Public sector procurement   **83**
Introduction   83
Objectives of this chapter   83
Part A   84
Context of public sector procurement   84
Historic background   84
UK National Health Service (NHS)   88
UK Metropolitan Police procurement   89
The Ministry of Defence (MoD)   90
Part B   97
The EU and procurement   97
EU competition procurement cycle for goods and services   97
EU procurement directives   98
The main provisions of the directives in relation to contracts   101
Contract pricing mechanisms   107
New developments   108
Summary   110
References and further reading   110

Part 2 KEY PROCUREMENT ISSUES   **113**

4 Outsourcing   **115**
Introduction   115
Objectives of this chapter   115
Outsourcing   115
Outsourcing methodologies   122
Outsourcing – pitfalls   125
How to avoid pitfalls   126
Summary   129
References and further reading   129

5 Quality management   **131**
Introduction   131

Objectives of this chapter   131
What is quality?   132
Statistical process control   134
Taguchi methods for the 'off-line' control of quality   136
Failure mode and effect analysis   139
Specification   140
Producing a specification   141
Early supplier involvement   143
Concurrent engineering   145
Standardisation   145
Supplier assessment   150
Economics of quality   153
Quality circles   154
The seven wastes   155
Value analysis/value engineering   156
Make-or-buy decisions   158
Summary   160
References and further reading   161

6 Inventory management   162

Introduction   162
Objectives of this chapter   162
Provisioning systems   162
Order quantities and stock control   163
Order quantities for production   171
Materials requirements planning (MRP)   171
Manufacturing resource planning (MRP2)   175
Distribution resource planning (DRP)   176
Enterprise resource planning (ERP)   177
Just-in-time (JIT)   177
Vendor managed inventory (VMI)   180
Late customisation   182
Summary   184
References and further reading   184

7 Lead time and time compression   186

Introduction   186
Objectives of this chapter   186
Time and competitive advantage   186
On-time delivery   187
Expediting   193
Liquidated damages   195
Summary   196
References and further reading   197

8 Sourcing strategies and relationships — 198

Introduction	198
Objectives of this chapter	198
The nature of the sourcing decision	198
Attributes of a good supplier	199
Different types of sourcing	200
Sourcing decisions	200
The sourcing process	203
Source location	203
Sources of information on potential suppliers	204
Supplier evaluation	205
The right relationship	210
Other aspects of sourcing	212
Partnering	219
Tiering of suppliers	221
Summary	224
References and further reading	224

9 Price and total cost of ownership (TCO) — 225

Introduction	225
Objectives of this chapter	225
Factors affecting pricing decisions	225
How buyers obtain prices	233
Auctions	234
Discounts	234
Price analysis and cost analysis	236
Pricing major contracts	239
Investment appraisal	243
Learning curves and experience curves	244
Conclusion	246
Summary	247
References and further reading	247

10 Negotiations — 248

Introduction	248
Objectives of this chapter	248
Negotiation	248
Negotiation skills	251
Preparation	252
The introductory stage	260
Discussion stage	261
Agreement stage	263
The post-negotiation stage	263
Competition and co-operation in negotiation	264

Body language 267
Negotiation strategies 268
Negotiation mix 268
Conclusion 269
Summary 270
References and further reading 271

Part 3 APPLICATIONS 273

11 Project procurement 275
Introduction 275
Objectives of this chapter 275
Introduction to projects 275
Project planning 277
Project control 278
Subcontracting 284
Network analysis 286
Summary 291
References and further reading 293

12 Procurement of commodities 294
Introduction 294
Objectives of this chapter 294
The principal commodities 295
Why do commodity prices fluctuate? 296
Price stabilisation schemes 298
The role of the speculator 299
Hedging with futures contracts 300
Some buying techniques 302
Indifference prices 304
Traded options 307
Glossary 308
Summary 308
References and further reading 309

13 International and global sourcing 310
Introduction 310
Objectives of this chapter 310
Global sourcing and international procurement 310
Why source internationally? 313
Problems with international sourcing 315
Incoterms 2000 320
Arbitration 322
Importing 323

How to change 323
Transport 325
Customs 325
Countertrade 326
Summary 329
References and further reading 330

14 Capital procurement 331

Introduction 331
Objectives of this chapter 331
The acquisition of capital equipment 331
What are capital items? 333
Leasing and hiring of capital equipment 334
Capital requisitions 335
Specification of capital equipment 336
The project approach 338
Lifetime costs 340
Investment appraisal 341
Investment appraisal criteria 342
Conclusion 347
Summary 348
References and further reading 348

15 Retail procurement and efficient consumer response (ECR) 349

Introduction 349
Objectives of this chapter 349
Retailing 350
Retailing research 351
Supply chains in retailing 351
Electronic point of sale (EPOS) 352
Merchandise planning 354
Stock analysis and sales analysis 355
Brands 357
Supplier selection 358
Developments in the retail sector 359
Efficient consumer response 359
Conclusion 362
Summary 362
References and further reading 363

16 Services procurement 364

Introduction 364
Objectives of this chapter 364
What is meant by 'services'? 365

Special factors 365
Procuring public relations (PR) 371
How to buy legal services 373
European Union Public Contracts Directive 374
Management in service provision 375
Summary 377
References and further reading 377

17 Corporate social responsibility 378

Introduction 378
Objectives of this chapter 378
Corporate social responsibility (CSR) 379
Public accountability 381
Business drivers for socially responsible procurement 384
Social Accountability 8000 (SA8000) 386
Summary 389
References and further reading 389

Part 4 E-PROCUREMENT SYSTEMS AND CONTRACT MANAGEMENT 391

18 E-procurement systems 393

Introduction 393
Objectives of this chapter 393
What is e-procurement? 393
The benefits of e-procurement 396
Complex procurement 398
Reverse auctions 398
The current state of e-procurement initiatives 401
The barriers 404
Measuring the benefits of e-procurement 405
What to measure 405
Electronic auctions (e-auctions) 407
The Electronic Commerce (EC Directive) Regulations 2002 415
Conclusions 416
Summary 416
References and further reading 416

19 Contract management and performance measurement 418

Introduction 418
Objectives of this chapter 418
Contract management 419
Examples of performance metrics 421
Pitfalls of traditional performance measurement 422
Performance measurement: effectiveness 423

Measuring procurement performance   425
Procurement as the intelligent customer   430
Benchmarking in procurement and supply   431
Reporting to management   433
Administration instructions   434
Disposing of redundant stock, scrap or waste   435
Summary   437
References and further reading   437

Index   439

Supporting resources

Visit **www.pearsoned.co.uk/baily** to find valuable online resources

For instructors
- An Instructor's Manual that includes learning objectives, a list of the case studies, figures and research boxes within each chapter and teaching notes.
- A set of PowerPoint slides from the book.

For more information please contact your local Pearson Education sales representative or visit **www.pearsoned.co.uk/baily**

Preface

As we said in our preface to the last edition, the original text was written over 30 years ago by Peter Baily and David Farmer and was in its day one of a very small (probably single figure) number of specialised texts relating to the field of purchasing and supply. We commented then that there were many excellent books on the subject, that purchasing and supply chain management had become recognised as a crucial strategic activity by those concerned with organisational management and as a recognised academic discipline with a growing number of university professors dedicated to the subject area. It is reassuring to note that the literature on the subject continues to expand, as does the amount of academic and practitioner interest in it, reflected in the now substantial number of university degrees available at both under- and postgraduate level. As we also said, the visionary and pioneering work that Peter and David took part in, probably to some extent as a gesture of faith, is now fully justified.

The book could not have survived for this length of time without continuous change, and of course the idea behind this new edition is to continue that process. It should be pointed out that the change process is evolutionary, and that we have taken care to balance the newer philosophies emerging in our profession with the proven and established thinking and practice. This book is not of the 'read this and it will change your life' genre; rather it is, we hope, a reflection of sound mainstream practice, accompanied by comment on the way things seem to be going, and by insights into developing ideas and approaches.

The revisions for the tenth edition include the addition of several new chapters, the substantial rewriting of several chapters, and the inclusion of much new material. We are very grateful for the contribution of Alexis Brooks CIMA and David Moore of Cranfield University to the revised Chapter 3 on the subject of buying for government and public services. We also thank Neil Fuller, a chief examiner for the Chartered Institute of Purchasing and Supply, for his help and advice, and for his contribution of material included in our treatment of the 'quality' theme. Readers will notice a feature not found in previous editions: the inclusion of mini case studies embedded in the text, showing the way in which some of the themes of the text are reflected in actual supply management.

The book is, as before, organised into four parts. The first, on the theme of objectives and organisations and covering Chapters 1–3, deals with the scope of purchasing activity and its evolution, relevant strategic issues and considerations, the structure and organisation of procurement, and public sector procurement. The second part, Chapters 4–10, looks at the key purchasing variables of quality, inventory, lead time, sourcing, total cost of ownership and price and negotiation. Part 3, Chapters 11–17, concerns itself with important purchasing activities and applications, dealing with processes associated with buying in particular markets or economic sectors. The final part, covering Chapters 18 and 19, deals with e-procurement systems and contract management and measurement.

We continue to hope that the book will appeal to those in the practitioner and academic communities. We have attempted to strike a balance between the demands of a pure academic text and the sometimes simplistic treatment of ideas encountered in the literature aimed at managers.

We are grateful for the help and support of many colleagues and friends who have contributed in a great variety of ways to the book, and to the copyright holders of some of the included material. Specific acknowledgements are, of course, made at the appropriate points in the text.

Barry Crocker
David Jessop
David Jones

Acknowledgements

We would like to thank the reviewers, Edmund Toal of London Metropolitan University, Gyongyi Kovacs of Hanken, Finland, Dr Herbert Kotzab of Copenhagen Business School, Denmark and Tom Chadwick of Heriot-Watt University for their valuable feedback.

We are grateful to the following for permission to reproduce copyright material:

Figure 1.8 from *Improve Purchase Performance*, Pitman, (Syson, R. 1992) and Figure 2.6 from *Corporate Strategy*, Harlow: Prentice Hall, (Lynch, R. 2002) with permission from Pearson Education Ltd; Figure 2.3 from *Turnaround: Managerial Recipes for Strategic Success*, Associated Business Press, (Grinyer, P. and Spender, J. 1979); Figure 2.9 Reprinted with the permission of The Free Press, a Division of Simon & Schuster Adult Publishing Group, from *Competitive Advantage*: Superior Performance by Michael E. Porter. Copyright © 1985, 1998 by Michael E. Porter. All rights reserved; Figure 2.25 from *CIPS Purchasing and Supply Management Model*; Figure 4.2 from *Outsourcing: A Business Guide to Risk Management Tools and Techniques*, Earlsgate Press, (Lonsdale, C. and Cox, A., 1998); Figure 8.3 with permission from PSL; Figure 17.1 from *Business and Society*, 3rd Edition, (Carroll, A.B., 1996); 'The pitch' (p. 371) with permission from the Incorporated Society of British Advertisers.

In some instances we have been unable to trace the owners of copyright material, and we would appreciate any information that would enable us to do so.

Part 1

Purchasing objectives and development

Chapter 1   Purchasing scope and development

Chapter 2   Strategic procurement and supply chain management

Chapter 3   Public sector procurement

1

Purchasing scope and development

Introduction

All organisations need inputs of goods and services from external suppliers or providers. In this chapter we examine the developing role of the purchasing and supply function in managing these inputs, and comment upon the ways in which the activity can contribute to the efficiency and effectiveness of the organisation, offering mini-case studies demonstrating how companies are developing their purchasing/procurement contribution. We will identify ways of measuring the stage of development reached by an organisation and demonstrate how the development stage reached can affect performance of the purchasing activity.

Objectives of this chapter

- To discuss the scope of purchasing
- To identify the purchasing cycle concept
- To discuss purchasing and supply as a service activity
- To discuss the changing role of purchasing and supply
- To explain how purchasing might develop from an independent function to an integrated activity
- To identify the internal and external influences which have affected the evolution of purchasing
- To examine the 'total acquisition cost' concept
- To consider the adoption of relationships based on mutual benefits as an alternative to the traditional transactional, adversarial approach
- To highlight the evolution of concepts relating to purchasing development
- To identify key practices encountered in developed strategic purchasing
- To provide mini-case studies demonstrating how companies are developing their purchasing functions

The scope of purchasing

A well-known statement of the objectives of purchasing is: to acquire the right quality of material, at the right time, in the right quantity, from the right source, at the right price. This statement is criticised by some as being rather superficial and simplistic. This is undoubtedly valid comment, though the definition does provide a practical starting point for discussion. For present purposes, the following broad statement of objectives is suggested:

- To supply the organisation with a flow of materials and services to meet its needs.
- To ensure continuity of supply by maintaining effective relationships with existing sources and by developing other sources of supply either as alternatives or to meet emerging or planned needs.
- To buy efficiently and wisely, obtaining by ethical means the best value for every pound spent.
- To maintain sound co-operative relationships with other departments, providing information and advice as necessary to ensure the effective operation of the organisation as a whole.
- To develop staff, policies, procedures and organisation to ensure the achievement of these objectives.

Mini case study – Hertz

Buyers have been urged to remember their business's overall strategy when trying to transform their procurement.

If procurement cannot align itself with what the organisation wants to achieve, it will not get the support for what it wants.

Case study – Nokia

Nokia re-examines its purchasing structure every year as part of its strategic review. In spring 2003, it dismantled the company's global category buying structure for indirect spend. The worldwide approach had been put in place for direct spend, which has global markets. But as the market for indirect spend varies from region to region, a local group was set up for each of Nokia's four global groups in London, Finland, Singapore and the US.

Research

Purchasing departments continue to operate in 'silo', with over half failing to fully integrate into their organisation.

That is one of the findings of a research study by Bristol Business School, commissioned by Oracle, CIPS and the Office of Government Commerce.

While 93 per cent of businesses had a formal purchasing department, just under half had buyers with specialist commodity experience. This was significant because departments with this experience were more likely to have greater market knowledge, better supplier relationships and achieve greater savings than generalist buyers. It was also an indication of investment in professional development.

Only 18 per cent of public sector respondents had a seat on the board, compared to 37 per cent of those in the private sector.

In addition, we might add some more specific objectives such as:

- To select the best suppliers in the market.
- To help generate the effective development of new products.
- To protect the company's cost structure.
- To maintain the correct quality/value balance.
- To monitor supply market trends.
- To negotiate effectively in order to work with suppliers who will seek mutual benefit through economically superior performance.
- To adopt environmentally responsible supply management.

Case study – Ford

Purchasing and supply management for many is now directly linked into their companies' business strategies and they recognise that it has a real impact on competitive advantage.

Ford Motor Company believes that procurement controls the ultimate profitability of the company.

Another viewpoint is summarised by Scheuing (1998) as follows:

Twenty-first century perspectives for procurement

1. Function will be sourcing* not purchasing	10. Long-term contracts to establish relationships	19. Benchmarking of best practice
2. A vision of competitiveness	11. Emphasise continuous improvements	20. Internal customer focus
3. Driven by customer requirement	12. Mutual cost management	21. Service level agreements established
4. Emphasising value creation	13. Early involvement in new product developments	22. Purchasing leadership/Empowered teams
5. Suppliers seen as external sources of ideas/ technologies/time compression	14. Skilled professionals in purchasing	23. Purchasing professionals involved in innovation
6. Bottom line focus not price	15. Outsourcing non-core activities	24. Cross-functional teams involving internal stakeholders to build and lead supplier relationships
7. Enhance competitiveness by using supplier capabilities	16. State of art IT systems	25. Sourcing a major contributor to organisational performance
8. Global sourcing	17. Purchasing involved in all non-direct spend	
9. Strategic alliances with key partners	18. Dramatic cycle time reduction	

(*Source*: After Scheuing, 1998)
Note: * Actually purchasing has become procurement in many world-class organisations.

In summary, firms need access to competitive and productive supply markets if they are to be in business at all. The trend is from tactical to strategic procurement, establishing collaborative relationships with external resources, and securing major business advantage from procurement.

■ The purchasing cycle

The main stages in the purchasing process may be summarised as follows:

- Recognition of need
- Specification
- Make-or-buy decision
- Source identification
- Source selection
- Contracting

- Contract management
- Receipt, possibly inspection
- Payment
- Fulfilment of need

The idea of the purchasing cycle is often employed to indicate the main activities in which purchasing might be involved. The activities included in the cycle do not cover all of those that a purchasing staff might be involved with; there are many activities such as, for example, negotiation, vendor rating and source development that are not specifically included. It will be noticed that, historically, the early and late stages in the cycle have not necessarily involved specialist purchasing staff, the core purchasing contribution to the cycle being the items included in the central part of the list. However, this has changed with early buyer involvement in design/specification work and greater involvement in ongoing contract management.

A limitation of the cycle concept is that it does not recognise the strategic contribution made by modern purchasing. We shall discuss this contribution within this chapter and more thoroughly in Chapter 2.

■ Is purchasing a service activity?

The thinking prevalent at the time of the first edition of this book was that purchasing was a service function, often subordinated to production or engineering in the manufacturing sector, or to finance in the service or public sectors. The idea was that specialist supplies staff could do the bidding of the more strategic elements of the organisation, and employ their skills at a secondary 'support' level. Thinking moved on, and there came a more general realisation that purchasing might contribute more effectively at a strategic as well as at an operational level. The idea that purchasing and supply was merely a support activity has been somewhat discredited, with a developing recognition that purchasing involvement in issues such as the 'make or buy' decision or strategic commercial relationship gave the function a central and strategic role in the competitive organisation.

Syson has stated that purchasing has been transformed from a service function whose aims were expressed in the price, quality and delivery equation to one which makes a contribution to sustainable competitive advantage by reducing the cost of ownership, cycle time reduction and improving time to market.

Simply to improve service levels or to cut costs is no longer enough. Purchasing must focus on its relationship to end-market performance. In many cases purchasing has moved through *evolution* of its role to *devolution* of much of the more straightforward buying activity, whilst retaining and developing its strategic contribution.

Research in 2006 (The 2006 Global Spend Agenda – The Ariba Study)

Three hundred and twenty-five purchasing heads from large organisations in Europe and the US revealed that there is an emergence of two groups of companies; one takes a rather conservative, traditional 'bookkeeper' approach while others are more bullish in their enthusiasm for innovation and aggressive cost reduction targets.

The bookkeepers are lagging because they do not have the strategic drive to know where they are going or how to get there. It concludes therefore that purchasing has to be innovative in structure and strategy so it can really grapple with complex spend categories, off-contract spend and compliance issues such as: almost two-thirds (59%) of suppliers working outside negotiated contracts and rogue spending occurring in 77% of businesses in Europe and 81% in the US. The study also found that procurement departments are still trying to reduce their supply base and still struggle with more complex spend areas such as services.

The changing role of purchasing and supply

As we have indicated, purchasing is seen by many of today's successful organisations as an activity of considerable strategic importance. The fact that the strategic role and contribution of purchasing and supply is well recognised in many leading commercial concerns has meant that the strategic purchasing decisions may be taken by purchasing involvement at board level, rather than by a departmental manager.

Mini case study – Nokia

The answer to whether procurement is strategic is yes, if one considers strategic contribution to an organisation to be any activity that drives market penetration, revenue growth, profit maximisation and shareholder value. For any function, including procurement, to be considered strategic then it must align itself directly with these organisational priorities.

The case for direct procurement as a strategic contributor to an organisation's agenda is well proven in many Fortune 500 organisations, like IBM and Ford, in which there are numerous examples of supply markets being managed to drive margin, market position and value.

There have been a number of well-publicised examples such as GlaxoSmithKline where the contribution of procurement has been an important part of post-merger cost efficiency improvement.

Nokia has been recognised as having designed and used all areas of its supply chain for competitive advantage.

Both financial and value benefits can be delivered from strategic procurement.

Their procurement professionals know that the segmentation of categories and supplier relationships are at the heart of delivering both strategic and tactical value to an organisation.

If this happens, the organisation can focus on managing its supply base for speed to market, cost advantage, innovation and value. This will always be of interest in the boardroom and can only be considered strategic.

There are a number of reasons for this shift in importance and recognition, and the main ones can be summarised as follows:

■ External organisational factors

Leading-edge concepts

Organisations employing leading-edge approaches to the management of materials are putting into practice integrative ideas, which are, at least in part, based on a strategic and integrated role for purchasing.

Approaches and concepts which might be considered under this heading are:

- best practice benchmarking;
- total quality management;
- just-in-time philosophies and lean production;
- supply chain concepts;
- tiering and empowerment of suppliers;
- relationship management;
- customer focus.

The expression 'world-class concepts' is sometimes employed to describe these, and in order to achieve such concepts, purchasing needs to be well developed and proactive.

Fewer but larger suppliers

Concentration in the supply market has had a profound effect in recent years. For example, the production of pharmaceutical products is almost entirely in the hands of a small number of large organisations; and only a handful of large European chemical companies remain. This process of concentration through amalgamations, takeovers and the failure of the smaller and less viable business units continues. It poses obvious problems for purchasing and supply, and ensures a higher profile and more strategic role for the function.

Increasing environmental awareness

The recognition has dawned, perhaps belatedly, that it is good business sense to be 'green', and to be seen to be responsible in this respect. Recycling, the specification of renewable raw materials, a greater concern with the effects of waste and by-products, wider concern for the use of returnable packaging, and many other related concerns, all have implications for purchasing and are affecting perceptions of the function. This area is examined in more detail in Chapter 17.

Competitor activity

When attempting to develop new ideas pressure is often placed on an organisation to look at what levels of performance competitors and other organisations are achieving. The term 'benchmarking' is often given to this process, but benchmarking is not simply copying good ideas. Demonstration of the real benefits that a developed supply function confers on the rest of an organisation has been a stimulant for other companies to improve that function, and this in turn has raised the profile of purchasing.

Customer demands

The customer is now seen by many as being all important. Philip Kotler, the marketing guru, talks about delighting the customer, i.e. exceeding customer expectations. Satisfying is silent while delighting is noisy. It is no longer acceptable to give second-best service if you want to remain profitable and retain market share. Organisations are more 'customer driven', and these driving forces impact upon purchasing.

Advancing technology

Technology and associated complexity has meant that most businesses now specialise in a narrower range of activities and are compelled to buy a greater proportion of their requirements from those who have the specialist expertise, patents, intellectual property or design rights associated with complex or advanced technology.

Finite resources

Some natural resources have, of course, always been finite. However, increasing recognition that their use and consumption needs to be planned has had a profound effect on the role of purchasing in contributing to the planned and responsible use of these resources, whether driven by simple economic forces or a growing sense of social responsibility. Corporate social responsibility is considered in detail in Chapter 17.

The Chartered Institute of Purchasing and Supply (CIPS) and the contribution of purchasing

In the early 1990s the Institute of Purchasing and Supply was granted a Royal Charter. This was a landmark in the development of the purchasing and supply function, and it is now more widely regarded as a truly professional activity. The Institute has spent considerable time and effort at a national level demonstrating the importance and contribution of effective purchasing in both the public and private sectors. Its examination scheme and courses have done much to enhance the status of the purchasing function, and the CIPS is now represented on many government committees where purchasing issues are discussed.

This heightened awareness of the purchasing and supply function is certainly a factor in improving the general development of the activity across the UK. This growth and development has also taken place in the professional bodies representing purchasing and supply professionals in many other countries.

Increasing proportion of revenue spent externally

As outlined in Table 1.1, organisations are spending a greater proportion of their income externally and less on internal costs such as wages and overheads. With the increased share of the expenditure comes an increasing responsibility for purchasing.

**Table 1.1
Some reasons for the increased importance and recognition of purchasing**

TOTAL ORGANISATIONAL EXPENDITURE	
Labour and overheads	**Externally provided resources**
Decreasing because of:	*Increasing because of:*
• automation	• greater specialisation on part of buying organisations
• more efficient work	• 'outsourcing' policies
• competitiveness depending on access to 'best practice'	• focus on core competencies
	• development of specialised contractors
	• easier access to world supply market
	• complex technology restricting breadth of 'make' capabilities
	• flexibility depending on external rather than dedicated 'owned' assets
	• closer co-ordination with key suppliers

Mini case study – IBM

In order to obtain greater leverage from its purchasing expenditure, IBM has since the late 1990s sourced a major proportion of its high value items on a global basis, achieving considerable cost savings. In order to achieve this it was necessary to employ integrated computer systems, and common coding systems were developed across all IBM operating locations. Global buyers now negotiate contracts that are used by the total organisation.

Innovation

The pace of change has quickened over the years. Organisations must be able to develop new practices and products quickly and effectively. This in turn requires significant improvements in the internal interface between purchasing on the one hand and production, marketing, finance etc. on the other, as well as with external suppliers and customers. As product life cycles get shorter, reaction times are being compressed. Purchasing must be prepared to help initiate new ideas and developments. A good deal of attention is being paid today to 'time to market' initiatives. New products cannot be developed and marketed rapidly without a proactive purchasing function.

Case study – BOC Group

BOC Group expects supply management to help the entire organisation create competitive advantage. It can do this in many ways, from identifying and developing sources of supply in emerging markets through to advising on mergers and acquisitions and facilitating new product design.

It needs to have a clear understanding of the business strategy and to work closely with other parts of the company in achieving their objectives.

E-commerce

The pace of technological progress means that organisations must have plans in place to handle development, and purchasing needs to be actively involved. An example may be found in the development of e-commerce. It is imperative that purchasing has an appropriate supplier base and is involved with suppliers who can jointly develop and use e-procurement approaches to business. E-procurement is discussed in detail in Chapter 18.

■ Internal organisational factors

Although there is considerable pressure from outside to develop the purchasing function, it is often internal influences that initiate the changes. These internal influences include the following factors.

Figure 1.1
The increasing importance of purchasing and supply in the manufacturing sector

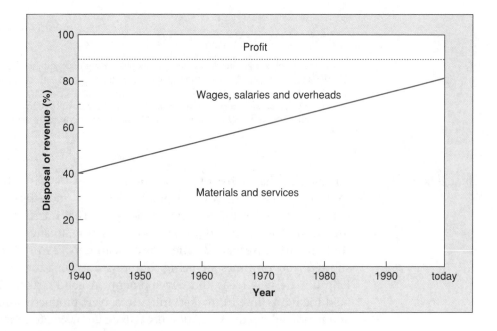

The level and percentage of purchased goods and services

Normally, as the external expenditure increases as a proportion of the total, greater attention is paid to the input activities. For example, in large automotive, electronic and retail organisations percentages of bought-out material and services expenditure in relation to sales income run at between 60 and 90 per cent. Clearly this expenditure is of crucial importance and needs close attention at policy level. It is interesting to note that this proportion has been increasing steadily for many years (see Figure 1.1).

Structural changes

Moves towards materials management, logistics and supply chain concepts have in turn helped to develop the purchasing and supply function. In almost all cases the amount of attention paid to purchasing and supply has risen.

Performance measurement

There has been more emphasis in recent years on measurement. Within organisations that measure the contribution of the purchasing and supply function, its status is usually affected in a positive way. Senior management have become aware of its contribution to cost reduction and its strategic capabilities, and in consequence are far more likely to promote its development. This topic is covered in full in Chapter 19.

Proactive purchasing

As the level of attention paid to purchasing and supply increases, the work tends to become more strategic in emphasis, concentrating more upon such activities as negotiating longer-term relationships, supplier development, and total cost reduction, rather than ordering and replenishing routines.

If we examine the responsibilities of buyers in organisations with a well-developed function – such as IBM, Nissan, Ford, Baxi, Hewlett Packard and others – we find that they spend only a small proportion of their time on administrative and clerical activities. Most of their activity concentrates on the establishment and development of appropriate relationships with suppliers. The emphasis in such organisations has evolved beyond simply reacting to the needs of users as and when they arise, to a forward-looking proactive approach that more fully reflects the contribution that the management of inputs can make.

Mini case study – Unisys

Since 1999 Unisys has streamlined its procurement. Like many organisations, procurement was disorganised and fragmented before the reorganisation began. The people doing the procurement were scattered throughout the organisation and were involved mainly in low-level administrative tasks.

Contracts with suppliers and partners were being agreed by people with no real knowledge of best practice procurement.

There was no company-wide system to tell employees what they were buying and how much they were spending. They were not buying as a multinational company, but as groups.

Experienced procurement professionals were drafted in from big name companies such as Fujitsu, Centrica, NatWest, BAE systems and Deutsche Telekom.

Latest figures show the dramatic effect it had. In 1999 there were three procurement teams, one for each business unit at Unisys, now there is just one. There were 78 people involved in procurement in five countries throughout the UK and Europe. That has gone down to 54 people in 14 countries. Most dramatic is the reduction in the supply base from 24,000 to below 5,500 with spending through the top 400 suppliers going up from 32 per cent to 83 per cent.

Now, out of the staff of 54 in the procurement department, about three-quarters are involved in high-level strategic activities.

Table 1.2 compares and contrasts reactive with proactive purchasing.

**Table 1.2
Changing purchasing roles: reactive and proactive buying**

Reactive buying	Proactive buying
Purchasing is a cost centre	Purchasing can add value
Purchasing receives specifications	Purchasing (and suppliers) contribute to specification
Purchasing rejects defective material	Purchasing avoids defective supplies
Purchasing reports to finance or production	Purchasing is a main management function
Buyers respond to market conditions	Purchasing contributes to making markets
Problems are supplier's responsibility	Problems are a shared responsibility
Price is key variable	Total cost and value are key variables
Emphasis on today	Emphasis strategic
Systems independent of suppliers	Systems may be integrated with suppliers' systems
Users or designers specify	Buyers and suppliers contribute to specification
Negotiations win/lose	Negotiations win–win (or better)
Plenty of suppliers = security	Plenty of suppliers = lost opportunities
Plenty of stock = security	Plenty of stock = waste
Information is power	Information is valuable if shared

■ The changing nature of relationships

A simplistic view of purchasing activity is that it is merely buying; that in essence it consists of finding a supplier who is willing to exchange the goods or services required for an agreed sum of money. This perception of purchasing has become known as the 'transactional' view, and is based on the idea that purchasing is concerned with simple exchanges, with buyer and seller interacting with each other on an arm's-length basis. The underlying interest of the buyer in this rather simple scenario is to acquire as much resource as possible for as little money as possible.

Case study – Feedwater

Feedwater believes purchasing should be as effective in promoting business growth as it is in controlling costs. By working cleverly with suppliers through strategic alliances – by sharing information, or getting goods on a just-in-time basis – they can deliver better value for money to clients and enhance profitability.

It is true to say that this transactional view is not obsolete; it is still an appropriate way of looking at the process whereby low-cost items, for which there are plenty of competing suppliers, might be purchased. However, it is no longer thought to be a suitable basis for most organisational purchasing expenditure.

Mini case study – BMW

In 1994 purchasing was essentially an administrative function, and morale in the department was low. This approach missed significant strategic potential to add value to a company through the purchasing function by driving innovations and superior long-term cost performance.

Transforming purchasing into such a strategic function requires a long-term perspective aimed at building 'networks of competence' – people who can cross boundaries and analyse the true costs of product and process proposals. It requires integrating purchasing into the beginning of a design or project rather than relegating it to the end of the process chain, where its role is viewed as simply buying the goods and services other departments need.

It requires a fundamentally different approach to recruiting and training employees, as well as reorientating the entire company to a holistic view of purchasing that looks across many functions and entire supply chains.

Beyond its contributions to product quality and business performance, a systematically orientated purchasing department can foster knowledge sharing and innovation both company-wide and across complex supply chains, a capability that is becoming a highly valuable strategic asset as manufacturers are increasingly held accountable for social and environmental impacts.

In this way, over the past 10 years, BMW's purchasing department has evolved into a strategic partner that influences numerous product and process design choices, realising significant savings for, and having a strategic impact on, all areas of the company, from services to production, from IT to development and from production facilities to construction.

The transformation was predicated on setting and meeting a number of mutually reinforcing goals:

- To change purchasing from an administrative function to one that influences demand;
- To concentrate on building and sharing deep knowledge;
- To work as a fair and competent partner with all internal and external business contacts;
- To commit to improvement in all areas and to becoming a benchmark for others;
- To develop a team approach that relies on shared values.

At BMW today purchasing associates' influence is wide-ranging. They play a role in key design and process purchasing choices that can have a significant overall financial impact. At the early concept stage of product development they have valuable input, suggesting how certain design features will affect the technical equipment at the factory or the level of investment that will be required to execute the design, which has saved 30 per cent on this significant cost company-wide.

They created an online system that allows people throughout the organisation to order their own supplies from the standard created. With pre-selected suppliers and negotiated contracts, it enables managers to determine their needs and to manage their ordering and procurement within clear criteria.

Much more attention has been paid in recent years to the development of 'mutual' supplier–buyer relationships, where the benefits of doing business together arise from ideas of *sharing* as well as *exchanging*. In a mutual relationship the emphasis is on building a satisfactory outcome together with, for example, such things as technology. Confidence and support are invested by both sides with the intention of adding value, a process not possible with a simple transaction. The organisations concerned seek to come closer together and to identify overlapping interests. These ideas will be referred to later in the text, but it is important at this stage to be aware of the developing nature of purchasing and supply work, and the complexity which accompanies this development.

Figures 1.2 and 1.3 enable a comparison between the transactional and the mutual relationship. The list of shared benefits is by way of example only and will vary between relationships.

Figure 1.2
The 'transactional' relationship

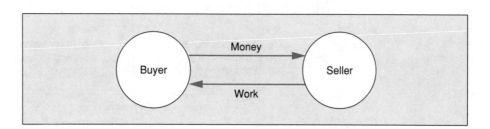

Figure 1.3
The 'mutual'
relationship

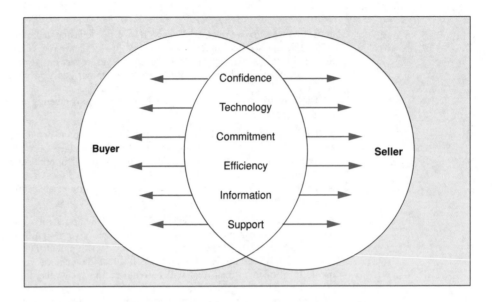

Procurement positioning

Of course, it is not the case that any organisation will wish to develop mutual or partnership relationships with all of its suppliers. Pareto's principle applies: it will generally be found that 80 per cent of expenditure will be with 20 per cent of suppliers; and it is likely to be the suppliers with whom large sums of money are spent that will be the ones with whom closer relationships are sought. A useful tool in determining those suppliers with whom close relationships might best be sought is the 'Procurement Positioning' tool based on the work of Kraljic (1983), illustrated by Figure 1.4. The vertical axis, labelled

Figure 1.4
The 'Procurement
Positioning' tool

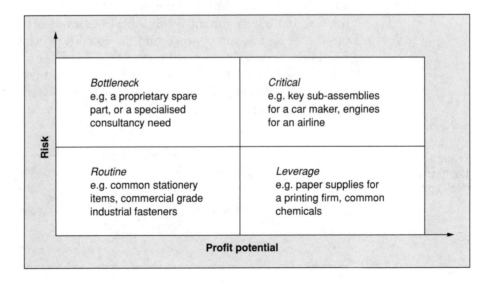

'Risk', is concerned with the degree of difficulty associated with sourcing a product or service, or the vulnerability of the client organisation to a failure of the supplier to provide the product or service on time, or to the failure 'in service' of a supply. The horizontal axis, 'Profit potential', is used to indicate the extent of the potential of the supply to contribute to the profitability (or efficiency) of the buying concern. This profit potential might be realised by achieving lower costs, either by paying a lower price for a good or service or by introducing more efficient buying methods.

It will readily be seen that there is no single best approach to relationships: a transactional approach might well be seen as appropriate for routine purchases, whereas a strategic approach will be of obvious benefit to a mutual relationship in the critical sector. A buyer is likely to be uncomfortable with suppliers of services or goods in the leverage sector, and may well wish to move the requirement to the routine sector – perhaps by developing additional suppliers – or to the critical sector, by attempting in some way to increase the seller's dependence. Where supplies and suppliers are in the leverage category, buyers are likely to feel quite comfortable, though of course we must expect that vendors will be keen to see their products or services repositioned as critical.

Case study – E.ON UK

E.ON is training the department's staff beyond traditional procurement skills, so that they see themselves as internal consultants. As they have developed, there is a greater focus on risk management.

The perception of purchasing used to be that it was about cutting costs and their targets centred around this. Now they focus on analysing opportunities and aligning them to the business strategy, sourcing appropriately and going through contracting and negotiation. The Board now is more concerned about spreading procurement's value around the organisation.

Total acquisition cost and total cost of ownership

Buying price is probably the factor most often associated with procurement responsibilities. The procurement function has an important role in judging the correct price for any purchase and this aspect of the task is seen at its most dramatic in the commodity markets. Since prices are affected by costs, at least in the long run, an important function of procurement is to work with colleagues and suppliers to eradicate unnecessary costs. These could result from over-specification; purchasing a non-standard item when a standard alternative is acceptable; unnecessary packaging; and, where significant transport costs are involved, the design of the product in terms of transportation utility.

Figure 1.5
The price/cost iceberg

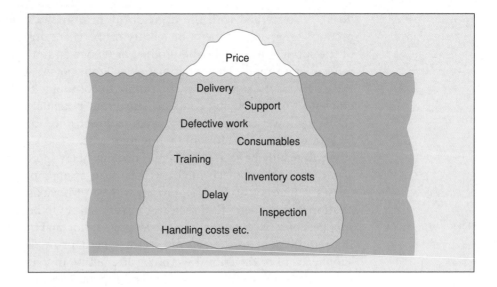

The total acquisition cost is more than simply price, and has a bearing on developing the wider role of purchasing into total cost management. It is the total you actually pay for goods and services, including such things as tooling, duty, inventory-carrying costs, inspection, remedy or rectification and so on. It is an obvious fact, yet a commonly ignored one, that a low price may lead to a high total acquisition cost. Of course, once materials or goods have been acquired, they may attract further costs while in use. With this in mind, some organisations prefer the expression 'Total Cost of Ownership' when referring to capital goods or materials that will be retained for some time.

Price is the most visible of the various costs, which arise from making most acquisitions, and in many cases it will be the biggest component of cost too. The 'price/cost iceberg' shown in Figure 1.5 helps us to remember the hidden costs, and to account for them in our business decision making.

The importance of purchasing and supply as a key function in the management of a business can be emphasised by considering the total acquisition cost of materials and services, and this is of course influenced by the *specification* being purchased. In turn, this may involve marketing and a desire to have an attractive product to sell. It will concern production and the need to minimise disruptions in production and can involve resulting scrap or waste and even transportation costs. As many value analysis studies have shown, the cost-saving potential in this area is considerable and the procurement function has a vital part to play in the search for the optimum specification. One problem in corporate management is that there tend to be dominant functions in particular companies; in one it will be marketing, in another finance or production. This results in that function being given attention at the expense of the overall operation. We shall return to the theme of price and total cost of ownership later in the book.

■ Specification

The procurement function has a part in working towards the optimum specification. This implies not only an attractive product for marketing to sell or for production to manufacture, but one which includes services, materials or components which are economic to purchase, and this in turn presupposes that they are attractive for the supplier to produce or provide. All this necessitates some degree of compromise between the parties involved. A weak procurement function, which simply purchases what, for example, production asks for, is missing the opportunity of contributing in this way. Clearly, it is not for procurement to usurp the design function or any other, but it should inform the various parties of the constraints and opportunities relating to the specifications and to delivery reliability.

Case study – Siemens

Siemens believes that with supplier partnerships, to take cost out of a supply chain is only one element of the partnership approach. Innovation, in the sense of developing new products and services and doing so quicker or better than competitors, is what differentiates successful companies from the rest.

The reason is that, these days, much of the innovation is likely to come from the supply base.

■ Quantity and timing

Total material cost is also affected by *inventory levels*, and procurement has an important role with respect to stocks of raw materials and bought-in parts, especially in times of rapid inflation. It is for procurement to judge supply market conditions with a view to assuring the necessary levels of materials required to meet production and marketing needs. Price movements, availability, possible shortages or surpluses, physical and financial limitations all need to be considered.

Another important point affecting material costs is *timing*. One aspect of this relates to assurance that deliveries of necessary materials will be made to meet activity schedules. Since inventory can be looked upon as insurance against supply failure, in theory perfect scheduling of deliveries would eliminate stocks. Whilst this is rarely possible in practice, purchasing can certainly work with suppliers towards this end. This will involve better information flow on manufacturing schedules and fewer changes to those schedules; and, if such changes are inevitable, ensure that they are announced as soon as possible. Procurement has an important role, too, in informing other functions of the costs related to such changes and working with them to reduce the number.

This includes making every effort to manage both internal and external environments in order to obviate unnecessary costs. For example, one company in the timber industry worked with its main suppliers to arrange shipments in 10 one-monthly lots instead of the traditional four- to eight-month period. Coupled with packages of uniform length, this resulted in significant reductions in average inventory and handling costs.

Market considerations

Other procurement responsibilities include monitoring market prices, not only of the products or materials purchased, but also of significant raw materials used in their manufacture; monitoring suppliers' prices, particularly where the item being purchased is 'special' to the buying company; and providing information on pending price changes as early as possible to facilitate pertinent action by colleagues. Procurement should contribute to the strategic management of the business. It should participate in corporate planning and policy making on, for example, key make-or-buy decisions, long-term economic availability of raw materials, price changes, and the development of alternative strategies.

Supply continuity

Another aspect of total acquisition cost is the negative effect of supply failure on company sales. Material economics and assurance of supply are critical in a capital-intensive assembly industry dealing with oligopolistic suppliers as supply failure may adversely affect corporate objectives. Apart from the direct impact on costs, competitors may gain larger sales if supply failure affects production.

Nissan has established itself in the north-east of the UK and part of its strategy has been to develop UK suppliers to meet its exacting needs. What has been significant in this exercise is not the shortage of components from local markets but the adherence of existing suppliers to Nissan specification and delivery schedule demands.

Nissan produces over 3 million cars annually from manufacturing plants in 21 countries, and works with suppliers to continually improve their performance using 'Kaizen' techniques. *Kaizen* translates from Japanese as 'constant improvement' and is pursued through slow, steady change. The *Kaizen* process encourages logical systematic thinking; it starts by recognising that things are never perfect and by identifying the areas where something can be done to improve matters. The role of the buyer in Nissan UK has changed dramatically since the formation of the company, from 'orderer' to 'consultant', spending time on strategic considerations.

Product development

Clearly purchasing has an important role with regard to *product development*. Contemporary industry structure includes considerable specialisation and, with faster developing technology in many industry sectors, product life has shortened as the pace of change has increased. It follows that where product life is shorter the importance of getting the product right first time and on time increases. It is true, too, that there is a vital role for purchasing to play in keeping colleagues informed of supply market developments. With increasing specialisation it is reasonable to argue that more products are developed from innovations in the supply market than within the company itself. The earlier that intelligence is available, and the closer the relationship with the suppliers, the more likely it is that the company can take advantage of the benefit. While the seller has an important part to play in informing the potential user of developments, the buyer too has a key role in searching for innovations. Indeed the buyer might even promote such developments, both in conventional markets and even more so in non-traditional markets.

In multinational companies another procurement task that can benefit the company as a whole is standardisation of components, materials or services between national units. For example, the car manufacturers, faced with national monopolies in certain key components, developed alternative 'foreign' sources. Then interchangeability of components within Europe affected vehicle design and thus marketing and manufacturing management. It appears that the emergence of the 'European car' may be as much the result of procurement considerations as of production and marketing strategy.

Table 1.3 shows a hypothetical example of a component which might be bought by IBM in the United Kingdom. The Japanese supplier is the cheapest, but the total acquisition cost would be much lower if the item were

Table 1.3
Comparative total acquisition costs of a commodity purchased by IBM

Procurement overview			
Commodity: Monitor	Description: Monochrome monitor		
Contract period: 52 weeks	Contract volume: 134 K		
Quote ref.: Example	Part no.: 1111111		
	Japan MATSUSUKI	Germany EUROMONITOR	Scotland VISIONTUBES
Ex-factory cost	10.000	11.000	11.500
Procurement m/power	0.070	0.154	0.057
Function manpower	0.050	0.165	0.034
Inventory finance	0.173	0.036	0.028
Capital tooling	0.037	0.060	0.022
Airfreight penalty	2.65	N/A	N/A
Freight – vendor	1.500	0.500	0.300
Freight – IBM estimate	0.300	0.120	0.100
Duty	0.490	N/A	N/A
IPO charge	0.066	N/A	N/A
Cancellation	1.400	0.440	0.230
Total uplift	5.236	0.974	0.472
Total cost	15.236	11.974	11.972
IBM contract spend	**20,416,763**	**16,046,453**	**16,043,581**

Note: The figures are hypothetical and the suppliers fictitious.

purchased from the supplier in Scotland. IBM defines total acquisition cost as: 'All costs, including the purchase price, related to the process of bringing a supplier's product and/or service to the point of consumption.'

Non-manufacturing organisations

There are two headings under which other forms of purchasing may be classified: purchasing for consumption and purchasing for resale. The latter grouping is dealt with in Chapter 15.

The first heading or classification mentioned above, purchasing for consumption, covers a wide variety of activities: the UK Procurement Executive, the National Health Service supply organisation, local authority supply organisations and the service sector such as banking are but some examples. Government organisations are increasingly being required to work with less money, which has meant that strenuous efforts have been made to reduce costs through more effective purchasing by such public organisations as the Prison Service, the Fire Service and the education sector. The task of the responsible executives in these services is to meet the demands that their service is intended to satisfy, within the constraints of lower budgets. Further discussion on these topics is contained in Chapter 3. In addition, purchasing specialists in organisations such as the railways, airlines, telecommunications and electricity help to maintain the service their industry provides. Given the size of these industries, vast sums are spent on capital projects, maintenance and in some cases goods for resale. Clearly it is important to the viability of each of these industries that the procurement function is performed effectively as part of an efficient business system.

Case study – Barclays Bank

At Barclays, purchasing has had to respond fast to changes in overall strategy.

Market managers now handle sourcing strategy and are responsible for making sourcing proactive by looking for developments such as new technologies and fresh suppliers. This leaves buyers to focus on deal making and contract management.

The four areas of sourcing – Barclays Global Investors, Barclaycard, Barclays Capital and the Barclays retail and corporate banking division – were combined into a single global organisation with £4.5 billion combined spend.

The orientation of the more highly developed purchasing role is now very clearly strategic, with the routine aspects of the activity either automated or undertaken by clerical staff. The strategic aspect is examined later. By way of example, Figure 1.6 shows some of the goods and services necessary to operate a passenger aircraft.

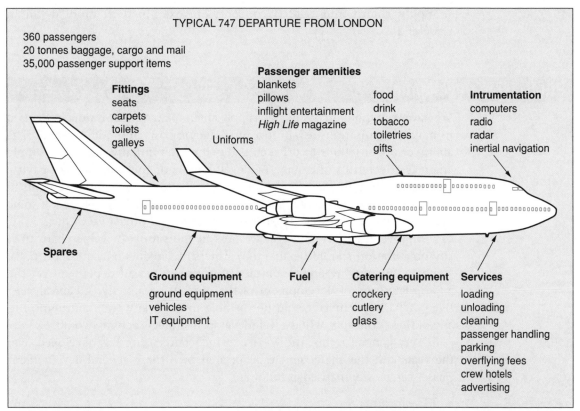

Figure 1.6 Example of the scope of a procurement function: some goods and services necessary to operate a passenger aircraft

(*Source*: Courtesy British Airways)

The supply chain concept

The perception that purchasing is no longer a routine, administrative 'ordering' activity is now widely, if not universally, held. The expression 'supply chain' has come into prominence, although there is competing terminology such as the expression 'value stream' preferred by the promoters of 'lean manufacturing'. 'Pipeline management' is another expression with a similar meaning, and there are advocates of the term 'networks'. All of these terms reflect the fact that purchasing is no longer just about ordering or buying, but has a strategic role, and is concerned with the flow of materials from raw state to use and disposal.

Mini case study – Bulwell Precision Engineers

Bulwell Precision Engineers confirms the importance of purchasing's strategic role. As a supplier of aero engines and airframes, Bulwell has found that big customers such as Rolls-Royce and Airbus are very interested in how it manages its own supply chain. The value of the service provided for them is crucial. That partly depends on the supply base, so they see purchasing and supply chain management as a selling point and a key to future growth.

Supply chains and related concepts are examined in more detail in Chapter 2.

Purchasing development

We have seen that purchasing and supply chain management is now recognised in major organisations as an area for reducing costs and adding value. The ability of organisations to drive costs down and eventually out of the supply chain is affected by the stage of development of the purchasing activity. Purchasing can only make operational, tactical and strategic improvements in the area of supply chain management if it is appropriately developed. If some organisations' purchasing departments, acting in a proactive strategic way, can improve efficiency and effectiveness in the supply or value chain then any organisation should be able to. Partnerships, reducing acquisition costs, strategic outsourcing and e-commerce, however, are all dependent on the appropriate level of development of the purchasing activity. A clerical reactive purchasing activity would not be able to make any real contribution to any of these concepts, while a well-developed strategic activity would.

In very general terms, the ways in which purchasing has developed over the years and the characteristics associated with these general development phases can be summarised as follows:

- **30 years ago**
  - Purchasing and supply was concerned with buying supplies at the lowest price. Activity was essentially clerical.
  - Little involvement with suppliers.
  - Reactive.
- **15 years ago**
  - Purchasing and supply was still concerned with lowest price but aware of other factors affecting price like quality and delivery.
  - More involved with suppliers and other internal functions.
- **Today**
  - Purchasing and supply is becoming strategically involved as purchasing is seen as giving the organisation a strategic advantage.
  - Closely involved with suppliers and other activities concerned more with true ownership cost than price.
  - Devolution of straightforward buying activities closer to the point of use.
- **The future**
  - Application of leading-edge concepts throughout the supply chain.
  - Value addition displaces cost reduction as primary role.
  - Potential of developing technology realised.
  - Total customer focus.

Many successful organisations have well-developed, strategically proactive purchasing departments that are capable of making major contributions to their organisation and the supply chains they are involved with, while there are other organisations where purchasing remains undeveloped and reactive, with all the characteristics of purchasing activities of 30 years ago.

Case study – Clarks

In the 2003 CIPS Supply Management Awards, the winner of the most improved purchasing operation accolade was footwear company Clarks.

The four-strong purchasing team was commended for 'throwing away the rule book' when it relaunched its department. The function now focuses on the business objectives of each division and regular review meetings with the various heads of department throughout the company. This results in a 'purchasing MOT' that measures the performance of each client against six key performance criteria: agreements, administration, sourcing, value tools, mind set and supplier development.

With each client they discuss how the client sees procurement playing a strategic role for them, its relevance to their operation and how they value the contribution of procurement. The strategic role means that the business is now really starting to see the benefits of the improved purchasing perform-ance. They now have confidence that key areas of expenditure are being managed more effectively – enabling Clarks to get value for money from their supply base and giving them the competitive advantage.

The awards judges commented: 'The Company presented a clear account of an organisation moving from a tactical procurement function to a strategic and valued operation.'

We therefore need to find a way of measuring the stage of development reached by an organisation in order to identify what it is capable of delivering in terms of performance.

■ Measurement of purchasing development

Measuring the stage of development reached by a purchasing organisation can indicate whether development is appropriate for the needs of the concern. For example, it could be totally inappropriate to expect an essentially reactive organisation to take on board leading concepts. Failure would be inevitable. It is helpful, therefore, to diagnose the stage of development reached by a pur-chasing function so that further development can be planned.

■ The evolution of purchasing development frameworks

Perhaps the first attempt at developing such a framework was that undertaken by Jones (1983). Jones developed his model in order to establish whether or not organisations with well-developed purchasing functions were more effective negotiators than those where purchasing was not developed. Various criteria were measured and profiles produced. He indeed found that where the activity was well developed, the organisation negotiated not necessarily better prices but better deals, that is, deals based on strategic acquisition cost.

Reck and Long produced a more involved four-stage purchasing development model in 1988 when they began investigating the contributions purchasing could make to organisational strategic roles. These four stages of development and the characteristics of each stage are shown in Figure 1.7. This framework moves us forward, but its major defect is that only four stages are contemplated and the variables are not operational. It does, though, offer an opportunity in general terms to indicate stages of purchasing development.

■ Area of focus

Russell Syson (1989) saw purchasing divided into three principal areas of focus: transaction, commercial and proactive. The more developed the purchasing activity, the greater its involvement in commercial and strategic activities. He illustrated the position of purchasing within the organisation in the two graphs shown in Figure 1.8. His illustrations show that the more involved purchasing becomes in commercial and strategic areas, the greater its effectiveness to the organisation.

■ Purchasing profile analysis

The final framework for us to examine is that developed by Jones in 1997 as part of his PhD thesis concerning stages of purchasing development. The most important outcome of this research is the suggestion that purchasing has five stages of measurable development, which Jones named:

1 Infant
2 Awakening
3 Developing
4 Mature
5 Advanced

Profiles can be produced for individual purchasing organisations identifying these stages of development, and indicating areas that may need further development. The framework is shown in Figure 1.9. Eighteen variables are assessed and profiles then produced.

From the research results it was possible:

■ To identify the development of profiles that aided development of organisational strategies.
■ To demonstrate that certain profiles, unless changed, could not support proposed organisational strategies.
■ To provide a benchmark against which strategies could be developed to improve the status of the function.

Figure 1.7
A four-stage purchasing development model

Passive

Definition
The purchasing function has no strategic direction and primarily reacts to the requests of other functions.

Characteristics
- High proportion of purchaser's time is spent on quick-fix and routine operations
- Purchasing function and individual performance are based on efficiency measures
- Little interfunctional communication takes place because of purchasing's low visibility
- Supplier selection is based on price and availability

Independent

Definition
The purchasing function adopts the latest purchasing techniques and practices, but its strategic direction is independent of the firm's competitive strategy.

Characteristics
- Performance is primarily based on cost reduction and efficiency measures
- Co-ordination links are established between purchasing and technical disciplines
- Top management recognises the importance of professional development
- Top management recognises the opportunities in purchasing for contributing to profitability

Supportive

Definition
The purchasing function supports the firm's competitive strategy by adopting purchasing techniques and practices which strengthen the firm's competitive position.

Characteristics
- Purchasers are included in sales proposal teams
- Suppliers are considered a resource which is carefully selected and motivated
- People are considered a resource with emphasis on experience, motivation, and attitude
- Markets, products, and suppliers are continuously monitored and analysed

Integrative

Definition
Purchasing's strategy is fully integrated into the firm's competitive strategy and constitutes part of an integrated effort among functional peers to formulate and implement a strategic plan.

Characteristics
- Cross-functional training of purchasing professionals/executives is made available
- Permanent lines of communication are established among other functional areas
- Professional development focuses on strategic elements of the competitive strategy
- Purchasing performance is measured in terms of contributions to the firm's success

(*Source*: Reck and Long, 1988)

Figure 1.8
The three principal areas of focus

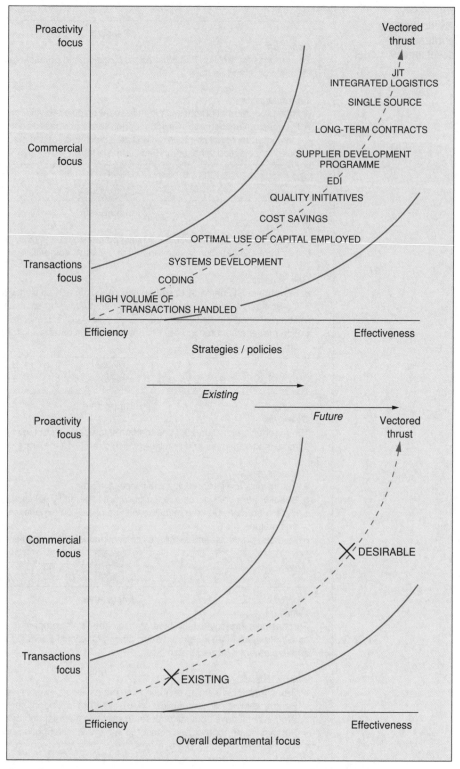

(*Source*: Syson, 1989)

MEASUREMENT AREA		STAGE OF DEVELOPMENT				
		1 Infant	2 Awakening	3 Developing	4 Mature	5 Advanced
1. Activity breakdown analysis	A1					
2. Purchasing organisational structure	A2					
3. Purchasing services	A3					
4. Function position in the business	B1/2					
5. Extent of training/development of buyer	B3					
6. Relative remuneration levels	B4					
7. Measurement of purchasing performance	B5					
8. Standard of information systems	E1					
9. Computer technology	E2					
10. Standard of operating procedures	F1					
11. Interface development (buying centre)	H1					
12. Buying process involvement	H2					
13. Buyer characteristics/development	I1					
14. Degree of purchasing specialism	I2					
15. Supplier interface development	J1					
16. Policy on ethics	J2					
17. Hospitality	J3					
18. Quality of buyer–supplier relationship	J4					

Figure 1.9 The purchasing development matrix

(*Source*: Jones, 1997)

29

- To show that 'best in class' organisations had very similar purchasing profiles.
- To establish that highly developed purchasing functions were better able to achieve optimisation of costs.

With the establishment of the purchasing development matrix it becomes possible for those managers responsible for the activity to identify where developments are required. The research has shown that developing some of the variables is more difficult than others. Attitudes are difficult to change, both within purchasing and in other parts of the organisation. It is important, therefore, that commitment to develop the purchasing function comes from the very top of the organisation.

▦ Outsourcing the purchasing activity

There have been numerous articles suggesting that the purchasing activity might be outsourced. Many of the arguments centre very much on the role of the activity and its contribution to the organisation.

Mini case study – Phillips

In 2007 Phillips announced a plan to outsource part of its procurement team. This covers finance, accounting, some transactional procurement including the processing of purchase orders, and hosting and maintaining the company's Enterprise Resource Planning (ERP) system. In 2006 the company centralised around 70 per cent of its spend and halved its supplier base to 25,000.

Most writers and practitioners seem to agree that the old clerically reactive and transactional style of purchasing has only a limited role today. Such an approach cannot give the organisation it represents a strategic advantage by effectively contributing to the integrated supply chain. A purchasing activity – whether it is a purchasing department or a devolved activity shared by a number of people in the organisation – that is poorly developed is likely to slow development of the whole organisation. In such cases it might make economic and practical sense to allocate the purchasing activity to an outside organisation where there is appropriate expertise and influence.

All those purchasing activities below stage 3 of development are likely to be considered for outsourcing if the organisation needs a strategically proactive purchasing activity quickly and cannot wait for or invest in the development of the purchasing activity that is required. Certain aspects of the purchasing activity, in particular the handling of low value and transactional purchasing, are likely to be devolved to users or requisitioners if the purchasing function is to spend more of its time on strategic acquisition and all that this involves. Such internal repositioning of the activity to other functions is likely to occur at stages 3 and 4, otherwise purchasing could have difficulty in making the

Stage of development	Example capabilities	Estimated contribution at each stage
Infant – Stage 1	Few; fragmented purchasing	None or low
Awakening – Stage 2	Emerging realisation of contribution through savings	Clerical efficiency; small savings of 2–5% through consolidation
Developing – Stage 3	Some control and development of purchasing price through negotiation	Price reductions of 5–10%
Mature – Stage 4	80/20 principle employed; specialist purchasing and supply staff; cost reduction focus; commencement of supplier base management	Price and cost reductions of 10–20%; acquisition cost reductions of 1–10%
Advanced – Stage 5	Devolution of routine purchasing to users; strong central control; supply-chain management concepts employed; leverage buying; global sourcing; understanding and practice of total acquisition cost and cost of ownership	Total cost of ownership reductions 25%, acquisition cost and supply-chain management cost reductions of 30%+

Table 1.4
Purchasing development stages and performance capabilities

'quantum leap' (Syson, 1989) to fully developed status where most of purchasing's involvement concentrates on strategic purchasing and supply chain management.

Table 1.4 is an attempt to indicate likely contributions of the purchasing activity at different stages of development. If organisations measure, using profile analysis, the stage of development reached by the purchasing activity, they can begin to reflect on its likely capability. Unfortunately, organisations often want the contribution offered by an advance on strategic purchasing activity but have not put the necessary corporate investment into the purchasing activity, which may still be at the awakening stage of development and not capable of making any real contribution to the organisation it represents.

Using the profiling technique, development shortcomings can be identified and appropriate development strategies produced.

■ Developments

In the Jones (1997) five-stage model the five stages of development are seen as:

1 Infant
2 Awakening
3 Developing
4 Mature
5 Advanced

A new, sixth stage could be added for those (relatively few) organisations that are truly global, operating a worldwide integrated purchasing activity. This might be called 'globally integrated strategic purchasing'. Hallmarks might include:

- Globally integrated purchasing systems and strategies.
- Integrated supply chains via Electronic Point of Sale (EPOS) or e-commerce.
- Major purchases across the global organisation handled by strategic supply chain managers and negotiators.
- Strategic logistics chain manager to integrate delivery of parts from suppliers to users throughout the organisation.

Best practice in strategic supply management

The following list includes many of the ideas taught to students of purchasing at all levels. Clearly, this good practice will not be practicable in an organisation with a less than fully developed purchasing function.

- Identify and work with key suppliers
- Develop openness and transparency
- Align systems with strategic initiatives
- Articulate mutual goals
- Forge partnerships where appropriate
- Use complementary competencies
- Employ dedicated complementary assets
- Employ appropriate technology
- Use appropriate e-technology/systems
- Share competencies and resources
- Establish common language
- Emphasise mutual benefits
- Implement *Kaizen*
- Remove decoupling points
- Empower individuals
- Empower suppliers
- Focus on customer needs
- Pursue and eliminate waste
- Consider core/non-core questions
- Build knowledge base
- Use knowledge base
- Be responsive, and ready to change

Summary

1 A broad introduction to the scope of purchasing is given.

2 We highlight the importance of a strategic purchasing function within organisations. It emphasises the necessity of purchasing being involved at all stages and levels of decision making.

3 Purchasing has had to adapt to becoming more proactive. More emphasis is given to supplier relationships with both sides investing time and support to achieve mutually beneficial goals.

4 Total cost is an all-inclusive measure of the cost of ownership. It is influenced by factors that can be improved with the involvement of an informed purchasing team.

5 The chapter suggests reasons why there has been increased pressure for purchasing and supply to develop.

6 Various purchasing development models are identified and reviewed in order to measure the stage of development reached.

7 Factors are identified that have a positive effect on development.

8 We identify that more advanced stages of purchasing development increase both the effectiveness and efficiency of the purchasing activity, and how 'best in class' organisations have similar profiles.

9 Characteristics of developed strategic purchasing are suggested.

References and further reading

Barnes, J G and McTavish, R (1983), 'Segmenting industrial markets by buyer sophistication', *European Journal of Marketing*, 17(6).

Benmeridja, M and Benmeridja, A (1996), 'Is it interesting for a company to outsource purchasing and under what conditions?' *1996 IPSERA Conference Papers*, April.

Caller, L (2003), Case Study – Unisys. *Supply Management*, October.

Carter, P L and Ogden, J A (1999), *The World Class Purchasing and Supply Organisation*, London: University of Arizona.

CIPS/Oracle/OGC (2006), Research Study, *Supply Management* (CIPS), March.

Ellinor, R (2006), 'Lack of involvement costs billions in missed savings', *Supply Management*, March.

Emmett, S and Crocker, B (2006), *The Relationship Driven Supply Chain*, Aldershot: Gower.

Erridge, A (1995), *Managing Purchasing*, Oxford: Butterworth Heinemann.

Gattorna, J L and Walters, D W (1996), *Managing the Supply Chain*, Basingstoke: Macmillan Business.

Geraint, J (2003), 'Your Chief Priorities', *Supply Management* (CIPS), September.

Hewitt, D (2004), 'Post-Modern Purchasing', *Supply Management* (CIPS), March.

Jones, D M (1983), unpublished essay, Lancaster University.

Jones, D M (1997), 'Purchasing Evolution and Development', unpublished PhD thesis, Strathclyde University.

Jones, D M (1999), 'Development models', *Supply Management*, March and April.

Kraljic, P (1983), 'Purchasing must become supply management', *Harvard Business Review*, September/October.

Lamming, R (1993), *Beyond Partnership: Strategies for Innovation and Lean Supply*, Hemel Hempstead: Prentice Hall International.

Lysons, K and Gillingham, M (2002), *Purchasing and Supply Chain Management*, London: Prentice Hall.

Mizik, N and Jacobson, R (2003), 'Trading off between value creation and value appropriation: the financial implications of shifts in strategic emphasis', *Journal of Marketing*, January.

Nelson, D *et al.* (2001), *The Purchasing Machine*, Aldershot: Gower.

Parker, R (2005), 'Restructuring', *Supply Management*, November.

Reck, R F and Long, B (1988), 'Purchasing, a competitive weapon', *Journal of Purchasing and Materials Management*, Fall.

Rich, N, Hines, P, Jones, T O and Francis, M (1996), 'Evidence of a watershed in the purchasing profession', *IPSERA Conference Papers*, April.

Russill, R (1997), 'Reassessing purchasing with a clear and fundamental role', *CIPS Annual Conference*.

Scheuing, E (1998), *Value Added Purchasing: Partnering for World Class Performance*, Menlo Park, CA: Crisp.

Smith, B and Vlamis, A (2001), *Business the Yahoo Way*, New York: Capstone.

Snell, P (2007), 'Strategy – buying plans must fit company's aim', *Supply Management*, March.

Snell, P (2007), 'Phillips in $250m outsourcing deal', *Supply Management*, August.

Spoor, R (2004), 'Is procurement really a strategic function?', *Supply Management*, May.

Stannack, P and Jones, M E (1996), 'The death of purchasing', *IPSERA Conference Papers*, April.

Syson, R (1989), 'The revolution in purchase', *Purchasing and Supply Management*, September.

Van Weele, A J (1994), *Purchasing Management*, Oxford: Chapman & Hall.

Van Weele, A J *et al.* (1999), 'Professional purchasing in organisations: towards a purchasing development model', *7th International IPSERA Conference*, April.

Wolf, H H (2005), 'Making the transition to strategic purchasing', *Sloan Management Review*, Summer.

Womack, J P and Jones, D T (1996), *Lean Thinking*, New York: Simon & Schuster.

2

Strategic procurement and supply chain management

Introduction

All organisations need to plan for the future; this requires the development of frameworks to allow the process to take place. Once strategic objectives have been agreed, the strategies themselves can be formulated. It is essential that all business functions, including purchasing, are involved in this process. In the past, purchasing tended to be involved in day-to-day operational activities, and has not always made the contribution to business that it is capable of. It has become involved in both tactical and strategic decision making in today's successful organisations.

In this chapter we will also examine how organisations structure their purchasing activities. The more developed the activity is, the more likely it is to be fully integrated with the rest of the organisation. There is no one 'best' type of organisational structure for purchasing, and supply structures that were appropriate five years ago may not be now. Strategies alter to meet these changes, so organisational structures will also need to be modified.

Objectives of this chapter

- To explain the growth in the strategic role of procurement, purchasing and supply
- To explain the concept of strategic management
- To identify various forms of purchasing strategy aimed at gaining competitive advantage and to examine influences on strategic choice
- To examine the issues of how decentralised v. centralised departmental organisations and support services affect the structure of the purchasing team
- To appreciate the importance of purchasing within the organisation's structure
- To consider the placing of purchasing in various types of organisation
- To consider the central role of contract management in the virtual organisation
- To identify the supply chain concept and to consider alternative 'supply chain' models
- To explain why it is important to be involved with the total supply chain

- To follow the supply chain concept investigating events from the primary supplier to the ultimate user
- To identify the relevance and importance of ethics in the supply chain
- To highlight the areas of environmental concern

Strategic procurement

A proactive strategic procurement operation can give the organisation it represents a competitive advantage by reducing waste in the value chain. Purchasing strategies, however, cannot be developed in isolation, they need to be integrated with corporate strategy to succeed. Figure 2.1 shows the involvement of purchasing at strategic, tactical and operational levels.

Historically, the functions of marketing, finance or production have tended to dominate organisations.

Growth in the strategic role of procurement, purchasing and supply

The main reasons for the growth in purchasing involvement in strategic decision making are as follows:

- Purchasing is seen as an area for *adding value*, not simply reducing costs.
- Rapid product innovation requires a more integrated management team, involving all functions, and adopting a process rather than functional approach to management.
- There has been a move to holistic views concerning the integration of material and information flows, both internally and externally, for example: materials requirements planning (MRP), manufacturing resource planning (MRP2), distribution resource planning (DRP), enterprise resource planning

Figure 2.1
The scope of the purchase function

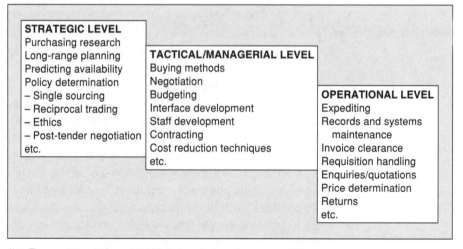

STRATEGIC LEVEL
Purchasing research
Long-range planning
Predicting availability
Policy determination
– Single sourcing
– Reciprocal trading
– Ethics
– Post-tender negotiation
etc.

TACTICAL/MANAGERIAL LEVEL
Buying methods
Negotiation
Budgeting
Interface development
Staff development
Contracting
Cost reduction techniques
etc.

OPERATIONAL LEVEL
Expediting
Records and systems
   maintenance
Invoice clearance
Requisition handling
Enquiries/quotations
Price determination
Returns
etc.

Note: The examples are for the purpose of illustration only. A complete statement of the scope would be very lengthy, and would vary greatly between one organisation and another.

(ERP) and integrated information systems associated with e-commerce; supply chain concepts such as value streams, lean and agile supply, and pipeline management.

- Awareness that active supplier involvement can increase efficiency and effectiveness.
- A developing recognition that concern with strategic costs of supply and total cost of ownership, rather than short-term price, is important.
- The growth and development of the Chartered Institute of Purchasing and Supply in supporting the role of the activity.
- A recognition of the growth in purchased materials and services.
- Increased recognition of the profit potential in purchasing.

One of the major problems faced by the purchasing and supply activity in many organisations has been the failure to take on board a proactive strategic role. How effective the function is will depend to a large extent on the stage of development, i.e. is it clerical or strategic, reactive or proactive?

During the 1990s purchasing evolved to be viewed as part of a broader function called 'procurement', defined as 'the systematic process of deciding what, when, and how many to purchase; the act of purchasing it; and the process of ensuring that what is required is received on time in the quantity and quality specified'. As a function, procurement includes purchasing, consumption management, vendor selection, contract negotiation and contract management. At the beginning of the 2000s, the terms 'purchasing' and 'procurement' became almost synonymous in the profession. In fact the following observation demonstrates that the term 'procurement' is now more dominant in many sectors.

Research

From a total of 29 purchasing and supply-related positions advertised in one edition of *CIPS Supply Management*, 18 were procurement positions, reflecting the increasing acceptance of the term in place of buying and purchasing.

■ Problems associated with activities and value

One of the major problems facing the traditional organisation has been the tendency to allocate and organise much of the work on a functional basis – purchasing, finance, production. This type of approach has led to demarcation disputes and sub-optimisation, i.e. each function attempting to achieve its objectives regardless of the others. Nowadays it is the norm for activities to be organised more on a process approach. This involves a team approach to problem solving and concern with getting the job done. This in turn requires a more integrated management approach than a segmental one.

Figure 2.2 illustrates how the structure of organisations may be forced to change in an attempt to provide a more streamlined approach to the flow of

Figure 2.2
Organisation structure and the flow of goods

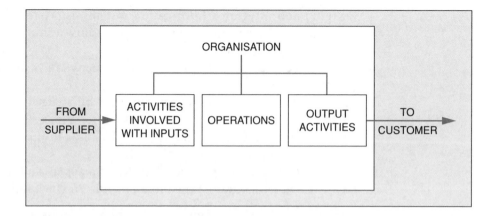

goods into, through and out of the organisation in an attempt to maximise added value and minimise costs. Such logistical structures are more concerned with overall efficiency than functional efficiency, and give organisations a much better chance of integrating strategies successfully at all levels. Organisations that fail to get purchasing involved in the strategies are likely to hinder or stop the development of such strategies.

The concept of strategy

■ Definitions

There is no one generally accepted definition of strategy but many, of which the following are examples:

> Strategy is the pattern or plan that integrates an organisation's major goals, policies and action sequences into a cohesive whole. A well formulated strategy helps to marshal and allocate an organisation's resources into a unique and viable posture based on its relative internal competencies and shortcomings, anticipated changes in the environment and contingent moves by intelligent opponents. (Quinn *et al.*, 1995)

> Corporate strategy can be described as an organisation's sense of purpose. (Lynch, 2005)

Many organisations indicate the strategies they are likely to follow in their mission statements. A mission or philosophy statement is a generalised objective or expression of an organisation's purpose – a master strategy.

■ Developing a strategy

In developing a strategy, the following need to be considered:

- What are target objectives?
- How are target objectives to be achieved?

Figure 2.3
A managerial recipe undergoing change

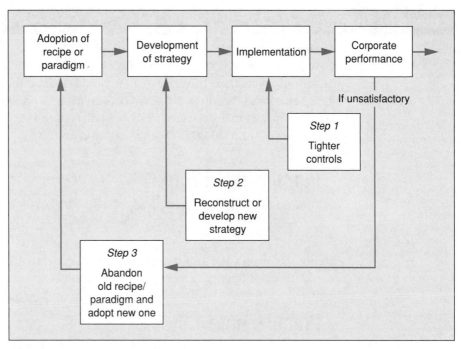

(*Source*: Johnson and Scholes, 2002)

Strategy covers:

- moves and approaches which are ongoing;
- new actions in the process of being mapped out;
- innovation, risk taking;
- choosing among alternatives;
- doing the right things at the right times.

Recipe/paradigm change

From Figure 2.3 it can be seen that if the recipe/paradigm is incorrect the organisation is likely to experience strategic drift. Typical symptoms of strategic drift are:

- poor performance;
- current culture/paradigm overly subscribed to;
- resistance to change;
- poor external focus.

The mission statement

This involves management's vision of what the business is, or should be. Once established, this vision serves to:

- shape the future direction the organisation should follow;
- establish a strong organisational profile; and
- identify core business.

Levels of strategy

Strategies may be determined for various levels in the organisation, as illustrated in Figure 2.4. If an organisation has successfully determined strategies at various levels then those strategies should operate together harmoniously. This, of course, requires total involvement and commitment by all concerned. Operational strategies are often reflected in vision statements, such as this example from IBM (UK) Manufacturing:

Purchasing Vision

To be the best of breed procurement organisation benchmarked within and without IBM, and to support our customers with a World Class supplier base.

Figure 2.5 shows the interrelationship between mission statements, results required and strategies.

Practice note

Some companies are introducing strategic improvement plans with their suppliers. Such schemes identify several areas where buying organisations would like to see considerable improvements leading to the elimination of problems. Such a vision might include:

- Nil defects
- Nil delivery times
- Nil administration errors
- Nil transaction costs
- Nil set-up costs
- Nil disputes

Members of the supply chain would work together to achieve such objectives.

Figure 2.4
Levels of strategy within an organisation

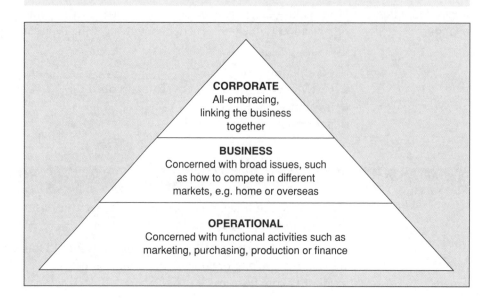

Figure 2.5 The interrelationship between mission statements, results required and strategies

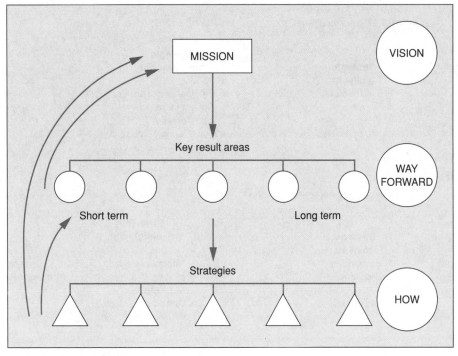

(*Source*: Based on Lynch, 2002)

Category management

Many procurement organisations are now implementing category management. What is category management?

> Continual monitoring of expenditures and supplier performance in specific buying categories with the intent of driving ongoing cost or supplier performance improvements.

Categories consist of items of:

- similar supplier sources;
- similar production processes;
- similar internal use;
- similar material content/complexity;
- similar specifications;
- similar underlying technology.

Categorisation looks at the inherent properties of categories. Once this has been carried out, staff can develop strategies for each category in order to maximise value for each particular category. The following paragraphs outline the various tools and techniques of strategic management which can be applied to each category.

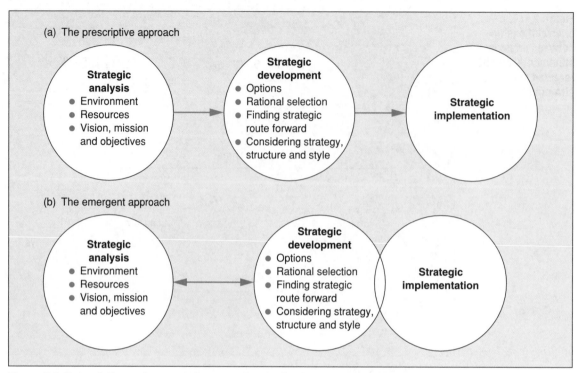

Figure 2.6 Prescriptive and emergent approaches to the three core elements

(*Source*: Lynch, 2002)

Strategic management

Strategic management can be divided into three major areas:

1 Strategic analysis – position facing the organisation.
2 Strategic choice – formulation of alternative courses of action.
3 Strategic implementation – planning how the choice of strategy can be put into effect.

Figure 2.6 indicates how these three areas interact depending on whether one sees strategy as a formalised prescriptive approach, that is planned, or emergent, that is evolving, incremental and continuous.

Analysis is of particular importance. The emergent approach is more concerned with choice and implementation of a strategy. The emergent approach argues that there is too much turbulence in the analysis stage to predict accurately.

Strategic analysis

Strategic analysis is to do with understanding the relationship between different factors affecting the organisation and its choice of strategies.

Table 2.1
Examples of tools of analysis

Analysis	Methodologies
Environmental analysis	● PEST (political, economic, social, technological) analysis ● SWOT (strengths, weaknesses, opportunities, threats) analysis ● Porter's five forces ● Competitor analysis
Competitive position	● Strategic group analysis ● Competitor analysis
Resource analysis, competencies and strategic capabilities	● Value chain analysis ● Resource audit ● Core business
Comparative analysis	● Historical and financial analysis ● Benchmarking
Organisational analysis	● SWOT analysis ● BCG (Boston Consulting Group) analysis ● Critical success factors (CSFs)
Stakeholders' perceptions	● Ethical considerations ● Stakeholder mapping ● Mission statements ● Culture ● Paradigms

The three main areas for analysis are:

- the environment;
- internal resources, competencies and strategic capabilities;
- stakeholders' expectations.

Some of the tools used in strategic analysis are shown in Table 2.1.

We are essentially thinking in terms of a PEST analysis, and this is illustrated in Figure 2.7, which shows the many factors – under the headings political, economic, social, technological – likely to affect an organisation.

Figure 2.7
PEST analysis

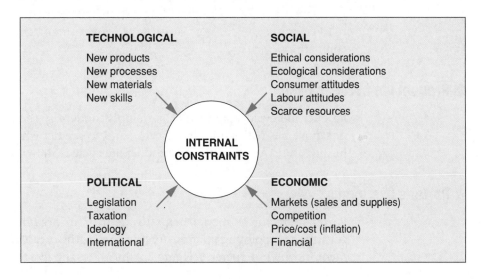

43

Figure 2.8
Product life cycle

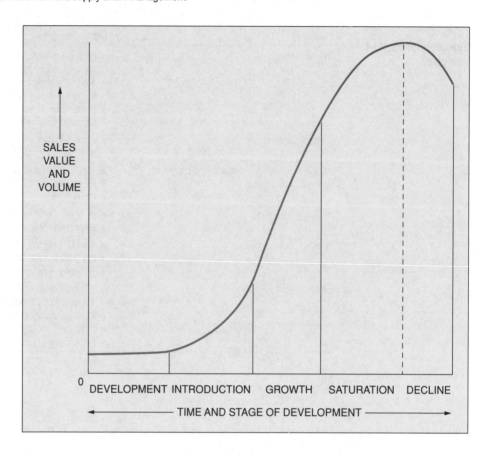

(The environment can also be analysed using Porter's five forces model, see Figure 2.9 below.) PEST can provide a checklist for evaluating different influences and makes it possible to pinpoint key factors currently affecting the organisation as well as longer-term areas for concern. Organisations concerned with a more global approach will identify key drivers such as market convergence, cost advantage, government influences and global competition.

■ Product life cycle analysis

Product life cycle analysis (PLC) attempts to identify the stage that a product or service has reached in its life cycle, and to predict what is likely to happen in the future. An example of a product life cycle is shown in Figure 2.8.

■ Porter's five forces

Porter's five forces model helps to identify an organisation's competitive advantage by pointing up those forces affecting the organisation in the environment in which it operates. Figure 2.9 illustrates the five forces:

Figure 2.9
Porter's five forces model

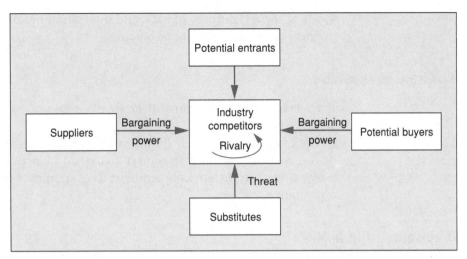

- bargaining power of suppliers;
- bargaining power of buyers;
- potential new entrants;
- substitutes;
- industry competition.

■ The power of suppliers and buyers

There are useful indicators of the extent of this power which can be used by the analyst. Supplier power is likely to be high when:

- there is concentration of suppliers rather than a fragmented source of supply;
- the 'switching costs' from one supplier to another in the industry are high, perhaps because a manufacturer's processes are dependent on the specialist products of a supplier;
- there is the possibility of suppliers integrating forward if they do not obtain the prices, and hence the margins, they seek;
- the supplier's customers and their long-term future are of little importance to the supplier.

Buyer power is likely to be high:

- when there is a concentration of buyers, particularly if the volume purchases of the buyers is high;
- when there are alternative sources of supply, perhaps because the product required is undifferentiated between suppliers;
- if the component or material cost is a high percentage of their total cost then buyers will be likely to 'shop around' to get the best price, and therefore 'squeeze' the suppliers;

- where there is a threat of backward integration by the buyer if satisfactory prices or suppliers cannot be obtained.

Threat of substitutes

If a market can be segmented it may be possible to avoid threats from substitutes, competition etc.

The first two stages of environmental analysis – understanding the nature of the environment and structural analysis – help to identify the general forces at work in the environment that have an impact on the strategy of the organisation.

Resource appraisal

It could well be that an organisation is failing to effectively utilise the resources available to it for all sorts of reasons. The question then becomes, 'What is our core business? Should we sell off some of these under-utilised resources?', e.g. real estate for US railways.

Some of the methods available for analysis are:

- structural analysis – identifies key variables;
- forecasting;
- strategic standing;
- resource audit – quality and quantity;
- resource utilisation;
- historical analysis of resources and their returns;
- flexibility analysis.

There are three main areas one needs to assess in this type of analysis:

- resources available;
- competence with which the activities of the organisation are undertaken;
- balance of resources and activities in the business.

Portfolio analysis

In a large and diverse organisation, a prime concern at the corporate level is achieving a balanced range or portfolio of business activities. The Boston Consulting Group (BCG) suggested a *matrix* analysis.

The BCG suggested the model of the product portfolio or the growth share matrix as a tool by which to consider product strategy. This product portfolio matrix is shown in Figure 2.10. The matrix combines market growth rate and market share and thus directly relates to the idea of the *experience curve*.

A *star* is a product (or business) which has a high market share in a growing market. As such the company may be spending heavily to gain that share, but the experience curve effect will mean that costs are reducing over time, and

Figure 2.10
The Boston Consulting Group product portfolio matrix

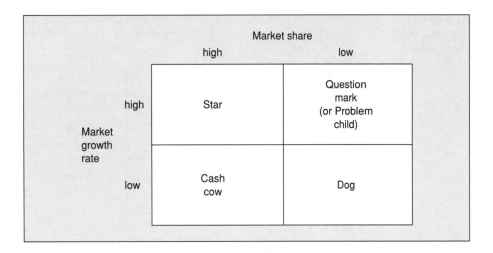

hopefully at a faster rate than the competition is. The product (or business) could then be self-financing.

The *question mark* (or problem child) is also in a growing market, but does not have a high market share. Its parent company may be spending heavily to increase market share, but if so it is unlikely that they are getting sufficient cost reductions to offset such investment because the experience gained is less than for a star, and costs will be reducing less quickly.

The *cash cow* is a product (or business) with high market share in a mature market. Because growth is low and market conditions more stable, the need for heavy marketing investment is less. High market share means that experience in relation to low share competition continues to grow and relative costs reduce. The cash cow is thus a cash *provider*.

Dogs have low share in static or declining markets and are thus the worst of all combinations. They are often a cash *drain* and use up a disproportionate amount of company time and resources.

The idea of a portfolio of interests emphasises the importance of having areas of activity which provide security and funds (cash cows) and others which provide for the future of the business (stars and question marks). The BCG emphasises the importance of a sensible flow of funds within the firm (i.e. the extent to which the products or businesses in maturity provide funds for the growth areas) to ensure long-term security.

■ Competition within the industry

This can best be assessed with SWOT analysis. SWOT is made up of the first letters in Strengths, Weaknesses, Opportunities and Threats. It:

■ involves assessing a company's internal strengths and weaknesses, and its external opportunities and threats;
■ is an easy-to-use tool for quickly coming up with an overview of a company's strategic situation;

**Figure 2.11
The basic SWOT
'cruciform'**

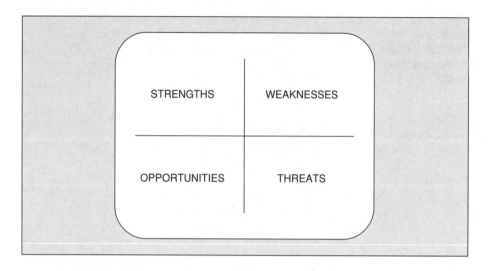

- introduces the point that strategy must produce a strong fit between a company's internal capability and its external situation.

It is normal to produce a 'cruciform' as shown in Figure 2.11. The various strengths, weaknesses, opportunities and threats can be listed under the appropriate headings, and a general appraisal made. After this initial analysis, further analysis can be undertaken to identify likely strategies the organisation might implement. Thus, if an organisation on balance has substantial internal strengths and numerous environmental opportunities, this would suggest it supports an aggressive strategy in Cell 1. If on the other hand it has substantial internal strengths and major environmental threats, then a diversification policy might be the order of the day. Similar analysis/strategy implications would be confirmed in Cell 3 or 4. An example of the cruciform strategy analysis is shown in Figure 2.12.

Strategic development

Once strategies have been developed they need to be delivered.

■ Generic strategies

Porter's model for strategic choice looks at three generic strategies:

- cost leadership;
- differentiation;
- focus.

We also need to identify clearly the basis for our strategy, which direction we should take and why. The Ansoff Matrix indicates directions for strategic development (see Figure 2.13).

Figure 2.12
Developing the
SWOT cruciform

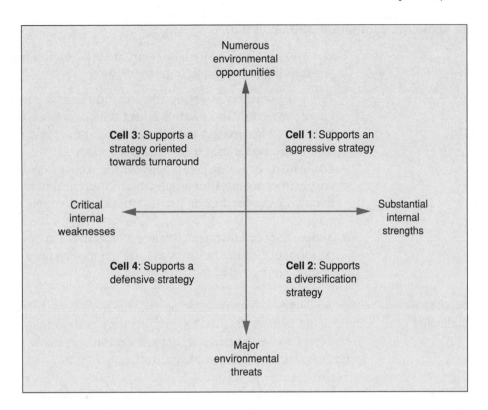

Figure 2.13
Directions
for strategy
development
from Ansoff

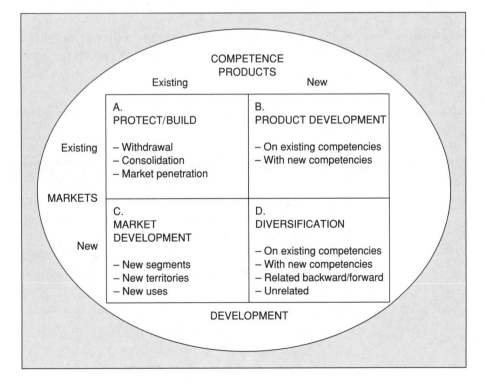

■ Strategic evaluation and selection

There are a number of criteria that any strategic option needs to satisfy to stay in the running for adoption implementation:

- *Suitability* – when assessing the suitability for a particular business, the chosen direction will need to reflect the circumstances currently in operation in the business. A strategic analysis should be undertaken to provide information on these business circumstances.
- *Feasibility* is concerned with whether the strategy could be made to operate within the organisational culture and environment. This will require a detailed examination of the resourcing and strategic capabilities of the business.
- *Acceptability* of an intended strategy is concerned with the expectation of performance of the business against the expectations of the various stakeholders connected with the business.

Assessing suitability

Assessing the suitability of an option will allow more incomplete options to be ruled out before more detailed analysis takes place. Any proposed strategy must be tested to see whether or not the option meets the circumstances of the business currently and in the future.

Ways of screening options

- Ranking – each option is assessed against agreed criteria.
- Decision trees – questions are asked of each option. The further they progress in a positive way, the more likely they will be adopted.

Feasibility

This is concerned with assessing whether or not the organisation has the resources to deliver the chosen strategy. Typical tools used are:

- funds flow analysis;
- break-even analysis;
- resource deployment analysis.

Strategy implementation

Having decided the strategic option, we need to implement the strategy. This involves resource allocation, planning and control, organisational aspects, human resource issues and management of change. Correct information is at the heart of the process. A time scale and action plan will need to be prepared. A typical implementation plan is shown in Figure 2.14 from Lynch.

Figure 2.14
The basic implementation plan from Lynch

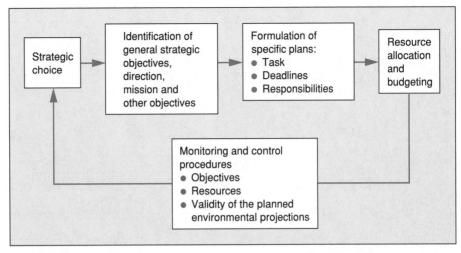

(*Source*: Adapted from Lynch, 2002)

Objectives for purchasing

It might be useful at this stage to consider purchasing objectives in the form of a 'hierarchy'. Figure 2.15 suggests the way in which this might be done, though of course the chart will differ from one organisation to another.

Strategies and their scope

It follows that whenever and wherever purchasing involvement in the development of business strategies is less than adequate, it is likely that exploitable opportunities will be lost while threats are neglected.

IBM (UK) has identified a class of supplier as 'strategic', and seeks in these suppliers technology leadership, highest product quality levels, design influence through early new product development, cost competitiveness, supply/market responsiveness, efficient administration and total customer orientation.

Some strategic options force the buying company to adopt a number of approaches so as to ensure success. For example, the much discussed just-in-time approach presupposes that the buying company can rely absolutely on the incoming goods being to specification. Further, it usually means that it is necessary for the supplier's plant to be reasonably close to that of the buyer. Where suppliers do not meet the buyers' requirements in one or more of these areas then a buyer might choose to upgrade its suppliers in order to achieve just-in-time performance. Rank Xerox in Holland followed this route with considerable success. Among the measures which it used in this work were:

- Statistical process control methods.
- A total quality control approach.

51

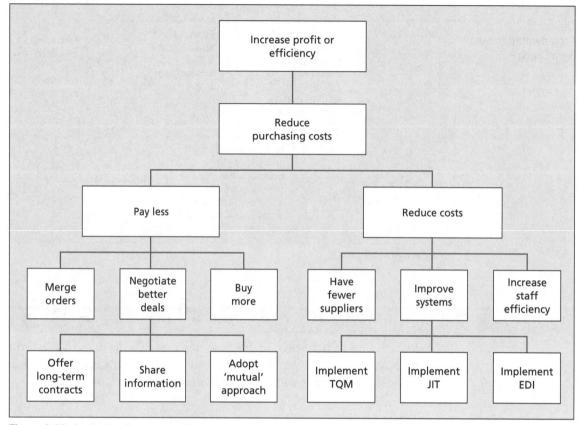

Figure 2.15 Analysis of cost reductions

- JIT application to manufacturing (its own and that of the supplier).
- Continuous supplier involvement.
- Supplier interface improvement through computer-aided manufacturing (CAM).
- Where applicable, computer-aided design (CAD) and electronic data interface (EDI).

Selecting a strategy

Figure 2.16 illustrates some of the factors involved in selecting and developing a strategy. Clearly, tactical and operational behaviour must support the strategic approach selected. For example, if the aim of the strategy was to set up a range of dedicated suppliers – that is, suppliers who are the sole source for a particular item – it would be nonsense for buyers to seek quotations from other suppliers during the period of the agreement (at least with the implication that business might be placed). If the strategy involved developing a local source to avoid reliance upon an overseas supplier (involving currency

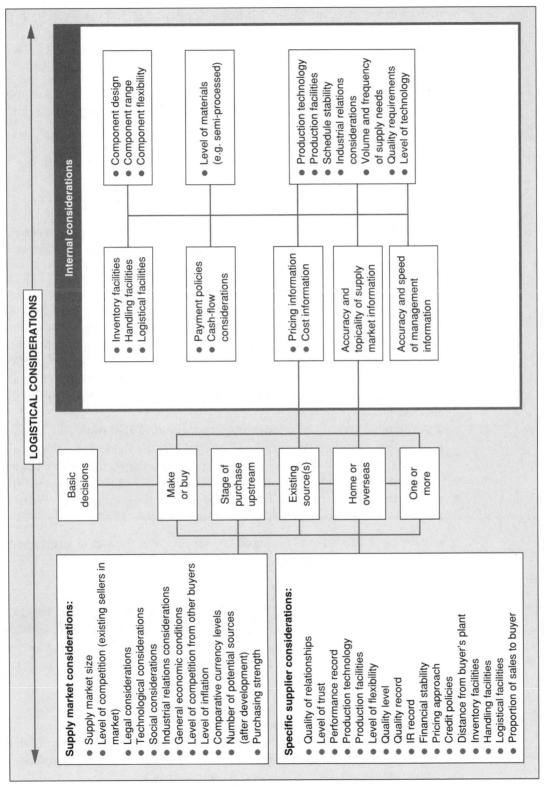

Figure 2.16 A framework for strategy development

management), it would be foolish not to support that supplier, even if, in the short term, it was more expensive.

As will be seen from Figure 2.16 many factors influence the choice of a strategy. Among them are:

- The position of the business in its supply chain. For example, is it a supplier of raw materials, components or finished product? How many competitors does it have in its supply and end markets?
- The number of effective sources in the company's supply market.
- The pace of technological development in the supply and end markets.
- The volatility of the supply and/or end markets.
- The degree of government involvement in the marketplace (e.g. the defence market).
- The ability of the buying company to manage a strategy (e.g. the quality and number of staff in the area and the ability to influence behaviour in the business).

The key criteria in the development of effective purchasing strategies are the same as those that apply to marketing strategies. They should focus on the areas of greatest potential in terms of contribution; exploit the competitive advantages available to the buying company as a consequence of its particular mix of resources; emphasise creative management in use of those resources vis-à-vis competition (buyers or sellers); stress consistency and feasibility and specify who, what, when, why, which and how through an effective plan.

Although there may be advantages in copying the strategies of competitors, they need to be considered carefully in the light of the company's own strengths and weaknesses. There may be advantages, too, with the same caveat, of considering the strategies of companies in other industries. What supply strategies currently being applied in other industries might be adaptable in our circumstances? (See Figure 2.17.)

- Have we developed our IT capabilities particularly in the area of e-commerce?
- How integrated are our supply chains?

Effective supply market strategies

Effective supply market strategies are based on analysis, weighing up probabilities, defining strategies and planning their implementation in detail. This involves:

1 Analysing the supply chains in order to find key points at which competitive advantage may be sought or threats exist.
2 Understanding the potential impact of particular strategic interventions upon the supply market; and being able to conceive of the likely rearrangements that may occur and how competitors may react.

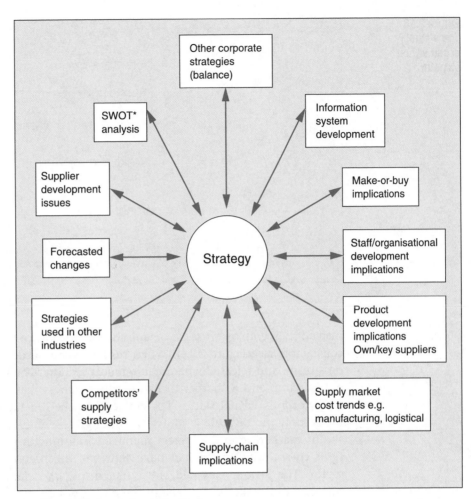

Figure 2.17
Some influences on strategy decisions

Strategy

- Other corporate strategies (balance)
- SWOT* analysis
- Information system development
- Supplier development issues
- Make-or-buy implications
- Forecasted changes
- Staff/organisational development implications
- Strategies used in other industries
- Product development implications Own/key suppliers
- Competitors' supply strategies
- Supply market cost trends e.g. manufacturing, logistical
- Supply-chain implications

Note: *Strengths, Weaknesses, Opportunities, Threats

Proactive purchasing activities need properly trained and developed buyers who can work well in teams and across functional barriers. If they have been trained as order clerks they will have great difficulty taking on strategic rules. The more developed the purchasing activity within an organisation, the better able it becomes to deliver its sources to the rest of the organisation and the supply chain. Procurement needs to take a thoroughly professional view of its role in the business as a whole and that must include planning.

■ Virtual organisations

Some organisations approach what is called 'virtual' status. The apparent contradiction in the term 'virtual organisation' is explained by the fact that such organisations do not produce anything that is sold to the customer.

Figure 2.18
The virtual organisation structure

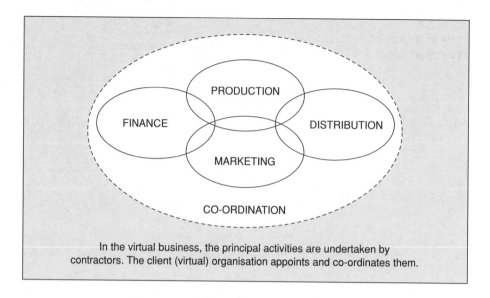

In the virtual business, the principal activities are undertaken by contractors. The client (virtual) organisation appoints and co-ordinates them.

Instead they employ strategic organisational skills to co-ordinate the work of contractors (see Figure 2.18). When resources are needed, they are brought on stream, and released when requirements are low. The trend towards more outsourcing, and a sharper focus on core business, has led many organisations towards virtual status. The concept can be illustrated by reference to the Nike brand of athletic footwear. Through the employment of extremely skilful marketing and expertly managed manufacturing and distribution skills the brand and product have achieved the premier position in their sector. The vision is owned and pursued by Nike management, but contractors undertake its actual fulfilment. Although we mention elsewhere in this text the possibility of purchasing and supply being outsourced, the central role in the virtual organisation is the identification and use of a team of ideal contractors. It is difficult to see how this role could be outsourced.

Purchasing and supply in different types of organisation

Organising the activity will obviously be influenced by the type of organisation concerned, and the 'culture' that permeates it. We shall now examine the likely characteristics of purchasing and supply in a number of different types of organisation.

Small single-product organisations

- Low pay and status.
- The activity is unlikely to have a say in strategy determination.
- Purchasing decision making fragmented.
- Head of the activity probably reports to finance or production executives.
- Purchasing and supply activity with little specialisation.

Flow production, e.g. car industry	■ Major say in corporate strategy.
	■ High degree of specialisation within the activity, e.g. expediting, material control, stores and stock control.
	■ Also specialisation within the purchasing activity, e.g. raw materials buyer, electrics buyer.
	■ A director of purchasing and supply would head the function.
	■ High salaries and status associated with those in the functions.
	■ Deployment of latest supply chain techniques such as lean supply.

Major manufacturing

■ Materials high proportion of cost.

■ Continuity of supply important.

■ Strong professional approach needed.

■ Head of procurement will be at board level, with a well-structured department containing experts in their particular field.

Process industry

■ High volume raw materials – major purchase.

■ Continuity of supply vital – continuous process.

■ Buying worldwide.

■ Category specialists.

Extractive industries e.g. oil, coal

■ No raw material purchases.

■ High capital expenditure.

■ Important spares and maintenance need.

■ Often in remote locations.

This is a production-orientated activity with the accent on plant and machinery and its operation. The spares inventory can be of high value. The procurement department has a considerable responsibility to control costs and keep stocks under control. For large companies purchasing may be under central direction with localised purchasing managers reporting to the local chief executive.

Distributive and retail

■ Goods sold as bought.

■ No perceived added value (no change of state by manufacturing).

■ Customer-related.

■ Affected by fashion.

■ Demand stimulated by advertising.

■ Buying around 80 per cent of total expense.

■ Choice and control of stock very important.

Net profit margins are low, usually below 5 per cent, and with the buying element being so high expertise is essential. Marketing and sales are closely linked and purchasing is represented at the highest level.

Service industries

The biggest part of a service industry is people, who provide the know-how, technique, etc. The physical materials are not a large element of the total expense, although the expenditure on capital goods might be high as in, for example, an airline. Where materials or equipment are significant, e.g. computers or transport, the purchase was often undertaken by the functional department rather than by purchasing, although nowadays there is a significant purchasing contribution in the more developed organisations.

The public sector This is a very large sector, with huge amounts of expenditure, represented by:

- utility industries;
- local authorities;
- government departments;
- health authorities;
- the armed forces.

Apart from the utility industries, these organisations have little or no sales income and their funds are provided through government taxes and local rates. The purchasing bill is the biggest item in their overall expenses. The importance in these areas is now well recognised, with the head of purchasing being at director or senior executive level. Often purchasing policy is decided by politics. Ethical standards are particularly important. Chapter 3 is devoted to this important area.

Multinational organisations These are large worldwide organisations, e.g. Ford, General Motors, Shell, Sony. They spend huge amounts of money on bought-out materials and supplies, for example Shell calculated its global expenditure on purchases in a recent year as $26 billion. Purchasing and supply is normally well developed.

Organisation of the activity

■ Centralisation/decentralisation

Most groups of companies or large organisations which operate several establishments adopt some compromise between buying everything centrally and buying everything locally, aiming to balance the advantages of strength with those of flexibility. Basically there are three alternatives:

1 complete decentralisation, allowing full autonomy in each of the units;
2 complete centralisation, which in practice means that apart from local purchases of small value, all purchases are made from a central office; or
3 a combination of the two.

The advantages usually cited for decentralisation are:

- The local buyer will have a better knowledge of the needs of his or her particular factory or unit, of local suppliers, and of transport and storage facilities.

■ He or she will be able to respond quicker to emergency requirements, partly because of shorter lines of communication and partly because he or she will have a greater awareness of local circumstances than someone sitting many miles away.

■ The local buyer's direct responsibility to his or her immediate management will produce better liaison and tighter control by local top management, particularly where they operate as a profit centre. Since materials represent such a large proportion of works cost in manufacturing, a common argument revolves around authority and responsibility. That argument runs: if local management are not allowed, for example, to select and deal with their own suppliers, how can they be held responsible for output which relies so heavily on supplier efficiency?

Complete centralisation, on the other hand, has advantages which include:

■ Economies obtained by consolidating like requirements of all units in the group, thereby improving purchasing strength in negotiating and facilitating supplier relationships.

■ Avoidance of price anomalies between group units and of competition between them for materials in short supply.

■ Better overall stock management and material utilisation.

■ Economies of staffing and clerical effort together with uniformity in procedures, forms, standards and specification.

Generally speaking, the advantages of one approach are the disadvantages of the other, thus a combination of both is often used to obtain the benefit from the best features of each, while avoiding their disadvantages. A typical structure in such an organisation is illustrated in Figure 2.19. In one of this nature the group or central office is often responsible for:

■ Determining policy, standards and procedures and group specifications.

■ The negotiation of contracts for common materials which are used by the group in any volume.

Figure 2.19
**A centralised/
decentralised
structure**

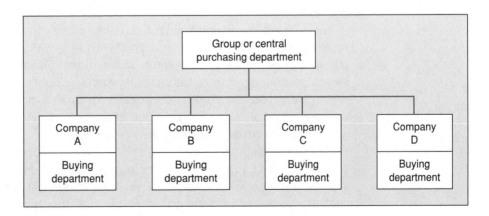

- Major plant and equipment and capital project contracts.
- Contracts for imported materials and for exports where relevant.
- Legal matters relating to supply.
- Co-ordination of group inventory.
- The education and development of supplies personnel within the group and the provision of advice on staffing and related recruitment.

Another approach sometimes used has a small group of staff which has a relatively limited policy and co-ordinating role, and the largest user of a particular commodity or material in the group negotiates on behalf of all group users as the 'lead' buyer. Thus, in the organisation illustrated in Figure 2.19 the buyer in company A might negotiate contracts for raw material X on behalf of companies B and C as well as their own. In the same way the buyer in, say, company D might do so on behalf of companies A and C.

In both systems, in matters outside the scope of the group office role local buyers act autonomously. In some groups, the local managers are directly responsible to a member of their own board and have only an indirect or professional accountability to the senior supplies person in the group office. Having established a particular approach within a group, it is still necessary to consider the problem of centralisation/decentralisation at plant or unit level. Over the last 30 years there has been a trend to centralise purchasing activity into one department.

However, there is considerable difference between companies as regards the effective centralisation of these activities. In some instances it is still the case that the purchasing department merely comprises a rubber stamp which signs orders that have been negotiated by whichever line manager is concerned with the material or service in question: in others, full authority is vested in the purchasing manager as the only executive able to commit the company to expenditure. Even though as official signatories to purchase orders both have the same legal authority, their levels of decision-making authority are at different extremes of a continuum. Between those extremes exists a variety of authority levels, most of which in analysis relate to the degree of confidence which the remainder of the organisation has in the professionalism of the incumbent.

The advantages of centralising purchasing activity in an enterprise depend on the ability of the executive entrusted with this work to use the company's purchasing power most effectively. This will include consolidating requirements, developing sources, rationalising stocks, simplifying procedures, working with suppliers to eliminate unnecessary cost to mutual advantage, and working with colleagues to ensure an effective flow of information that will enable the objectives of the enterprise to be met.

Effective centralisation does not imply that the supplies manager dictates which piece of equipment is to be purchased. Nor does it imply that the supplies manager's only role is to vet the commercial technicalities of the contract for the equipment, try to ensure that the price is competitive and that the equipment is delivered on time. For the best effect, the manager will be involved in decision making from the initial stages where the need for equipment to perform the necessary function is identified: advising colleagues on sources and working closely with them on evaluating the alternatives. The supplies manager should be seen by prospective suppliers as the decision-making authority, even if only in allowing commercial leverage in discussion with them. This does not imply that technical matters should be subordinated to commercial ones, but suggests that both are considered in parallel. Too often the converse is true and the buyer is given little scope to perform his or her function. If suppliers know that technical factors dominate and the order is theirs, the buyer has to negotiate with extremely limited power.

To take this example further, among the commercial factors which the buyer should take into consideration are: guarantees on the life of the machine, the position regarding spares, breakdown service, operative training, payment terms and conditions, delivery programme and check points, logistic and installation implications, price breakdown and relationship with the programme, level of after-service, etc. It is important to remember that effective comparison between alternatives at the quotation stage should include these and other considerations as well as the technical specification.

■ Various methods of organising the function

There are many ways of organising the purchasing and supply function, taking into account organisational objectives and strategies. The possibilities include:

- *Organisation by end product*
  Here the section is within the purchasing and supply department under a team leader and is responsible for buying all materials associated with a particular end product.
- *Organisation by category, i.e. category management*
  Teams are responsible for buying families of materials (such as timber, paper products, plastics, castings, forgings). They buy all the requirements of the company which fall within their category grouping.
- *Organisation by value classification*
  Areas of high cost become the responsibility of a senior buyer with minor items assigned to more junior staff.
- *Organisation by profit centre*
  This is in addition to the style of organisation discussed immediately above but where the department effectively becomes a supplier to the user, whose operating costs are added to the material cost for charging purposes. Costs of purchasing operation become self-liquidating, reducing overheads and on-costs normally charged. Detailed operating budgets and cost control are necessary.

Figure 2.20
**A typical small
department
structure**

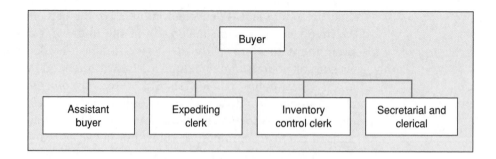

◼ Departmental organisation

At departmental level the number of people employed, the volume and variety of goods and services purchased, the ability and authority of the departmental head, the capabilities of the people employed in the department, and the importance of the supply function to the operation of the enterprise concerned are among the factors which will affect the decision on the structure of the organisation.

Nevertheless, there are basic organisation patterns around which variations occur. A simple form in a small department is often something like that shown in Figure 2.20. With the exclusion in some cases of the stock-control function from the buyer's responsibilities, this pattern is reasonably typical of a small departmental structure. Most departments, in the UK at least, are composed of fewer than four people. The division of responsibilities shown in Figure 2.20 is generally quite straightforward. The buyer assumes responsibility for the more important purchases, and an assistant deals with the more routine matters. In practice, the classic 80/20 relationship is evident in this division, for most of the money spent by the organisation will tend to be concentrated on a relatively small number of items. (The 80/20 relationship is one application of the Pareto Principle in that the significant items in a given group tend to be concentrated in a small area within that group. Eighty per cent of a company's purchases by value tend to be concentrated with 20 per cent of their suppliers: indeed in some cases the ratio can be as much as 90/10.)

Figure 2.21 (with similar caveats to those mentioned for Figure 2.20) illustrates one approach to organisational structure in a larger department. It can be seen that the allocation of responsibilities within the department is more complex. Generally speaking the chief buyer is responsible for policy making as well as the efficient management of the department as an element in the company organisation. The chief buyer usually retains responsibility, too, for the most important contracts and purchasing decisions. In this type of structure a decision has to be taken as to how best to group the purchasing activities so as to be most effective. One increasingly common approach is to do this by category of materials, where each buyer deals with a particular range of items. For example, one buyer may be responsible for raw materials, another for mechanical components and another for electrical/electronic

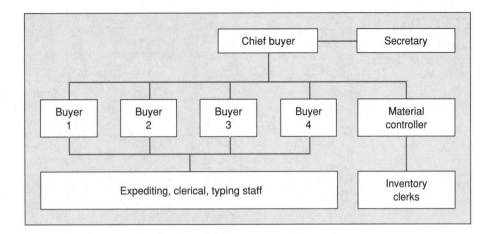

Figure 2.21
A medium-sized departmental structure

materials. Apart from the advantage of specialisation in a particular range of goods, category management helps to avoid duplication of research and negotiation effort at plant level. It should also facilitate data collection and communication inside the department and with other sections of the company as a whole. It can strengthen the buyer's negotiating position through consolidation of total requirements and can reduce time spent in negotiation. In addition, liaison with suppliers is often improved by this means as the supplier base is consolidated.

However, if this approach to division of work is followed, it is important to bear in mind that provision should be made whereby a colleague can take over responsibility for a particular group of materials in the absence of the buyer normally responsible. One method commonly used to deal with this is to pair buyers. Not only can this help to overcome such temporary problems, but it can be a useful means of staff development. In the organisation shown in Figure 2.21, buyers 1 and 2 and buyers 3 and 4 might work together in this manner. In larger organisations (a typical example of which is shown in Figure 2.22), each section will tend to become self-sufficient in this way. Development of staff in such cases, however, may involve moving people between sections.

Purchasing in the organisation structure

Where should purchasing be in the organisation structure? In some cases the function may not be significant, and will be placed in a subordinate position in the hierarchy. The converse is true when the size of purchase expenditure relative to corporate turnover is such that a very senior executive is appointed to control the function, or when key supplies emanate from volatile markets, or when the proportion of the cost of a product which is bought in is significant. Between these extremes, on what might be thought of as a continuum, lie many variants.

Figure 2.22
A departmental organisation in a large single-factory enterprise

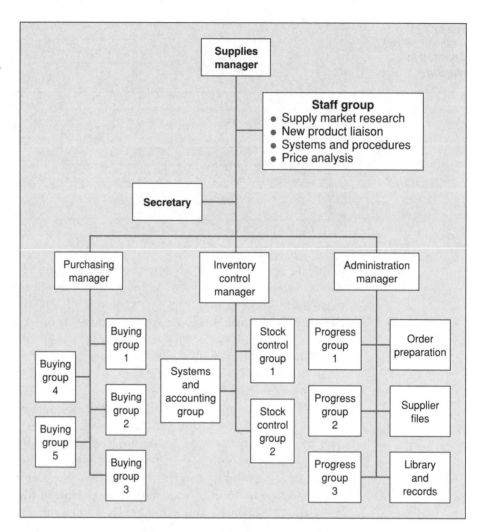

Figure 2.23
Outline organisation of a medium-sized manufacturing company

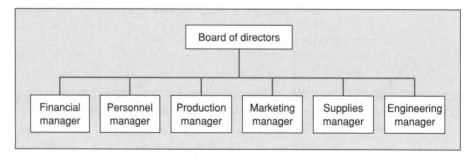

Figure 2.23 is the outline organisation of a medium-sized manufacturing concern in which the purchasing function is recognised as a key element in company operations. Depending upon the perceived importance of purchasing, the function may also be represented at board level either in its own right or through a director with related interests.

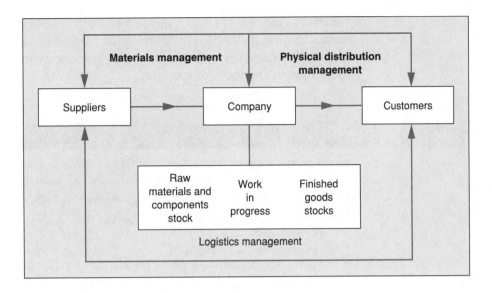

Figure 2.24
A model of a manufacturing company's materials systems

■ The broader approaches

Several references have been made in this chapter to systems approaches. In broad terms these differ from conventional functional organisation systems in that they seek to avoid functional sub-optimisation while pursuing system-wide effectiveness. As implied earlier, this always involves trade-off decisions being made between departmental objectives. 'Materials management', 'logistics management', 'physical distribution management' and 'materials administration' are examples of such approaches.

Figure 2.24 illustrates what are generally regarded as the spheres of activity for each of these approaches. However, it is important to recognise that some advocates of, for example, 'materials management' and 'physical distribution management' define their scope of influence as being that of 'logistics management' or supply chain management.

Purchasing devolution

As purchasing takes on a more strategic role it will release much of the routine purchasing to budget-holders, particularly in the areas where purchasing can add little value. As purchasing evolves to become strategically proactive so it must devolve. New structures have now come into place, with a small strategically tasked purchasing activity responsible for managing the supply chains, determining overall purchasing policy and involved with major negotiations, while routine, lower value items are handled on a day-to-day basis by budget-holders.

Clearly e-procurement facilitates call-offs using desk-top catalogues by local users. Chapter 18 discusses this application in greater detail. Within each functional area or operating unit profit centre, individual budget-holders would be delegated to 'buy' within agreed parameters laid down by purchasing. A strategic purchasing activity would have to contribute to the development of staff, and monitor activities.

The supply chain

Supply chain management is concerned with the co-ordinated flow of materials and services from origins through suppliers into and through the organisation and on to the ultimate consumer in such a way as to maximise value added and minimise cost. Associated flows of information and funds are also included.

The supply chain includes all those involved in organising and converting materials through the input stages (raw materials), conversion phase (work-in-progress), and outputs (finished products). The cycle is often repeated several times in the journey from the initial producer to the ultimate customer as one organisation's finished good is another's input.

The Chartered Institute of Purchasing and Supply indicate the role of purchasing in the supply chain process (see Figure 2.25).

The structural entity of the supply chain is concerned with activities such as make, transform, move and store. Capacity location also needs to be considered. Further decisions will need to be taken with regard to internal/external transport. The supply chain could be local, national or international. The supply chain may be complex, and will affect everyone involved in it.

■ Primary and support supply chains

Primary supply chains are those that ultimately provide the goods/services to the customer, for example:

Raw materials → components → sub-assemblies → finished product → customer

Support chains are regarded as those that supply consumables or maintenance, repair and operating (MRO) items and capital items to support the above activity.

■ Supply chains and 'value added' ideas

It is desirable that developing good practices and concepts is implemented throughout the supply chain by migrating these ideas both upstream and downstream. This will require inter-organisation co-operation, and may involve such factors as cross-functional teams, recognition of the need to delight both internal and external customers, empowerment, more flexible management structures, effective partnerships, etc. Such developments will reduce costs and add value throughout the supply chain. This requires a

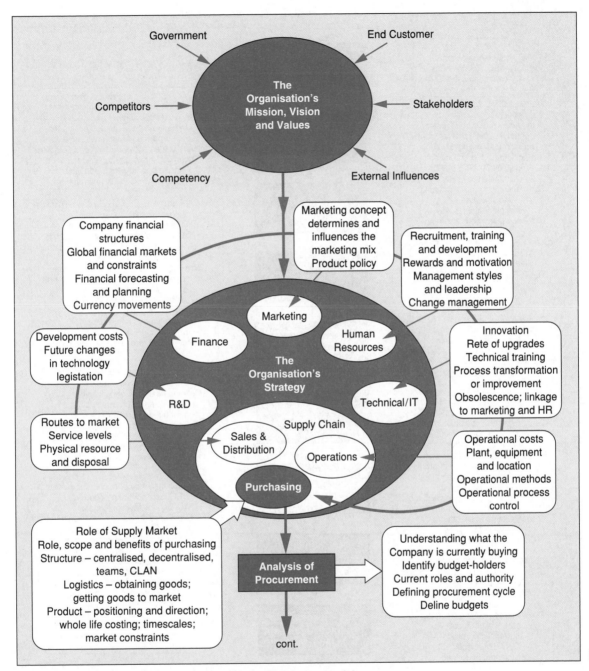

Figure 2.25 The CIPS purchasing and supply chain process model

(*Source*: CIPS)

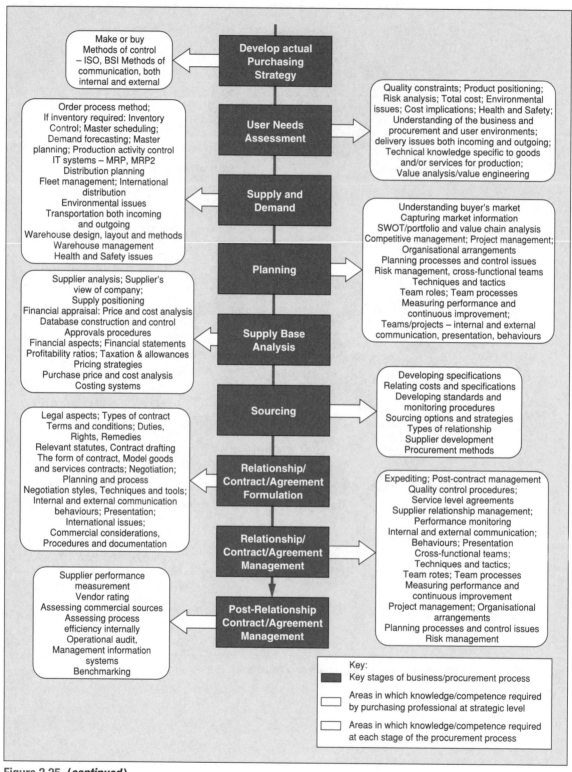

Figure 2.25 (*continued*)

review of the concepts of cost and value, with an emphasis on total cost of acquisition and use of strategic acquisition cost with less emphasis on traditional price-based approaches.

Some ideas that are pursued by those concerned with supply chain management are:

- reverse engineering;
- value engineering;
- value adding relationships and negotiations;
- supplier integration;
- tiering of suppliers;
- value added chains;
- lean supply;
- agile supply;
- supply pipeline management;
- value streams;
- network sourcing.

The list is far from exhaustive, but indicates something of the scope of the contemporary thinking and that of the recent past that has contributed to the elevation of supply chain management to a recognised major strategic contributor to the organisation.

The supply chain concept in action

The perception that purchasing is no longer a routine, administrative 'ordering' activity is now widely, if not universally, held. The expression 'supply chain' has come into prominence, although there is competing terminology such as the expression 'value stream' preferred by the promoters of 'lean manufacturing'. 'Pipeline management' is another expression with a comparable meaning, as is 'network sourcing'. Not only is there competing terminology, there are also alternative definitions of the term 'supply chain' itself, some regarding it as another name for the procurement cycle, and others linking the term with logistics, i.e. movement, storage and distribution activities.

What supply chain management is about is the linkage of the immediate seller/buyer relationship into a longer series of events. A company's suppliers have their own suppliers, and often the direct customers are not the ultimate consumers. Supply chain management sees the various buyers and sellers as being part of a continuum, and recognises the benefit to be derived from attempting to take a strategic and integrated view of the chain, rather than focusing on the individual links and thereby sub-optimising. In other words, the focus of managerial attention is not just the individual company or organisation, but the interactions between the series of organisations that constitute the chain. It might be helpful to visualise the firms in the chain and the flows of goods or services and information passing between them as links. Figure 2.26 may help in this respect.

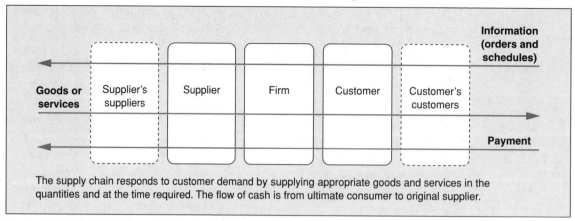

The supply chain responds to customer demand by supplying appropriate goods and services in the quantities and at the time required. The flow of cash is from ultimate consumer to original supplier.

Figure 2.26 **Supply chains and the principal 'flows'**

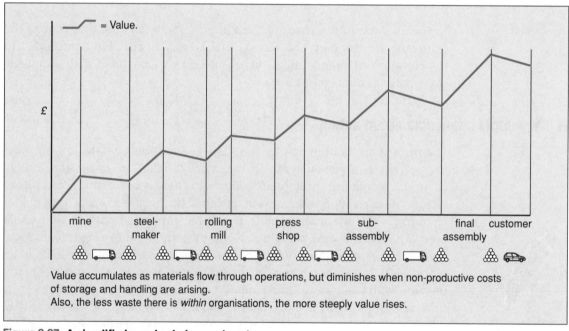

Value accumulates as materials flow through operations, but diminishes when non-productive costs of storage and handling are arising.
Also, the less waste there is *within* organisations, the more steeply value rises.

Figure 2.27 **A simplified supply chain or value stream**

Consider Figure 2.27. It shows some of the major steps in the production of an automobile component in the form of a steel pressing. Iron ore is mined and converted into steel which is rolled into strip form, the component is pressed from the strip and then it is assembled, with others, to form the automobile. In practice there would almost certainly be many more steps, for example the steel component would be rather likely to become part of a sub-assembly prior to being incorporated into the car.

As work proceeds, value is added to the material (for the purpose of this illustration value is represented as the amount that the next 'customer' in the chain from iron mine to driver pays for the material, less any costs of process or conversion). The various conversion or production operations begin with stocks of incoming material, and end with inventories of goods ready for the next operation. Transportation links the programmes.

The diagram shows that cost is being added during storage and movement, but not value, and that if storage and movement can be minimised, value increases more steeply. In addition to the costs which are apparent *between* the main stages, there are also, of course, intra-organisational costs (costs *within* the main stages). For example, if the steelmaker can become more efficient through the reduction of wastes associated with the steelmaking process, then the value added slope will be a steeper one for that part of the chain. Value will be added more quickly.

Womack and Jones (1996) described the value stream for a soft drink can (Figure 2.28), recognising that the most difficult component of a can of cola to produce is the can itself. They highlight the stark contrast between the actual value adding process time and the storage and movement time. They report that around 11 months elapse between the extraction of bauxite (aluminium ore) and the consumption of the contents of the can leading to disposal. Of these 11 months, only approximately 3 hours are spent on conversion of the product. In other words, for more than 99 per cent of the time the value stream is not flowing; the muda (waste) of waiting and queuing is being funded.

Professor Dan Jones has referred to purchasing and supply professionals as 'the architects of the value stream'. There is a good deal of inefficiency in most supply chains; as purchasing develops its more strategic and holistic view of supply as constituting an extended process linking consumers with raw materials, it is predicted that the benefits from increased efficiency will be great.

Improving the efficiency of the supply chain

■ Convergence and divergence in the supply chain

It will be easily seen that the supply chain concept is a convenient idea for study purposes, but that in practice there are very few goods that flow in a single stream from origin to point of use or consumption. The closest we get to this is perhaps in the supply of certain food or drink items, where growers such as farmers or gatherers such as fishermen make the produce available for consumption. Even here, though, taking the supply of milk as an example, the commodity cannot be taken to final market without associated supplies of such things as energy, packaging or transportation, so we do not really have a single strand from beginning to end. It is also worth considering that the

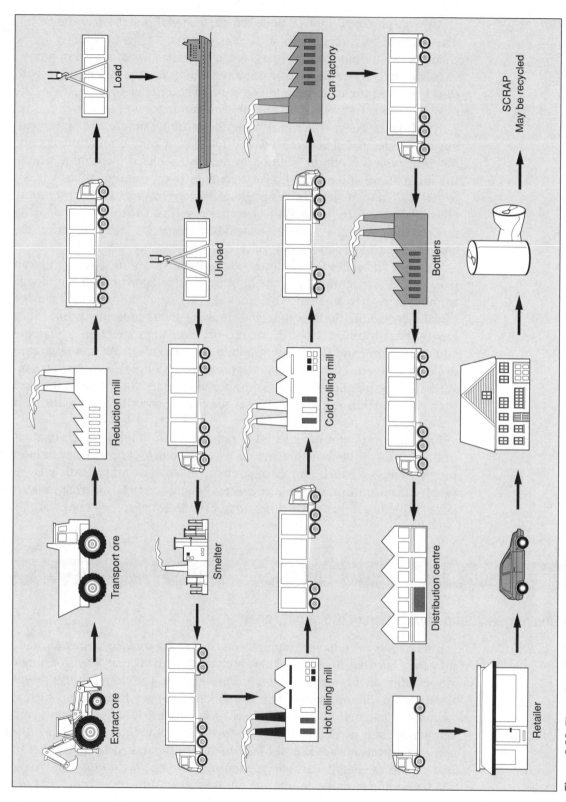

Figure 2.28 The value stream of a soft drink can

product itself, milk, finds its way to market in either a fresh or preserved state, as cheese or butter, or as an ingredient in a wide range of food products.

If we follow a supply chain from the upstream or producer's end, we are likely to see a great deal of divergence. In other words, the material can find its way into a range, sometimes a huge range, of different products. Copper ore might eventually become any one of the millions of items that are made from this metal, or one of its alloys. If we start with a final product, a sewing machine for example, we see convergence. Different types of metal, plastics, electrical and mechanical components are embodied in the item. Many different supply chains converge at this product. While each individual component might, at least in some cases, have its own supply chain, once we begin assembly, or sub-assembly, then we have convergence.

Most materials diverge from their source, and converge on the finished product. Figure 2.29 shows the ideas of convergence and divergence and their combination.

Types of supply chain

Hughes, Ralf and Michels (1999) suggest that there are several types of supply chain, and that relations between different types of chain may be either collaborative or competitive. Figure 2.30 shows diagrams adapted from their work that illustrate this point.

Strategic development of purchasing

As organisations became more involved with such leading-edge concepts as just-in-time (JIT) and total quality management (TQM), it was soon realised that a major contribution could be achieved from the input activities, particularly purchasing, if they became more involved in managing the supplier base effectively. Reductions in the number and increases in the quality of suppliers could reduce input costs considerably and increase organisational efficiency, with consequent increases in customer satisfaction.

■ Internal purchasing involvement

While it was seen that the purchasing and supply activity could make an important contribution externally through its relationships with suppliers, it was increasingly recognised that it could also make an equally important contribution internally, and with the final customer, the consumer, if it became more strategically proactive. Thus the idea was to extend its influence backward strategically in terms of managing the supplier base, and forward so that it became more involved with internal strategic decision making and with the ultimate customer.

Figure 2.29
Convergent and divergent elements in a supply chain

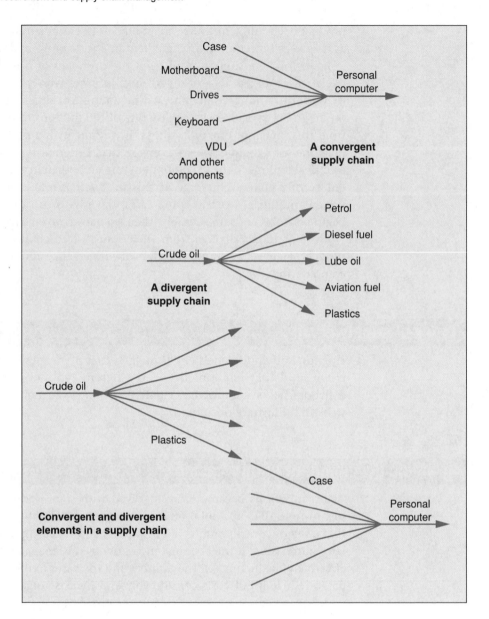

■ Strategic input supply chain management

Clearly, if purchasing is to be actively involved in improving and developing the input part of the supply chain, it will need to be sufficiently well developed itself and proactive. This would imply that over a period of time there had already been a recognition within the buying organisation of the strategic importance of purchasing. We have already examined stages of purchasing development in Chapter 1.

If purchasing is essentially reactive and clerical, it will find it impossible to improve the supplier base strategically. Buyers need to be well trained, with

Arm's length: open competition	**Commodity trading** A sells to B or C, B sells to A or C, C sells to A or B	**Partnering for customer delight**
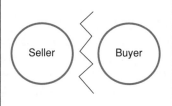	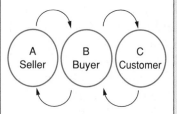	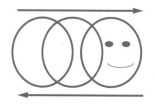
Competitive bids, tenders and market testing. Emphasise rigour and tough bargaining	Independent trading driven by the deal. Emphasis on need to manage volatility with commodities	Openness, trust and shared deliverables
From supplier's suppliers to customer's customers	**Lean supply chains and systems integration**	**Competing constellations of linked companies**
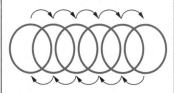		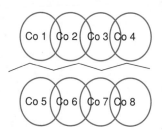
Link up all the players in a horizontal supply chain. Emphasise seamless delivery, optimisation and integration	War on waste and step change cost transformation. Emphasise lean as in *fit*, not starving	First movers link up with the best players. Emphasise capability, competence and cultural compatibility
Interlocking supply between competitors	**Asset control supply: dominate or die**	**Virtual supply: no production, only customers**
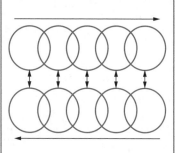	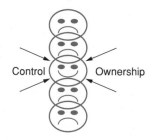	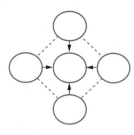
Link up for incremental business. Emphasise an association where little competitive advantage arises	Gain control of the assets and leverage them. Emphasise staying the right side of monopoly abuse	Low fixed costs and subcontracted production. Emphasis on marketing skills and superb distribution

Figure 2.30 Types of supply chain

(*Source*: Based on Hughes *et al.*, 1999)

the necessary skills to carry out such work. If, however, the purchasing activity is well developed and works well with others in its own organisation, who are needed in supplier management teams, the strategic input improvements are likely to proceed with greater success.

In some organisations concepts such as JIT, TQM and agile supply are putting pressure on the need for a smaller, more efficient, rationalised supplier base tending towards single sourcing. Other organisations have a policy of having all major supplies dual-sourced. This dual or multiple sourcing requirement may have arisen because of customer requirements, or questions concerning the quality or reliability of existing suppliers. Before reducing the number of suppliers, purchasing would have to review the reasons for multiple sourcing, and take steps to address those reasons if still present. It has been known for organisations simply to reduce the number of suppliers without addressing the reasons for having more than one supplier, with resulting major problems.

If the supplier base is to be reduced, it is vital that those suppliers left are able to meet the purchasing organisation's future requirements, and are prepared to improve on a continuous basis the quality and delivery of the goods and services they provide. Safeguards must be established to make sure that the remaining key suppliers, i.e. strategic suppliers, do not exploit their new single-supplier status. One way of overcoming some of these problems is to enter into a partnership or collaborative agreement with those suppliers. In exchange for preferred status, the supplier and buyer organisations would have to agree to such considerations as:

- Looking on a continuous basis at ways of reducing costs and improving performances.
- Being prepared to grow together, in terms of both size and direction. It would be expected that the supplier and buyer might invest in complementary technology.
- The disclosure or exchange of costs and financial information so that unnecessarily expensive operations could be reduced.
- Conducting negotiations between the two sides on a win/win basis, with the emphasis on joint pursuit of efficiencies.

For this type of commitment to be entered into there needs to be considerable trust between the two sides. The relationship must be mutual, in that costs and benefits are shared by both sides. By reducing unnecessary costs and activities in the supply chain, lead times and prices can be reduced, making both supplier and buying organisations more competitive.

Once the supplier base has been reduced, the remaining strategic suppliers might agree to strategic improvement targets in relation to such considerations as:

- quality;
- delivery;

- operations;
- systems;
- development of innovative concepts.

A more dedicated and powerful supplier base is not achieved by getting suppliers to cut profits, but by working together with the buying organisation to eliminate unnecessary costs and to seek opportunities to add value.

If purchasing and supply is to adopt responsibility, or at least a leading role in supply chain management, it must be supported by strategies from the top. This requires continual investment in the purchasing and related functions, and in commitment from senior management to such developments.

Purchasing within a group (intra-group buying)

Sometimes group companies compel the purchasing staff to acquire, where possible, items from within the group. There is nothing wrong with this, provided that those organisations from within the group offer at least comparable products or services as could be purchased from external suppliers. There have, however, been many cases where the group supplier is more expensive, or quality and delivery are not as good as with outside suppliers. The net effect of this is that costs rise and the organisation becomes less competitive. If such a state of affairs continues for too long the organisation could be affected adversely. It is therefore necessary that policies that require purchasing to source within the group also provide safeguards, so that, for instance, if an internal part of the company cannot match outside deals within a specified time period, then the buyer is allowed to source such goods or services with external suppliers.

The CIPS Ethical Code

Precepts

Members shall never use their authority or office for personal gain and shall seek to uphold and enhance the standing of the purchasing and supply profession and the Institute by:

- maintaining an unimpeachable standard of integrity in all their business relationships, both inside and outside the organisation in which they are employed;
- fostering the highest possible standards of professional competence amongst those for whom they are responsible;
- optimising the use of resources for which they are responsible to provide the maximum benefit to their employing organisation;
- complying both with the letter and the spirit of: (a) the law of the country in which they practice; and (b) such guidance on professional practice as may be issued by the Institute from time to time;
- rejecting any business practice which might reasonably be deemed improper.

Guidelines

In applying these precepts, members should follow the guidance set out below:

■ **Declaration of interest**. Any personal interest which may impinge or might reasonably be deemed by others to impinge on a member's impartiality in any matter relevant to his or her duties should be declared.

■ **Confidentiality and accuracy of information**. The confidentiality of information received in the course of duty should be respected and should never be used for personal gain; information given in the course of duty should be true and fair and never designed to mislead.

■ **Competition**. While bearing in mind the advantages to the member's employing organisation of maintaining a continuing relationship with a supplier, any arrangement which might, in the long term, prevent the effective operation of fair competition should be avoided.

■ **Business gifts**. Business gifts other than items of very small intrinsic value such as business diaries or calendars should not be accepted.

■ **Hospitality**. Modest hospitality is an accepted courtesy of a business relationship. However, the recipient should not allow him or herself to reach a position whereby he or she might be, or might be deemed by others to have been, influenced in making a business decision as a consequence of accepting such hospitality. The frequency and scale of hospitality accepted should not be significantly greater than the recipient's employer would be likely to provide in return.

■ When it is not easy to decide between what is and is not acceptable in terms of gifts or hospitality, the offer should be declined or advice sought from the member's superior.

Ethical behaviour and relationships with suppliers

Allegations of corruption have long been a factor in business dealings, and these have focused attention on business ethics. Without a rigid self-imposed and universally accepted ethical tradition, purchasing could not be regarded as a true profession. It is only to be expected, then, that the Chartered Institute of Purchasing and Supply should publish a Code of Conduct and Guide to Good Practice containing many references to basic ethical considerations (as shown). In particular, reference is made to:

■ respect for the confidentiality of information which comes to members in the course of their work – speculation in the shares of a supplier is discouraged, for instance;

■ refraining from any activity which may impair impartiality and disclosing any personal interest;

■ placing orders with a company in which there is a financial interest for the buyer, or taking a financial interest in a supplier;

■ observing contractual obligations as strictly as the buyer intends they should be observed;

- refusing to accept arrangements which falsify the process of tendering and open competition;
- ensuring that the legitimate interests of suppliers are not put at risk;
- aiming at a mutually satisfactory relationship with suppliers rather than short-term advantage;
- discouraging practices which lead to commercial or other corruption;
- promoting the development of high standards of professional conduct and competence.

One of the major reasons for developing and enforcing such codes throughout the organisation is to assist in the development of integrated, effective supply chains. Suppliers involved in such chains need to be reassured that they are dealing with purchasing organisations that have their long-term strategic interests in mind; that they are not going to be involved in various sharp practices; will get paid on time; will not suddenly lose the business because the buyer is unfairly cutting prices. Such ethics are also important for the buyer as they become involved in partnerships.

Organisations such as IBM, Shell, Hewlett-Packard and other 'blue chip' companies all have well-developed ethical practices and interestingly have some of the best-developed integrated supply chains.

■ Environmental procurement and the supply chain

These days it is essential that the purchasing activity examines its supply chain to ensure environmental factors are being assessed.

BS7750/ISO14001/2 requires organisations to manage environmental issues effectively. New suppliers must provide details of their environmental intent. While value for money is important it must not be achieved by sacrificing environmental factors. Factors that the buyer needs to investigate are:

- biodegradability of products at the end of their product life cycle;
- ways of reducing waste;
- impact on the environment of waste products;
- design influences to produce a more friendly product;
- sustainability of raw materials used and alternative products;
- new legislation and its impact on the supply chain.

Organisations might find some of the processes employed in their production methods could become outlawed in the future. As an example, IBM had to change the way it cleaned its computer boards, from using a chemical cleaner to 'charged water'. The cost of the change was high but it was required under environmental legislation.

Buyers need to investigate their supply chains and such issues as:

- the use of CFC and ozone-depleting substances;
- making the important distinction between recycled and environmentally friendly products;

- promoting and developing environmental issues with suppliers;
- energy consumption and efficiency of the product when in use, and its disposal;
- the extent and nature of the emissions from the equipment or product under normal use and under situations of abuse;
- the consumption of non-renewable natural resources associated with the product and the use to which it will be put;
- the amount and type of packaging material and disposal arrangements required to get rid of it;
- the ability of the product to be recycled and/or disposal arrangements likely to be required when it reaches the end of its product life cycle;
- the lifetime cost of ownership and overall value for money of the commodity;
- the materials involved and any process which generates excessive waste and problems;
- the environmental implications of using particular suppliers, and their improvement plans;
- long-term strategic plans for improvements.

Summary

1 The chapter considers growth in the strategic role of procurement, purchasing and supply and how an organisation's view of its business profile develops its Mission Statement, which, in turn, determines its strategies.

2 Viewing purchasing objectives as a hierarchy, world-class concepts and co-makership principles are at the foundation level leading up to the ultimate objectives of increasing efficiency and profits.

3 The external environment influences strategy selection. The perceptions of managers at all levels, the company culture and experience will influence the effectiveness of those strategies adopted. The chapter stresses the need to adopt strategies which will develop and maintain competitive advantage.

4 It is vital that purchasing be well informed on the external environment and its influences in order that it can provide effective input as part of the organisation's integrated planning activity.

5 We have considered the implications of the term 'supply chain', the role of purchasing in upstream and downstream management, and different types of supply chains have been identified.

6 Aspects of purchasing and supply management within and between organisations have been identified and discussed.

7 There is no generally applicable organisational structure as each enterprise is unique. The size of the organisation, the type of market which it serves, the technology and processes involved and many other factors will all determine the structure.

8 Systems approaches can be used to explain the development of organisation structure. The more integrated the system, the better the chance of success.

9 The adoption of leading-edge concepts means purchasing has to extend its involvement down to the levels of supply and up to the final customer, i.e. buyers must become familiar with the total supply chain in order to reduce costs and waste.

10 Organisational structures should be tailored to meet specific needs taking into account the external environment and the objectives and strategies laid out.

11 Purchasing activities of a routine nature will be devolved to users, and can be outsourced.

12 Virtual organisations have procurement strategy as their central role.

13 Ethical and environmental issues and the supply chain have been recognised.

References and further reading

Appointments (2007), *Supply Management*, March.

Birchall, D (1993), 'Managing the supply chain', *Logistics*, April.

Cox, A (2003), 'Horses for courses', *Supply Management*, January.

Department of Trade and Industry (1991), 'Building a purchasing strategy', *Enterprise Initiative 1991*.

Emmett, S and Crocker, B (2006), *The Relationship Driven Supply Chain*, Aldershot: Gower.

Evans, E and Maguire, R (1993), 'Purchasing fraud', *Purchasing and Supply Chain Management*.

Freeman, V and Cavatino, J (1990), 'Fitting purchasing to the strategic firm: framework, processes and values', *International Journal of Purchasing and Materials Management*, 26 (1), Winter.

Gundlach, G T, Bolumole, Y A, Eltantawy, R A and Frankel, R (2006), 'The changing landscape of supply chain management, marketing channels of distribution, logistics and purchasing', *Journal of Business and Industrial Marketing*, 2 (7).

Hadfield, R and Nichols, E (2002), *Supply Chain Redesign*, Oxford: Financial Times Prentice Hall.

Hoagland, J H (1999), 'Fifty years of purchasing; progress, problems and potential', *7th IPSERA Conference*, April.

Hughes, J (1998), 'Force pretenders', *Supply Management*, July.

Hughes, J, Ralf, M and Michels, B (1999), *Transform your Supply Chain*, London: International Thomson Press.

Johnson, G and Scholes, K (2002), *Exploring Corporate Strategy*, Harlow: Prentice Hall.

Kelley, B (1999), *Ethics at Work*, Aldershot: Gower.

Kraljic, P (1983), 'Purchasing must become supply management', *Harvard Business Review*, September/October.

Li, L (2002), 'Information sharing in a supply chain with horizontal competition', *Management Science*, 48 (9), September.

Lynch, R (2002), *Corporate Strategy*, Harlow: Prentice Hall.

Lynch, R (2005), *Corporate Strategy*, Harlow: Financial Times Prentice Hall.

Manion, D (1993), 'Partnership selection at ICL', in Jessop, O and Hines, P (eds), *Selected Readings in Purchasing and Supply*, Ascot: CIPS.

Mintzberg, H (1995), 'Five Ps for strategy', in *The Strategy Process*, Hemel Hempstead: Prentice Hall.

Morris, N and Calantone, R (1991), 'Redefining the purchasing function: an entrepreneurial perspective', *International Journal of Purchasing and Materials Management*, Fall.

Nicholson, A (1993), 'Strategic management for the professional', *Purchasing and Supply Management*, April.

Pearson, J and Gritzmacher, G H (1990), 'Integrated purchasing', *Long Range Planning*, 23 (3).

Quinn, J B, Mintzber, H and Ghoshal, S (1995), *Strategies for Change: The Strategy Process*, Englewood Cliffs, NJ: Prentice Hall.

Rumelt, R P (1995), 'Evaluating Business Strategy', in Mintzberg, H, Quinn, J B and Goshal, S (eds), *The Strategy Process*, Englewood Cliffs, NJ: Prentice Hall.

Rajagopal, S and Bernard, K (1993), 'Strategic procurement and competitive advantage', *International Journal of Purchasing and Materials Management*, Fall.

Rich, N, Hines, P, Jones, O and Francis, M (1996), 'Evidence of a watershed in the purchasing function', *IPSERA Conference Papers*, April.

Sammons, P (1999), 'Cut it out', *Supply Management*, July.

Simon, J (2000), 'Ethics', *Supply Management*, June.

Spekman, R E (1989), 'A strategic approach to procurement planning', *Journal of Purchasing and Supplies Management*, Spring.

Spinks, T (1993), 'Gaining a strategic advantage', *European Purchasing and Materials Management*.

Womack, J P and Jones, D (1996), *Lean Thinking*, New York: Simon and Schuster.

3

Public sector procurement

Introduction

Government expenditure on non-pay-related areas covers a vast range of equipment, goods and services: weapons systems, stationery, furniture, uniforms, food, capital projects including consultancy services, banking services, information systems and services, the management of facilities, as well as medical services, road building and maintenance and utilities. This requires an insight into the background and context of government procurement and the changing and challenging nature of such procurement in the light of commercial best practice. It will also require an overview of EU procurement regulations.

Objectives of this chapter

Part A

- To appreciate the context and background of public sector procurement
- To recognise the distinctive challenges of government procurement
- To examine the ways in which strategic procurement best practice has been adopted and adapted within major public sector organisations, such as Police, National Health Service (NHS), and Ministry of Defence (MoD)

Part B

- To appreciate the EU procurement directives
- To outline the main provisions of the directives
- To outline the main changes introduced in the revised EU directives (2000)
- To consider contract pricing mechanisms

Part A

Context of public sector procurement

Initiatives and policies such as market testing, contracting out, private finance initiative, competing for quality, NHS internal market, facilities management and partnering all affect how equipment, goods and services are procured within government and the public sector. They help to shape the approach to the market, the preparation of the specification and evaluation of the most economically advantageous tender followed by pertinent relationships in order to meet the requirement. However, in order to appreciate this contextual setting it is useful briefly to consider the background to the current public sector procurement environment.

Historic background

The government's first major statement on procurement strategy was set out in a report to the Prime Minister in 1984, *Government Purchasing: A Multi-department Review of Government Contract and Procurement Procedures* (Cabinet Office, 1984).

> [To] provide the accounting officer, and through him Parliament and the taxpayer, with value for money from expenditure on procurement. (Cabinet Office, 1984: Para. 1.4)

In May 1995, the government published its second procurement strategy in the form of a white paper, *Setting New Standards: A Strategy for Government Procurement* (HM Treasury, 1995). This identified ambitious proposals for the public sector including:

- seeking to develop world-class professional procurement staff;
- seeking to introduce best practice in terms of whole-life cost savings;
- highest standard benchmarking;
- co-operative relationships with contractors and suppliers within the constraints of competition;
- the promotion of continuous improvement (*Kaizen*).

This recognised that since the mid 1970s the influence of Japanese management philosophies and their subsequent derivatives have had a considerable impact on the survival and profitability of commercial organisations. Approaches such as JIT, TQM, the recognition of the importance of customer–supplier relationships, the increasing strategic significance of supply chain management and the adoption and adaptation of lean and agile concepts have all had major impacts upon the commercial sector. The beneficial effects of these, within the public sector, could not be ignored and government departments, local authorities, NHS and others have been keen to utilise these within their need for public accountability.

Once again a primary objective was stated as being the achievement of value for money. The strategy went further though in providing a definition of best value for money, namely:

The optimum combination of whole life cycle costs and quality to meet the customers' requirements. (HM Treasury, 1995: 2–3)

In 1998, Peter Gershon, Head of the Office of Government Commerce reviewed:

Civil procurement in Central Government in the light of the government's objectives on efficiency, modernisation and competitiveness in the short and medium term. (Gershon, 1999)

Gershon echoed the previous reviews, particularly regarding the primary objective of government procurement being the achievement of value for money.

From the above it is clear that delivering best value for money is accepted as the primary UK public sector procurement objective. Amazingly though, for a strategic objective at public policy level, no clear guidelines existed. The National Audit Office (1999) has, however, sought to remedy that situation through articulating value for money principles, namely:

- have a procurement strategy;
- plan early and agree requirements;
- actively manage contracts;
- think about the supply chain;
- seek continuous improvement;
- monitor performance.

Telgen and Sitar (2001) conclude that it is possible to generalise for every type of organisation that value can be added by the procurement department through:

- better contracts;
- improved purchasing efficiency;
- customer satisfaction (improved quality and service);
- closer and more co-operative relationships with suppliers;
- reduced costs, improved quality and time to market (as a result of being involved in the new product design process).

■ Public accountability

Considerable sums of money are spent annually in the public sector on goods and services. The procurement of these is for the good of the population at large and the expenditure that is incurred is, in effect, the taxpayers' money. Public sector buyers are accountable to the public whose money is being spent, *including disappointed tenderers and potential suppliers*. They must produce procedures and practices which will stand up either to scrutiny during government audits or to the challenge through the courts of any purchasing decision that has been made. A primary purpose of public accountability is to prevent abuses of taxpayers' money. A secondary purpose is to let it be seen that any such abuses have been prevented.

General principles of government procurement

The approach that has been taken for many years within the public sector can be summarised as follows:

- Purchasing should be based on value for money.
- Competition should be used to acquire goods and services (unless there are convincing reasons to the contrary).
- There should be clear definition of the roles and responsibilities of personnel involved in specifying the need, giving financial authority, and making procurement commitments.
- There should be separation of the financial authority and the purchasing authority.
- There should be separation of duties between personnel who make contracts, those who receive the goods or services and those who authorise payments.
- Requirements which are above a certain financial threshold are normally required to be advertised in accordance with EU regulations on public procurement.

Value for money

There was a widely held belief that government and public sector procurement decision making is based upon 'the lowest price'. This is not now the case. Purchasing decisions must be made on the basis of best 'value for money' criteria. This requires a consideration of many factors including, for example:

- costs over the lifetime of the goods or services;
- status and standing of suppliers;
- exact details of equipment, goods or services offered;
- financial aspects including payment terms, basis of contractual price, transport, etc.;
- operating costs;
- extent of support through life;
- assistance with disposal, etc.

As Behan (1994) has pointed out, the real value for money question is 'How much will the item or service purchased cost to *own and use*?'

Figure 3.1
Variables contributing to the Best Value concept

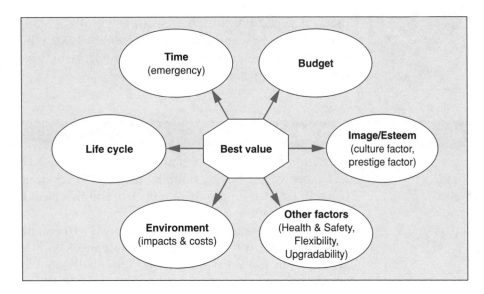

Targeting optimum value in public sector projects is best achieved through 'best value' focused contractor selection.

The best value concept is ambiguous and there may not be a commonly agreed definition for 'best value' (Palaneeswaran *et al.*, 2003), as shown in Figure 3.1. When selecting a 'best value' proposal the public clients should carefully balance the procurement objectives and 'value for money' within the constraints of public procurement principles and governing rules/regulations in a public accountability framework.

■ Tensions

Procurement of equipment, goods and services for the government and the public sector generally is complex. On one hand there is a need to ensure best value for money on behalf of the taxpayer, and the need to ensure that the processes to achieve this are fair and open to scrutiny. On the other hand there is considerable pressure to make savings (especially in the light of constantly reducing budgets) and to utilise some or all of the best practice philosophies mentioned earlier. This has led to many challenges for those undertaking procurement. Many observers will comment that procurement in the public sector is about following procedures and yet, many say, if the procedures are followed then innovation and improvement in cost performance (in line with commercial best practice) can be stifled.

■ Professionalism in public sector procurement

In order to ensure public accountability, yet to gain optimum impact through the use of commercial best practice, there is a need for professional training and education of those personnel responsible for the strategic direction and practical application of procurement action. Professionalism can only come from a full understanding of all the issues involved, a sound knowledge of the legal and commercial aspects and the confidence to make decisions that effectively balance these tensions.

UK National Health Service (NHS)

A decision was made to outsource the work of the NHS Logistics Authority and much of the buying done by the NHS Purchasing and Supply Agency (Pasa) to German supply chain firm DHL and its subcontractor, US healthcare company Novation.

The deal is expected recoup £1 billion over its 10-year lifetime. Under the new agreement, DHL will manage the entire supply chain. If they can deliver leverage they can not only use it to get lower prices but also it becomes more attractive for suppliers to work with them. Previously, that was not happening across a range of products as suppliers were going round the trusts and doing separate deals. They now need to work over time to get more commitment from the customer base so that they can work with them to deliver long-term value.

Elsewhere, areas such as IT and stationery, which have a large number of suppliers, will be rationalised. Through the DHL managed catalogue, suppliers have their products presented to 80,000 ordering points in the NHS. It is believed that the innovative contract will radically improve performance and cost in the health service and that it will in effect create strategic procurement in the NHS for the first time.

Less than £1 billion of the £3.7 billion spend is currently supplied through the central channel. Reverse e-auctions carried out for hospitals averaged a 25 per cent saving in price against delivered prices from the NHS Logistics catalogue. If that can be done with individual hospitals in isolation, then with the volumes being bought DHL should be able to make bigger savings.

Case study – How the NHS supply chain will work

Under the agreement, DHL will run NHS Supply Chain on behalf of NHS Business Services Authority (responsible for managing core public sector support services). It will be responsible for delivering all procurement and logistics services across an initial 500,000 products to support 600 hospitals and other providers in England. By focusing on procurement, supply, logistics and delivery of hospital goods, it claims it will enable healthcare providers to better manage their cost base and focus on patient care.

Goods will be procured from 10 categories (the parts of Pasa covered under the outsourcing):

Medical supplies
Food and kitchen
Print and stationery
Laundry and cleaning
Bedding and linen
Dressings
Uniforms and clothing
Patient appliances
Lab equipment and furniture and office equipment

The £3.7 billion a year contract is expected to save £1 billion over 10 years – the lifetime of the contract – by offering a wider range of goods to NHS trusts at lower prices.

In 2008, DHL will open a 250,000 square foot distribution centre (DC) to act as a stockholding hub for food and other products. It is expected that about 1000 extra employees will be recruited to manage this centre and an additional DC in 2012.

UK Metropolitan Police procurement

The London Metropolitan Police force has 44,000 staff supported by a £500 million annual procurement budget, managed by the Metropolitan Police's procurement department, comprised of 50 plus staff.

Yet until the authority was created as part of the Mayor of London's remit in 2000 its procurement policy barely existed. Goods were purchased on price alone, procurement officers handled orders as they arrived without any market specialisation and only three out of the 40 staff had CIPS qualifications. They had to introduce processes and procedures, training and development, tools and techniques that delivered best value for the authority. Staff were encouraged to gain CIPS qualifications.

Before the authority was established, procurement staff simply handled orders as they arrived, often with no prior warning, and did not have any particular familiarity with specific markets. Now staff specialise in one or two market areas and are switched around every 18 months or so to gain experience in other commodities or services. It has moved them from simply doing what they are told to knowing they have a valuable part to play in strategic decision making and operational delivery. They have cut the their 2000 suppliers by 30 per cent, buying from longer-term, 'higher value' relationships.

An example of improvements is as follows: for yellow waterproof jackets, a 40 per cent saving was delivered by aggregating their own requirements. In the police environment, availability and performance of equipment come first – operational support and quality are paramount and only then do they think about saving money.

They have begun to put in place contracts that give them clear perform-ance measures and improvement targets. They used to buy always on lowest price. Now they use the whole-life costing approach.

The Ministry of Defence (MoD)

The Ministry of Defence (MoD) buys a vast array of equipment, goods and services, spending nearly £10 billion annually. However, because it had not undergone the changes that affected the other public sector organisations, it still operated without having fully taken on board many of the ideas and con-cepts discussed earlier; still working in a bureaucratic manner in respect of tendering, contracting and commercial relationships. Kincaid (1999, 2002) christened it a 'dinosaur'. In many ways, the MoD could be seen as the last bastion of the 'old way' of procurement within the government and public sector. Yet it encapsulates all of the key aspects mentioned earlier and because it buys all manner of equipment, goods and services (from warships to grass-cutting equipment, medicine to consultancy services, food to fuel, etc.), it is an excellent example of how a major public sector organisation can recog-nise, adopt, adapt and develop new ideas and concepts within a rule-bound environment, and produce considerable savings in respect of value for money on behalf on the taxpayer. The following section will give an insight into the background and introduction of the new initiative at the MoD.

■ Procurement in the Ministry of Defence

The *Strategic Defence Review* (MoD, 1998) introduced a new philosophy, known as the 'Smart Procurement Initiative' (and subsequently renamed 'Smart Acquisition' in order to recognise an integrated, holistic, whole-life perspective), which brought a renewed focus on gaining *value for money* in the defence environment. This was to be achieved by bringing best practice from the commercial business world into public sector bureaucracy (MoD, 1998). This reflects the view that this was the 'new public management' environment to which the entire public sector had been exposed. This, in turn, follows legisla-tion that allows greater competition for professional services in the public sector and this is particularly manifest in the search for greater *economy, efficiency and effectiveness*. In essence, like the rest of the public sector, the Ministry of Defence had to improve financial performance, especially in respect of procurement. There has been a need therefore to ensure that personnel, who have been operating under the old regime and approach, are now able to work effectively in the new environment. This has required a cultural change; indeed a new 'mind set' (Moore and Antill, 2001) has been identified as a key to developing personnel and bringing about performance enhancements.

In many ways defence procurement is a reflection of the public sector generally with its bureaucracy and the need for public accountability, yet this is the same environment into which this new philosophy is to bring its commercial ethos and approach. A key defining feature, however, of the public sector based defence procurement environment is that if commercialism is not introduced optimally, then deaths could result.

■ Defence acquisition environment

The defence acquisition environment now encompasses a number of functional entities; it is spread across a number of management processes and is subject to considerable political, social and economic pressures. It also includes commercial organisations (as contractors and suppliers).

Within this environment there is the need to ensure that equipment, goods, supplies and services are effectively and efficiently specified, procured and subsequently supported in service (and ultimately disposed of) so that the armed forces can be effective in all activities that they are required to undertake.

In essence, the acquisition environment encompasses those who consider the capability required of the armed forces (specification), those involved in converting the specification, or requirement, into tangible equipment, goods, supplies and services (procurement), and those involved in ensuring that such equipment is supported with supplies, goods, services, maintenance, etc. (support). The *specification* element can be classified as Customer One, whilst the *support* element and ultimate user can be classified as Customer Two. The link between these differing classifications of customers is the *procurement* element (see Figure 3.2).

Additionally at each stage there will be the involvement of, and relationships with, a range of commercial organisations (from small and medium enterprises to large multinational private and publicly owned businesses).

Customer One (specification) broadly equates to equipment capability, Customer Two to the Defence Logistics Organisation and front-line commands (support) and the link between them as the Defence Procurement

**Figure 3.2
The defence
acquisition
environment**

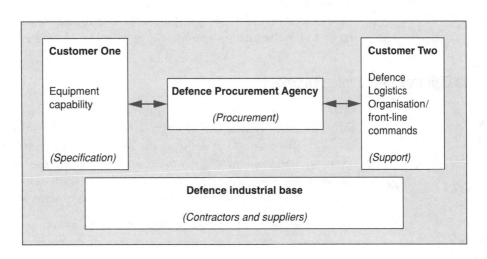

91

Agency (procurement). The defence industrial base (commercial organisations) can be involved, to a lesser or greater extent, in all areas.

Nonetheless, this is further complicated by the Customer Two area, under the mantle of support (and bearing in mind that support projects and activities can last for many years), having considerable scope to buy equipment, goods, supplies and services (i.e. procurement) in its own right.

■ Previous emphasis and approach

The *Strategic Defence Review* (*SDR*) was preceded by reforms introduced by Sir Peter Levene as Chief of Defence Procurement (CDP) in 1981, which looked at value for money in defence procurement with an emphasis on *competition*. This theme of 'competition' is a recurring one and has driven much of the changes to public sector expenditure, and thus procurement, from the mid 1980s through to the present. Hence, even though governments have come and gone, public sector policies continued to seek competitive means of gaining improved efficiencies against a background of budgets that were constantly being decreased.

Nevertheless, the experience (for commercial organisations) of dealing with the MoD had remained markedly unchanged, the culture characterised by 'an excess of bureaucracy, slow decision-making and a belief that procedure (rather than innovation or judgement) would deliver value-for-money' (Boyce, 2000: 1).

This was always justified by the blanket explanation that such features are a necessity in order to provide (or as a result of) *public accountability*. However, rigidly following these characteristics would constantly result in disappointment and criticism from the National Audit Office (NAO) in its regular reviews of MoD major projects, due to the unending problems (delay, poor performance and cost overruns) and frustration at the intractability of such problems. This had been exacerbated within the defence industry where there was inherent conservatism, inefficiencies which had developed during, and carried on after, the 'cost-plus' contracting and Cold War eras, and a tendency to lay the blame squarely with the MoD (Boyce, 2000).

■ Failures of the 'old' approach

The system was failing because there was no clear customer focus within the MoD and the system was effectively broken up into a number of linked but separate phases (such as defining the requirement, researching potential technology, management of the project and supporting the project once it was in service) managed separately within the MoD, making an effective through-life management approach impossible. Other key problems were:

■ Insufficient resources being made available in the early stages of the procurement project meaning that important decisions had to be made with inadequate information and understanding of the risks involved, often resulting in a need for greater expenditure at a later stage.

- Procedures were not inherently flexible enough to cater for the fact that they had different tasks to carry out.
- Delegation of authority was inadequate at all levels and stages of the life cycle.
- The process for approval of project expenditure was inherently cumbersome and caused delay and inefficiencies.
- Incentives available to the stakeholders were ineffective and innovative contracting solutions that could have led to improvements were discouraged as they fell outside the bureaucratic rigidity of procedural guidelines.

These criticisms effectively undermined procedure and policy that had been in place for over a quarter of a century. With so many agencies and individuals involved with the procedures and processes *before*, let alone after, the letting of a contract, there were problems with communication, co-ordination and coherence. (Some of the organisations were: the service user, Operational Requirements branch, sponsors, scientific adviser, scrutinisers, budget-holders, research establishments, test and trials establishments, policy advisers, legal advisers, accountants and the Contracts Branch – and this only represents officials within the MoD.) The old functionally based approach which contained disparate processes, insufficient resources at an early stage, a lack of flexibility and inadequate delegation made it very difficult for the commercial sector to know how best to deal and communicate with the MoD as a customer. A wide variety of personnel would interact with each other at differing levels often with divergent results, inevitably impairing ultimate performance (Boyce, 2000).

■ A new approach

Arising from this, an organisational review, carried out as part of *SDR*, identified the need for change by highlighting problems with the then defence procurement system:

- Defence projects continued to incur both cost and time overruns (exceeding by large margins performance targets that had been agreed between the MoD and the Treasury as part of the MoD's forward expenditure plan).
- Defence equipment in general had become more complex and diverse requiring more flexible and shorter acquisition procedures.
- The new defence environment meant that the UK armed forces faced more diverse and wide-ranging threats, which required the new technology to be introduced faster.
- The MoD needed a new basis for its relationship with industry, built not on competition that saw possible suppliers as adversaries, but rather as *possible partners working together for mutual benefit* (as with the increasingly accepted philosophy in the private commercial business sector).

Commercial organisations supported the need for change. Delays and cost overruns in projects both before a contract is awarded and after it is awarded severely compromise a procurement project.

■ Smart procurement/acquisition

Specific aims of smart acquisition are:

■ To deliver projects within the performance, time and cost parameters approved when the major investment decision is taken.
■ To install a procurement process that acquires military capability in a progressive way, at lower risk and with the optimisation of trade-offs between military capability, time and through-life cost.
■ To reduce the time taken for new technology to reach the frontline where it is needed to secure military advantage and industrial competitiveness. (MoD, 2002)

A subject as diverse and as complex as defence acquisition needs a suitable organisational structure, the ability to manage corporate knowledge and the retention of a suitable skills mix. Within the new philosophy a more co-ordinated and focused approach that achieves this can be enabled. It is predicated upon a matrix-based integrated project team (IPT) structure that cuts across functional boundaries and focuses upon processes. The overall strategy leading to relevant processes and organisation is shown in Figure 3.3.

The key features of smart acquisition are:

■ The process adopts a whole-life approach, embodied in the IPT, that brings together the main stakeholders in the project.
■ There is a clearly defined set of customers for the IPT. This necessitates a *central customer* (Customer One) within the MoD that is organised around

Figure 3.3
Smart acquisition strategy

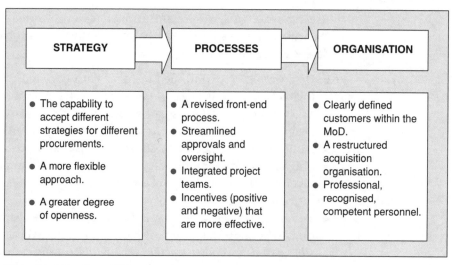

(*Source*: Adapted from Boyce, 2000)

capabilities, and provides funding and a clear and consistent direction to the IPT through all the phases of the procurement cycle. The *second customer* (Customer Two) acts as a customer for the equipment when it is in service.

- A greater willingness to identify, evaluate and implement trade-offs between performance, time and cost.
- A more open and relaxed relationship with industry that is based on the principles of partnering and the identification of common goals and opportunities for gain-share that is underpinned by competitive contractor selection if this will provide value for money.
- The introduction of new shorter procurement processes.
- Empowerment of the IPT to undertake procurement decisions based upon commercial judgement in line with public sector guidelines.
- Projects have procurement time scales that are sharper and have a simpler, streamlined process for approval.
- A larger percentage of investment being undertaken earlier in the project in order to reduce risk before binding parameters are set with regard to performance, cost and time.

■ Professional culture change

In order to be successful the culture of both the MoD and industry must adapt to the new philosophies and practices. It has been suggested (Boyce, 2000) that those who are likely to make the most effective contribution to smart acquisition share the following beliefs and values:

- An understanding of the customer and the customer's needs and a commitment to fulfilling their needs on time and to cost.
- A commitment to deliver a strong level of performance as a result of effective project management and monitoring a project's progress against a set of agreed target milestones.
- A desire to work closely with fellow team members (amongst others), valuing the diversity within the team and understanding the different roles colleagues will have and contributions they can make.
- A willingness to share ideas, thoughts and data and to overcome problems when they occur.
- A commitment to challenge conventions, rules, procedures and dogma and not hide behind the rules when it is convenient and be satisfied with taken-for-granted performance standards.

These cultural issues posed a considerable challenge to the successful and sustained development of this new approach for defence procurement. In effect, following the similar changes that have been introduced into areas of both private and public sector organisational life, there was a requirement to 're-engineer business processes'. This has not proved easy within the private sector generally but has been particularly difficult in the public sector. For the Ministry of Defence, many civil service personnel were brought up in a culture that emphasised compliance with procedure rather than the conviction that the customer's needs come first, while the culture of the armed forces personnel is one of hierarchy and acceptance of orders rather than questioning of activities or reasoning of decisions.

Further, team working is a challenge with which the new organisational structures have had to cope. Tensions between various parts of the MoD structure have existed in the past (including inter-service rivalry) that were caused by conflicting interests, differing agendas, misunderstanding and 'blame avoidance'. However, not only have teams been effectively set up with personnel from different areas of the MoD but contractors have also been included within the teams.

Movement to a joint team working approach is being built upon the development of mutual trust and confidence, underpinned by contracts that encourage co-operation. These are the very tenets of commercial best practice which had its origins in the Japanese philosophies that commenced with 'just-in-time' and now are inculcated within most of the government initiatives such as partnering.

■ The integrated project team (IPT)

The role of the IPT is central and crucial to the success of smart acquisition; it is widely drawn and has a wide area of responsibility. The ethos behind the IPT is that it focuses on the whole-life management of a project (known as the CADMID cycle, i.e. Concept, Assessment, Development, Manufacture, In service, Disposal – often referred to as 'cradle to grave' life-cycle management). Membership of the IPT draws in many stakeholders, bringing together large numbers of highly skilled, highly trained and motivated personnel *who focus upon the management of achievement and not upon procedure.*

The working practices between the IPT and the customer are laid out in a customer–supplier agreement, which records as a minimum the expected levels of performance, in-service date and cost parameters and the range within which the IPT leader can work. In line with commercial best practice there is considerable emphasis upon the (internal and external) customer–supplier relationship.

Typically it is expected that the core members of the IPT are likely to have skills in the following areas (Boyce, 2000):

- Requirements management.
- Project and risk management experience.
- Knowledge of project engineering and technical, quality and reliability expertise.
- Experience in integrated logistic support (ILS) management as well as the traditional equipment support functions.
- Knowledge and experience of commercial management.

- Knowledge of financial management.
- Secretariat skills.
- General industrial and commercial expertise.

People bringing skills in each of these areas will have an important part to play, but their exact contribution and relative importance will vary between the different phases of the project's life cycle. (On occasion the IPT will draw on experience, skills and competencies from beyond those included within the core of the team.)

Practice note

The Ministry of Defence has a £6 billion programme to build the British Army's next generation of air-portable armoured vehicles. The Defence Procurement Agency has announced that technology consultants will play a key role in providing an objective view of the choices available. This is a major departure from the traditional approach of dealing directly with competing manufacturers.

Part B

The EU and procurement

All procurement made within the public sector should follow the EU's *Good Procurement Practice* guidance, which advises:

- A set of clear and concise objectives.
- A full understanding of the market and the law.
- A clear specification.
- Good sourcing and careful consideration when choosing suppliers, service providers and contractors.
- Well-considered award criteria.
- Effective contract management.
- A sound supplier and contract performance review process.

EU competition procurement cycle for goods and services

The EU procurement cycle is shown in Figure 3.4. The objective is to ensure that a contractual relationship is formed with the most suitable supplier of goods or services in the market.

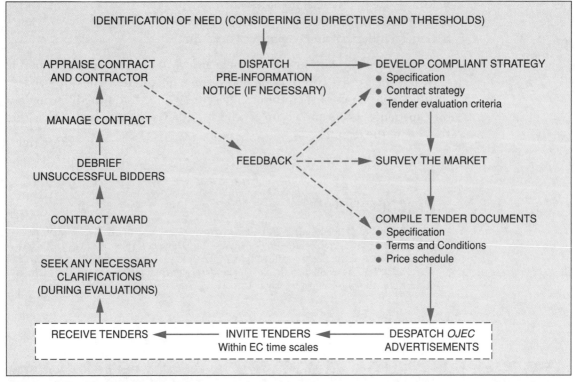

Figure 3.4 The EU procurement cycle

EU procurement directives

■ Origins of the European procurement law

The underlying legal basis for the EU procurement directives are contained in the Treaty of Rome, March 1957. The main principles of this Treaty which carry through to the procurement directives aim to:

- Increase the transparency of procurement procedures and practices throughout the community.
- Aid the free movement of goods, services, capital and people between member states.
- Develop effective competition for public sector contracts.
- Standardise specifications.
- Provide advance information of procurement needs to the marketplace.

European directives become directly applicable to all member states from their date of implementation, but are translated to have the same meaning as the original law into national law as Public Sector Procurement Regulations.

The European Commission sets a time frame within which such ratification must occur. As a result, any public sector purchasing decisions which violate the Treaty may be challenged in the European Court of Justice by the European Commission or a member state through the national court system.

The General Agreement on Tariffs and Trade (GATT) has had an impact upon the effects of this legislation on particular entities of the public sector. This agreement identified a series of entities which were included as those who must follow the full rigour of the EU procurement law. The GATT agreement was designed to establish an international framework of rights and obligations with respect to government procurement, and with a view to achieving liberalisation and expansion of world trade. (It thus had a lot in common with the procurement directives that were to follow.) This agreement has been superseded by the General Procurement Agreement derived from a more recently designated worldwide organisation – the World Trade Organization. Nevertheless, the original parameters set by the GATT agreement in respect of identifying those entities that should follow the law still have effect. All government departments and their agencies, local authorities, and health trusts are mostly subject to this legislation. A complete revision of the range of procurement directives is planned, which will no doubt reflect the development of various newer entities brought about through changes to the public sector's organisation and structure.

It is clear that the impact of the European Union's directives has been far-reaching across the public sector. Heads of procurement organisations (contracting authorities) have been given the responsibility of ensuring compliance with the directives throughout their organisation, a task which has been particularly difficult in those departments where the purchase of goods and services has been fragmented.

In those areas where planned and systematic approaches to procurement do not yet exist there is a danger that the directives are seen as a burden rather than a means of achieving better overall value for money. The procurement directives are having an effect on the organisational structure of procurement and supply units across government departments as a whole as they wrestle with the massive obligation to co-ordinate, aggregate, plan and forecast need over longer and longer periods of time. The EU directives tend to operate best within a co-ordinated structure such as a centralised, commodity procurement groups or satellite configuration. Decentralised procurement structures work less well since there is not the scope for the necessary co-ordination and management across the departments and agencies.

■ Enforcement of the directives

As a result of implementing the obligations of the compliance directive into UK law, aggrieved supplies and service providers can take action against non-complaint contracting authorities in the courts of the UK. They may take the form of, for example:

- claims arising from a company's belief that they would have been awarded the contract had the procurement process been properly conducted, e.g. the use of discriminatory specifications;
- claims that the *Official Journal of the European Communities* advertisement was improperly worded, leading to failure of the company to respond;
- claims that the company was improperly excluded from the procurement process, e.g. by the use of unfair evaluation criteria.

■ Definitions of public supply, services and works contracts

It is important to be aware of the various types of contract and their relationship to procurement practices and EU directives.

Public supply contracts

A public supply contract is when the buying authority engages a contractor (the service provider) to provide services. There are two categories of services: Part A, priority services (to which the services regulations apply in full) and Part B, residual services (where the tender is only subject to some of the requirements in the regulations, e.g. technical specifications, publishing of the contract post-award, and making statistical reports to the Treasury).

Design contests

Design contests are procedures for obtaining plans or designs which involve a jury panel and offer prizes or payments or which may lead to the award of a services contract.

Public works contracts

A public works contract is where the contract is for civil engineering or building works or where the contracting authority engages a third party to carry out work corresponding to specified requirements on their behalf.

Work concessions contracts

Works concessions contracts are works contracts where the consideration given by the buying authority consists of or includes the right to exploit the work or works to be carried out under the contract.

Subsidised works contracts

Subsidised works contracts are works contracts which are awarded by a body other than a public authority for certain types of works where a public authority contributes more than half the cost.

The distinction between 'work' and 'works' used within the Public Works Regulations has been explained as applying to contracts which involve building and civil engineering activities whether in the form of a specific service, i.e. a 'work' – e.g. painting, or in the form of a series of services leading to the completion of a work that has an economic or technical function – or 'works' – e.g. the construction of a building.

The main provisions of the directives in relation to contracts

The provisions relating to contracts do vary from directive to directive in some aspects. However, the following section outlines the main elements of the directives:

- Thresholds;
- Aggregation rules;
- Advertisements;
- Procurement procedures;
- Technical standards and specifications;
- Evaluation criteria
  - Supplier's or service provider's appraisal;
  - Supplier's or service provider's bid;
- Contract award.

Thresholds

The proposed tender will fall within the procurement directives if the estimated value is greater than the prescribed threshold. The threshold is calculated and revised bi-annually. All threshold figures are exclusive of VAT. The directives provide guidance on how to estimate the value of proposed tenders. These are referred to as aggregation rules.

Aggregation rules

The method of calculating the value of the proposed services and supplies contracts depends upon the type of contract that is to be used. The rules generally offer four types of contractual procurement circumstances and, alongside each, a method of calculation relating to that circumstance is given.

- If the contract is for a one-off purchase, then estimate the total value including all component parts, transportation costs, installation and commissioning, etc.
- The value of a series of contracts, or repeat orders, for the same or similar 'products' should be estimated over a 12-month span (either historically or for the future). The requirement cannot be disaggregated to avoid the regulations.
- Fixed term contracts should be estimated for the full duration of the expenditure over the three years that represent the estimated amount. Similarly, if a contract is fixed for one year with two further year options to extend, then it is the three-year figure that should be taken as the estimate.
- For series of contracts for an indefinite term or uncertain period, the total value should be calculated by multiplying the estimated monthly value by 48.
- Where there is a single requirement for services, and a number of service contracts have been or are to be entered into, then the total value of all the

101

individual contracts may be removed from the total contract (if each contract is valued at less than €80,000 and taken together they represent less than 20 per cent of the total overall valuation).

Aggregation rules which apply to public works contracts use similar principles. The estimated value applied for such contracts is the estimate of the value of the whole works contract.

■ Advertisements

There is a requirement for the majority of EU procurements to be advertised in the *Official Journal of the European Communities* (OJEC) to comply with the aim to provide advance information. The Official Publications Office of the EU normally has 12 days in which to publish the notice in the *OJEC* supplement, starting from the date of dispatch of the notice from the contracting authority. (As well as appearing in the *OJEC* supplement, tender notices are accessed by subscribers to the Tenders Electronic Daily (TED) database.) There are three kinds of advertisement that could be applied.

Pre-information notices

These have to be issued in respect of both supply and service requirements. It is required that:

■ Notices are published at the commencement of the financial year or as soon as possible after forming the intention to procure.
■ Only one notice must be published for the specific 'product' for each contracting authority.
■ Notices contain the total estimated contract value of the requirements for the coming 12 months.
■ Notices must be issued where total estimated requirements equal or exceed a threshold.

Individual contract notices

If the estimated value of a contract requirement is equal to or exceeds the relevant threshold then the anticipated contract in the majority of cases has to be advertised by the contracting authority using one of these notices.

Contract award notices

It is the requirement of the EU procurement directives that a contract award notice is published no later than 48 days after the date of the contract. Furthermore, a contract award notice is required for any contract falling within the provisions of the directives even if it was not originally advertised in the *OJEC*. This applies whichever procurement procedure has been followed. The details to be published in the *OJEC* supplement include:

■ The contract award criteria.
■ The name and address of the selected supplier.
■ The nature of the goods or services.
■ The contract price or range of prices tendered.

■ Procurement procedures

There are three main types of European procurement procedure that can be chosen by a contracting authority, the *open* procedure, the *restricted* procedure and the *negotiated* procedure. The opportunity exists to *accelerate* two of the procedures in circumstances of extreme urgency outside the contracting authority's control.

The open procedure

The open procedure is generally used where the contracting authority anticipates that competition is likely to be very limited because of the few known available suppliers or the specialist nature of the goods or service. The use of the open procedure increases the level of interest and competition to the maximum available, since all interested suppliers are invited to tender. The procedure is represented in Figure 3.5.

Figure 3.5
Flow chart showing the process of the open procedure

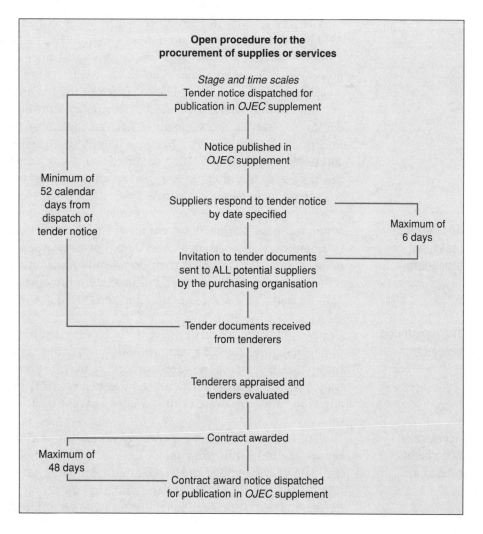

Open procedure for the procurement of supplies or services

Stage and time scales
Tender notice dispatched for publication in *OJEC* supplement

Notice published in *OJEC* supplement

Minimum of 52 calendar days from dispatch of tender notice

Suppliers respond to tender notice by date specified

Maximum of 6 days

Invitation to tender documents sent to ALL potential suppliers by the purchasing organisation

Tender documents received from tenderers

Tenderers appraised and tenders evaluated

Contract awarded

Maximum of 48 days

Contract award notice dispatched for publication in *OJEC* supplement

The restricted procedure

The restricted procedure has a two-stage process and, as the name suggests, restricts the number of competitors that the contracting authority permits to enter the competition. This is the procedure most commonly used by UK government departments for their supplies and service requirements.

The open and restricted procedures have been placed on the same footing as each other, so as to provide a free choice for contracting authorities to use either of these procedures. The open procedure has high resource and time implications, the restricted procedure aids the minimisation of such implications through the ability to select those it is felt most suit the criteria and legitimately reject the rest.

Under the restricted procedure, a tender notice advertising the requirement is dispatched and published in the *OJEC* supplement. Interested suppliers will then notify the contracting authority of their interest. Under the open procedure *all* of these will be invited to tender. Under the restricted procedure the contracting authority will select from among the interested parties those who may submit tenders.

With the normal restricted procedure, a prescribed minimum period of 37 days is set aside from the date of dispatch of the tender notice to give interested suppliers sufficient time to respond. Under the normal restricted procedure, using the normal time scales, tenderers are given a minimum of 40 calendar days from the date of dispatch of the tender documents in which to complete and return their tender. This period may be reduced to 26 calendar days in service procurements where an indicative notice under the pre-information procedure has been used. When requested by the tenderers, additional information relating to the tender documents must be supplied by the buying organisation not less than six calendar days before the deadline for receipt of the tenders. The restricted procedure is represented in Figure 3.6.

Accelerated restricted procedure

When using the restricted procedure, the normal time scale may be shortened by adopting the accelerated procedure, but only when operational urgency makes impracticable any of the normal minimum time limits. The justification for the use of the accelerated procedure must be stated by the buying organisation in the notice published in the *OJEC*.

The negotiated procedure

Under the EU procurement directives it is permitted in certain circumstances to negotiate the terms of a contract with one or more suppliers. Depending on the circumstances, the use of this procedure may first need to be advertised in the *OJEC* with a negotiated procedures notice, or it may only need to be advertised after the award of the procurement contract.

Accelerated negotiated procedure

Under EU procurement it is permitted to use an accelerated negotiated procedure but only with prior publication of a tender notice. The period from the date of dispatch of the accelerated negotiated procedure notice to the deadline for receipt of requests to participate must not be less than 15 calendar days. The justification for the use of the accelerated procedure must be

Figure 3.6
Flow chart showing the process of the restricted procedure

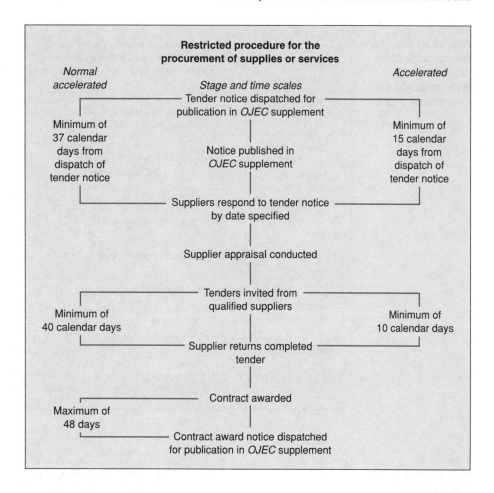

Restricted procedure for the procurement of supplies or services

Normal accelerated | *Stage and time scales* | *Accelerated*

Tender notice dispatched for publication in *OJEC* supplement

Minimum of 37 calendar days from dispatch of tender notice

Notice published in *OJEC* supplement

Minimum of 15 calendar days from dispatch of tender notice

Suppliers respond to tender notice by date specified

Supplier appraisal conducted

Tenders invited from qualified suppliers

Minimum of 40 calendar days

Minimum of 10 calendar days

Supplier returns completed tender

Contract awarded

Maximum of 48 days

Contract award notice dispatched for publication in *OJEC* supplement

stated by the buying organisation in the notice published in the *OJEC*. The procedure is outlined in Figure 3.7.

Negotiated procedure without prior publication of a tender notice

The negotiated procedure may be used without prior publication of a negotiated procedures notice in certain circumstances and this is outlined in Figure 3.8.

■ Technical standards and specifications

The EU procurement regulations require the contracting authority to use certain non-discriminatory terminology in pursuance of the aims of both the Treaty of Rome and the procurement directives. Specification detail needs to include such factors as the standards of quality, performance and safety required. In this respect, it is the responsibility of the buying organisation to ensure compliance with the requirements of the EU procurement directives upon the use of European Standards and common technical specifications.

Figure 3.7
Flow chart showing the negotiated procedure with prior publication of a procedure notice

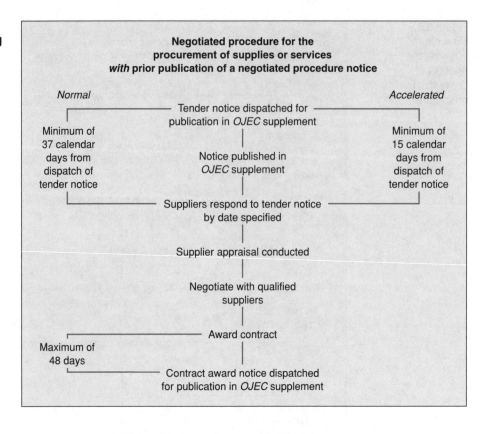

Negotiated procedure for the procurement of supplies or services *with* prior publication of a negotiated procedure notice

Normal   *Accelerated*

Tender notice dispatched for publication in *OJEC* supplement

Minimum of 37 calendar days from dispatch of tender notice

Minimum of 15 calendar days from dispatch of tender notice

Notice published in *OJEC* supplement

Suppliers respond to tender notice by date specified

Supplier appraisal conducted

Negotiate with qualified suppliers

Award contract

Maximum of 48 days

Contract award notice dispatched for publication in *OJEC* supplement

Figure 3.8
Flow chart showing the negotiated procedure without prior publication of a procedure notice

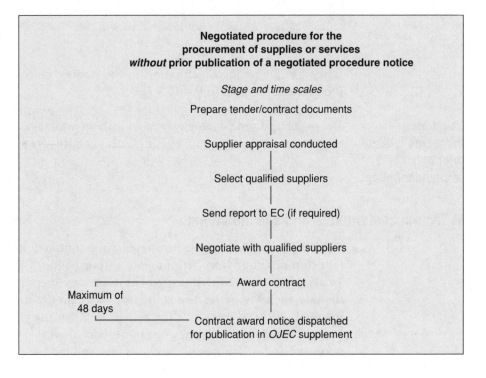

Negotiated procedure for the procurement of supplies or services *without* prior publication of a negotiated procedure notice

Stage and time scales

Prepare tender/contract documents

Supplier appraisal conducted

Select qualified suppliers

Send report to EC (if required)

Negotiate with qualified suppliers

Award contract

Maximum of 48 days

Contract award notice dispatched for publication in *OJEC* supplement

A common technical specification is a technical specification laid down in accordance with the procedure recognised by member states with a view to uniform application across the EU.

◼ Evaluation criteria

Supplier (or service provider) appraisal

The supplier appraisal conducted when using one of the procedures prescribed under the EU procurement directives follows the same general methodology as that of any supplier appraisal. Typically, there are three main factors to consider:

1 Legality to operate as a supplier or service provider.
2 Minimum economic and financial standing.
3 Technical capacity to perform.

Supplier's (or service provider's) bid

Within the EU procurement directives, a requirement exists to be open about the criteria to be used to select or reject a bid in the form of a tender from a potential supplier or service provider. The directives offer two criteria upon which to base the choice:

- lowest price only, where the contracting authority may select only the lowest priced bid without consideration of any other factor; or
- the most economically advantageous tender where the various cited value-for-money factors are weighed off against the price to allow recognition of quality, durability, delivery, after-sales service etc. in the choice of the best offer to meet the requirement.

It is public sector practice to choose the value-for-money option when procuring goods, services and works contracts.

◼ Contract award

There is now a requirement within EU procurement directives to operate a debriefing policy for unsuccessful suppliers. The law states that if a request for a debrief from an unsuccessful tenderer is made to a public sector contracting authority then it must be met with a response within 15 days of that request.

Contract pricing mechanisms

Once a contract is agreed, both parties are legally bound to fulfil their contractual obligations: in essence, the contractor completes the work in accordance with the specification with regard to quality and time, etc.; the contracting authority promptly pays the agreed price for all such work carried out.

It is a principle of government contracting that firm price contracts should be used whenever possible (firm prices are those prices not subject to any provision for variation). Firm price contracts are the most desirable types of contracts for a buying organisation because they provide a level of certainty and they give the contractor the strongest incentive for *economy, efficiency and effectiveness*. The overall aim is to encourage the contractor to keep costs under control while maintaining the contract quality requirements.

To obtain such a price from the market requires a clear, unambiguous specification and a relatively stable economy, so as to allow suppliers to cost the requirement with some certainty. For just as all cost savings below the contract price can be *retained* by the contractor, so all costs incurred above the price will be *paid* by the contractor.

However, as soon as the risk of a loss is foreseen, the supply market may be less willing to contract on a firm price basis. It may be that a *target cost incentive contract arrangement* could be used. It would not be necessary to agree a price with the contractor, merely a target cost, a target fee and a share ratio. Such an incentivised arrangement can be beneficial but it is essential that the output required from the contract is specified clearly to ensure that the full performance requirement is achieved. Quality or timing issues may also be incentivised.

New developments

Revised EU procurement directives

On 31 January 2006 new procurement directives (public sector 2004/18/EC, often referred to as 'the classic directive' and utilities 2004/17/EC) came into force. The classic directive provides a framework within which public procurement must be conducted. Primarily it consolidates the separate directives into one and removes many inconsistencies. There have also been significant additions, mainly the introduction of a new procurement procedure called competitive dialogue which covers the award of public works, public supply and public services contracts.

Competitive dialogue

This is a new route for contracting authorities to procure complex contracts for public works, supplies and services. It allows for a significant degree of dialogue with potential suppliers prior to receipt of final offers. It was introduced to counter the criticism that previous procedures did not offer sufficient flexibility in complex projects. Examples include integrated transport infrastructure projects, large computer networks or projects involving complicated and structured financing where the financial and legal make-up cannot be defined in advance.

The new process can be used only in the case of particularly complex contracts, where use of the open or restricted procedure will not allow the award of the deal. 'Particularly complex' is defined as where contracting authorities:

- are not objectively able to define the technical means of satisfying their needs or objectives;

- are not objectively able to specify the legal and/or financial make-up of the project.

Framework agreements

Although framework agreements have been used as a procurement method in the public sector for years, this is the first time express mention of them has been made.

Central purchasing bodies

The classic directive explicitly recognises that there are central contracting authorities that purchase goods and services on behalf of other contracting authorities, whether through frameworks or through straightforward sale arrangements. The public sector regulations provide that a contracting authority that acquires works, goods or services from or through a central purchasing body (CPB) shall be deemed to have complied with the public sector regulations in so far as the CPB has complied with them in the original acquisition or award.

Dynamic purchasing systems

A dynamic purchasing system (DPS) is a new form of purchasing arrangement introduced in the classic directive. It is a completely electronic system which may be established by a contracting authority to purchase commonly used goods, works or services.

Electronic auctions

For the first time provisions dealing with e-auctions have been included. Provided a contract notice refers to possible use of e-auctions, this method may be used as part of the open and restricted procedure on the opening for competition of contracts to be awarded through a DPS, or the reopening of competition within a framework.

E-communications

The basis of the new regime is that e-communication mechanisms should be available to participants in procurement processes on a par with traditional communication mechanisms. However, in practice the new provisions have the result that e-tendering solutions are required to be purchased by contracting authorities in order to electronically receive requests to participate and tender.

Checklist – Key changes

- In official tender notices, purchasers will have to include more details of the criteria used to select suppliers for a tender list.
- New 'competitive dialogue' procedure will offer extra scope for discussing the most appropriate solution with suppliers.
- The new procedures legitimise the framework approach to purchasing.
- The directives allow purchasers to follow shorter time scales on electronic tenders and clarify the rules on reverse auctions.

Summary

1 Considerable amounts of taxpayers' money are spent on procuring a wide range of goods and services.

2 While there is a need for public accountability there is also recognition that utilising commercial best practice can bring improvements in performance.

3 Procurement (acquisition) within the National Health Service (NHS), Police forces and Ministry of Defence (MoD) provide excellent examples of the approaches necessary in order to meet public accountability yet still utilise, by adaptation, commercial best practice.

4 European directives on procurement take precedence over national law and dictate open, fair and non-discriminatory policies.

5 Threshold values indicate whether or not a contract falls under the scope of the full procedures.

6 European procurement has three types of procedure: open, restricted and negotiated.

7 Revised EU Directives (2006) have been outlined.

References and further reading

Arminas, D (2001), 'Making a business of better services', *Supply Management*, July.

Behan, P (1994), *Purchasing in Government*, Ascot: Longman, in association with the Civil Service College.

Bickerstaff, R and Kingston, H (2006), 'EU procurement directives – one rule for all', *Supply Management*, May.

Boyce, T (2000), *Understanding Smart Procurement in the Ministry of Defence*, London: Hawksmere.

Boyle, E (1993), 'Managing organisational networks – defining the core', *Management Decision*, 31 (7).

Byatt, I (2002), 'Diversity will deliver', *Supply Management*, November.

Cabinet Office (1984), *Government Purchasing: A Multi-department Review of Government Contract and Procurement Procedures*, London: HMSO.

Central Unit on Procurement (1997), *Contracting for Strategic Services*, London: HM Treasury.

Fletcher, G (2004), 'Updated regulations', *Supply Management*, March.

Gershon, P (1999), *Review of Civil Procurement in Central Government*, London: HM Treasury.

Gilbert, H (2006), 'What the doctor ordered?', *Supply Management*, November.

Hiles, A (1993), *Service Level Agreements*, London: Chapman & Hall.

HM Treasury (1995), *Setting New Standards: A Strategy for Government Procurement*, London: HMSO.

HM Treasury/Cabinet Office (1998), 'Efficiency in Civil Government Procurement'.

Kincaid, B (2002), *Dinosaur in Permafrost*, Walton-on-Thames: The SAURUS.

Kincaid, B (1999), *Dancing with the Dinosaur*, Newcastle-upon-Tyne: UK Defence Forum.

Ministry of Defence (1998), *Strategic Defence Review*, CM3999, London: The Stationery Office.

Ministry of Defence (2002), *The Acquisition Handbook – A Guide to Smart Procurement*, 3rd edn.

Moore, D M and Antill, P D (2001), 'Integrated project teams: the way forward for UK defence procurement', *European Journal of Purchasing and Supply Management*, 7(3).

Murray, J G (2002), 'New roles for purchasing: researchers, detectives, teachers, doctors and architects', *International Journal of Public Sector Management*, 15 (4).

National Audit Office (1999), *Modernising Procurement*, London: The Stationery Office.

Pagnoncelli, D (1993), 'Managed outsourcing: a strategy for a competitive company in the 1990s', *Management Decision*, 31 (7).

Palaneeswaran, E, Kumaraswamy, M and Ng, T (2003), 'Targeting optimum value in public sector projects through "best value" focused contractor selection', *Engineering, Construction and Architectural Management*, 10 (6).

Pears, M and Wright, A (2000), 'Buy by the rules', *Supply Management*, September.

Smulian, M (2004), 'A force for good purchasing', *Supply Management*, August.

Takal, P F (1993), 'Outsourcing technology', *Management Decision*, 31 (7).

Telgen, J and Sitar, C P (2001), 'Possible kinds of value added by the purchasing department', *Proceedings of the 10th International Annual IPSERA Conference*, Jonkoping.

The Public Supplies Contract Regulations 1991, SI No. 2680.

The Public Supplies Contract Regulations 1993, SI No. 3228.

The Public Supplies Contract Regulations 1995, SI No. 201.

Trepte, P-A (1993), *Public Procurement in the EC*, Oxford: CCH Editions.

White, R and James, B (1996), *The Outsourcing Manual*, Aldershot: Gower.

Part 2

Key procurement issues

Chapter 4   Outsourcing

Chapter 5   Quality management

Chapter 6   Inventory management

Chapter 7   Lead time and time compression

Chapter 8   Sourcing strategies and relationships

Chapter 9   Price, cost and total cost of ownership (TCO)

Chapter 10   Negotiations

4

Outsourcing

Introduction

The Outsourcing Institute has defined outsourcing as: 'The strategic use of outside resources to perform activities traditionally handled by internal staff and resources.' So, outsourcing is not a synonym for procurement. It is concerned with the external provision of functional activity, and therefore outsourcing decisions are strategic in nature. They impact upon the nature and scope of the organisation. As such they are not taken at the operational level, but involve top management, and the consideration of a great variety of variables such as:

- Do we have candidate functions for outsourcing?
- How do we select?
- How do we assess ourselves?
- Who are the potential providers?
- How do we assess them?
- What sort of relationship will we form?
- How will we manage it?
- How do we ensure efficiency?

Objectives of this chapter

- To discuss the concept of outsourcing
- To highlight the basics of a best practice approach to outsourcing, including outsourcing methodologies
- To outline the pitfalls of outsourcing
- To outline the use of service level agreements (SLAs)

Outsourcing

Outsourcing is, essentially, the contracting out of non-core activities. That is not to say that the activities are unimportant; for example the government has outsourced much of the computing activity required by various Civil

Service departments and agencies. A difficulty is, of course, that a decision has to be made as to what really is core activity, and what is not. Mention is made in Chapter 2 of the concept of the virtual organisation, whose core activity will be managing and orchestrating contractors.

Prahalad and Hamel (1990) wrote that business development would depend on a corporation's ability to identify, to cultivate and to use its core competencies. These were prophetic words. Many organisations, large and small, in both manufacturing and service operations, have invested, and continue to invest, great effort in attempting to do just this. The fundamental questions of 'What business are we in?' and 'What business do we want to be in?' are at the root of corporate strategy. No commercial or public sector concern can undertake all the production of goods and services necessary to the business, and decisions of a strategic nature will need to be taken and adopted as a matter of policy for the concern in question. Decisions as to which classes of goods and services to outsource and, if partial outsourcing is to be pursued, what the proportions should be are core issues which in many respects actually define the business. Major issues of investment, location, planning and direction are, to a large extent, dependent on the make/do-or-buy decision. These strategic decisions will be informed by many considerations, amongst them:

- Financial constraints. If we cannot invest in everything connected with supplying the needs of our organisation then which factors do we invest in and which do we outsource?
- Which of our capabilities provide competitive advantage? Should we outsource those which do not?

Once, outsourcing meant handing over functions such as catering and security to third-party specialists, allowing businesses to concentrate better on their core competences. Many of the deals being announced these days come dangerously close to having an impact on companies' critical competencies – handing over the entire IT function, for example, or passing responsibility for warehousing and distribution, or customer service. Companies should ask themselves:

- Will integration (vertical or horizontal) bring benefits to our organisation? If so, how do we pursue this?
- What services, goods or commodities are difficult to acquire externally? Should we develop our own capability?
- If 'downsizing' seems to be an option for us, which bits of our operation do we shed, and which do we retain?
- Are we in the right business? Are we making things when selling them is what we're really good at, or are there opportunities to become producers of the goods or services that we sell?

Recently, some companies have been bringing back in-house activities that were formerly outsourced. For example, RMC, a cement company which had outsourced in the expectation of cost reduction, found that costs were going up instead, and decided to improve its control by reverting back to in-house provision.

Nor is the improved service that companies expect from outsourcing necessarily the service they receive in practice. Many companies report that rather than improving control, they are actually losing effective control.

One common problem is outsourcing for the wrong reason. If the company is already efficient and effective then it is unlikely that the desired cost savings will be achieved. If the objective is cost savings, or improved service, or being better able to cope with flexible demand, then outsourcing offerings should be evaluated and monitored in that light.

The reaction of many companies is 'outsource and forget' when instead it should be 'outsource and manage'. Within the contract a number of specific key performance indicators (KPIs) should be made explicit, and the results should be both produced and reviewed in a timely manner.

Mini case study – Vita phone

At Vita phone, a German company producing mobile phones for medical and emergency applications, the decision to outsource the making of the devices to US-based contract electronics manufacturer Flextronics was based partly on the supplier's commitment to provide such metrics. But more important was Flextronics's parallel commitment to engage with Vita phone to review, interpret and use the figures to drive improvements.

They have a regular schedule of monthly meetings, where issues such as quality, cost reduction, adherence to delivery schedules and other measures are reviewed.

What is important to the company is to be able to see trend information. How long is it taking to process a claim? How many claims are processed per employee? Moreover, that trend information is seen with ample time to act upon it.

It is often said that the secret of successful outsourcing is a solid relationship between the two parties. Original contract negotiations often failed to fully appreciate the links between pricing, the required service level measurements and the specified scope of the services provided. Both sides often fail to fully define the process.

Most outsourcing service level agreements (SLAs) do not incentivise the correct behaviour from the outsourcer. 'Risk and reward' contracts, in which both parties to the deal share the risks and the rewards, have been found to achieve mutually acceptable levels of performance.

■ Best practice – team approach

The cornerstone of a successful outsourcing project is the creation of an effective team, one that provides a pool of talent and represents all the stakeholders. KPIs relating to quality, speed, flexibility, dependability and cost frequently form the basis for continuous improvement plans. They provide a measurement system for management to gauge the effectiveness of the outsourcing decision and communicate results to a wider audience.

Conversely, they also help to increase expectations over time, with pressure to meet tough new business goals, stretch service performance and improve business growth. Plans are not complete without a termination clause and an exit strategy with clearly identified switching costs, allowing an efficient switch to an alternative supplier or in-sourcing with minimal disruption to the buyer's business.

■ Best practice – drivers

The main driver of outsourcing is the need for focused competitiveness:

- Outsource where others can do it better.
- Outsource to focus on core business.
- Outsource to reduce cost base.

■ Why outsource?

There are many considerations that might influence an organisation, such as:

- External supplier has better capability.
- External supplier has greater or more appropriate capacity.
- Freeing resources for other purposes.
- Reduction in operating costs.
- Infusion of cash by selling asset to provider.
- Reducing or spreading risk.
- Lack of internal resource.
- Desire to focus more tightly on core business.
- Economies of scale.

Unfortunately, rarely is there a clear organisational focus for determining which activities are 'core competences' or for determining strategic impact.

Most important contributors to success

- Activity well defined.
- Roles and responsibilities of all parties clear.
- Good relationship with supplier.
- High quality of supplier.
- Effective contract management/monitoring.

An important part of managing outsourcing is the consideration of potential exit strategies. Indeed, as mentioned earlier, there are many instances where outsourced services have been taken back in-house – clear evidence that even if companies outsource they can eventually retain long-term control.

Best practice – contract management skills

Buyers need to carry out better planning and post-contract management to prevent outsourcing ideals collapsing, according to outsourcing advisory firm, Orbys. In a report, 'Managing Outsourcing for maximum value', Orbys found that nearly a quarter of the UK's biggest firms have brought an outsourced function back in-house after failed expectations.

According to interviews with 82 manufacturing, financial services and retail firms with a UK presence – including Kellogg's, Selfridges, Dixons, Boots and Citibank, 43 per cent said their supplier had failed to meet expectations and 23 per cent have brought work back into their own business as a result. Traditionally procurement focuses on the procurement process rather than the planning and post-contract management, which is where real benefits and value can be identified.

Contractual relationships

Outsourced functions normally lead to relationships where the vendor is providing services on a continuous basis. The determination of an appropriate relationship within which this continuous service is to be provided is likely to require a very great investment of time and effort at the planning stage. Additionally, of course, as with all relationships, there will be evolutionary change; change which will itself need to be managed.

- Reward good performance.
- Share the risk and reward.
- Perceive the contractor as a potential partner.

Most of those who are looking to make increased use of open book mechanisms or performance-based contracts currently have very little experience of doing so. Nor is the experience with monitoring mechanisms reassuring. The level of skill and sophistication necessary for effective monitoring is clearly increasing beyond the current capability of many organisations.

Strategic sourcers manage relationships as well as contracts. It is as important to manage the relationships between the customer and the supplier as it is to manage the contract. In pursuit of this, strategic sourcers are more willing to share risk and reward and less likely to rely on penalising poor performance. This is in line with a greater use of partnership-type contracts, where incentives and the sharing of risk and reward are more common features.

There is a demonstrable correlation between the adoption of a strategic approach to outsourcing and the achievement of satisfactory outcomes.

■ An approach to market testing

In making the decision whether to outsource or not, it might be helpful to undertake a market testing exercise whereby one's own commercial and technical capabilities are benchmarked against providers in the external market. This process requires some analysis and evaluation of current and projected needs and capabilities, the reduction of the product of this analysis to a clear specification, and the invitation of external providers to bid against this specification. Analysis of provider bids might result in a decision not to proceed, but if it is determined at this stage that outsourcing might be appropriate then a thorough but conventional contractor selection and evaluation exercise will follow, and a contract will be drawn up. The contract will most likely be based on agreed, measurable service levels (see below).

Important considerations

It is essential that both the client and the external provider under consideration have a clear and shared understanding not only of the specification but also of goals and objectives, and that this understanding is translated into a workable strategic plan. Following the careful and rigorous procedures necessary for appointment of an external provider there will need to be a well-designed and mutually acceptable contract, and an open and continuous working relationship underpinned by senior management support from both organisations.

Service level agreements

Service level agreements may be entered into between a client and a supplier of services. They may be defined as an agreement between customer and service provider in which quantified elements of the service provision are determined. Most services are built up from a number of individual components, and a complete service level agreement will cover these in some detail. Examples are:

- Time of provision of each type of service.
- Points of service delivery.
- Nominated service provider.
- Responsiveness.
- Documentation.
- Emergency arrangements.
- Hotline support.
- Dispute procedures.
- Training and staff development.

Figure 4.1 demonstrates the relationship between the key stakeholders involved in service level agreements.

Figure 4.1
Three main players involved in SLAs

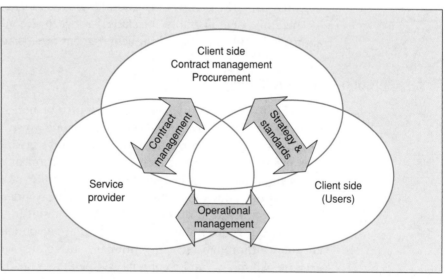

(*Source*: Crocker after Hiles, 1993)

Best practice – Outsourcing: the long view

A recent Dun & Bradstreet global outsourcing survey of 1000 companies on its database reported that a quarter had terminated at least one outsourced relationship before its due date. Dataquest also reported that more than 50 per cent of oursourcers surveyed had renegotiated a contract mid-term, resulting in 25 per cent of the incumbent providers losing the account. Why?

What can be said with some degree of certainty is that if the needs and expectations have been clearly defined, communicated and understood during the selection process then the execution, measurement and subsequent review will be far more focused and cohesive.

The value proposition for outsourcing must be to shift the business's focus from managing its own resources to one of managing the provider's results. This demands a more advanced approach to selecting the right partner and to the performance management of the contract. The business needs, the desired results, must be defined in clear and measurable terms. This needs to be in conjunction with all interested parties (or stakeholders).

The required results must reflect the time requirements of the business and, as importantly, they must be owned, measured, reported and modified as business needs change.

However, performance is two-way, and the customer will also have to meet obligations in terms of 'owning' the relationship.

There is a strong correlation between the (good) performance of outsourced service providers and clear lines of responsibility, authority and accountability being established for the outsourced relationship.

There must be an ability to amend or change the outsourcing requirements over time. It must be recognised that there will be cost and performance factors associated with such changes. Include provisions for external benchmarking to stimulate the opportunities for continuous improvement.

A Warwick Business School research study found that 4–8 per cent of internal management time is applied to managing relationships.

There needs to be a focus on soft skills such as mutual problem solving, listening, error-cause removal, force field analysis (the factors in favour of and against change), risk and vulnerability analysis.

Clear escalation and resolution procedures for conflicts should be developed.

■ Key contractual elements

- Comprehensive service definition – what is actually required?
- Process for service evolution – ongoing continuous improvement.
- Ability to add/delete service.
- Volumetric change.
- Service levels (meaningful measure/targets).
- Service credits/bonuses (shared risk and reward).
- Objectives to be delivered by both sides.
- Supplier responsibilities – contract management.
- Customer responsibilities – partnership concept of win–win.
- *Force majeure*.
- Change control processes.
- Avoid undue 'lock-in' to:
  - Particular technology
  - Particular solution/service

- Particular supplier – although outsourcing contracts are longer term by their very nature.
- Ongoing market testing/benchmarking.
- Dispute resolution.
- Termination procedures.

Outsourcing methodologies

Lonsdale and Cox (McIvor, 2000) revealed that outsourcing decisions are rarely taken within a thoroughly strategic perspective, with many firms adopting short-term solutions for cost reductions. Elsewhere in this chapter, we support the statement with examples of research which demonstrate the same phenomenon.

Many companies have no formal outsourcing process, and make short-term decisions based on reduction of head count and costs, rather than managing the risks and securing added value and continuous improvement. In this section we highlight three frameworks or methodologies for effective outsourcing strategies, all of which are examining risks at each stage of the process in terms of a decision tree approach, allowing companies to consider the full implications of their actions. The first of these was introduced by Lonsdale and Cox (1998), and is shown in Figure 4.2.

This very useful model allows companies to assess the risks of outsourcing in terms of non-core/core competencies and the criticality of the activity. Companies must have a clear understanding of what business they are in, how value is sustained and, therefore, what activities are non-core and low risk in terms of outsourcing.

**Figure 4.2
The outsourcing process**

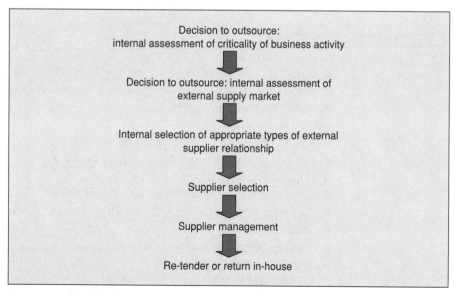

(*Source*: Lonsdale and Cox, 1998)

Moreover, it indicates the importance of assessing the supply market; it is imperative that we select suppliers/providers who have more specialist knowledge in order that they can provide superior levels of service and continuous improvement. If the market is not sufficiently 'mature', in that there are many providers but there is a lack of a sufficient level of competence, then clearly it may not be appropriate to outsource at this stage.

Supplier management in the form of effective contract management and performance monitoring with appropriate partnership/collaborative approaches is imperative if benefits of outsourcing are to be realised.

Finally, the re-tender or return to in-house decision must be managed effectively since badly managed termination of provision can cause interruptions in service levels and an unprofessional reputation in the marketplace.

A second outsourcing framework is provided by McIvor (2000), again in the form of a decision tree involving four key stages.

Stage 1:
'Define core activities'

It is essential to distinguish between non-core and core activities (those adding value to the customer and therefore key sources of competitive advantage). Companies such as Honda, Apple, IBM and Digital build their strategies around their core activities and outsource as much of the remainder as possible.

Stage 2:
'Evaluate relevant value chain activities'

This involves analysing the competence of the company compared to those of the potential providers, comparing the ability to add value and the implications for the total cost of ownership.

Activities for which the company has neither a strategic need nor special capabilities can be outsourced to more competent providers who have a lower cost base.

Stage 3:
'Total cost analysis'

At this stage, if after analysis of total costs the company is more capable than the external sources then it should retain in-house capability. If a number of capable suppliers exist, then move to the final stage.

Stage 4:
'Relationship analysis'

At this stage companies are attempting to select suppliers who have the ability to initiate and develop suitable relationships which will add value and provide continuous improvements.

Again, elsewhere in this chapter we demonstrated the importance of relationship management in several research findings.

If no suppliers are suitable, then again the risk is too high and therefore the decision should be to retain in-house capability. If companies follow such an approach then they will manage the risks associated with outsourcing more successfully.

Finally, a third framework is provided by Galetto, Pignatelli and Varetto (2003). Again, there are several stages associated with:

- Core competency evaluation.
- Identification of process to be outsourced.
- Types of relationships.
- Prioritisation of activities to be outsourced (criteria at this stage are capabilities, total cost and control).
- External benchmarking.
- Supplier selection.
- Establishment of service level agreements and suitable relationships, involving future targets for continuous improvements.
- Management of the outsourcing process.

Essentially, this highlights the importance of ongoing contract management and regular reviews. Again, this was found to be most important to users in research findings presented elsewhere in this chapter.

In summary, if companies adopt formal strategic thinking such as outlined in these frameworks then it is likely that the percentage of successful outsourced contracts reported would increase dramatically.

Mini case study – Goodyear

The Goodyear Tire & Rubber Company in North America is outsourcing more than 40 indirect spend categories in a drive to cut costs.

A Goodyear spokeswoman claimed the deal 'will help save $1 billion by 2008 and allow buyers to focus on strategic and direct spending'.

Outsourced categories include:

Transportation
Distribution
Maintenance
Repair
Operations
Packaging
Energy
Marketing services

In March 2004 Goodyear Dunlop Tires Europe outsourced all its indirect spend to IBM for 10 years. It estimated that procurement savings of €50 million would be achieved within two years.

A study from PA Consulting found 58 per cent of clients carried out no due diligence on potential suppliers, 44 per cent admitted to underestimating the effort involved in managing their supplier and half of the lawyers believed that less than 10 per cent of their clients understood what partnership meant.

A study by outsourcing adviser TPI said outsourcing a function saves on average 15 per cent. A company must retain a small team with the commercial and technical credibility to mange the contractual relationship and mange supplier performance over the life of the contract.

Clients also have to specify what services they need. They need a format that sets out qualitative requirements combining outputs, measurable results, and key inputs. Often, specifications are a wish list of outputs that bears no relation to current performance. This may result in the contractor having to improve the service from a low starting point without adequate resources or time. If can also increase costs beyond the means of the client organisation. There is a need to specify 'fit for purpose' service requirements just as with any other purchase.

It is also often the case that clients do not know the true cost of current services as costs are hidden, delegated or not reported accurately.

Only 21 per cent of suppliers in a survey (2006) felt that clients communicated their objectives well. With a figure this low, it is no wonder that their expectations are failing to be met.

Forty-four per cent of clients surveyed underestimated the effort involved in managing a supplier.

Both customer and providers fail to appreciate the complexity of the contract and the resources needed to manage a structured relationship effectively. Effectively this demonstrates a lack of meaningful engagement between suppliers and clients.

Mini case study – Accenture

Unless companies understand what they want to achieve, whether it is cost savings or innovation, it will not be achieved.

The firm's new 10-year £23 million IT outsourcing contract with retailer New Look is a success story. The deal was built on an eight-year relationship, and to ensure smooth running the team meets with New Look daily to review the previous day and plan for the next 24 hours.

Ongoing contract management is often either non-existent or far too simplistic. Success lies in a tailored deal that is flexible enough to meet changing business models over the life of the contract. Active management of performance, service and relationship, and measuring these against the market performance, are vital to ensure that mutually acceptable objectives are met.

How to avoid pitfalls

More often than not outsourcing contracts collapse because of a lack of communication between suppliers and buyers. Two out of three clients said they wished they had focused more on their supplier's ability to deliver on their promises.

Many of the problems that arise during the course of a contract could have been readily resolved at the outset. This is why buyers and suppliers need to agree exactly what the supplier will deliver, the time frame for delivery and targets that need to be met. A key performance indicator of 20 per cent savings, for example, is not enough; buyers need to be explicit about the benefits they want to achieve, the risks involved and the scope of activities covered. The buyer needs to be aware of what level of service the end user expects and ensure this is part of the service procured from the suppliers.

Outsourcing deals are more successful when the buying team works closely with the department being outsourced to agree equally beneficial KPIs. This is crucial when outsourcing areas of the business that cannot always be measured in hard metrics, such as HR or training.

Once the KPIs are set, discussions between buyers and suppliers should continue through monthly reviews, with agreed delivery dates and escalation processes should anything go wrong. It is the supplier's responsibility not just to meet the terms of the contract, but also to prompt the buyer on measuring its success at meeting KPIs.

Taking a partnership approach can reap dividends in this respect. One strategy is to outsource work in stages. This way, a relationship is established and the supplier gains an understanding of the buyer organisation and its needs whilst the buyer learns how outsourcing works.

■ TUPE

Transfer of Undertakings (Protection of Employment) Regulations 1981 (TUPE) requires that where an undertaking is transferred from one employer to another, i.e. outsourced, the following, with the exception of pension rights, are taken over by the new employer:

- the contracts of employment;
- the rights and obligations arising from these contracts;
- the rights and obligations arising from the relationship between the transferor and the employees working in that undertaking;
- any existing collective agreements.

Employees who are employed by the original employer at the time of transfer automatically become employees of the new employer, as if their contracts of employment were originally made with the new employer; service is counted as continuous from the date on which employment commenced with the first employer.

All employees transferred must, under TUPE, retain all their current employment rights and conditions. The employees cannot be dismissed for a transfer-related reason without such dismissal being ruled by an industrial tribunal to be automatically unfair.

The virtual organisation

Some companies are using outsourced services to the point of retaining control, but in an almost 'virtual' capacity. Until recently, functions, services, products and processes that were considered core to the success of a company, such as customer care, had to remain in-house to maintain control, maximise potential advantage and minimise risk. Many of these areas are now emerging as potential candidates for outsourcing. Ford considers virtually anything outside design and final assembly as non-core.

Procurement – a candidate for outsourcing?

A number of authorities have argued that if an organisation is to concentrate on its core competencies then procurement activity may well not be one of them, and the activity might itself be placed in the hands of an external agency. A number of contributors to the 1996 International Purchasing and Supply Education and Research Association (IPSERA) conference held at the University of Eindhoven in the Netherlands presented papers suggesting or predicting the end of 'purchasing' in the traditional or established sense. Benmaridja and Benmaridja (1996) suggested outsourcing the non-critical part of procurement, and proposed a methodology for determining exactly what the non-critical parts are. Stannack and Jones (1996) argued convincingly that purchasing as defined by Burt (1984) – 'the systematic process of deciding what, when, and how much to purchase, the act of purchasing it and the process of ensuring that what is required is received in the quantity specified on time' – was dying, to be replaced by 'the assessment, management and monitoring of supplier behaviour to optimise organisational inputs'. Compelling though the arguments put forward by Stannack and Jones are, the fact remains that at least some the operations suggested by Burt's definition need to be undertaken by somebody somewhere. Perhaps that somebody might be a specialist services contractor, or a vendor rather than a buyer, and perhaps that somewhere will be remote from the customer's place of business.

Evans (1996) reported the case of an organisation which developed its interface with suppliers to such an extent that it had a small cadre of well-regarded suppliers who worked strategically in alliance with the company. Supplier appraisal or sourcing work was no longer necessary, negotiations no longer took place, and the routine requisitioning, ordering acknowledgements and payments work took place electronically and automatically. Procurement had improved to such an extent that there was no longer a need for the function. Quality issues were resolved by the quality department, manufacturing teams met regularly to discuss initiatives, and the accountants worked closely with their counterparts at suppliers where prices were concerned. So, with no more need for a procurement department the staff were redeployed and the department closed. Of course, this does not mean that the activities that many regard as being part of the role of procurement had all been rendered obsolete, but rather that they had been relocated to a more appropriate place in the organisation and its interface with suppliers. Direct supplier/customer linkages at the appropriate level and between appropriate managers had obviated the need for procurement in an intermediary role. So, there was not 'outsourcing' of procurement in this case, but some degree of internal re-sourcing.

Many commentators report benefits of outsourcing procurement, such as:

■ improved return on investments through improved use of resources;
■ a focus on core competence;
■ access to greater economies of scale.

Others point to the negative effects, such as:

■ conflict of interest;
■ loss of control;
■ outsourcing core activities by mistake.

Mini case study – Roadchef Motorway Services

In 2004 Roadchef outsourced both direct and indirect spend.

Shortage of internal category knowledge prevented the company from realising its true purchasing leverage and potential.

Benefits have been reduced costs, simplified processes, best practice procurement, quality products, and improved KPIs overall.

Unless companies have a robust contract with their service providers which contains such provisions as

■ prescriptive arrangements relating to the sharing of gains,
■ commitment to realising and capturing real savings,
■ agreed processes, and
■ clear scope of work for the services to be provided,

they may find that many of the expected cost savings do not materialise and that the outsourcing is actually unsuccessful.

Of paramount importance is the safeguarding of quality by ensuring satisfactory provisions for supplier selection and maintenance of quality standards whilst producing year on year total costs of ownership reduction.

Summary

1 The concept of outsourcing was introduced with examples of best practice outsourcing which highlight various strategies employed.

2 The reasons companies outsource are varied and factors such as the removal of non-core activities from the company are cited.

3 Critical success factors for effective outsourcing are included, such as a well-defined activity, a good relationship with a good supplier, and an effective system for contract management and reporting.

4 Appropriate relationships with outsourced providers are of paramount importance, including the sharing of risk and reward, and mutual trust.

5 Service level agreements (SLAs) were discussed in addition to the key contractual elements to be included.

6 Outsourcing methodologies were reviewed in detail, emphasising the need to assess risk at each stage of the outsourcing decision-making process.

7 Outsourcing pitfalls were included with best practice adoption advice.

8 The concept of the virtual organisation was discussed, whilst procurement itself was posited as a candidate for outsourcing.

References and further reading

Benmaridja, M and Benmaridja, A (1996), 'Is it interesting for a company to outsource purchasing and under what conditions?' Paper presented at IPSERA Conference, Eindhoven University of Technology.

Benn, I *et al.* (2003), *Strategic Outsourcing*, London: Gower.

Bradley, A (2006a), 'Tire giant outsources to save a billion', *Supply Management*, March.

Bradley, A (2006b), 'Complacent IT deals are fraught with error', *Supply Management*, April.

Bradley, A (2006c), 'Outsourcing – call to develop post contract skills', *Supply Management*, May.

Burt, D N (1984), *Proactive Procurement*, Englewood Cliffs, NJ: Prentice-Hall.

Cha, A (2007), 'Outsourcing procurement from the inside out', *Supply Management*, May.

Cooper, A (2007), 'To outsource or not to outsource?', *Supply Management*, May.

Evans, E (1996), 'The disappearing department', *Supply Management*, July.

Galetto, F F, Pignatelli, A and Varetto, M (2003), 'Outsourcing guidelines for a structure approach', *Benchmarking: An International Journal*, 10 (3).

Hiles, A (1993), *Service Level Agreements*, London: Chapman & Hall.

Hunt, M (2004), 'Teaming with talent', *Supply Management*, August.

Lonsdale, C and Cox, A (1998), *Outsourcing: A Business Guide to Risk Management Tools and Technique*, Boston: Earlsgate Press.

Matthews, J (2004), 'Outsourcing – the rise of the virtual company', *Supply Management*, July.

McIvor, R (2000), 'A practical framework for understanding the outsourcing process', *Supply Chain Management: An International Journal*, 5 (1).

PA Consulting Group (1996), 'International Survey on Outsourcing'.

Prahalad, C K and Hamel, G (1990), 'The core competence of the corporation', *Harvard Business Review*, May/June.

Sellis, M (2006), 'Outsourcing: getting closer', *Supply Management*, April.

Snell, P (2006), 'Are we getting the message?', *Supply Management*, April.

Stannack, P and Jones, M (1996), 'The death of purchasing?' Paper presented at IPSERA Conference, Eindhoven University of Technology.

Varley, P (2000), 'Serviceable solutions to all-out chaos', *Supply Management*, January.

Wheatley, M (2004), 'Outsourcing: getting the measure of services', *Supply Management*, September.

Wilson, D (2002), 'A facility for friction', *Supply Management*, October.

5

Quality management

Introduction

Product or service quality is increasingly seen as a 'qualifier' which must be demonstrably attainable before a supplier can merit consideration. Unless specifications can be understood and consistently met, a potential supplier is unlikely to win business from a buying organisation taking a professional view of the need to do business only with vendors who are tuned in to, and able to respond to, the particular needs of customers. The shift in business and commercial practice from quality control to quality assurance is reflected in the chapter, as is the developing extent to which attention is paid to the management systems employed by suppliers rather than the measurement or assessment of their products or services. In this chapter we consider the question 'What is quality?' We discuss approaches to specification, and some of the relevant commercial practices. A note on value analysis and value engineering is included. Firms need to convince their customers that they can meet quality requirements before they can compete on price, and so ISO 9000, now firmly established as a key 'must know' for the procurement professional, is outlined in the chapter.

Objectives of this chapter

- To indicate the move away from quality control (inspection techniques) towards quality assurance (prevention of defective work)
- To discuss statistical process control (SPC) and off-line control
- To introduce the concept of failure mode and effect analysis
- To examine the different approaches to producing a specification and the role of value analysis, including the idea of early supplier involvement
- To consider the fact that total quality management requires the involvement of all suppliers and subcontractors, ideally at an early stage, and to outline the concept of concurrent engineering
- To comment on the benefits of standardisation
- To introduce the standards BS EN ISO 9000 on quality assurance
- To discuss value analysis (VA) and value engineering (VE)
- To comment on the economics of quality
- To identify what drives make-or-buy decisions

What is quality?

Quality is a word with several meanings and connotations. For example, it can mean excellence, as in 'this is a quality product', or it can be thought of as the extent to which a product or service achieves customer satisfaction. An idea gaining widespread support is that 'Quality is whatever the customer says it is'. The quality gurus (Deming, Juran) have been extremely influential, and have taught us that quality is an issue related to strategic advantage. Womack and Jones (1996) have advocated the pursuit of perfection, meaning the avoidance of all waste, though they state: 'Perfection is like infinity. Trying to envision it (and to get there) is actually impossible, *but the effort to do so provides inspiration and direction essential to making progress along the path.*' So, quality can be defined in many ways. However, for the purposes of this text it might appropriately be defined or specified as the whole set of features and characteristics of a product or service that are relevant to meeting requirements. These can be few, or many (as shown in the coffee profile in Figure 5.1).

So, for the rather restricted purposes of this chapter, 'quality' is simply 'fitness for purpose', or 'suitability'. There is a popular saying, 'There's no point in buying a Rolls-Royce to do the job of a Ford', and this sums up the concept adequately.

Quality for a given application can be either too low or too high. The British Standards Institution has defined quality as 'The totality of features and characteristics of a product or service that bear on its ability to satisfy a given need'.

Performance quality and conformance quality

Supplies staff are concerned with quality from two points of view:

1 Quality of design or specification. Have we specified the right material for the job, and have we communicated our requirement to the supplier in a clear and unambiguous way? This is performance quality.
2 Conformance quality. Has the supplier provided material in accordance with the specification? We usually establish the answer to this question by inspection.

The words performance and conformance occur again later in the chapter, at the point at which we discuss specifications. Care is needed to avoid confusing performance quality with a performance specification.

Attributes and variables

When inspecting goods we may be looking at attributes or variables. It is relatively easy to check for attributes, since they are either present or not. A domestic appliance is checked to see if the power lead accompanies it; a circuit board has 17 components attached; a gasket set has no missing items.

Figure 5.1
Multidimensional quality analysis

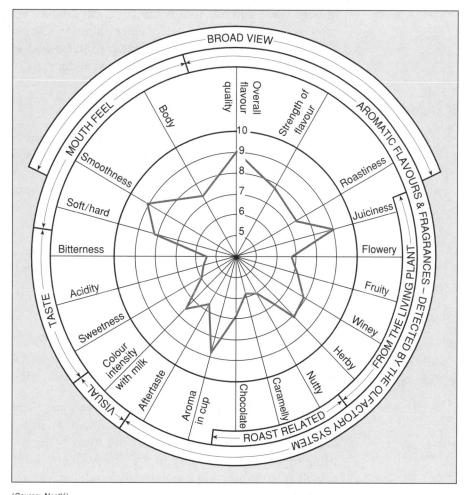

(*Source*: Nestlé)

These are all checks for attributes. Variables are much more difficult to inspect. A variable is something which needs to be assessed or measured, such as the dimensions of a mechanical part, the mass of a package of material, or the shade of colour of a printing paper. It is often economically sound policy to devise pass/fail tests of some kind that can enable variables to be assessed as attributes. Thus the inspection process becomes 'Does this item pass the test?' The answer, which can only be 'yes' or 'no', is an attribute of the item.

Simple devices known as 'go/no go' gauges can be helpful in inspection for attributes. The idea can be illustrated by means of example. Suppose a small cylindrical component must have an external diameter within a certain tolerance range. A piece of steel might have two holes carefully machined in it, one of which is set at the minimum diameter of the component, the other at the maximum. A component that is within tolerance will 'go' into the larger hole, but will not go into the smaller one. A component that is too small will 'go'

133

in both cases, and one that is too large will produce a 'no go' result in both cases. A correctly machined piece will produce the desired 'go/no go' result.

Gauges based on this general principle can be used to test many variables; the diameter of a work piece is just one example.

■ Quality control and quality assurance

Inspection activities can be classified as quality control processes, along with the other activities that involve monitoring to ensure that defectives (or potential defectives) are spotted. Quality assurance can be contrasted with control in that assurance includes all the activities connected with the attainment of quality, such as:

- design, including proving and testing;
- specification, which must be clear and unambiguous;
- assessment of suppliers, to ensure that they can perform;
- motivation of all concerned;
- education and training of supplies staff;
- inspection and testing;
- feedback, to ensure that all measures are effective.

■ Total quality management

The 'total quality' philosophy takes matters a stage further, and is based on the active involvement of all concerned. Attention is paid to systems procedures and processes rather than the focus being on the good or service being supplied. Total quality in the supply chain would mean that suppliers, as well as customers and the company's own workforce, would be involved in determining quality. Inspection and supplier assessment are superseded by a shared approach to the elimination of defective work, with the emphasis on prevention rather than detection and cure. Suppliers must be seen as allies in this process; it is no longer appropriate that buyers should 'vet' suppliers, who should be bringing as much enthusiasm and commitment to quality management as their customers. Key ideas associated with TQM as a policy are 'teamwork', 'involvement' and 'process'.

Statistical process control

Statistical process control (SPC), an aspect of quality management, is often seen as a key part of a quality strategy. Basically, the idea is that statistical methods are employed to ensure that a quality capability is possessed by an organisation, and that quality is maintained by a monitoring, feedback and adjustment system (see Figure 5.2). SPC is not, however, just a set of techniques. The idea is that a proactive approach is taken to the prevention of

Figure 5.2
Feedback loops in statistical process control

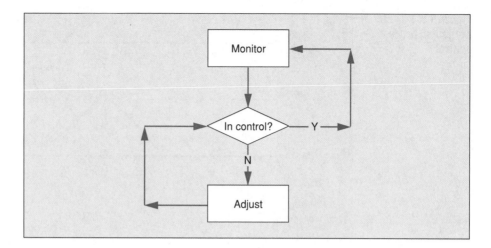

defective material or service, rather than the reactive 'correcting' approach of seeking to identify defective work already done.

SPC is not an approach confined in its application simply to the manufacturing context; the ideas may be applied in any situation where a process takes place. Every useful task or recognised activity may be viewed as a process. The inputs may be materials, information, skills, knowledge, tools and equipment, or any other factor which the task or process requires. Outputs may be products, services, information, documents or anything else that a customer requires.

A high concentration of effort on inspection or checking at the end of a process is indicative that attempts are being made to inspect quality in. This is contrary to the SPC goal of building quality in. If the inputs and process are co-ordinated properly, the outputs will meet the specification. This fact is of particular significance to the procurement function. The goods and services acquired as inputs for the organisation are, of course, somebody else's outputs. If SPC is properly employed by the supplier then we can have confidence that our inputs will be in accordance with the specification and requirements agreed.

SPC depends upon the operators of the process taking responsibility for quality. Inspection, in the traditional sense, is redundant. Attention must be paid to ensuring that the process is capable of meeting requirements; to ascertaining that the process is actually meeting requirements at all times; and to the empowerment of operators to make adjustment to the process so that outputs can be kept in control. Figure 5.3 shows in schematic form the process of monitoring and adjustment on which SPC is based.

A commonly employed approach in SPC is the use of control charts, which are designed to ensure that deviations outside a band of acceptability are detected in sufficient time to enable corrective action to be taken before defective items are produced. Figure 5.3 is an example of one type of chart; there are, of course, other types of control chart and, indeed, numerous other techniques employed in SPC.

Figure 5.3
Statistical process control

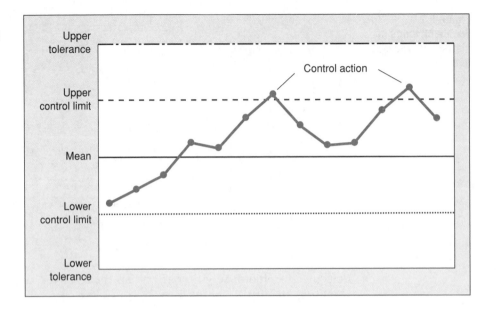

Procurement managers may derive benefit from working with suppliers on the implementation of SPC. There are potential benefits for both.

Taguchi methods for the 'off-line' control of quality

The management of quality has been at the forefront of the improvement process in industry throughout the 1990s and 2000s. The writings of the quality gurus such as Deming, Crosby and Feigenbaum are all now familiar to both students and practitioners in the field of quality, have been the subject of numerous articles, and have formed the basis of most quality management systems in use today.

One of the characteristics of existing quality control techniques, however, is that they tend to involve the online control of quality, i.e. the control of quality at various stages in the supply chain. Such controls are, of course, vital in reducing the costs of quality. However, further cost reductions may require the control of quality to move to an earlier stage in the production process – to the control of quality at the design stage. Such controls are referred to as 'off-line' quality control procedures.

Off-line control procedures have, of course, one great benefit – if good design can prevent quality failure at a later stage then the cost of bad quality never arises in the first instance, which is clearly a more attractive prospect than the finding of bad quality from any form of inspection or control method, no matter how rigorously applied. To quote Martyn House (author of 'Confessions of a Quality Expert') 'the world can be changed at the stroke of a pen at the design stage'. Consider the worldwide recall of a car model due to a minor design fault and compare the cost of this to the cost of improvement at the design stage. This can be thought of in terms of the Japanese concept 'invest first, not last', meaning that they prefer to make greater investment at the design stage rather than correct faults later, as in Western manufacturing.

Although there are various techniques of off-line control, the methods that are attracting most attention from world-class manufacturers are those of Genichi Taguchi. Possibly Deming's greatest contribution was to convince companies to shift quality improvements back to the statistical control of the production process. Taguchi takes this a stage further from production to design, with the objective of making a design that is robust in terms of both production and end-user environments.

The Taguchi definition of quality is 'Quality is the (minimum) loss imparted to society from the time the product is shipped'. This loss includes customer dissatisfaction that leads to the loss of market standing by the company in addition to the usual costs of quality such as scrap and rework. Customer satisfaction is deemed to be the most important part of a process. It is the total financial loss to society that is the true cost – a very broad view of cost, which also incorporates factors such as environmental costs. This methodology suggests that traditional measures of quality underestimate the costs of poor quality.

The Taguchi approach requires that quality be built into the product from the design stage and the 'quadratic loss function' measures quality (see Figure 5.4). In the traditional approaches to quality management, such as Crosby's 'zero defects' approach, quality is defined in terms of a specification with upper and lower tolerances and an item is acceptable provided it lies within these two parameters. However, according to Taguchi, performance begins to deteriorate as soon as the design parameters deviate from their target values. Hence the loss function is measured by the deviation from the ideal or target value. This target value, rather than the usual expression of quality in terms of nominal values and tolerances, is central to Taguchi's loss function. Loss (or cost) increases exponentially as the parameter value moves away from the target, and is at its minimum when the product or service is at the target value.

The loss function is continuous and indicates that producing products within the traditional limits does not necessarily mean that the product is of good quality. Good quality is now achieved by minimising variation around a target value.

The implication here is that the zero defects approach of Crosby *et al.* may not be a sufficient condition for the achievement of good quality. Crosby defines quality in terms of conformance with requirements, i.e. within specification. This implies that a part is acceptable where it is within tolerance. Taguchi methods imply that this may result in poor performance and high costs due to variability around the target value. Furthermore, this variability will be even greater if during the assembly process a part near to its

**Figure 5.4
The quadratic
loss function**

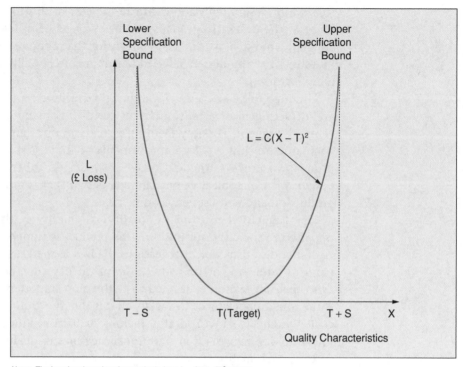

Notes: The loss function takes the quadratic form $L = C(X - T)^2$ where:
L = the money loss (£s), C = cost, T = target value, X = the point where the quality characteristic is actually set. Note that as upper $(T + S)$ and lower $(T - S)$ specification limits are approached costs rise exponentially. Costs are only minimised when the parameter is at its target value.

upper limit is combined with a part near to its lower limit: the total variation will be unacceptably high leading to poor performance during assembly and in the field.

Control of quality in the Taguchi methodology consists of three elements: system design, parameter design and tolerance design.

System design is achieved through the careful selection of parts, materials and equipment, frequently involving brainstorming by engineers, designers and buyers.

The objective of parameter design is to produce a robust product or process. A robust product is one which remains close to its target value and will perform well under a range of variations in its production environment and under a range of conditions in the end-user market. Robust products are said to have a high 'signal to noise ratio', which refers to the ability to cope with external factors or 'noise' – e.g. a television could be expected to operate under different weather conditions and reasonable variation in current. Parameter design for robust products is achieved through statistical experimentation using the method of orthogonal arrays. The method allows for the design of statistical experiments to determine the optimal levels for control factors. It quantifies all the likely interactions between variables and optimises factor levels.

Tolerance design is used to tighten tolerances on those factors that have a large impact on variation in order to further reduce variation around the target value. By using statistical experimentation at the design stage both time and costs are saved and robust products produced which will continue to please customers, reduce costs, and increase market share.

Failure mode and effect analysis

Failure mode and effect analysis (FMEA) is a technique used to eliminate potential faults in product design and manufacturing process of that product. The objective is to ensure that the product can be manufactured consistently to the requirements, taking into account the probability of failure occurring, the severity of a failure should it occur, and the probability of detection of faults. There are two basic approaches to FMEA: *design FMEA*, which analyses potential failure of the design and indicates where modifications need to be made, and *process FMEA*, which analyses potential failures to produce to specification and identifies corrective actions. Process FMEA is almost identical to design FMEA but obviously considers manufacturing processes instead of designs.

Many of the systems are statistically based and involve the ranking of the key factors of:

- severity of failure;
- probability of detection;
- probability of an occurrence.

The rankings produced are combined by addition or multiplication to produce a risk priority number (RPN). These are then reviewed and a minimum calculated. When the RPN associated with a particular failure mode exceeds the possible minimum, corrective action is required. This will involve changes which would, wherever possible, eliminate the mode of failure, or reduce the severity of the effects of failure by introducing fail-safe mechanisms. After corrective action the resulting RPN must be recalculated and the process repeated until the value falls to a minimum (process improvement).

Correct documentation is essential in order to operate the technique. All actions and records must be completed and include:

- a complete FMEA record;
- engineering specification changes;
- a production layout;
- storing the FMEA for future use.

The use of FMEA should lead to a reduction in:

- defects during the production of initial samples and in volume production;
- customer complaints;
- failures in the field;

- performance related deficiencies (these are less likely if a detailed development plan is generated from the design FMEA);
- warranty claims.

In addition there will be improved customer satisfaction and confidence as products and services are produced from robust and reliable production and delivery methods.

The process of FMEA is one of progressive iteration. In brief it involves the following steps:

- It starts by focusing on the function of the product, service and/or process.
- It identifies potential failure modes.
- It assesses the effects of each potential failure.
- It examines the causes of potential failure.
- It reviews current controls.
- It determines a risk priority number.
- It recommends the corrective action which is to be taken to help eliminate potential concerns.
- It monitors the corrective actions and counter-measures which have been put in place.

Specification

There are basically two approaches to specification: performance and conformance.

■ Performance specifications

The idea of performance specification is that a clear indication of the purpose, function, application and performance expected of the supplied material or service is communicated, and the supplier is allowed or encouraged to provide an appropriate product. The detailed specification is in the hands of the supplier. Where applicable, performance specifications are to be preferred in that they allow a wider competition and enable suppliers to suggest new or improved ways of meeting the requirement. It is frequently the case that when services are being acquired or purchased it is not possible to prescribe a conformance specification due to the fact that the service provider alone knows how to do the work required and the customer is able only to convey the intended outcome.

■ Conformance specifications

A slogan encountered in the purchasing function of British Airways states: 'Specifications restrict Innovation.' This is, of course, particularly true of conformance specifications – specifications where the buying organisation lays down clear and unambiguous requirements that must be met. The specification is of the product, not the application. This type of specification is necessary where, for example, items for incorporation in an assembly are to be bought, or where a certain chemical product is to be acquired for a production process. Nevertheless, the production of effective conformance specifications is rather difficult to achieve on occasion. Even in situations where the greatest care has been taken, it is sometimes the case that a supplier will deliver material that meets the specification as they understand it, while the customer complains that the specification means something different and seeks to reject the supplies. Conformance specifications take a variety of forms and can be drawn up by various departments.

Producing a specification

In manufacturing, a design or engineering department usually has the responsibility for product design, which includes the specification of parts and materials. In service industries, user departments often prepare specifications. In distributive industries, which sell the merchandise they buy rather than products they have manufactured, the selection of supplier-specified goods and the development of specifications for purchaser-specified goods is of central importance both in buying and in marketing, and reflects the organisation's policy on merchandising. In buying supplier-specified goods, retailers pick a brand or a make, or buy by sample, but in specification buying they draw up their own specifications, which are usually very detailed and thorough.

Preparing specifications is essentially a technical rather than a commercial activity. However, commercial staff have an important support role for their technical colleagues, in providing information about relative price trends and availability, keeping in touch with new developments, arranging contacts with essential suppliers and obtaining supplier help in formulating specifications. Formal detailed specifications are not drawn up for the majority of relatively unimportant purchases. If the quality required is well within the range which is commercially available then it is usually left to the procurement department to pick the appropriate make or brand. If the article required is not a constituent of the product, or is bought for internal use rather than for resale (such as factory seating or overalls), it will again often fall to the procurement department to specify what is to be purchased. The department is acting on behalf of the organisation as a whole in making such decisions, and care should be taken to seek the reaction and obtain the support of users before making a final choice between the alternatives available.

It can, of course, happen that procurement staff are technical experts in what they purchase and carry primary responsibility for specification. The wool buyer for a textile manufacturer may well be responsible for specifying, as well as arranging for the supply of, the grades of wool which satisfy the particular needs of the manufacturer. Specialist buyers of print, packaging or furniture may also have this dual role, first, to collect and interpret the organisation's requirements to arrive at a specification and, second, to review the market and negotiate a contract. The technical role of specification is in these cases not an extension of the commercial role of procurement; it is a different role carried out by a single person because his or her qualifications make him or her the most suitable person for both roles.

An important stage in specification is to review alternative ways of satisfying a given need. Commercial as well as technical considerations affect the choice. For instance, copper is used more widely than silver for electrical conductors for commercial rather than technical reasons: silver has a higher conductivity but is more expensive. Aluminium has a lower conductivity than copper but is lighter, so that for overhead power cables where weight is important it can be a better buy than copper, depending on the relative prices of the two materials.

These price relativities change, and a specification which at the time it was drawn up represented the best buy may be capable of improvement in the conditions which apply in a later stage of manufacture. There is often little to choose technically between zinc alloy and aluminium alloy for pressure die-castings, but there may be a price difference. Natural rubber (latex) prices fluctuate and affect the commercial choice between rubber and synthetics such as neoprene. The choice of production method is affected both by production volume and by technological development, which makes new options available. For instance, a part might be purchased in small quantities as a mild steel fabrication for £50 apiece. In large quantities, a similar part might be purchased as a pressing for 50p apiece, once a press tool had been laid down for more than 2000 or so. Or technological innovation might provide some different way to produce an equivalent part at a lower cost.

Specifications usually state a tolerance: the permissible variation in important characteristics such as size and weight. Close tolerances simplify assembly and promote interchangeability, but increase the costs of production and inspection, and thus of the purchase. In one case it was found that a dimensional tolerance of 0.0001 in. for grinding added 33 per cent to machining cost and 100 per cent to inspection cost compared with a tolerance of 0.001 in. It is widely accepted that some specifiers play safe by over-specifying, for instance by prescribing tolerances and limits which are too tight. These are some of the reasons why value analysis examines such questions as:

- Would a cheaper material do as well?
- Is it made on the right tooling in view of volume?
- Are limits and tolerances too tight?

In some instances a technically equivalent end-product can be made to a variety of recipes using different ingredients. For instance, cattle feed cakes can be made from 70 different ingredients, from herrings to molasses, which can be combined in various ways to produce cakes having the same iron content, nutritional value, etc. Possible ingredients are mostly primary commodities and their prices vary rapidly and by large amounts. The choice of which ingredients to buy and, consequently, which recipe to use at a particular time is a commercial rather than a technical decision. It is thus a decision taken by procurement staff, usually after carrying out a linear programming calculation on the computer.

Specifications take a variety of forms, from a pile of drawings inches thick to a brand name. Every purchase order, large or small, critical or not, must communicate the requirement to the supplier, but the expense of preparing a detailed specification is justifiable only when the requirement is critical or unusual or volume is great and cost high.

One of the simplest forms of description is a brand name. If there is only one brand which meets requirements then this is the obvious way to specify. But if one brand has been tested and found satisfactory and other brands exist which may be just as satisfactory and have not been tested then it is preferable to specify in the form 'Brand X or equal'. Suppliers sometimes change the specification without changing the brand name, which can cause problems for the buying organisation. Where possible, national or international standards should be adopted in preference to specifications which are peculiar to the buying organisation. If minor amendments would make a public standard appropriate to the need, it is good practice to state this specifically at the outset: 'generally to British Standard XYZ but with closer tolerance and harder temper', for instance.

Early supplier involvement

When a new product is being designed and specified, decisions need to be made about the extent (if any) and the timing of supplier involvement. While there are possible disadvantages associated with supplier participation in specification writing, there are many potential benefits. If there is to be involvement, then the sooner the better is the rule, since the further a design proceeds, the less the opportunity to influence it.

Possible disadvantages of early supplier involvement are:

- Supplier develops a complacent view as preferred source.
- Risk of leakage of commercial or technical confidential information.
- Competition may be reduced or eliminated.
- Buying organisation may lose ownership or control of technology.
- Potential valuable innovation from other sources may become unavailable.

Notwithstanding the above issues, there are many potential benefits to the buying concern if the supplier is brought on board at an early stage. A fundamental consideration is the fact that the supplier will, in all probability, be the 'expert' in the relationship, knowing a good deal more than the customer does about the technical and commercial aspects of the good or service in question. From this expert position, the supplier will possibly be able to advise on:

- developing ideas;
- materials employed;

- appropriate methods of manufacture;
- materials availability;
- alternative technologies;
- alternative materials;
- methods of manufacture and supply;
- present and predicted materials costs;
- sources of appropriate manufacturing capability;
- extent of competing demand for parts etc.;
- information on patents, copyrights and other protection of design.

There are also issues connected with the relationship between buyer and seller that influence, and are influenced by, early supplier involvement. The involved supplier will be part of the customer's team, and the developing 'value stream' and 'supply chain' philosophies require a close bonding between companies. This bonding requires mutual involvement.

Early involvement of and collaboration between supply function, suppliers and the rest of the design team might involve the following stages:

1 Identify the relevant stakeholders in the design and product development activity. These might, for example, be:
   - engineering;
   - production;
   - marketing;
   - finance;
   - supply department;
   - supplier(s).
2 Organise cross-functional activities between relevant internal stakeholders to examine such questions as commercial feasibility, technical feasibility, time requirements, quality issues, customer wishes and needs and so on.
3 Involve external stakeholders, including trusted supplier, working with them on technical and commercial issues relating to product development.
4 Work together to consider the development of appropriate information systems and the possible use of e-commerce approaches so that planning, scheduling and delivery of materials can be harmonised with the customer's build or manufacturing programme.

Mini case study – Neilsen Media Research

At Neilsen Media Research, Dunedin, Florida, procurement's involvement in the IT buy continues to grow. 'We are focusing on our capital spending', says Tim Russell, Procurement Manager. 'We are making greater efforts to involve major technology manufacturers into our IT plans earlier and more frequently. To lead these efforts, we have developed a solid team of representatives of IT, technical support, national contract administration, and purchasing. Through the cross-functional team's effort, we continue to stay up with or ahead of new technologies in the marketplace. Adding to this effort, our end users/customers provide early information on their needs.'

Figure 5.5
Concurrent engineering contrasted with consecutive engineering

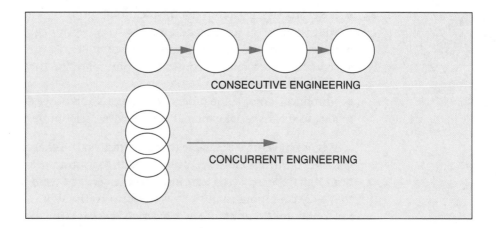

CONSECUTIVE ENGINEERING

CONCURRENT ENGINEERING

Concurrent engineering

There has been a good deal of attention paid in recent years to the concept of concurrent (or simultaneous) engineering. The approach has been defined as

> Getting the right people together at the right time to identify and resolve design problems. Concurrent engineering is designing for assembly, availability, cost, customer satisfaction, maintainability, manageability, manufacturability, operability, performance, quality, risk, safety, schedule, social acceptability and all other attributes of the product. (Dean and Unal, 1992)

The idea is that all the concerned parties work together at the same time, rather than in sequence, thus achieving a clearer understanding of each other's needs and contributions, and a much shorter elapsed time between conception of a need and its fulfilment. Figure 5.5 shows the concept of concurrent rather than serial working, each node representing a participant in the design process.

It can be seen that any organisation pursuing the concurrent engineering approach will require the active involvement of procurement staff, and in many cases that of vendors.

Standardisation

The systematic formulation and adoption of standards is referred to as standardisation. It is usually accompanied by variety reduction: a reduction in the range of items used, stocked, bought or made. This is not a process which happens naturally: engineers call for special parts which seem to them just a little better for the purpose than standard parts, users indulge individual preferences or even whims, and as a result the stores accumulate extensive ranges of different items to serve requirements which really differ little, if at all. A systematic standardisation and variety reduction programme can then be well worth launching. The benefits this can bring include:

- fewer stock items and reduced stockholdings;
- wider choices of supplier and increased scope for negotiation;
- larger orders and the possibility of lower prices;
- reduction to a simple routine of some parts of the work of design and purchase;
- simplification of some orders, requisitions and other documents; and
- less need for special explanations by letter, telephone, interview, etc.

It is not in general advisable to standardise on the cheapest, since when many versions of an article have been bought for substantially the same application, it may be expected that just as some versions were too good in the sense that they cost more than they were worth to the user, so other versions were not quite good enough. The objective in standardising is to select not the least expensive or the most expensive, but the right quality to meet the need.

No standardisation programme can succeed unless users are convinced that it is worthwhile. It needs to be marketed from the outset, and it is important to involve users in the variety reduction process; where possible, users themselves should decide which version will best suit their needs. Simply to issue a management edict that all standards must be rigidly adhered to does not work well. Ignoring legitimate differences in need provokes people to develop their private differences in preference into apparent differences in real need. But just offering standards as available options does not seem to work well either, because of organisational inertia. In practice, standards are often mandatory for minor items where users' needs are unlikely to differ much, but for more complex items they become increasingly optional.

Most countries have national standardisation bodies. The British Standards Institution (BSI) is linked with similar bodies in other countries through such supranational organisations as the European Committee for Standardization (CEN) and the International Organization for Standardization (ISO).

European Union national standards bodies have worked hard to harmonise their standards, although much remains to be done before the EU is really operating on common standards throughout.

■ BS EN ISO 9000

The predecessor to this series of standards, British Standard 5750, was first published in 1979 and gained widespread recognition in the United Kingdom as an indication that companies which had gained registration were consistently able to supply their product or service to a stated level of quality. As such, BS 5750 certification became widely recognised by the procurement and supply profession as a desirable characteristic in suppliers. This in turn led to competitive benefits being experienced by registered suppliers, and a rapid expansion in the number of registered organisations.

Following the introduction of BS 5750 many other countries saw the benefits associated with the scheme, and the idea was widely adopted abroad, usually with the support of the British Standards Institution. This wider interest in quality standards of this kind gave rise to the International Standards Organisation developing an international equivalent. This was published in 1987 as the 1SO 9000 series of five standards. In turn, the British Standards Institution adopted, without amendment, ISO 9000 as the new (1987) edition of BS 5750. This adoption recognised the fact that ISO 9000 reflected several years of British experience with BS 5750, and was of international relevance.

The ISO 9000 series was also adopted as European Standard EN 29000, 1987. Thus for many practical purposes BS 5750, ISO 9000 and EN 29000 are the same. The name adopted by the British Standards Institution for the standards has itself been standardised as BS EN ISO 9000.

The standards have a number of constituent parts, and contain three assessable quality assurance standards:

1 BS EN ISO 9001: A model for quality assurance in design, development, production, installation and servicing.
2 BS EN ISO 9002: A model for quality assurance in production, installation and servicing.
3 BS EN ISO 9003: A model for quality assurance in final inspection and testing.

Firms need apply only one of these parts. A company producing or supplying a simple standard product with little or no design input may well work to BS EN ISO 9002, whereas if product design or development is undertaken by the firm then BS EN ISO 9001 will be more appropriate. If final inspection is the most appropriate way of assuring quality, then BS EN ISO 9003 is likely to be adopted as the standard. An example of this type of activity might be contract cleaning services. It should be recognised that the standards are applicable to organisations producing services as well as goods: the requirements relate to the ways in which the firms operate and are managed, not to the products of the firms.

The BS EN ISO 9000 series of standards is of great interest to those responsible for identifying and selecting appropriate suppliers in that they provide evidence that a certificated organisation is employing appropriate quality systems. They are not applicable to the products of the supplier, be they goods or services, but to the manner in which the supplier organises and conducts those aspects of the business with a bearing upon quality. The standard is employed by all major public sector procurement organisations in the UK as a basis for determining a supplier's ability to produce satisfactory goods and services.

The following guidance notes are reproduced by permission of the Department of Trade and Industry and are adapted from their booklet *Purchasers and BS EN 9000*.

Claims of compliance with BS EN ISO 9000

A firm can implement a quality management system that follows the principles of BS EN ISO 9001/2/3, benefit from doing so and tell you about it. They are not legally obliged to have it independently assessed, but they cannot claim BS EN ISO 9000 registration until they have done so. If they are not registered, this does not lessen their achievement. But equally it does not give you the same assurance that an independent assessment does.

Claims of compliance with BS EN ISO 9000 may be based on:

Assessment by the supplier themselves: This is not very common, and such claims are of limited value, as they lack any input either from you the buyer or any independent body. If you are buying from a self-assessed firm, you should:

■ Check that the process is supervised, preferably by people who have experience of or professional qualifications in quality assurance.

■ Check they have proof of their ability to deliver to your requirements.

■ Check that they can provide evidence that their system follows BS EN ISO 9000.

Assessment by a second party: This may be by:

■ Acceptance on the tender list of an internationally recognised quality led company which assesses suppliers against its own quality system requirements, based on BS EN ISO 9000 (e.g. Ford, Rover, Cores, Marks & Spencer).

■ A few major organisations have schemes for assessing and certifying the quality systems of their suppliers. These schemes are assessed by UKAS on the same criteria as those used to assess accredited third party certification schemes, and they are recognised as Second Party Certification schemes.

Assessment by an independent third party: Explained in the note that follows.

Alternatively, suppliers may provide evidence from other customers that they have delivered reliable and consistent products or service, to specification, over a long period. While this does not prove compliance with BS EN ISO 9000 it is likely to provide an indication that the company manages its procedures to assure consistency of supply.

Independent assessment and registration

Independent assessment gives the buying organisation an impartial assessment of a supplier's system; if an assessment is successful the applicant company is awarded a certificate and included in the assessment body's own register of successful assessments. There are over 70 independent certification bodies, increasingly referred to as 'registrars', operating in the UK market. In January 1996, 51 of these were accredited by UKAS (see below), and three have been recognised as second party assessment bodies by UKAS. These 54 bodies are expected to provide assessment to the highest possible standards.

Accreditation is awarded to a third party, independent certification body as recognition that the body has met internationally accepted criteria covering integrity and technical competence, and that its assessors have the capability to assess companies against the requirements of BS EN ISO 9000 in specific business areas to a consistent level. These bodies are assessed and accredited in the UK by the United Kingdom Accreditation Service (UKAS).

In recognition of their status, the UK government permits accredited bodies to use the National Accreditation Mark of Certification Bodies. Companies assessed by an accredited body may also use the Mark, subject to a registration within the certification body's accredited scope. The Mark is a clear and public demonstration that a competent and independent body has assessed a company's quality system. It is recognised internationally.

There are three levels of independent third party assessment. When considering the merits of using registered suppliers, you may wish to consider which level of assessment gives the amount of assurance you need. The highest of these levels results in a certificate of registration issued by an accredited certification body under its accredited scope. The next level is a certificate issued by an accredited body but outside its accredited scope. The third level is a certificate issued by a non-accredited body.

It is worthwhile remembering when considering the level of assurance you require that although accredited bodies are prohibited, for impartiality reasons, from providing consultancy services to the companies they assess, a number of non-accredited bodies both provide clients with their quality manuals and assess compliance to the manual against companies they assess. A number of non-accredited bodies both provide clients with their quality manuals and assess compliance to the manual against BS EN ISO 9000.

When specifying BS EN ISO 9000, government purchasers wherever possible specify an accredited certificate. When this, or a second party certificate, is not available then a non-accredited certificate from an accredited body is acceptable to most government purchasers. A certificate issued by a non-accredited body is generally treated with great circumspection. You may wish to adopt a similar strategy when considering using BS EN ISO 9000 registered suppliers. Remember: the National Accreditation Mark is the mark to look for from companies claiming an accredited registration. However, when you use a supplier with an accredited registration it is important that you ensure their scope of registration is applicable to your needs.

An organisation wishing to achieve certification must, of course, first ensure that it has a quality system which meets the requirements of the standard. If advice and help is needed, then the regional offices of the Department of Trade and Industry are able to offer advice, and in the case of small companies, subsidised consultancy. Having developed and implemented a conforming quality system, then the company will be 'vetted' by an appropriate accredited certification body. The BSI does not itself offer certification. What happens is that the Secretary of State, following the assessment of a body by the National Accreditation Council for Certification Bodies, issues a statement that the body is competent to issue certificates within certain specified areas. This process is called 'accreditation' (see below).

It is important to remember that the BSI says that a company ought not to be rejected as a supplier solely because the supplier does not have a quality management system or ISO 9000 provided the company can provide other acceptable quality assurances. There has been some resistance to ISO 9000 by some small and medium-sized enterprises, who see the standard as imposing systems and procedures that are too rigid and bureaucratic, and which add cost without adding real value. Many larger concerns, while recognising the importance and value of ISO 9000, also recognise that it is not appropriate for all their suppliers. For example, RS Components, a leading stockist and supplier of electronic components, is a large and successful organisation which might be expected to require all suppliers to demonstrate that they are accredited under ISO 9000. However, they regard this as inappropriate and impracticable, and instead insist that suppliers demonstrate that they have an appropriate quality regime in place that is working satisfactorily. Many companies in such industries as automotive and aerospace have their own quality systems and procedures, which are rather more rigorous than ISO 9000. In the case of such concerns, accreditation would serve no useful purpose.

Supplier assessment

The next stage in the process of buying quality assurance, after defining the specification, is to select one or more suppliers capable of working to the specification. Five methods used in assessing supplier capability in this connection are based on:

- past performance;
- reputation;
- visit and appraisal;
- third-party certification; and
- evaluation of sample products.

Vendor appraisal, supplier evaluation and vendor rating are procedures used in this connection. Vendor appraisal is the term used when the performance of potential suppliers is assessed before an order is placed with them. Supplier evaluation refers to assessment after orders have been placed. Supplier rating (or vendor rating, as it is often called) refers to the calculation of an index of actual performance.

■ Past performance

The first method, basing the choice on past performance, can only be used for supplier selection when items are bought in large quantities from several suppliers. Records of quality performance need to be available to the buying organisation's decision maker. Such records may also include quantitative data on delivery, performance, service, price and other matters considered relevant, which may be summarised and combined into a supplier rating. Buyers use this information not only to give more business to better suppliers, and to phase out inadequate suppliers, but also to urge weak suppliers to improve their performance.

■ Reputation

The second method is widely used. A good reputation for quality can be a valuable trade asset, and in industrial markets it is mainly based on actual performance rather than advertising and other forms of publicity. Experienced buyers build up a lot of market knowledge, which they add to by talking to colleagues, sales representatives and buyers in other organisations. Potential suppliers can be asked to give references: the names of three customers who can be approached for a confidential report.

■ Visit and appraisal

The third method involves a visit to the supplier in order to make an assessment of quality capability. This takes time and can be expensive, but the expense may be a small price to pay for quality assurance. Quality control staff, procurement staff or an interdepartmental team may make the visit. The procurement representative be make sure to meet any people who may need to be contacted if delivery or other problems occur. But since the purpose of the visit is to assess quality capability, most of the time will be taken up in examining production methods and facilities; inspection, test and measurement facilities both in production and in inspection departments; check and calibration routines for gauges and other test devices. Quality control procedures in use, including the use of control charts and other records, and the way in which corrective action is taken will also be considered, an attempt made to assess the standard of work in progress, policies and attitudes in relation to quality, and, so far as possible in a short visit, the quality of management. More detail is given in Chapter 8, which also includes an example of a checklist such as most organisations use on these visits.

■ Third-party certification

Third-party certification is the term used for visits and appraisals made by some independent body – neither the first party, or buyer, nor the second party, or seller – the results of which are then published or made available to clients or subscribers in the form of a certificate of quality assessment.

■ Evaluation of products

The final stage in the process is the delivery of satisfactory goods by the supplier and their acceptance by the customer, thus completing the transaction once payment has been made. This used to be considered the key to the whole of quality control: the inspection stage, when the buying organisation checked deliveries and either accepted or rejected them. Now the view is that it is the supplier's responsibility to deliver goods which are acceptable, as conforming with specified requirements. Rather than inspect the goods, the buying organisation inspects the supplier's arrangements for ensuring that the goods are acceptable. The earlier notes on BS EN ISO 9000 are relevant here. Some goods still call for 100 per cent inspection, and there are also some goods which do not require technical inspection. Examples of the latter are works and office supplies, most branded goods, standard machine screws or cans of paint, and low-priced goods of minor importance. Sampling inspection methods are now very widely used, especially when goods are delivered in large lots or batches. Checking every single one of a large batch of goods is tedious, time-consuming and expensive, and because of human errors it seems not to be as effective as checking a sample chosen on the basis of probability theory. Sampling procedures and tables for inspection by attributes are given in BS 6001, and BS 6000 explains clearly how to use these procedures.

A sample is taken from the batch, and the whole batch is rejected if more than a certain proportion is defective, or it is accepted if less than this proportion is defective. As quality expectations rise, the standard is becoming more severe. In the early 1980s 5 per cent defective was often considered acceptable. Now 0.2 per cent or 200 parts per million is considered a normal target, with some companies looking for 50 to 100 parts per million and beyond. The pursuit of 'zero defects' reflects a philosophy that perfection should be the goal.

Prompt notification to the supplier, and if relevant to the transport firm which made the delivery, should be given if goods are rejected. Any delay could affect the legal position if a claim has to be made. Several alternatives are open when defective goods are received. Goods which are unacceptable are not all unacceptable for the same reason. The buying organisation may:

- refuse to accept the batch;
- return the batch for replacement;
- return the batch for credit;
- arrange for the supplier to make a 100 per cent inspection at the buyer's establishment to sort defective parts from good parts; or
- make this 100 per cent inspection using the buyer's inspection staff.

Following the 100 per cent inspection, there are three further alternatives:

1 to return defective parts for credit or replacement;
2 to correct or rework defective parts; or
3 to use the defective parts, but with special care or for special applications.

In addition:

4 A lower price would be negotiated for the last two of these alternatives.

Serious or persistent quality problems call for a thorough review of the situation and perhaps a visit to the supplier's establishment to see the problem in the field and discuss it with production and quality control staff. Points to check include the following:

- Are specifications clear, explicit, unambiguous?
- Has the supplier understood them?
- Do they specify the right quality or are they too demanding?
- Is there any assistance we can give in quality control or production methods?
- Or in training staff?
- Should we change to a different supplier?

■ Vendor accreditation

Many major organisations have vendor accreditation schemes. These are mentioned in Chapter 8 on source decision making. An important aspect of performance monitoring is the rating of quality, and statistics will normally be gathered on the quality of supplies received. From these statistics supplier incentive schemes can be derived, such as supplier league tables, or 'vendor of the month' awards. Figure 5.6 illustrates the certification scheme used by Kodak in the UK, the idea being that suppliers will strive to qualify for a 'gold' certificate.

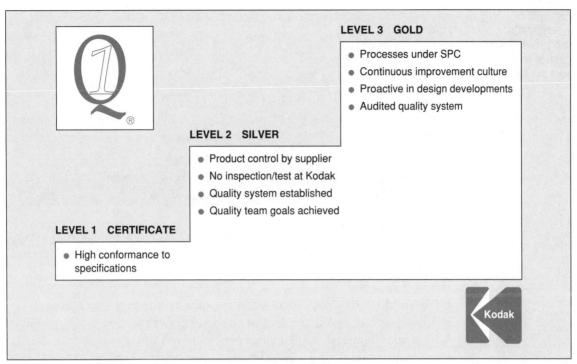

Figure 5.6 'Quality first' supplier programme: award recognition levels

(*Source*: Kodak)

Economics of quality

It used to be the case that the level of quality control activity expressed as a cost worth incurring could be determined by looking at the cost of inspection, and at the cost associated with accepting defective supplies and detecting them later, perhaps at the time of use. No expenditure on inspection would result in all defective supplies finding their way into the system, and would result in high costs. One hundred per cent inspection would, for most supplies, be prohibitively expensive, so some optimum level of quality control was sought, seeking to minimise the total cost of quality. It was widely taught that the economic level of inspection would be attained where the cost of inspection was equal to the cost of failure. In this situation the important total cost would be minimised. What this concept failed to recognise was that the money spent on inspection and detection of defectives could be turned into an investment rather than a sunk cost if feedback was in place so as to prevent a repetition of the defective work. If such investments can be made and managed, the incidence of defective supply will become less, and the cost of quality will reduce over time. Current thinking on quality, inspired by the charismatic individuals known as the quality gurus, suggests that we consider four costs of quality:

Figure 5.7
A schematic representation of change in quality cost over time

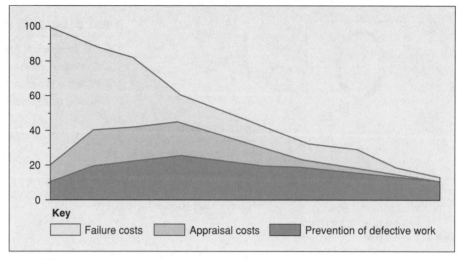

Key
☐ Failure costs   ▨ Appraisal costs   ■ Prevention of defective work

Note: Base cost index = 100.
Shift is from no quality management to quality control to quality assurance.

1 Prevention costs – costs incurred in avoiding failure in the first place.
2 Appraisal costs – costs incurred in checking and inspection.
3 Internal failure costs – arising from errors within the operation.
4 External failure costs – arising from an error being passed on to an external customer.

The last two items in the list are covered by the term 'failure costs' in Figure 5.7.

Quality circles

Quality circles have become a popular approach to the improvement not only of product quality but also of other aspects of company performance and the quality of working life. They go by various names: General Motors calls them employee participation groups; Toyota refers to small group improvement activities.

They originated in Japan. Groups of up to 12 workers plus one or two supervisors or managers from the same department would meet once or twice a week on a voluntary basis to find better ways to do things: improving quality, increasing output, easier work, or getting along with each other better. They have been adopted enthusiastically by British and American firms trying to improve quality and reliability, although there have been some difficulties. Management and workforce have to overcome traditional adversarial attitudes and learn how to collaborate in their common interest. This has often proved to be hard for both sides. Several attempts have sometimes been required before getting it right.

Quality circles seem to have made big contributions to the improvement of quality and reliability, as well as to other aspects of company performance, in those organisations which have managed to develop the right attitudes to make them work. The same can be said of a much earlier approach, which also relies on part-time group work: value analysis (see below).

The seven wastes

Taiichi Ohno, the former chief engineer of Toyota in Japan, was influential in the development of what is now widely known as 'lean thinking'. He suggested seven common 'wastes', or non-value-adding activities, which are summarised below (see Womack and Jones, 1996):

1 The waste of overproduction. Symptoms of this waste are:
   - just-in-case manufacture or supply;
   - working ahead of need;
   - excessive lead times;
   - excessive storage;
   - excessive work in progress.
2 The waste of waiting. Symptoms are:
   - ineffective use of time;
   - lack of motion;
   - lumpy flow;
   - opportunity cost of waiting time.
3 The waste of unnecessary transportation. Key observations are:
   - customers do not pay for movement;
   - handling is a form of transportation;
   - better communication can lead to less transportation;
   - people, plants and processes should, where possible, be linked;
   - the number of steps in a process should be minimised.
4 The waste of inappropriate processing. Key ideas are:
   - processes need to be both efficient and effective;
   - focus on process not product;
   - avoid 'monoliths' (expensive, often 'high tech' investments over-specified in relation to the real need);
   - ensure quality capability at all stages.
5 The waste of unnecessary inventory. Negative aspects of inventory include:
   - inventory tends to mask problems;
   - inventory generates ownership cost;
   - inventory generates opportunity cost;
   - inventory impairs flexibility.
6 The waste of unnecessary motions. Be concerned with ergonomics, and avoid such activities as:
   - stooping;
   - bending;
   - lifting;
   - reaching;
   - over-exertion.

7 The waste of defects. Key ideas are:

- poor quality = cost = waste;
- quality assurance is an investment (not a cost);
- a defect should be seen as a challenge.

The Japanese word 'muda' was employed by Ohno to describe waste in the manufacturing and supply context, and has been widely adopted by managers and scholars in the West. Ohno's thinking has led to what might almost be called a waste elimination industry, and today many more kinds of waste have been identified beyond this original seven.

Value analysis/value engineering

Value analysis (VA) and value engineering (VE) are terms which both refer to the same basic techniques. Sometimes the term 'value engineering' is used when new specifications are being refined before they are finalised, and 'value analysis' when the methods are used to reconsider existing specifications that have been in use for some time. Others prefer VE when the engineering design department takes the lead in implementing the technique, and VA when it is the procurement department that takes the lead. Often the two terms seem to be used interchangeably. The same technique is referred to, with the same aim of increasing value for money whether by reducing the cost of providing a part, product or service to satisfy given needs, or by increasing the satisfaction resulting from a given part, product or service. Applied at the initial design stage, VA/VE assists in the launch of an attractive and competitive product; applied in the mature or declining phases of the product life cycle, it helps to prolong the profitable life and defend the market share of the product.

Successful VA/VE exercises have in thousands of instances produced savings very much greater than the cost of the exercise: savings not only in purchase cost or production cost, but also in the less quantifiable results of better co-operation between departments and more constructive relationships with suppliers.

The basic procedure is to ask: What is this? What is it for? What does it cost? What else would do the job? What would that cost? Usually a value analysis team is set up (a team, not a committee) with representatives at middle management level from such departments as procurement, production, design, costing and, perhaps, marketing. The members are there not so much as departmental representatives, more because their departmental interests and their personal capability enable them to make contributions from different angles and with different kinds of expertise. The team operates part time, and this is considered important because it means that members retain their main commitment to their departments. It is usually necessary to have one member who works full time on value projects; that member is the designated value analyst and may act as chair or secretary. The team should meet regularly, for instance once a week for three hours at the same time and place.

Having set up the team, the next steps are to select targets for analysis, preferably starting with profitable, high-volume items where reasonable prospects exist of making substantial savings, and to proceed systematically through the successive phases:

- information;
- speculation;
- investigation;
- recommendation;
- implementation.

The information stage calls for the collection of facts and figures about the target item: its shape and size and cost of production or purchase, its weight, material analysis, processing and assembly operations, etc.

The speculation phase is seen as the heart of value analysis. It is a deliberate attempt to stimulate creative thought about the item. A common starting point is to attempt to define the function of an item in two words – a verb and a noun. Of course, an item may have more than one function; but the object of this exercise is to concentrate attention on what a thing is for, or what it does. Occasionally, it is found that what the item is for is lost in past history and what it does now is nothing, so that useful savings can be made by simply eliminating it. Defining the function in this way concentrates attention on the cost of performing the required function, rather than on the cost of whatever happens at present to be used for the purpose. What else could be used? Brainstorming, consulting suppliers, function/cost matrices, and other techniques have been mentioned as sources of ideas. When new ideas are put forward it is important to accentuate the positive and eliminate the negative; for instance, a poster may be displayed at team meetings which lists stock responses such as:

'Let somebody else try it first.'
'It's not the way we do things.'
'The customers will never agree.'
'Our business is different.'
'We've tried it before.'
'We've never tried it before.'

The investigation phase probes the merit of proposals and provides hard evidence for the next phase, the recommendation to management. The final phase, implementation, could be regarded as a routine matter once management approval has been received. Unfortunately, organisational inertia and individual resistance can frustrate the whole exercise unless as much effort is put into implementation as into earlier phases.

Footnote

NASA spent a great deal of money in encouraging the US pen manufacturer, Fisher, to develop and produce a pen for use in space. It had to be able to write upside down, and function in zero gravity situations. The Soviets came up with a better value solution to the same problem. They used pencils.

Make-or-buy decisions

If it proves impossible to secure quality fit for purpose from an external resource then companies have investigated the possibility of bringing production back in-house. This is known as the make-or-buy decision.

Make-or-buy decisions are decisions about the source of materials, goods or services. The choice to be made is to produce the materials and goods or provide the service internally, or to purchase from a source external to the organisation.

Mini case study – Mitel

Mitel, a manufacturer of telecommunications equipment, experienced difficulty in sourcing components that embodied a certain emerging technology. There was undercapacity in the market. The company made the necessary investments to bring the technology in-house and developed capacity sufficient to meet internal needs and to sell components profitably to external customers.

Tactical make-or-buy decisions will be reviewed as circumstances change. Some exigency is the usual reason for review, and some common reasons for make-or-buy decisions at lower levels are:

- Deterioration in an existing supplier's quality performance.
- Delivery failure or poor service by existing source.
- Large price increase.
- Volume changes; much larger or smaller quantity requirement for item concerned.
- Pressure to reduce costs.
- Desire to concentrate internal resources on areas of special competence.
- Need for design secrecy.

■ Operational decisions

A general rule is that prior to making a make-or-buy decision a comparison should be made between the costs of making in-house or buying in. If it is found to be cheaper to make then make; if cheaper to buy, then that is what will be chosen. The following decisions need to be made before a comparative evaluation can begin:

- What volume do we expect to require?
- What capital investment is required to make the goods?
- What will be our peak demand?
- How much risk is associated with the technology required?
- How much wastage (or cost of reworking) can we expect?
- What level of inventory will we (and our supplier) hold?
- For how long will the contract apply?

- What variations can be expected in materials costs?
- Can we make more by concentrating on our special competencies than we can save by carrying out the work internally?

Even when we have answered these questions there will be more; some more difficult, such as how much of our overhead should we attribute to the cost of making this item? If substantial capital investment in specialist equipment is required to produce goods internally, then the decision cannot be reversed within the economic life of the plant without losing money on the remaining capital value. Table 5.1 provides a checklist which may help to ensure that relevant factors are not overlooked.

Table 5.1
A make-or-buy checklist

If currently purchased from an outside source	If currently being manufactured within the company
• Does capacity exist within our own company?	• Is there a matter of secrecy to be considered?
• If so, is such capacity likely to be available for the planning period involved?	• If the item is withdrawn from production, would redundancies result?
• Is the necessary raw material available now at economic rates?	• If 'yes', what action would need to be taken by management regarding those redundancies?
• Will that material continue to be available at economic rates for the planning period?	• If tooling is involved, what is its condition? Can it be used by the prospective source?
• If tooling is involved: (a) what is the cost? (b) what is the expected life? (c) what is the delivery?	• Will the machinery involved on current manufacture be fully utilised for alternative work if the part is withdrawn?
• Are we satisfied that the current supplier is the most economic source?	• Is there a possibility of development work being done on the part? If so, can this be done satisfactorily in conjunction with an outside supplier?
• Is there a patent and thus the possibility of royalties to be paid?	
• Is VAT chargeable (e.g. printing)?	• Will the quantities involved interest an outside supplier?
• Is the current supplier doing development work towards an improved version of the item?	• Do we know the true cost of alternative supply against manufacture (e.g. transport and handling costs) – present and forward?
• Has the current supplier had difficulty with either quality, quantity or time factors, and have their costs escalated as a result, thus affecting their selling price?	• Is the item part of an integrated production route involving several stages of manufacture? If so, can outside manufacture be satisfactorily co-ordinated with production schedules and machine loading in our shops?
• If their quality has been affected: (a) has the supplier's quality system been vetted? (b) what has been the extent of quality failures? (c) is our production department confident that the specified quality can be economically maintained in internal production? (d) are we over-specifying?	• What is the forward market position for the item concerned for the relevant planning period?
• If their other costs are escalating: (a) what are the reasons? (b) are we confident that we will not be affected in the same way?	• Are all drawings correct?
	• Is there any advantage in supplying raw materials/components if a decision is taken to buy?
• If the item is currently being imported, what is the cost breakdown? If duty is payable, what rate is applied? What duty, if any, will be payable on the relevant raw materials/components if they are imported?	• Can we indicate to the potential supplier the remaining life of the product?
	• Can the potential supplier suggest ideas for taking cost out of the product?

One important consideration concerns the ability of the specialist supplier to innovate and find ways of improving the product or service.

Mini case study – Lucas Engineering

Lucas Engineering and Systems take the following considerations (amongst others) into account when making the make-or-buy decision in relation to a process.

- How important is the process to our business?
- How competitive are we in relation to others undertaking this process?
- How strongly does this process impact on our measures of business performance?
- To what extent does the process have an impact on other products/processes?
- Is the process linked to any of the strategic issues confronting the business?

The information gathered in response to these questions is brought together on a chart, which enables some comparisons to be made between the processes which might be candidates for a changed make-or-buy status. Of course, financial models and projections are used too.

Summary

1 Quality means different things to different people. It can be defined as 'fitness for purpose'. More strategically, it can be viewed as an issue related to competitive advantage.

2 Statistical process control (SPC) is a mathematical system used to monitor an organisation's quality capability. It is a proactive approach to preventing defective work being produced. SPC devolves responsibility for quality down to the operator who is authorised to take corrective action should measurements stray outside of acceptable limits.

3 'Off-line' approaches to quality assurance have assumed a greater prominence in recent years. The work of Taguchi in connection with the quadratic loss function has been extremely influential in this regard. Ideas such as failure mode and effect analysis and early supplier involvement exemplify other 'off-line' approaches.

4 Performance specifications encourage the supplier to be innovative in providing an appropriate product/service to meet the need. Conformance specifications are clear and unambiguous, relating to the product/service rather than its application.

5 Standardisation can be a difficult and lengthy process as it often requires individual preferences to be ignored. However, the benefits of variety reduction, lower stockholding costs, economies of scale on larger orders, etc., can make the exercise well worthwhile.

6 An organisation wishing to achieve ISO certification must ensure that it has a quality system that meets the requirements of the standard. While it is a useful award to hold, it may not be appropriate for all suppliers. For some the procedures may be too rigid, adding cost without adding value. (These companies should not be rejected if they can provide some other acceptable quality assurance system.) Other companies may employ far more rigorous quality procedures in which case accreditation would serve no purpose.

References and further reading

Call, J (1993), *TQM for Purchasing Management*, New York: McGraw-Hill.

Calvi, R *et al.* (2001), 'How to manage early supplier involvement into the new product development process', 10th International IPSERA Conference.

Dean, G B and Unal, R (1992), 'Elements of Designing for Cost', AIAA Aerospace Design Conference, Irvine, CA.

Department of Trade and Industry (1995), *Purchasers and BS EN 9000*, London: DTI.

Disney, J and Bendell, A (1994), 'Taguchi methods', in Dale, B G (ed), *Managing Quality*, 2nd edn, London: Prentice-Hall.

Erridge, A *et al.* (2001), *Best Practice Procurement*, Aldershot: Gower.

Emmett, S (2005), *Supply Chain in 90 Minutes*, Cambridge: Management Books 2000 Ltd.

Giunipero, L and Brewer, D (1993), 'Performance based evaluation systems under TQM', *International Journal of Purchasing and Materials Management*, 29 (1), Winter.

Jackson, P and Ashton, M (1993), *Implementing Quality through BS 5750 (ISO 9000)*, London: Kogan Page.

Jessop, D and Jones, O (2000), 'Less distant relations', *Supply Management*, May.

Juran, J and Gryna, J (1993), *Quality Planning and Analysis*, New York: McGraw-Hill.

Oakland, J (1990), *Statistical Process Control: A Practical Guide*, Oxford: Heinemann-Newnes.

Oakland, J (1993), *Total Quality Management: The Route to Improving Performance*, Oxford: Butterworth–Heinemann.

Oakland, J S (1995), *Total Quality Management*, Oxford: Butterworth–Heinemann.

Plank, R and Kjjewski, V (1991), 'The use of approved supplier lists', *International Journal of Purchasing and Materials Management*, 27 (2), Spring.

Taguchi, G and Clausing, D (1990), 'Robust quality', *Harvard Business Review*, January.

Womack, J P and Jones, D T (1996), *Lean Thinking*, New York: Simon & Schuster.

Wynstra, F *et al.* (1999), 'Purchasing involvement in product development', *European Journal of Purchasing*, 6.

6

Inventory management

Introduction

Holding inventory costs money, and therefore reduces profitability. That inventory is designed to support production and service operations. Some level of inventory is essential in order to provide continuity of service and to avoid costly downtime and service disruption and non-availability, but inventory reduction and, therefore, the release of cash and reduced operating costs remain essential concerns of inventory management.

Objectives of this chapter

- To consider provisioning systems for stock and production purposes
- To examine positive and negative reasons for holding stock and approaches to reducing inventories
- To identify methods of stock control and their application
- To explain the EOQ concept
- To discuss the usefulness and limitations of forecasting in the supply context
- To develop an appreciation of MRP, MRP2, DRP and ERP systems
- To discuss 'just-in-time' and related philosophies
- To explain late customisation as a provisioning policy

Provisioning systems

Regular requirements are bought either for stock, or for direct use in operations or production. Part of the function of stock or production planning and control is to calculate what quantities are needed and when they are needed to meet requirements for stock or for production.

Stock control could be defined as the policies and procedures which systematically determine and regulate which things are kept in stock and what quantities of them are stocked. For each item stocked decisions are needed as to the size of the requirement, the time at which further supplies should be ordered, and the quantity which should be ordered. Production planning and control could be defined as the policies and procedures which systematically determine and regulate manufacturing programmes and which establish requirements for parts and materials to support production. For each item required decisions are needed as to the size of the requirement, the time at which it should be ordered and the order quantity.

Requirement quantities can be aggregated or subdivided in various ways, and the quantity notified to the procurement department as required is not necessarily the same as the quantity the procurement department orders from suppliers.

Ordering policies used by procurement include:

- Blanket orders which group many small requirements together for contractual purposes.
- Capacity booking orders, which reserve supplier capacity for the production of various parts, used in conjunction with make orders which specify later which parts are to be made. This type of purchasing is becoming more commonplace as supply chains become more flexible or agile.
- Period contracts stating an estimated total quantity for the period and the agreed price, in conjunction with call-off orders which state delivery date and quantity.
- Period contracts which specify a series of delivery dates and quantities (e.g. '1000 during the first week of each month').
- Spot contracts and futures contracts in various combinations.
- 'Open-to-buy' (OTB) and the similar 'order-up-to' systems sometimes used by stock controllers in the retailing sector.
- Part-period balancing, lot-for-lot, and other approaches favoured by production controllers in conjunction with materials requirement planning (MRP) or kanban systems.
- The economic order quantity (EOQ).

We go on to consider order quantities in connection, first, with stock control and, second, with production control.

Order quantities and stock control

Every organisation holds some things in stock. Stock can be a nuisance, a necessity, or a convenience. Retailers and wholesalers see stock as the central feature of their businesses: what they sell is what they buy, and they aim to sell from stock rather than from future deliveries which have yet to arrive. Organisations such as some manufacturers, health-care institutions and other service providers place stock in a subsidiary rather than a central position, but it is still an important element in operational effectiveness and often appears on the balance sheet as the biggest of current assets, locking up a lot of money.

Why do we carry stock? The reasons include:

- the convenience of having things available as and when required without making special arrangements;
- cost reduction through purchase or production of optimum quantities;
- protection against the effects of forecast error, inaccurate records or mistakes in planning; and
- provision for fluctuations in sales or production.

Carrying stock is expensive, and it is accepted that many organisations carry too much stock. A continuing drive to reduce stock without reducing service is needed to combat the natural tendency of stock to increase. Constructive approaches to stock reduction include:

- Arranging for things to be made and delivered just in time instead of stock-piling just in case a need arises.
- Devising ways to reduce ordering costs, set-up costs, and lead times so that optimum quantities are smaller.
- Making forecasts more accurate, ensuring that records are right, and better planning.

Order quantities directly affect the size of the stockpile. If 12 months' requirements arrive in one lot, and consumption takes place at a steady rate, average stock over the whole year (neglecting buffer stock) is equivalent to six months' requirements. But if only one month's requirements arrive, average stock over the whole year is equivalent to only half a month's supply. Frequent small orders for such regular requirements, instead of occasional large orders, can result in substantial reductions in the size of stocks. Unfortunately, this can also result in substantial increases in paperwork and administrative effort.

Essentially, the role of the stock controller is to achieve a balance. Too little stock and the organisation will suffer from delayed production, poor customer service or lack of ability to respond to new requirements; too much stock and the funds of the organisation will be tied up, thus impairing opportunities to invest or spend elsewhere. A well-known 'rule of thumb' is that the cost of carrying stock is 25 per cent per annum. While this is merely a guide, and the costs for a particular organisation may well be somewhat higher or indeed lower, it is clearly important to be extremely cautious about making an 'investment' with this very high negative return.

■ Inventory (stock) as waste

Influential thinkers in supply chain management have suggested that inventory is waste, and should be avoided wherever possible. The reasons behind this view are that stocks of materials can adversely impact any organisation because they:

- tie up capital;
- impair cash flow;

- impair flexibility;
- need to be stored (at a cost);
- need to be handled (at a cost);
- need to be managed (at a cost);
- are at risk of loss through fire, theft and many other possible misfortunes;
- usually depreciate in value.

It is also argued that stocks are frequently held for the wrong reasons, sometimes to mask inefficiencies in the management of the organisation. Examples include:

- Masking poor quality – 'If this one is faulty, we have a reserve in the stores.'
- Masking poor planning – 'We haven't worked out exactly what to do as yet, we'd better stock items to include all possibilities.'
- Masking poor suppliers (or poor relationships with suppliers) – 'We can't always rely on them to deliver, but carrying some stock protects us from this uncertainty.'

We should critically evaluate decisions as to whether to adopt an item as a stocked line, and take care to see that the justification is sound. The important thing to remember is that it is unnecessary inventory that constitutes waste; the important question is, 'is it necessary?'

■ Approaches to control

There are many systems employed for the purposes of determining when, and in what quantities, to replenish stocks. These systems are based on either some form of 'action level' approach, or the periodic review system (see Figure 6.1).

■ Economic order quantities

Analysis of the costs involved led to the devising of formulae which enable an economic order quantity (EOQ) to be derived for any combination of the variables of price, rate of usage or demand, and internal costs. The EOQ is the quantity that results in the lowest total of variable costs. It should not be surprising to find that if the annual usage value is low in relation to the cost of ordering and processing deliveries then the formula indicates that orders should be placed infrequently, whereas if it costs appreciably more to hold a month's supply in stock than it does to order it then the formula indicates that frequent orders should be placed. For those of us who are not mathematicians, it may, however, be surprising to find that order quantity is proportional not to the annual usage value but to its square root; so that if annual demand doubles, the order quantity should be increased by about 40 per cent. Properly applied, the EOQ formula does in fact work well, resulting in lower stocks, fewer orders, and no reduction in service, and thus justifying

Figure 6.1
Requirement
profiles:
(a) constant rate;
(b) increasing rate;
(c) seasonal rate;
(d) periodic rate

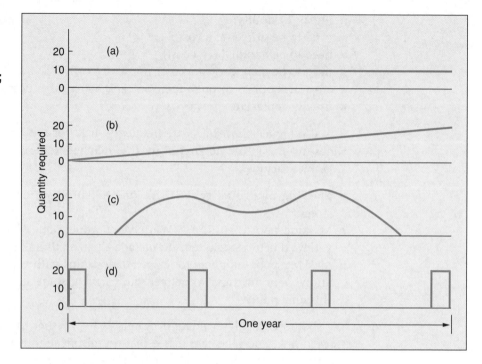

its name. It is economic in the sense that it is a thrifty, efficient order quantity which avoids needless cost. But it has often been applied inappropriately, and much of the criticism of EOQ approaches arose because many firms used them in situations for which they were unsuitable, with unfortunate results.

EOQ formulae

The basic EOQ formula is:

$$EOQ = \sqrt{\frac{2 \times \text{annual usage quantity} \times \text{ordering cost}}{\text{unit cost} \times \text{stockholding}}}$$

Writing u for annual demand or usage quantity;
   p for the paperwork and administrative cost associated with an order;
   c for unit cost or price each;
   s for the cost of holding stock as a decimal fraction of average stock value, the formula becomes:

$$EOQ = \sqrt{2up/cs} \tag{1}$$

Alternative versions can be derived from this, which show how many weeks' or months' supply to cover with an order, how many orders to place in a year, or which use weekly or monthly demand instead of annual demand. The derivation of the formula is straightforward. Demand is not affected by order quantity, and as a first approximation it may be assumed that buffer stock and price are not affected by order quantity. The total variable cost is then the sum of the remaining cost factors, the stockholding cost and the cost associated with ordering.

Since the average stock without taking account of buffer stock will be half the order quantity, q, the stockholding cost is given by

$$q/2 \times cs$$

and the cost associated with ordering is given by the cost per order, p, multiplied by the number of orders placed:

$$u/q \times p$$

Hence:

$$\text{Total variable cost (TVC)} = qcs/2 + up/q$$

This is a minimum when

$$\frac{d(\text{TVC})}{dq} = 0 \tag{2}$$

Differentiating (2) with respect to q, rearranging and taking the square root, we arrive at the EOQ formula already given as (1).

The application of the formula is not difficult in practice. It can be solved on any pocket calculator which has a square root facility.

If, as is usual, stock records are computerised, suggested order quantities can be computed automatically, or a short table of representative values can be used. EOQ formulae can be used with advantage if the stock range includes many minor stock items, used on a variety of products, for which detailed calculation of exact requirements and scheduling of as-required deliveries would not be feasible. For such items, using the EOQ can cut both the size of the stockpile and the number of orders placed.

EOQ formulae should not be used if price fluctuates, if the rate of use or demand is not approximately constant, or if the lead time is long and uncertain.

Of the various requirement profiles shown in Figure 6.1, the constant-rate requirement (a) is the only one which is really suitable for use of the EOQ.

The EOQ approach has several limitations in practice, although most software-driven provisioning systems incorporate a version of the formula and will recommend a purchase quantity. Amongst these limitations are:

- It requires the cost of carrying stock as an input. This cost is somewhat difficult to determine accurately.
- It requires the cost of ordering or acquisition to be input. This also is difficult.
- It does not cope well with varying demand patterns.
- It does not relate well to the economics of manufacturing or supply.

Stock-turn rate and EOQ

Two common measures of stock control performance are service level and stock-turn rate. Service level measures success in meeting demand off the shelf. If every request can be met immediately then the service level is 100 per cent; if only eight out of ten then it is 80 per cent. The adoption of EOQ does not in principle affect the service level, although methods used to achieve the service level may not be the same for frequently ordered items as for infrequently ordered items.

Stock-turn rate measures not the effectiveness of stock control in meeting demand but its efficiency in doing so economically. It relates the amount of money invested in stock to the use that is made of it. Achieving a high service level by ample stocks of everything that could conceivably be needed would result in a very low stock-turn rate. At the other extreme, a high stock-turn rate could be achieved by hardly stocking anything except the essential, very frequently used items – with, of course, a low service level as a result.

Stock-turn rate is calculated by dividing average stock for a period of time into total usage for the same period. The formula is:

[Annual Usage Value / Average Inventory Value]

This measures how quickly the inventory is used. The larger the ratio, the better the inventory is being used.

Thus if stock on the first day of June is £100,000 and stock on the last day of June is £110,000, then average stock for the month is £105,000. And if the cash value of issues for the month (or sales) is £52,500, then stock-turn rate is given by 52,500/105,000. The stock is 'turned over' 0.5 times a month; or once in two months, or six times a year.

In considering the effect of the adoption of EOQ on stock-turn rate it must be borne in mind that the latter is intended to evaluate the efficiency of the total stock investment rather than a single stock item. If the annual demand for a particular stock item is low in relation to the cost of procuring it then the EOQ formula will balance stockholding cost against procurement cost and indicate that a year's supply or more should be ordered. For that item, the stock-turn rate will not improve, but fewer orders will be placed. Because a typical stock range includes a large number of items with a low annual usage value, the result is greatly to reduce the number of orders placed compared with an ordering policy which treats all items alike, for instance ordering three months' supply whenever a stock item needs to be replenished.

Stock-turn rate for a high usage value item will, on the other hand, improve when instead of ordering three months' supply the EOQ formula is used. Although high usage value items form quite a small proportion of the total stock range, they also tend to account for a large proportion of the sum shown in the accounts for stock. Usually EOQ policies improve the overall stock-turn rate by frequent ordering of high usage value items, as well as reducing the number of orders placed by less frequent ordering of low usage value items. An example of the effect on profit of improving stock-turn rate is shown in Table 6.1.

Price breaks and quantity discounts   Although EOQ methods are not used when price fluctuates, they are used when lower prices are available if larger quantities are ordered for delivery in

Table 6.1 **Effect on profit of improving stock-turn rate**

	Firm A	Firm B
Sales revenue	100	100.00
Cost of goods sold	60	60.00
Gross margin	40	40.00
General and administrative overhead	27	27.00
Cost of holding stock	5	1.25
Gross profit	**8**	**11.75**
		(46.9% more)

one lot. These lower prices may be expressed as percentage reductions to the nominal price, i.e. quantity discounts; or alternatively as progressive reductions in the net price as the quantity ordered increases, sometimes called price breaks. The foregoing analysis provides a systematic procedure to evaluate these. The basis of the procedure is to compare the gross saving due to a price reduction with the extra cost due to increased stocks in order to arrive at the net saving, if any. The gross saving is calculated by multiplying the annual requirement quantity by the difference between the normal price and the discounted price. The extra cost is calculated from formula (2), first by using the normal price and order quantity and second by using the discount price and order quantity. The net saving, if any, can then be calculated. Sometimes the order quantity required to qualify for a lower price is excessive. In view of uncertainties about the future, it may not be safe to order more than a year's supply, and it is often not safe to order more than two years' supply.

For example, the annual requirement for part X125 is 10,000 and the normal price £1 each. With the stockholding cost estimated at 20 per cent and the ordering cost at £10, the EOQ is 1000. Now the supplier offers a 10 per cent discount for deliveries of 5000 instead of 1000. Is it worth accepting? The difference between normal price and discounted price is 10 per cent of £1, and with an annual requirement of 10,000, the gross annual saving is £1000. The extra cost (from formula (2)) is £270. The net saving is thus £730 a year. Financially the offer is attractive. If the discount offered is 2.5 per cent instead of 10 per cent, the gross annual saving is only £250. The extra cost is £307.50, so there is a net loss rather than a net saving. Accepting this offer would add to costs rather than reduce them.

Other methods in stock control

Reorder-level methods of stock control are procedures in which whenever the stock of an individual item is down to a quantity called reorder level (or order level, or order point) an order is initiated to obtain more stock. The order level is the average quantity required in the lead time plus buffer stock. Buffer stock is a reserve to take care of requirements running at above the average rate, or of delivery periods which exceed the normal lead time. The order quantity may be the EOQ, or may be determined in some other way.

Periodic review methods of stock control review large groups of stock items periodically. Stock on hand may be compared with a target stock figure for each item, and enough ordered to bring stock up to target. Target stock is typically enough to last until the next review, plus the quantity likely to be used in the lead time, plus buffer stock to cover variations. In many systems, orders need not be placed for every item which is below target level. Modifiers are incorporated, such as minimum orders (don't order until you need at least 12, for instance), order with (if you're going to order A, order some B as well), etc.

■ Forecasting

A forecast is a projection of patterns in past events into the future. All forecasts have one thing in common: they are generally wrong! That is not to suggest that forecasting for stock control is a pointless activity. Forecasts can enable you to have a more reliable idea about the future than you would otherwise have and, of course, the selection and application of an appropriate forecasting technique can enable you to be less wrong than a competitor or other person taking a less suitable approach.

The reasons for projections being inaccurate to some degree are usually:

- The perceived pattern is not continued into the future.
- The past pattern has not been adequately understood.
- Random fluctuations have prevented the pattern from being recognised.

Of these three sources of error the first cannot be avoided other than by looking for indications that the pattern might change. These are called 'leading indicators', and might be such things as population trends, changes in government policy, etc. The second source of inaccuracy can be reduced by careful analysis, and the third isolated and allowed for when taking decisions.

We have all met individuals who display an almost religious reverence for 'the forecast'. However, in practice it is true that forecasts cannot be relied upon. This is what a middle manager of one FMCG manufacturer had to say about the performance of his organisation's forecasting department:

> Fifty per cent of the time they get it right. That is, their forecasts are within 10% of actual demand. Our problem is that we're never sure beforehand which 50% will be correct!

Faced with this problem we must choose between two options. Either we can endeavour to find a better way of forecasting; or we can accept that forecasts are always likely to be flawed and therefore the appropriate response is to reduce the organisation's reliance on forecasts. That means that the organisation must find ways to respond to unexpected events, or reduce the incidence of these.

There are many approaches to forecasting, ranging from simple time series analysis or the charting of trends through to highly complex modelling systems, some of which are 'adaptive' in that the forecasting system monitors its own performance, and makes changes to the algorithms on which it operates according to experience. In other words, the system learns as it goes. It should be borne in mind, however, that sophistication cannot guarantee success; the future can never be made certain.

Order quantities for production

Manufacturing industries were the basis of the British economy for two centuries. While still of importance, they no longer perform this fundamental role. They are classified by product in the standard industrial classification used in official statistics, and the products cover an enormous range: transistors, electric motors, machine tools, cranes, small tools, lawn mowers, refrigerators, motor cars, double-glazed windows, garments, food products, garden gnomes, and furniture, for instance. Some make to customers' order, others make or stock in anticipation of orders. Thousands of process technologies exist, but four fundamental approaches to their organisation are in use: project organisation, job shop organisation, batch production, and continuous production.

Project organisation is used for a single major product such as a bridge, a dam, a factory, or an oil rig. The project contract establishes the relationships between customer and contractor. Components, materials and services are ordered in the quantities specified in the contract for delivery at the time scheduled. At the other extreme, *continuous production* is typified by an electrical power station or by any other plant which is designed to produce its output in a continuous stream. Between these extremes, at least two-thirds of manufacturing industry exists. *Job shops* go into production when they get a job from a customer. *Batch producers* make their products in small batches – perhaps six machine tools at a time – or large batches – for example 1000 agricultural machines at a time.

Materials requirements planning (MRP)

The standard system for calculating the quantities of components, sub-assemblies and material required to carry out a production programme for complex products is called materials requirements planning (MRP). This can be carried out by manual methods but is more easily done by computer software. Indeed, MRP was an early computer application in supply chain management, involving as it does the manipulation of large amounts of data.

The MRP process starts with a production programme, or, as it is often called, a master production schedule (MPS), which schedules the end products to be completed week by week during the planning period. It is based on customer orders, sales forecasts, and manufacturing policy. There is quite an art to getting it right. Most software packages include facilities for making rough

Figure 6.2
**Developing
the master
production schedule**

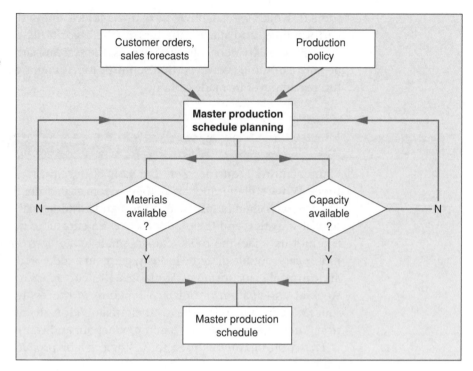

checks during planning to allow for capacity bottlenecks or scarce material constraints, as shown in Figure 6.2, so that a realistic production programme which can be made to work is scheduled. The next stage is to explode the master schedule into detailed lists of all the parts required to make each product by means of parts lists, sometimes called bills of material (BOMs). MRP procedure calculates gross requirements level by level, adjusting at each level for stock on hand and orders due in to get net requirements. These are offset by lead times to arrive at dates at which orders should be placed if net requirements are to be available in time. Planned purchase orders and planned works orders are calculated in the order generation part of the procedure, but remain in the system and are subject to amendment unless designated as firm orders. They become actual orders when released, and are then printed out or otherwise communicated to suppliers and to internal production. Realistic, achievable production programmes and accurate information about stock on hand and orders due in are vital to success, and failure to provide them has led to many unsuccessful applications. Stock must be counted and stock records must be right (and the reconciliation of physical stocks with the relevant records cannot be done by computer) before the order generation process (which can be done by computer) will work properly.

Nevertheless, MRP has notched up many successes, typically when organisations which had used inappropriate stock control methods for production planning reverted to common sense. Stock control is appropriate to a situation in which the demand for each stock item is independent of the demand for any other stock item, as in a retail shop where the demand for shirts in no way depends on the demand for shoes. In production planning, the demand for all the parts used to make a product is dependent on the demand for that product. Thus, if a car is supplied with five wheels (assuming each car has a spare), in planning the production of a batch of 6000 cars we know that we need 30,000 wheels. We do not need to apply stock control techniques of demand forecasting and provision of buffer stocks for forecast errors as if the demand for wheels occurred independently of the demand for cars, except in allowing for orders for spares and replacements. MRP is the process, simple in principle, of calculating in detail the net demand for the components and material required to implement a given production programme, and allowing for lead times in order to plan production and purchase orders. Several techniques are used in deciding on order quantities. The simplest is lot for lot, in which the order quantity is the same as the minimum quantity required for production:

Period	1	2	3	4	5	6	7	8	9
Net requirement	24				24				24
Planned order	24				24				24

The EOQ approach is quite unsuitable for use when the net requirement occurs in lumps at intervals of time, when another batch of the product is put into production as in the above example and as shown in Figure 6.1(d). If the EOQ worked out at less than 24, the order would not be enough to meet the net requirement. If it worked out at more than 24, the excess would just lie in stock until the next requirement date. The EOQ is based on the assumption that stock is consumed at an approximately constant rate, which is not valid for this sort of intermittent, lumpy demand. If, however, there is some net requirement in most periods, unlike the above example, there is a case for applying the idea on which the EOQ is based, of balancing set-up costs or ordering costs on the one hand, and stockholding costs on the other, to arrive at a least cost solution. A version which has had some success calculates the cost of holding stock period by period, as in the following example.

In Table 6.2, net requirements for nine periods are taken as 40, 20, 0, 80, 0, 20, 35, 40 and 45. Stockholding cost is taken as £0.50 per unit per period, and ordering cost as £25. The procedure is to calculate total ordering and stock-holding costs for successively larger lots and to choose the order quantities which give the lowest cost per unit. The result is:

Period	1	2	3	4	5	6	7	8	9
Net requirement	40	20	0	80	0	20	35	40	45
Planned order	60			80		55		85	

This approach, which can easily be applied by computer, is called part-periods balancing because the stockholding cost and ordering cost are balanced period by period to give the lowest cost per part. It has the same basis as the

Table 6.2
Part-periods balancing

Period	Net requirement	Order quantity	Periods stocked	Stock cost (£)	Stock + order cost (£)	Cost per unit (£)
1	40	40	0	0	25	0.625
2	20	60	1	10	35	0.583
3	0					
4	80	140	3	130	155	1.107

First order is 60 parts to cover periods 1 and 2

Period	Net requirement	Order quantity	Periods stocked	Stock cost (£)	Stock + order cost (£)	Cost per unit (£)
4	80	80	0	0	25	0.312
5	0					
6	20	100	2	20	45	0.450

Second order is 80 parts to cover period 4

Period	Net requirement	Order quantity	Periods stocked	Stock cost (£)	Stock + order cost (£)	Cost per unit (£)
6	20	20	0	0	25	1.250
7	35	55	1	17.5	42.5	0.773
8	40	95	2	57.5	82.5	0.868

Third order is 55 parts to cover periods 6 and 7

Period	Net requirement	Order quantity	Periods stocked	Stock cost (£)	Stock + order cost (£)	Cost per unit (£)
8	40	40	0	0	25	0.625
9	45	85	1	22.5	47.5	0.559

Fourth order is 85 parts to cover periods 8 and 9

EOQ in that it balances costs to arrive at a least cost solution, but it does not require the assumption that stock is depleted at a uniform rate over the year. A simpler way to calculate these order quantities on a similar basis is sometimes called the least cost algorithm. The cost of holding one part in stock for one period, taken above as £0.50, is divided into the ordering cost, taken above as £25, to obtain the part-period value, in this example 50. This part-period value means that it is economical to carry 50 part-periods, whether this is 50 for one period or five for 10 periods or one for 50 periods. In practice these figures are rounded up where appropriate. So, applying it to the net requirement figures in the previous example: period 1 requires 40, periods 1 and 2 require 60, which is over the part-periods value, so the first order is for 60. Period 3 requires 0, period 4, 80, so the second order is for 80. If the calculation is continued, it will be found that the same order quantities are obtained as by the previous, more laborious method.

Software packages usually include lot-sizing rules for determining quantity, such as predetermined order quantity or predetermined supply period, which can be useful. They also include modifiers, which can be extremely useful in the special circumstances for which they are intended, such as 'order with' to enable items that are related, for instance by coming from the same supplier or using the same tooling, to be ordered at the same time, or 'minimum' and 'maximum' to set upper and lower limits on the order quantity. Unthinking application of mathematical formulae can lead to ridiculous order quantities of 1.5 days' supply, or 10 years' supply. These can be avoided by use of modifiers in the order quantity algorithms, as well as by making sure that the

Figure 6.3
Flows of information (-- ►) **and materials** (—►) **in a material requirements planning system**

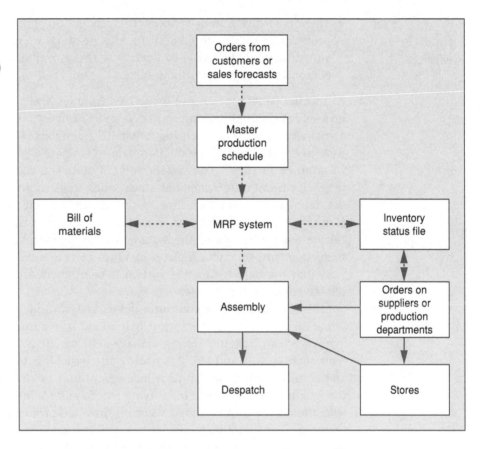

people responsible for order quantity decisions know what they are doing. Both information and materials will flow in the system (see Figure 6.3).

Manufacturing resource planning (MRP2)

MRP2 is an extension of MRP. The first stage in the conversion of MRP into MRP2 is the development of a 'closed-loop' MRP system. Closed-loop MRP means that the various functions in production planning and control (capacity planning, inventory management and shop-floor control) have all been integrated into a single system. This represents an improvement over MRP because it provides a number of additional features.

- Priority planning – 'rush' jobs can be brought forward in time and others put back in time and the necessary adjustments made to material delivery schedules.
- Integration of related functions into the system (in particular capacity planning, inventory management and shop-floor control) allows feedback from them, making sure that the production plan is constantly kept up to date.

- There is feedback from vendors, the production shop, stores, etc. when a problem arises in implementing the production plan, which enables adjustments to be made to overcome these problems immediately, i.e. before they become insurmountable.

Another benefit which can be derived from an MRP2 system is that it can be used for simulation purposes. This can be done by taking a 'cut' or section across the database and posing 'what if?' questions. For example, we may wish to bring forward a production date so we pose the question 'what if we work an extra shift?' The system will simulate the consequences for order releases, current order schedules, inventories, work in progress, finished product, labour costs and cash flow. If this is not a viable proposition then an alternative can be tested, and once this is found the necessary adjustments can be made throughout the system. The same approach can be used with financial plans, production plans, inventory levels and so on. It is, of course, vital that the data within the system is completely accurate, otherwise the results will not be as reliable.

MRP2 is obviously a computer-based system and simulations utilising visual display units can be a most helpful aid in planning, as the alternative 'scenarios' can be tested during management meetings. The objective of systems such as MRP and MRP2 is really quite basic: it is to give greater control and accountability but also to reduce inventories to a minimum and reduce the length of time between identifying a need and fulfilling it to the customer with the ultimate aim of improved cash flow and profitability. Do not forget, however, that MRP2 in particular is a *management system* and all good management puts people at the forefront of its operations.

Mini case study – Reckitt & Colman

Reckitt & Colman (Pharmaceutical Division) Suppliers' Guide defines MRP2 in this way. This is an example of sound management philosophy.

MRP2 is a way of planning and controlling the business – a company philosophy led by people not computer.

The computer is an aid. People lead the business.

Distribution resource planning (DRP)

DRP is a system for forecasting or projecting requirements for finished products at the point of demand. From these projections, aggregated, time-phased requirements schedules for each echelon in the distribution system can be derived. As with MRP, inventories themselves are essentially secondary to this process. The system works to the elimination of inventory.

DRP is a 'pull' approach to replenishment in that it depends on awareness of customers' (end users') requirements, which pulls the rest of the system through the echelons of the distribution system.

If DRP is a 'pull' system linked to the customer (end user), MRP is (in end-user terms) a 'push' system linked to the master production schedule.

The problem of aggregate demand forecasting in DRP is that at each stage of the distribution system demand becomes more 'lumpy' or, rather, presented in bigger and more irregular increments. These irregularities are cushioned in the traditional stock point generation systems – in DRP they require careful planning, communications and customer contact to prevent bottlenecks.

Briefly, manufacturing resource planning (MRP2) systems and distribution resource planning (DRP) systems are organisational processes enabling physical resources requirements to be planned together with production and purchasing control. This combines production resources planning with materials and distribution requirements planning. In combination, these systems establish logistics resources planning (LRP), a control of the entire logistics system. It is always possible to go even wider in search for integration.

Enterprise resource planning (ERP)

The concept of 'ERP' can be mentioned here. It is, as its name suggests, an approach whereby the resource requirements of the entire organisation, with reference to those of its neighbours in the supply chain, can be taken into account in planning. ERP is a multi-mode suite of software, operating on a company-wide basis, which might be concerned with all aspects of the business including, for example, procurement, inventories, production, sales, human resource management, marketing, engineering and cash flows. All departments operate with the same data. This recognises the interaction of all business activities; what happens in one area has direct effects elsewhere and these effects are captured by the system which adjusts throughout each area. In all areas the data is reduced to the common denominator of financial data which provide management with the information it needs to manage the business successfully; for example, the values of inventories, status of work in progress, finished goods, etc., are known at all times. Many large organisations in recent years have adopted ERP systems from major software houses such as SAP, J. D. Edwards, Oracle and Peoplesoft. There are a good number of competing products in this market.

Just-in-time (JIT)

The just-in-time philosophy – requiring production when, and not before, a customer requires something, and the pursuit and elimination of waste in production and associated planning and purchasing – was developed mainly by Japanese manufacturers, and was so conspicuously successful that everyone wanted to know how it was done and if they could do it too. The basic idea is simple. If made-in parts are produced in just the quantity required for the next stage in the process, just in time for the next operation to be carried out, then work-in-progress stocks are almost eliminated. If bought-out parts are delivered direct to the production line without delays in stores or inspection, just in time for the needs of production and in just the quantity needed, then material stocks are largely eliminated too. Stock-turn rates of better than 30 have been achieved (although after years of effort and not overnight), compared with the rates of 5 to 8 which comparable businesses were getting with traditional methods. Stock-turn rate is closely linked with profitability. If firm B achieves a stock-turn rate four times as high as firm A, assuming that the two firms are in all other respects similar, then firm B will incur only a quarter of the stockholding costs incurred by firm A. Firm B could be much more profitable, as shown in Table 6.1.

Perhaps the best known of the JIT systems is the kanban system developed by Toyota. 'Kanban' is a Japanese word which means (among other things) the travelling requisition card on which the system depends. Two types are used: move cards and make cards. Both form part of a manual, visual control system, which is itself a sub-system of a more comprehensive process of planning resources and scheduling output, as shown in Figure 6.4. Kanban is similar to the MRP planning system previously considered. The main difference is that, in order to make the kanban system work, it is necessary to smooth product

Figure 6.4
A simple kanban system

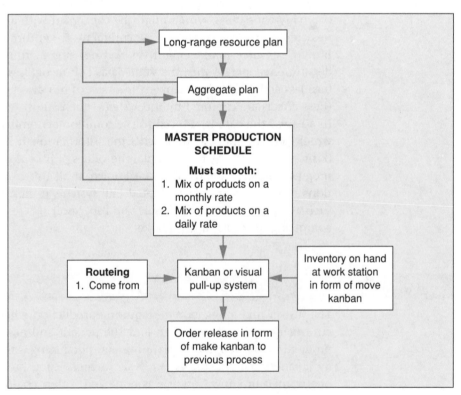

(*Source*: Hahn *et al.*, 1983)

mix, monthly and daily. So far as possible, batch production is made similar to continuous production. Master schedules are smoothed so that ideally every product is made every day, and from day to day the same mix of end products is produced, giving a smooth and continuous flow of parts through all work centres to the final assembly line. Changes in product mix are introduced gradually. Dramatic examples of reduced set-up and changeover time have been reported. For instance, Toyota cut changeover time on a bolt maker from 8 hours to less than 1 minute, and set-up time for a wing and bonnet stamping operation from 6 hours to 12 minutes. Short changeover times increase flexibility and reduce lead times, thus greatly facilitating rescheduling to cope with such hazards of manufacturing as scrap, tool breakage, wrong forecasts, late deliveries by suppliers or revisions to the parts list.

A long process of small improvements leads eventually to a situation in which stock is much easier to manage because there is so much less of it, and it is out in the open where it can be seen, in production or in assembly. Buffer stocks are not provided. Consequently, shortages (for whatever reason), bottlenecks and queues are highlighted rather than hidden. Vigorous attempts are at once made to find what causes the trouble and to devise a solution. Better quality control, training more people, and increasing available machine capacity (for instance by reducing set-up time) may provide a cure. What is sought is a solution to the problem, whereas buffer stocks are a way of living with the problem rather than solving it.

It is sometimes observed that the JIT approach leads inevitably to more frequent deliveries of small batches of goods, and this in turn leads to high transportation costs and road congestion. This may in some cases be true, but the 'milk round' approach to collection mitigates these adverse effects, and may in some cases lead to savings. Where possible, vehicles are routed in such a way that goods can be loaded in the appropriate sequence for delivery to the appropriate point on the production line. Figure 6.5 gives a schematic illustration of the 'milk round' principle.

For bought-out parts, suppliers must be selected who can be relied on to deliver to the day and the hour stated on the order, straight to the production line without going through inspection and stores. Suppliers must have reliable quality control for this to be possible. Transport arrangements have to be reliable too, which has led to a strong preference for local sources using their own transport for delivery.

At a time when General Motors was dealing with nearly 4000 suppliers, Toyota had less than 300. Today the figure is much lower again, with a single-figure (i.e. fewer than 10) direct supplier base per model achieved by Toyota. Note that we are referring here to the *direct* supplier base; a tiered structure enables the retention of larger numbers of indirect suppliers, with whom Toyota has no direct dealings. If production depends on suppliers delivering acceptable parts on time every time, then suppliers need to be co-ordinated well so that they always meet requirements. Another reason for having fewer suppliers is the kind of relationship with suppliers that is required for JIT. The

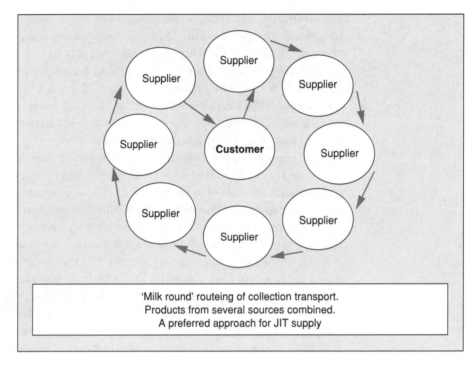

Figure 6.5
The 'milk round' routeing of collection transport

'Milk round' routeing of collection transport.
Products from several sources combined.
A preferred approach for JIT supply

adversarial relationship, playing one supplier off against another, which has been traditional in Europe and America does not readily lead to long-term co-operation in reducing cost and increasing efficiency. Co-operative relationships with fewer suppliers are preferred.

Order quantities are also affected. Traditional approaches such as EOQ, part-periods balancing and the least cost algorithm tend to take the internal cost figures for buying and stockholding as constants and use them to calculate order quantities. JIT systems treat nothing as constant. The cost figures can be driven down and Hahn *et al.* (1983) explained how. Ordering cost included six elements, it was argued: negotiation, paperwork, expediting, receiving count, receiving inspection, and transport. Transport and negotiation cannot be dispensed with, but when JIT is operating properly there is little need for paperwork, expediting, receiving count and inspection. So buying costs are lower; and, according to the formula, order quantities become smaller.

Vendor managed inventory (VMI)

Conventionally, inventories are managed by their owners. A company buys materials for resale or consumption and, in circumstances where it is not possible to match supply with demand exactly, places these materials in stock, and manages issues and replenishments systematically. Ownership, possession and control all rest with the same organisation. This traditional approach is not always the best approach. It might well be the case, for example, that a vendor will carry stocks to compensate for or accommodate unpredictable or erratic demands from a given customer, and that same customer may be carrying stocks in an attempt to cope with erratic internal demand, or uncertainty further along the supply chain. The customer organisation may also be seeking, through inventories, protection against possible variations in availability of supplies. This traditional approach, whereby every organisation in a supply chain acts independently in protecting its own position, may be effective but is not necessarily efficient. It provides an example of sub-optimisation, in that the needs of the various elements of the supply chain, managed in isolation, give rise to duplication of stocks and do not minimise total costs. Researchers at Cardiff Business School have defined VMI as follows:

> VMI is a collaborative strategy between a customer and supplier to optimise the availability of products at a minimal cost to the two companies. The supplier takes the responsibility for the operational management of the inventory within a mutually agreed framework of performance targets which are constantly monitored and updated to create an environment of continuous improvement.

Whilst others may prefer to define the concept differently, this definition does provide us with the key concepts underpinning the VMI approach. These are:

- *Collaboration*. Readers will be aware of the implications of this word, and the associated concepts of trust and transparency. VMI, if adopted, is a decision taken jointly with a full appreciation of the relevant factors.
- *Minimal cost to the two companies*. VMI is not about cost allocation, in other words the 'Who pays?' question, it is about cost removal.
- *Framework*. The parties involved understand their responsibilities, and have agreed targets in view. Questions such as 'Where will the inventory be located? When does payment take place? Is there a management charge, and if so how much?' will be answered and those answers embodied in the framework agreement.
- *Continuous improvement*. This pervasive concept is very important here. Supplier and customer can share in the pursuit and avoidance of waste.

As is the case with many topical issues in supply chain management, there is nothing really new about the concept of VMI. What is new is the degree of attention that it is receiving. The long-established merchandising approach whereby, for example, a supplier of greetings cards manages a display inside a retail outlet, visiting at intervals to replenish the stocks, and charging the retailer for the cards which have been sold, is a VMI approach. The idea of placing stocks by a supplier on the premises of a customer, with the supplier determining stock levels and replenishment policies, and retaining ownership until issue takes place, is a similarly well-established VMI approach.

A well-designed and developed approach to VMI can lead not only to reductions in inventory levels in the supply chain, but also to secondary savings arising from simplification of systems and procedures. A supplier of industrial fasteners to a customer in the automotive industry supplies track-side and assembly positions, and is paid a predetermined sum for each vehicle completed and shipped. This approach avoids accounting for single or small quantities of low-cost items, and consolidates what would otherwise be a large number of small payments into a smaller number of larger payments. The benefits are shared.

There may be other benefits. Users should receive higher service levels, and improved cash flows, and vendors enjoy better visibility of changing demand and greater customer loyalty. The real benefits are those which attach neither to the buyer nor the seller in particular, but to the supply chain as a whole. These include management undertaken by whoever is best positioned or qualified, a smoother flow of materials, an enhanced flow of information, simplified administrative procedures, and the placing of the competencies of supply more firmly with the supplier.

It is unlikely that vendor management will be seen as appropriate for all classes of inventory. Generally speaking, it is likely that category C items (wide range, low cost) might be seen as being particularly appropriate, especially those items such as stationery, where there is a wide market and a number of suppliers wishing to differentiate their offerings by virtue of service. Items where there is a strong interdependence between seller and buyer might also attract consideration of the possibilities of VMI, for example a sole supplier with a piece of machinery or other asset specifically dedicated to the needs of a particular customer might be pleased to collaborate closely with the customer so as better to manage the employment of that asset. This collaboration, in an appropriate atmosphere of trust, might extend to VMI.

Late customisation

The further that materials pass down the supply chain from original raw materials to ultimate consumer, the more the product becomes dedicated to its final application. This poses something of a dilemma for those concerned with efficiency in materials management, in that a fully manufactured product, made available close to its point of final sale or use, can be drawn from stock and used without any significant delay. Unfortunately, providing materials in this way requires copious amounts of stock, and there is a great risk that 'just-in-case' materials provided in this way will in fact never be used, and be a source of waste rather than value. Moving stocks of materials further upstream, away from their final destination, increases the power and usefulness of the stock. For example, a central warehouse might serve several clients, with the allocation of stock taking place in response to actual demand from an operating location. The introduction of a 'pull' approach to supply at the end of the chain can lead to a much smaller investment in stock serving a wider range of customers.

Many readers will be familiar with the problem of the informal private stocks, sometimes known as 'squirrel stores', held by individuals in their organisation. The practice is frowned upon because taking possession of materials in this way deprives other possible users of availability. Stocks held in the formal stores system are employed more efficiently.

Mini case study – Benetton

Benetton, the Italian fashion knitwear company, provide a good example of late customisation and its benefits. Traditionally, knitted garments are made from dyed yarn, the colour of the garment being determined by the colour of the wool used. This meant for Benetton that there was a need to keep stocks of a given design of garment in several sizes and in several colours. The company felt that if garments could be made from undyed yarn, and stocked in this neutral colour, then when a demand for a particular colour arose the actual garment could be dyed. Suppliers at first said that this approach was unfeasible, in that dying a finished garment posed technical problems of some magnitude. However, persistent attempts to solve this problem finally paid off, and the company has enjoyed the benefit of much reduced inventory as a result.

In Figure 6.6 we see the principle of late customisation, and the potential benefits. Iron, not yet converted into steel, has an immense range of possible applications: it can potentially be converted into tens of thousands of final products, anything made from iron or steel in fact. Once the iron has been converted into a certain grade of steel, then the range of possible applications diminishes, although there is the benefit of the material being closer to its

Figure 6.6
The power of late customisation

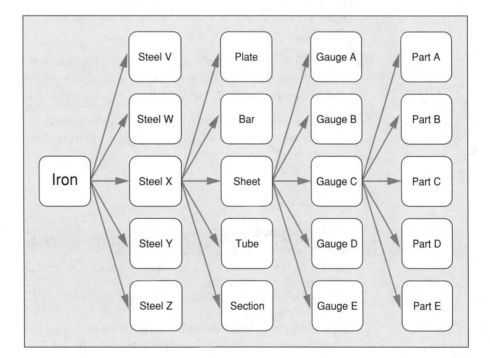

market in terms of time. Conversion of the grade of steel into a particular shape or form takes it closer to the market, but further diminishes the range of possible applications. At the final extreme, a particular item or part in the hands of the consumer has no alternative use, but has a lead time of zero. The supply chain takes materials from the state of wide possible application but long lead time, to narrow application but short lead time. Lean, agile and other developing supply philosophies tend to reduce inventories close to the point of use, replacing them with responsive supply systems.

Summary

1 Ordering policies used include blanket orders; capacity booking orders; part-periods balancing and EOQ. The method used depends upon the industry, the usage, the production technique and the cost of ordering.

2 Stock is expensive to hold, therefore it is advantageous to reduce levels. The chapter explains the EOQ method of deriving an order quantity which results in the lowest total of variable costs. This technique works well for minor items used on a variety of products but makes limiting assumptions that price is stable and usage steady. It ignores lead time.

3 MRP uses a master production schedule, which it explodes into a bill of materials. Allowing for stock and orders due in, a net requirement of components required is produced. This initiates purchase and work orders taking account of lead times. The process can be computerised using specially designed software packages and is appropriate for dependent items for which there is 'lumpy' demand.

4 Just-in-time assumes made-in parts are produced in just the quantity required for the next stage and bought-out parts are delivered direct to the production line as they are needed. Thus work in progress and stock are eliminated.

5 Vendor-managed inventory and late customisation are ideas that have recently received close attention in supply chain management.

6 Late customisation increases versatility of inventory, but with a lead-time penalty.

References and further reading

Barekat, M (1993), 'MRP2 is dead – long live MRP2', *Selected Readings in Purchasing and Supply*, vol. 1, Ascot: CIPS.

Bauer, R S *et al.* (1994), *Shop Floor Control Systems: From Design to Implementation*, London: Chapman & Hall.

Brown, A (1993), 'Understanding technological change: the case for MRP2', *International Journal of Operations and Production Management*, 13 (12).

Chopra, S and Meindl, P (2001), *Supply Chain Management*, New York: Prentice Hall.

Cusumano, M (1991), *The Japanese Automobile Industry: Technology and Masnagement at Nissan and Toyota*, Cambridge, MA: Harvard University Press.

Emmett, S and Granville, D (2007), *Excellence in Inventory Management*, Cambridge: Cambridge Academic.

Hahn, C K, Pinto, P A and Bragg, D J (1983), 'Just-in-time production and purchasing', *Journal of Purchasing and Materials Management*, Autumn.

Hill, T (2000), *Operations Management*, London: Macmillan.

Jessop, D and Morrison, A (1994), *Storage and Supply of Materials*, 6th edn, London: Pitman.

Offodile, T and Arington, J (1992), 'Support of successful just-in-time implementation: the changing role of purchasing', *International Journal of Physical Distribution and Logistics Management*, 22 (5).

Russill, R (1997), *Purchasing Power: Your Suppliers, Your Profits*, New York: Pitman.

Womack, J P, Jones, D T and Roos, D (1990), *The Machine that Changed the World*, Oxford: Maxwell Macmillan International.

7

Lead time and time compression

Introduction

This chapter is concerned with the importance of on-time supply, and includes a discussion of lead times and techniques employed in achieving time compression. The recognition of 'time' as a key variable, and the need to minimise time as waste in the supply chain, has led to an increased degree of concern with time and responsiveness in recent years. Attention is being paid to the benefits which might arise from increasing responsiveness at all stages.

Objectives of this chapter

- To emphasise the importance of responsiveness to customer needs
- To consider differing perceptions of 'lead time'
- To explain the importance of lead time variability
- To outline the component parts of lead times
- To explain the need for expediting, how it is prioritised and organised and how it can be reduced
- To introduce network analysis and Gantt charts
- To consider the inclusion of liquidated damages, penalty and force majeure clauses in a contract

Time and competitive advantage

Companies that can react promptly and accurately to the needs of their customers are, obviously, more likely to attract orders than those that cannot. Thus it can be seen that ideas such as responsiveness, time compression and time to market rightly earn their place in the developing management philosophies of the new century.

Christopher (1992) stated that in the past it was often the case that price was paramount as an influence on the buying decision. He went on to suggest that, while price is still important, a major determinant of choice of supplier or brand is the cost of time. The cost of time is simply the additional costs that a customer must bear while waiting for delivery or seeking out alternatives.

If a company is seeking competitive advantage by becoming better able to respond to customer needs as they arise, then it follows that the company will require a greater degree of responsiveness from its own suppliers. While it might be argued that the possession of appropriate inventories might facilitate the same degree of 'responsiveness', it is unlikely that an organisation can carry the high levels of stock that such a policy would call for, yet still remain price competitive. Even organisations which have promoted themselves as 'stockists' are beginning to question the value of substantial inventories, and are seeking to continue to provide high levels of customer service economically through working with suppliers who can themselves behave responsively.

Traditional 'batch and queue' manufacturing and supply is challenged by approaches based on 'pull' and 'flow'. The production resources held by firms in supply chains are maintained in a state of readiness rather than employed on large batch production, and materials are made and supplied only when they are needed. The economies arising from the avoidance of waste when such approaches are adopted can more than outweigh the so-called economies of scale generated by the production of large quantities for stock.

On-time delivery

The achievement of delivery on time is a standard procurement objective. If goods and material arrive late or work is not completed at the right time, sales may be lost, production halted, and damages clauses may be invoked by dissatisfied customers. In addition, most organisations regard cash as committed once an order has been placed; failure to achieve supply on time may slow down the cash-to-cash cycle, thus reducing the organisation's efficiency or profitability (see Figure 7.1).

Figure 7.1
Delay in supply of goods or services results in a slower cycle time and adversely impacts on cash flow

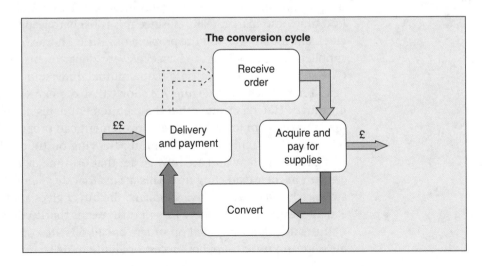

Buyers are blamed, sometimes rightly, by user department colleagues if suppliers fail to deliver on time. To obtain on-time delivery, however, it is vital to ensure that user departments know what lead times apply, and any other necessary information. However, measures of this kind are not enough. Procurement has a practical role in supply markets, convincing suppliers that they must deliver as and when agreed.

Most buyers and buying organisations throughout industry and commerce are happy with delivery times for most of their purchases, and regard late delivery as an exceptional event which might require crisis action. Pharmaceutical wholesalers normally deliver two or three times a day, with a two to three hour delivery period for orders. Many building suppliers not only give same-day delivery but find it confusing to get more than 24 hours' notice of requirements. Mainly it has been with suppliers producing goods to customers' specifications, and whose work typically takes several weeks to complete, that problems have occurred in delivering on time.

Sometimes suppliers quote delivery dates which they cannot achieve. This may be an unscrupulous device to get the order, or the quote may be given in good faith but circumstances change and delivery dates are rescheduled. Sometimes the firms which fail to deliver on time may not be competent at production planning and control. Frequently, of course, buying organisations are themselves the source of the delivery problem, through issuing inaccurate delivery schedules, continually amended, or by allowing insufficient time for delivery.

The first step to obtaining delivery on time is to decide firmly and precisely what is required and when it is required. Only in exceptional cases is this the responsibility of procurement per se. Normally it is a materials-related department such as stock control or production planning and control which works out the timed requirement schedule, as explained in the last chapter. For occasional – as distinct from regular – requirements, it is often the user department which says when something is required. It is obviously not good practice for these requirement dates to be specified without regard to supplier lead times and market realities, since this is likely to lead to late deliveries. Procurement should work on the problem of getting shorter lead times (and reliable suppliers) and should ensure that relevant departments know what they are. Care should be taken to ensure that a mutual understanding of the expression 'lead time' is achieved. Figure 7.2 shows that the expression has a variety of meanings. Having ensured that the requirement dates notified to the procurement department are achievable, procurement can properly be expected to go out and achieve them. A vital step in achieving on-time delivery is to ensure that suppliers know and are fully aware that on-time delivery is an important element in their marketing mix. This means that they know that, when making a choice between alternative suppliers, the buyer gives a lot of weight to their actual delivery performance. This in turn means that records need to be kept.

If the due dates specified on orders or call-offs are correct then it is easy to measure and record supplier success or failure in delivering on time, and to tell

Figure 7.2
Some perceptions of 'lead time'

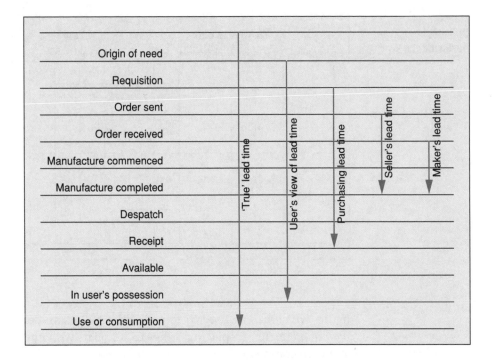

suppliers how well they are doing. Delivery performance in many instances has improved significantly when recorded performance is used as a basis for talks with suppliers. In fact, experience shows that 94 per cent on-time delivery is often achieved when suppliers come to realise that requirement dates as stated on orders and call-off schedules are accurate, are reminded that whenever they fail to deliver on time they will have to explain it, and that on-time delivery counts for a lot in the future allocation of business.

In the case of suppliers making regular deliveries, a simple way to assess delivery performance is the percentage of deliveries in each review period which were behind schedule. This can be shown on a graph (see Figure 7.3). Here it can be seen that supplier B's performance is getting better, whereas supplier A's is getting substantially worse, and calls for corrective action by the buyer. A more complicated assessment would take account of the length of time by which a delivery was behind schedule as well as the number of late deliveries. In one scheme this was applied as follows:

Days late	Weighting
Fewer than 11	1
11–20	2
21–25	3
More than 25	4

Mathematical or theoretical perfection is not what is sought; the aim of these schemes is to apply data available in goods received records to produce

Figure 7.3
Delivery
performance

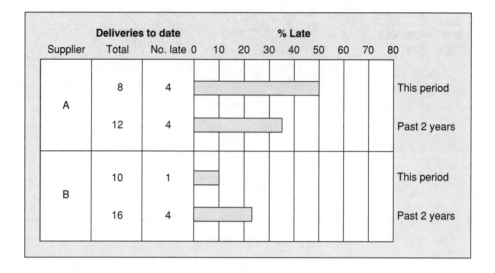

figures which can be used (i) to persuade suppliers to deliver on time, and (ii) to give preference in placing orders to suppliers who have demonstrated their ability to comply with delivery requirements.

■ Lead time and lead time variability

Lead time is perhaps the critical component in SCM; however, it is usually viewed incrementally and sub-optimally. Just as time is cash, and cash flow is important to a business, also important are the associated flows of goods and information that have generated the cash flow in the first place. The cash-to-cash cycle time (C2C) is at the root of cash flow and reducing the time from buying to the receipt of payment for sales is therefore critical. What follows is a basic view of lead time covering all the elements involved: first, by looking at the eight types of lead time; then followed by an analysis of the component parts of these eight types.

Eight types of lead time

Lead time	Action	By
Pre-order planning	User	Customer
Procurement	Order placing	Customer to supplier
Supplier	Order despatching	Supplier
Production	Making to order	Supplier
Warehouse	Supplying from stock	Supplier
Transit	Transporting	Supplier
Receivers	Receiving	Customer
Payment	Paying	Customer to supplier

Component parts of lead times

Lead time	Lead time stage	Steps, by time
Pre-order planning	User need	Analysing status to determining need to order
	User requisition	Need to order to date of order requisition
Procurement	Order preparation	Order requisition to order release date
	Order confirmation	Order release to date of confirmation
Supplier (see also the production and warehouse lead times)	All the stages here are in the following production and warehouse lead times	Confirmation to order despatched date
Production (for example, made to order)	Order processing	Date of order receipt to date order accepted/confirmed
	Preparation	Order accepted to date manufacture starts
	Manufacture (queue time, set up, machine/operator time, inspect/put away times)	Start of manufacture to date it finishes
	Pack/load (to warehouse or to transit LT)	Finished manufacture to date order despatched
Warehouse (for example, available ex stock)	In stock	Date goods arrived to date of order receipt
	Order processing	Order receipt to date order is accepted or confirmed
	Picking	Date order accepted to date order is available/picked
	Pack/load (to warehouse or to transit LT)	Order available to date order despatched
Transit		Date despatched to date order received
Receiving		Date order received to date available for issue/use
Payment	Credit	Date invoice received or other trigger to date payment received
	Payment processing	Date payment received to date cash available for use

Supply lead time

The supply lead time (SLT) used in inventory management should not be confused with the above mentioned supplier lead time. The supply lead time is actually the total of all the above lead times, excluding the payment lead times. Effectively therefore the supply lead time is from the pre-order planning lead time (from analysing the order status/determining the need to order), right through all the above steps and stages to the receiving lead time (date order received to date available for use/issue). It involves many different parties internally in a business and also externally, including both the supplier and the customer.

191

Lead time examination

Lead times must be examined using real examples, whilst ensuring that all appropriate stages and steps are included. There may also be additional lead times for some players; for example, with imports, the customs clearance lead time.

An example below, using chocolate confectionery, shows some abbreviated results found on lead times:

> supply lead time (cocoa): 180 days on average (once per year crop) with a company in-stock lead time of 70 days (traders are also holding some external stocks);
>
> supply lead time (ingredients): for example, with nuts 80 days on average (range 10–120 days) and the in-stock lead time of 80 days maximum;
>
> supply lead time (sugar) 1–2 days with in-stock lead time of 2 days;
>
> supply lead time (packaging): 1–3 days with in-stock lead time of 3 days maximum;
>
> production lead time: 1–2 days but product line batch scheduling can mean waiting for 30 days before the next production run;
>
> warehouse and transit lead times (distribution): 1–5 days with in-stock lead time of 30 days minimum to cover for the production lead time.

After each lead time stage has been quantified, analysis will show if there is a way to do things better. It can be expected that many reductions in lead times will come from the optimising of information flows and not from the goods flows. For example, ICT can rapidly transfer to suppliers the end-user demand of a customer and bypass all the customer's internal organisation departments. This will give immediate visibility of requirements to the supplier, enabling them to make decisions in real time and not be subject to processing delays.

Lead time variability

A crucial aspect when examining lead time is variability. When lead times are realistically looked at, then a range of times will be found; for example from 2 to 8 days. This range represents the variability of lead time. Average calculations are of little practical assistance and can be dangerous if used for planning and decision making.

It is this variability that so often represents the uncertainty found in the supply chain. This is traditionally dealt with by holding safety stocks to cover against the uncertainty.

The variability must, however, be examined by all those involved. Then the variability and the uncertainty can be targeted for replacement with fixed and known and reliable lead times.

The problem of lead variability can be illustrated as follows. If lead time (LT) is halved from 12 to 6 weeks and lead time variability (LTV) stays the same at +4 weeks, then:

Current LT			New LT		
LTV	LT	LTV	LTV	LT	LTV
−4	12	+4	−4	6	+4
Total LT = 8 to 16 weeks			*Total LT* = 2 to 10 weeks		
(Index 100 to 200)			(Index 100 to 500)		

So, if LTV stays the same then there is higher disruption/cost and reduced speed (index of 1 to 2 from 1 to 5).

The following are some ways to consider reducing lead time variability:

1 Demand LTV:
   - predictable known orders/size/make-up;
   - predictable order times;
   - data accuracy on what customers want/when/price;
   - is it the real end users' demand or has it been institutionalised by passing through and influenced by internal and/or external supply chain players who do not communicate with each other efficiently?
2 Supply LTV:
   - predictable known LT;
   - get correct quantity first time;
   - get correct quality first time;
   - data accuracy on what is supplied/price.

The importance of lead time variability in inventory can be seen in the expression, 'Uncertainty is the mother of inventory'. The length of lead time is of secondary importance to the variability and uncertainty in the lead time. Fixed reliable lead times are more important than the length of the lead time.

Expediting

In order to achieve procurement's responsibility of delivery on time expediting is frequently undertaken. Systems employed in the application of proactive contract management will be based on the application of effort where it is likely to be needed, and before the problem of late delivery arises.

It can be argued that expediting work does not add value to an organisation's activities or products in any way, and a principal objective of many concerns, achieved in some, is to reduce the need for expediting work to zero. In other words, to obviate it. The approach of continuous improvement is highly relevant here, and the 'partnership' philosophy of buyer–seller relationships can lead to significant improvements in this area. Nevertheless, it would not be true to claim that expediting work is no longer a major aspect of procurement – it is. In this chapter, therefore, it is appropriate that we take a look at an aspect of the work.

■ Prioritisation in expediting

If we accept that expediting work is to be undertaken, and that it ought to be proactive, then an obvious first question is: 'Where do we apply expediting effort?' It is possible to devise a points-based system which can be used to indicate in a reasonably objective way the contracts or orders where expediting work might be undertaken, and to suggest the degree of priority that might be given. The following factors exemplify the kinds of variable that might be taken into account when devising such a system.

Supplier

1 How good is their record?
2 What is their reputation?
3 How often do we use them?
4 How important is our order to them?
5 Have they a good record of co-operation?

Criticality

1 How serious are the consequences of late delivery likely to be?
2 Is the material of:
   a) high priority (e.g. raw materials, key assemblies, fuel, production materials)
   b) medium priority (e.g. standard components, parts for planned maintenance, furniture, packaging materials); or
   c) standard priority (e.g. cleaning materials, internal stationery, paint (for buildings), office supplies)?

Alternatives

1 If the material is late do we have a substitute?
2 Is there an alternative supplier?
3 Are stocks held somewhere?
4 Do we know another user?

■ Organisation of expediting work

It is common practice for expediting work to be undertaken by the buyer, and it is a natural responsibility of the buyer to work with suppliers on the 'time' variable where a mutual 'partnership' type relationship has been established. However, it is commonly the case that a separate expediting section exists within the procurement department, with expediting activities being either at the direction of the relevant buyers or at the discretion of the expediting staff themselves, sometimes liaising with user departments. The expediting group may be attached to the planning department, or to the function requiring the goods or services, the justification for this approach being that these people are better able to determine priorities. Another possible variation is that the expediter is attached to a particular buyer, and performs expediting tasks (and possibly other duties too) as required by the buyer.

■ Reduction in expediting

The need for expediting may be reduced by ensuring that:

1 Lead times are known and accepted.
2 Mutual concern exists between buyer and seller.
3 Information is shared by buyer and seller.

4 Users do not frequently reschedule requirements.

5 Expediters do not raise the alarm too often unnecessarily.

6 Capacity and capability of suppliers is checked pre-contract.

7 Specifications are clear, understood by seller and fall within seller's technical capability.

8 Specifications are not frequently altered.

9 Delivery required is specified properly (not, routinely, as 'ASAP', 'urgent' or 'ex stock').

10 What the salesman says can be done reflects the actual situation.

This 10-point checklist is not intended to be exhaustive, but is indicative of the fact that the need for expediting is perhaps as likely to arise through buyer shortcomings as seller failures.

Liquidated damages

In ordinary English law, a supplier who is in breach of contract by failing to deliver on time becomes liable to the buying organisation to pay a sum decided by the courts, known as damages, to compensate the buying organisation for any loss actually suffered, including loss of profits, as a result of this late delivery. Litigation is not part of normal procurement procedure. Expense, delay and uncertainty associated with litigation make it a remedy of last resort. There is a practical alternative based on this legal principle which is widely used in contracts for capital equipment and in major engineering and construction projects and this is to include in the contract a liquidated damages clause. In this phrase the word 'liquidated' appears to mean 'decided in advance and expressed in monetary terms'. It is a quirk of the English legal system that the law courts reserve for themselves the right to impose penalties, but allows the parties to a contract to decide in advance between themselves the loss likely to be suffered by the buying organisation as a result of late delivery, and to specify this loss in cash terms in the contract. Provided that the sum specified can be shown to be a genuine pre-estimate of loss rather than an arbitrary sum picked out of the air to frighten the supplier into compliance with the contract, the courts will enforce it in the unlikely event of litigation being required.

In some other legal systems it is open to the contracting parties to include in the contract a penalty clause, and this penalty may be payable in addition to any damages recovered by legal action. In the English legal system, the liquidated damages clause, which is often called a penalty clause in common parlance, is not seen as a penalty but as an agreement as to the amount payable by way of damages. Consequently some clauses emphasise this aspect by using such wording as: 'seller shall pay to buyer 1 per cent of the contract price for each week of delay up to a maximum of x per cent of the contract price by way of liquidated damages and not as a penalty'.

The advantage to the buyer of such clauses is that they strongly motivate the supplier to deliver on time, and in case of difficulties with delivery they provide the expediter with a powerful argument: 'It's going to cost you a lot of money if you don't deliver.' However, they also have advantages to the seller. They limit the seller's liability to a known amount. Marsh (2000) argued that 'no contractor can afford to be liable for a risk against which it is difficult to insure and which is out of all proportion to the value of the contract and to his anticipated profit' and that in such cases the supplier needs a liquidated damages clause as protection. The supplier also needs the further protection of an additional clause offering exemption from liability if the delay is due to causes completely out of the supplier's control. Such clauses are often called *force majeure* clauses.

■ Force majeure

If either party is prevented from carrying out contract obligations by circumstances beyond their reasonable control, including government intervention, strikes and lockouts but not including weather conditions, then the party affected shall not be liable for any delay resulting from such circumstances for as long as they last. If such delay extends for an unreasonable time the other party may cancel the contract without liability to either party, and buyer shall pay to seller an equitable sum for work done before cancellation.

Summary

1 Price used to be of paramount importance in choosing between suppliers – now it is the 'cost of time' that makes the decision.

2 Competitive advantage can be gained by being able to respond to customers' needs as soon as they arise. This demands that not only is the supplier responsive but that their suppliers are too.

3 Late delivery can mean lost sales, production downtime and invoke damage clauses. All of these have an effect on cash flow, reducing the company's efficiency and profits.

4 Network analysis is a visual representation of the events of a project and the activities which have to be performed to achieve them. Timings to each activity give the critical path and the minimum duration of the total project. While costly to set up, the savings made in operating costs are normally far greater.

5 Liquidated damages seek recompense for the buyer for the late delivery of an order. This is a sum agreed between the parties to represent a realistic pre-estimate of loss. Penalties may be in addition to damages, although the supplier's liability is limited.

References and further reading

Christopher, M (1992), *Logistics and Supply Chain Management*, London: Pitman.

Emmett, S and Crocker, B (2006), *The Relationship Driven Supply Chain*, Aldershot: Gower.

Emmett, S (2005), *Supply Chain in 90 Minutes*, Cambridge: Management Books 2000 Ltd.

Emmett, S (2006), *Logistics Freight Transport: Domestic and International*, Cambridge: Cambridge Academic.

Jensen, A (1992), 'Stockout costs in distribution systems for spare parts', *International Journal of Physical Distribution and Logistics Management*, 22 (1).

Marsh, P D V (2000), *Contracting for Engineering and Construction Projects*, Aldershot: Gower.

8

Sourcing strategies and relationships

Introduction

It would be possible to argue that the most important procurement decisions are concerned with selecting the right sources of supply; that is, if the correct source decision is made in a particular instance, then the buying company's needs should be met perfectly. In such circumstances it would receive the required goods or services at all times. However, the very simplicity of this statement belies the complexity of source decision making, for in arriving at the right decision many factors have to be considered. This chapter is concerned with many of the issues that are involved.

Objectives of this chapter

- To suggest the attributes of a good supplier
- To examine the 'relationships spectrum', and the move towards more mutuality in appropriate buyer/seller relationships
- To discuss the advantages and disadvantages of different procurement policies

The nature of the sourcing decision

Effective source decisions will only be made when all relevant factors have been considered and weighted against the risks and opportunities which apply. Not all source decisions will justify the same level of attention, but major purchases will always repay careful decision making. For example, significant buying organisations that dominate the demand side of a market need to devote a good deal of thought and time to the optimum supply market structure, and sometimes take direct action to develop new suppliers or support minor competitors. If one or two large companies dominate the supply side of a market, it may well be to the long-term advantage of buying organisations to place orders in a way which keeps competition alive and prevents the market from degenerating into a monopoly. Conversely, in order to obtain the greatest benefits from longer-term relationships, the buying company might seek deliberately to develop a mutual relationship, sometimes called partnership sourcing or co-makership.

Sourcing thus involves much more than simply picking a supplier or contractor for each requirement in isolation. It involves continuing relationships, both with preferred sources which are actually supplying goods and services, and with potential sources which may have been passed over for the present but are still in the running. It involves decisions about how to allocate the available business, and what terms to do business on.

For its proper performance sourcing requires supply market research. This is a normal part of procurement and supply work, undertaken informally by buyers when they talk to representatives, visit exhibitions, read trade journals, and investigate the market before placing orders. Additionally it may be undertaken more formally as a support function to buyers by full-time procurement research staff in a procurement services section, perhaps located at corporate headquarters. Supply market research identifies the set of actual and potential sources which constitute the supply side of a market, investigates their capabilities, examines market trends and long-term supply prospects, and generally keeps an ear to the ground. It is part of the procurement department's research.

Attributes of a good supplier

While a definition of a good supplier which would be acceptable to everybody would be difficult to write, there are a number of attributes which might be regarded as desirable for a typical relationship. The following list is given by way of suggestion only:

- Delivers on time.
- Provides consistent quality.
- Gives a good price.
- Has a stable background.
- Provides good service back-up.
- Is responsive to our needs.
- Keeps promises.
- Provides technical support.
- Keeps the buyer informed on progress.

Most procurement and supply staff have little difficulty in identifying the characteristics that they require in a supplier, for they see the identification and selection of appropriate sources as one of their primary roles. However, there is, generally speaking, a lower level of concern in connection with the attributes of a good customer, or buyer. The traditional view is that the buyer is spending money and suppliers should be encouraged to compete vigorously in order to gain acceptance. However, this view is not so widely held these days, and there is an increasing belief that buyers and sellers may be seeking a mutually beneficial long-term relationship through which advantages will arise for both participants in the trading process. The idea is that through bringing together complementary assets value might be created through a relationship. Terms such as *synergy* or *symbiosis* are used to describe this relationship, indicating that an ideal arrangement leads to a '2 + 2 = 5' situation, where additional benefits arise out of an association between buyer and seller. Nonetheless, if such a relationship is to come about, one of the first things a buyer needs to do is to discover what suppliers are seeking in a customer, and attempt to meet these requirements.

Different types of sourcing

Before developing the present discussion it is worth recognising that the many implications of source decision making may vary by the type of purchase being made. For example, among the many different types of source decisions are:

- consumable supplies;
- production materials and components;
- capital purchases (e.g. machinery);
- intellectual property (e.g. software);
- subcontractors; and
- services.

Each type will involve different factors. For example, a mineral may only be available from a single country. However, it could be bought direct or through an agent or a distributor. Computer equipment may be bought outright or leased, and among the many factors involved in these decisions may be whether the proposed equipment is compatible with that which exists. On the question of production materials it will be necessary to consider the logistical implications, the proximity of the supplier and the frequency of delivery. Then decisions about subcontractors may involve consideration of the individuals who are to service the contract and the liabilities of the two parties.

Sourcing decisions

The traditional approach to source decision making involves the buying organisation in:

1 establishing which suppliers make or supply the product or service – often by referring to a buyer's guide or industrial directory;
2 selecting a shortlist (say three) from those available;

3 sending an enquiry to each of those three setting out the requirements;

4 selecting the best supplier from those who quoted by comparing the offers; and

5 placing the purchase order with them, specifying such matters as volume, schedule, place of delivery, price and quality required.

Major buyers, of course, augment this procedure by a closer involvement with suppliers. Indeed, in recent years many major buyers have laid great emphasis on quality management at their supplier's plants. For example, Rank Xerox in Holland had, at one time, 70 quality engineering staff working with suppliers to help them improve their performance. In addition, they ran training programmes for the staff of certain suppliers in order to hasten that improvement and took groups of suppliers to Japan to see what was being done there. Obviously, this kind of approach necessitates the use of far more resources than the traditional approach would require. However, Rank Xerox believed that it was necessary to take this action, did so and obtained some remarkable results. It is interesting to note that one factor which allowed them to pay so much attention to individual suppliers was their decision to reduce their direct supplier base. Their strategy here involved reducing the number of production suppliers from 3000 to 500. Obviously, the fewer suppliers, the greater the time that can be spent with each. It was also true that the company utilised a larger number of staff of better calibre. The results demonstrated that the effort paid off.

It follows that when less than adequate attention is paid to buying decisions, supplier performance reflects that state of affairs. Since the source decision is so vital it is clear that, where proper attention is paid to such matters, the outcome will be of great benefit to the buying company. It is a fact that a greater awareness of this truth by successful manufacturing companies has been a major factor in their success in Europe and the United States.

■ Finding the right suppliers

As we indicated earlier, in order for buyers to be able to make the right source decisions they must know their markets. They need to know their main suppliers well, to visit them and talk to the people who process their orders and make decisions about them, to keep in touch with business plans, product developments, and what is going on inside key supply organisations. This could be described as part of demand marketing, which is not a new idea, even though in recent years marketing experts have concentrated almost exclusively on supply marketing, aimed at both current and potential buyers and buying organisations rather than sellers. In addition, buyers should know where other potential suppliers are based and be aware of production costs, wages and distribution costs which apply in particular markets. Further, they should have clear criteria against which they will be able to judge the suitability of a particular supplier to meet the needs which they have.

Today, enlightened buyers are seeking suppliers with whom they can work to mutual benefit. This means that, in some cases, suppliers are selected prior to a design being prepared, on the basis that they are the kind of company with whom the buying firm wishes to do business. Such judgement, of course, must be based upon thorough assessment involving technical and commercial factors.

Major buyers expect key suppliers, selected after thorough appraisal, to set up production near their own plants. This, of course, implies what has been called quasi-vertical integration, where the buyer and seller, although owned by different shareholders, form an alliance. Philips, the Dutch-based multinational, called this 'co-makership' – a term which is now widely used – where the source of supply is selected with a long-term relationship in view. Obviously, where a supplier agrees to erect a factory near to that of the buying company there must be a long-term arrangement in the minds of both parties. In such cases effective source selection becomes even more important.

■ Some criteria

In most cases where such decisions are made the selection process is comprehensive. Included among the criteria used by one company was the requirement that the supplier should have the 'necessary capabilities and experience'. This meant that a potential supplier:

- Was viable in the longer term financially, technically, and in production terms.
- Would be able to participate in the early phases of product design and development as a full partner in the process.
- Would openly share information on the functional, assembly and in-service requirements of the parts, including cost and quality targets.
- Would be orientated towards taking cost out of product and improving total system performance to mutual benefit.
- Would be able to develop prototypes as well as manufacture volume production.
- Would be prepared to agree cost structure targets.
- Would work with the buying company so as to increase flexibility in meeting changing demands and operate on a pull rather than a push basis in the process, reducing its own wastes such as inventory holding, unnecessary inspection and excess work in progress as well as those of the buying company.

Another multinational, seeking partner suppliers of the same kind, formulated the following criteria. The supplier should have:

- Sound business sense and attitude.
- A good track record in supplying the market in which the buyer operates (or similar).

- A sound financial base.
- A suitable technical capability with modern facilities.
- A total quality orientation.
- Cost-effective management.
- Effective buying – acquisition and control.
- Good morale among the workforce.
- Effective logistical arrangements.
- A customer service mentality.

The sourcing process

There are two ways to look at the sourcing process. So far in this chapter we have been looking at the big picture, at the major problem of matching total supply capability with total demand. In this section we look at the countless relatively minor problems which buyers deal with every day, of where and how to place orders for all the requirements notified to them: that is, how to match individual demand with supply availability.

The process usually starts with a requisition which informs procurement that something needs to be bought. The buyer would check first if there is already some commitment by long-term contract, in which case an order could be placed immediately. In the absence of such agreement, the buyer would ask if there is an existing source of supply whose performance is satisfactory; if so, the usual practice is to reorder from that source unless there is reason to review the position. Reasons for reviewing the position include price increase request, failure to meet specification, unsatisfactory performance as demonstrated by vendor ratings, internal pressure to save money, or simply that some time has elapsed since the position was last reviewed.

Research confirms that buyers are reluctant to change sources for regular purchases without good reason, and suggests indeed that they sometimes stay too long with a source which is not as satisfactory as others on the market.

Source location

The location of potentially useful sources of supply is a major responsibility of the procurement and supply executive. It is widely believed that there is normally a queue of suppliers who are willing to compete to meet the buyer's needs, but the reality is often very different, and the location of potential suppliers can be quite a challenge. Three principal reasons why the location of suppliers might be difficult are:

1 *Technological advances*. The buyer's needs are becoming more complex and difficult to meet, and fewer suppliers are willing or able to do so.

2 *Increasing 'concentration' in supply markets*. The continuing process of mergers and takeovers is leading, in many industries, to a situation where there are very few, very large suppliers who have less need actively to pursue business which will inevitably come their way.

3 *Increased specialisation*. Specialisation among manufacturing concerns tends to lead to more 'buy' rather than 'make' decisions. This in turn means that a greater proportion of their needs are acquired from outside sources. These sources may not be aware of the developing needs, and will have to be actively sought by the buyer.

Mini case study – Ikea

IKEA, the Scandinavian-based international retailer of furniture and related products, attributes a share of the reasons for its success to its suppliers. IKEA has followed a policy of developing relations with the most economical suppliers rather than necessarily dealing with traditional suppliers to the furnishing business. As an example of this, the company chose to buy seat covers from a shirt manufacturer.

Sources of information on potential suppliers

When collecting and collating information on potential suppliers, the Internet has revolutionised companies' ability to locate potential suppliers. In addition, the following points ought to be considered:

- *Reputation*. The reputation of a particular source may be ascertained through talking to professional contacts and colleagues.
- *Appraisal*. A detailed investigation of potential suppliers may be carried out (see below).
- *Recorded performance*. The procurement department may maintain records which provide information on the past performance of suppliers who have been used.
- *Approved lists*. Individual organisations may maintain lists of companies who have been assessed and approved. The approved lists of other organisations such as the MoD may be useful. Approval under ISO 9000 may be a qualification.
- *Online catalogue library*. Some companies keep a special library file containing the catalogues, price lists and other literature from potential suppliers.
- *Online publications*. The general or specialist trade press often contains information on the activities of companies that might be potential suppliers.
- *Online trade directories*. Online access to specialist skills by category.
- *Sourcing services*. A number of agencies will provide information to buyers about potential sources of supply.
- *Representatives*. Suppliers' representatives are useful sources of information on supply sources. They may disclose details of similar and competing products as well as their own.

- *Exhibitions*. These events may provide the buyer with an opportunity to compare similar products from different sources.
- *Colleagues*. Personnel in other departments within a company are often knowledgeable about sources of materials relating to their specialism.
- *Other buyers*. Communications with fellow professionals in the buying field might be helpful in discovering new sources.
- *Agents*. Stockists and distributors might provide comparative information on different manufacturers and their products.
- *Organisations promoting trade*. Embassies and commercial attachés are usually keen to help buyers to find sources of supply in the territories they represent.

Supplier evaluation

The evaluation of actual and potential sources is a continuing process in procurement departments. Actual sources with which one is dealing regularly can be evaluated largely on their track record, on the actual experience of working with them. This is often known as vendor rating, and a number of schemes have been devised for doing it systematically, as considered later. There is currently a movement towards the evaluation of *relationships* rather than vendors, reflecting the fact that if something is going wrong in connection with the supply of goods or services both participants in the trading process – buyer and seller – might derive best benefit by seeking to solve the shared problem rather than to cast the buyer in the role of paragon of virtue, and the seller as potential problem creator. Potential sources can be evaluated only by judgement of their capabilities. The extent of investigation into suppliers will be affected by the volume and value of possible expenditure. Most organisations spend 80 per cent of their annual budget with 20 per cent of their suppliers, and probably on 20 per cent of the range of items bought, and these big-spend articles justify thorough investigation. Unusual or first-time purchases, where the buyer has little or no experience to call on, may justify extensive investigation, especially if the wrong choice of supplier could have expensive consequences. Parts made to a buying organisation's specification require more careful assessment of supplier capability than standard parts available off the shelf or from several satisfactory sources. Task variables which determine the choice of supplier are traditionally stated as: quality; quantity; timing; service; and price.

Service includes before-sales service for some products, and after-sales service for others. Prompt and accurate quotations, reliable delivery times, ease of contact with persons in authority, technical advice and service, availability of test facilities, willingness to hold stocks; these are just some of the varied things that make up the package called service. Good service by the supplier reduces the buyer's workload, increases the usefulness or availability of the product, and diminishes the uncertainty associated with making the buying decision.

Financial stability is one of several supplier characteristics not mentioned as a 'task variable', but which is nevertheless important. Buyers prefer suppliers to be reasonably profitable because they are interested in continuity and on-time delivery. A supplier with cash-flow problems will have difficulty paying bills, and consequently in obtaining materials; delivery times and possibly product quality could also suffer. A supplier who becomes insolvent can be as big an embarrassment as a customer in similar difficulties. Good management is also important. Well-managed suppliers improve methods, reduce costs, develop better products, deliver on time, have fewer defective products, and build high morale in their workforce.

On-the-spot surveys of facilities and personnel by technical and commercial representatives of the buying organisation are often carried out to evaluate potential suppliers – although sometimes it may be possible to eliminate this on the basis of a supplier's reputation as obtained from word-of-mouth and published information. If the supplier's establishment is to be visited for evaluation purposes, most buyers prepare in advance a checklist to remind investigators of what to look for and to record their findings.

Many firms use multi-page checklists, asking a great many questions such as 'What percentage of their tooling do they design themselves?' and 'What is the labour turnover?' Based on the answers, an analysis is completed, incorporating a marking scheme which might, for example, be divided into four areas: tooling (capability), machines, planning, and quality control. Finally, the supplier is evaluated for named products or processes as fully approved, approved, conditionally approved, or unapproved (see Figure 8.1). Variations of the checklist approach are legion, and changes and improvements are incorporated as the needs of the organisation change.

Typical checklist questions are:

- Do they trade with our competitors?
- Are confidential documents properly controlled?
- Does the buyer have technical support?
- How do they search the market and how often?
- How long have they been established?
- What are their investment plans?

Overhead allocation, whether cost breakdowns are provided, the state of the order book, and the names of persons with authority to make decisions on delivery dates are also looked into. The type of labour available in the areas is investigated, by observation, questions and, if necessary, consulting the local Department for Employment and Skills office. Again, the checklist is used to fill out the form, with its marking scheme, and to arrive at a final judgement of the supplier as fully approved, approved, requiring minor improvement, or unapproved. The contents of such checklists are devised to suit individual requirements. For checking the quality capability of a supplier it is, however, possible to standardise checklists to a greater extent, as considered in Chapter 5.

Figure 8.1
Supplier evaluation

Procurement Engineer's Vendor Evaluation Rating Form

Vendor name ....

Date of evaluation ....

Address ....

Commodity or process
under review

....

....

....

....

Evaluators: Commercial ....

Technical ....

SUMMARY

As a result of this evaluation, the above vendor is

Fully approved .... 25 all areas ☐

Approved .... 20 all areas ☐

* Conditionally approved .... 18 all areas ☐   *Tick appropriate box*

* Unapproved .... less than 18 any area ☐

For the following commodities

_____

Product description

_____

Range of recommended

_____

Preferred quantity

_____

Precision class

_____

* Reason for vendor's conditionally approved/unapproved status

....

....

....

....

Evaluator's signature .... Procurement Engineering Dept

Figure 8.1
(*continued*)

Procurement Engineer's Vendor Evaluation Rating Form

VENDOR RATING FORM

Rate factors	1 Fully approved
	0.8 Meets minimum requirements
	0 Unacceptable

	Rate	Wtg	Total
(a) Tooling capability			
1 Design		9	
2 Manufacture		6	
3 Maintenance		4	
4 Storage		3	
5 Tooling control		3	
Total		25 max	
(b) Machines			
1 Capacity		6	
2 Capability		6	
3 Operator skills		6	
4 Maintenance		4	
5 Environment safety – layout		3	
Total		25 max	
(c) Planning			
1 Detail method planning Operation sheets		8	
2 Detail estimating by operation		5	
3 Responsible to eng. change activity		2	
4 Work study practices		5	
5 Cost reduction consciousness		5	
Total		25 max	

Figure 8.1
(*continued*)

Procurement Engineer's Vendor Evaluation Rating Form

(d) Quality control systems

	Receiving inspection			Control of manufacture			Final inspection		
	Rate	Wtg	Total	Rate	Wtg	Total	Rate	Wtg	Total
1 Quality assurance management		3			3			3	
2 Quality assurance planning		3			3			3	
3 Record systems		3			3			3	
4 Equipment and calibration		3			3			3	
5 Drawing and change control		2			2			2	
6 Corrective action procedures		4			4			4	
7 Non-conforming material		3			2			3	
8 Handling/Storage/ Shipping		1			1			1	
9 Environment/ General		1			1			1	
10 Personnel experience		2			3			2	
Total (25 max)									

RATING SUMMARY

Area of evaluation	Total rating	Status
Production tooling		
Production machines		
Production planning		
Receiving inspection		
QC of manufacture		
Final inspection		

Status rating: 25 fully approved

20 approved

18 conditionally approved

Less than 18 unapproved

Another requirement of some buying organisations necessitates the sellers being electronic data interchange (EDI) connected. EDI is a method of sending information electronically between, for example, buyer and seller. By this means both parties eliminate paperwork, reduce transmission errors and speed the information flows. Retailers and motor manufacturers have been early users of this process and most frequently it has been the buying company which has promoted the establishment of the facility. The advantages to the buying companies in helping minimise inventory whilst facilitating greater flexibility in response to demand are likely to result in fast adoption of the approach.

A further requirement in mass production industries in particular is for the supplier to be capable of delivering against a just-in-time (JIT) schedule. In this context JIT implies a supplier's manufacturing and delivery process capable of immediate response to a demand from the buying company, thus eliminating the need for the latter to hold anything other than a minimum inventory.

It is interesting to note the additional criteria which one company has developed to help ensure success in selecting this type of supplier. JIT arrangements are made with companies with which the buyer wishes to form a long-term liaison. The approach necessitates absolute reliability in both quality and schedule terms. Thus potential suppliers have to satisfy the buying company on these counts. In most cases the company concerned has found that it has had to develop potential suppliers to the required level. They start by looking for suppliers that are located near the plant. Where that is not possible they have frequently persuaded effective suppliers to relocate.

Their initial focus is upon ensuring the quality of performance which they require, that is, specification and delivery schedule. In the process they work with the supplier in analysing the specification of the product so as to give the supplier every chance of producing the material or service as efficiently as possible. The specification includes statements like 'it must be possible for us to run our machinery at X units per minute'. The company makes every effort to develop mutual trust in the process. They aim to work with the supplier in partnership while 'eliminating 43-page contracts', and the aim of the partnership is continually to improve process quality control from an agreed level to a better one by a particular date. A team drawn from both companies works on a continuing basis with the brief 'How can we improve performance, e.g. quality, logistics, price?' One important factor from the buying company's viewpoint is that it agrees a target profit level with the suppliers and then works with them to take cost out of the process.

The right relationship

In recent years, much attention has been paid both by practitioners and academics to this theme. There is now a greater recognition that there is a wide spectrum of relationship types, and that there is no single 'best approach'. The view that relationships were either mutual or adversarial is now seen as a major oversimplification. These relationship types are opposite extremes. The arm's length, transactional way of doing business is entirely appropriate in certain, perhaps most, circumstances. At the other end of the spectrum the long-term joint alliance between buyer and seller has its place, but in practice many relationships will fall between the two extremes. There is also a more developed body of knowledge surrounding the factors that impact upon relationships and have a bearing on the determination of the style to be adopted.

There are many factors that might make such a partnership inappropriate or unlikely.

We might first consider power as a factor. A large corporation is unlikely to seek strategic close relationships with a much smaller client organisation, or with a firm that might be appropriately large, but which only provides a small fraction of the selling firm's business. The same sort of thing will apply in reverse; a large buyer in terms of absolute size, or in respect of the value of contracts placed, will not necessarily see it as being advantageous to relate to suppliers as 'partners'. Full but fair use of the customer's buying power will probably be seen as the appropriate basis for relationships. Power does not, of course, stem only from size. There will be plenty of small suppliers who can exercise a great deal of power through their exclusive ownership or control of some good or service sought by the buyer. Registered designs, patents and other forms of intellectual property might fall into this category. Similarly, it is sometimes the case that a small buyer can have a disproportionate amount of power. An example of this might be the situation where an agent has sole distribution rights in an export territory attractive to the seller. Many readers will be aware that the application of appropriate 'matrix' tools of analysis can be helpful in relating issues such as this to relationships.

The idea of power as a determinant of relationships can also be examined in connection with the strategic intention of firms as members of supply chains. A major food retailer might, for example, seek to pursue waste elimination by working closely with key suppliers, seeking a jointly owned supply process that might lead to mutual trust, a shared goal, and a close relationship. Another company in the same business might see benefit in achieving a position of power in the supply chain, and might seek dominance through exploitation of its key position in order to direct and control the chain.

Power is not, of course, the only factor impacting upon relationship issues. Another important consideration is that of compatibility, or 'fit'. This question of compatibility can be looked at in various ways. For example, there is the issue of *cultural* fit. A buying company may well find itself attracted to a closer relationship with a certain supplier for a variety of reasons, but might be concerned about the supplier's attitudes and beliefs in relation to, say, environmental issues, working practices or long-term plans. If the buyer concludes that the seller, while perfectly well qualified and appropriate technically, is not subscribing to values broadly similar to those held by the buyer, then anything beyond a transactional relationship is unlikely. It is perfectly possible that the seller will wish to remain at some distance from the buyer for the same reason.

There is also the question of *technological* fit. If organisations possess complementary technologies then the probability of close commercial relationships is increased. A manufacturer of steel strip for the automotive industry is likely to wish to bond closely with a car maker, and this desire for closeness is likely to be reciprocated. There is a clear interdependence between these companies. Asset specificity is another factor to be borne in mind. A supplier who is considering investment in plant or equipment developed and commissioned for the specific purpose of serving a particular customer will find it difficult to justify this expenditure unless there is some degree of commitment from the customer. The basis of the arrangement is likely to be that the buyer undertakes to commit long-term business to the seller in exchange for the better prices, delivery, quality or reliability made possible by the new plant. Clear mutual benefit will lead to a closer relationship.

Mini case study – The Body Shop

The Body Shop is a company well known for its environmental concerns. Guidance is given to suppliers in this respect. As an example, specifications for packaging include consideration of the need to minimise packaging, reduce the number of different types of plastics used and to facilitate recycling.

Other aspects of sourcing

■ One or more suppliers?

Earlier we discussed cases where the buyer deliberately gives all business of a particular type to one supplier. This is a single source approach and it is becoming increasingly popular. However, this is not always the right decision to make; in some circumstances it is better to have more than one source. Many factors have to be taken into account before the right decision is made. In some instances there is no choice to make as only one supplier can be used because of patents, or technical or economic monopoly. In other instances there is little real choice because the amount of business is too small to be worth dividing, or because one supplier is outstanding and without serious rivals. Where scope exists for a real choice, valid arguments can be made on both sides, and examples can be found where single sourcing has paid off handsomely as well as where advantages have been gained by dividing the business. There is no simple answer; each situation needs to be analysed. Some of the considerations which need to be evaluated are:

■ *Effect on price*: aggregating orders with a single source may mean a lower unit price because of greater volume, will certainly reduce tooling costs if moulds, dies, or other costly equipment would have to be duplicated for dual sourcing, and may bring savings in transport costs. Splitting the business between several suppliers may, on the other hand, bring lower prices because of competition between them.

■ *Effect on security of supply*: scheduling is simpler with a single source, stockless buying or consignment stocking may be available, and the supplier is motivated to give a good service because they have been entrusted with all the business. On the other hand, with a second source there is greater security if fire, flood, plant breakdown or strike interrupts supplies from the first source.

■ *Effect on supplier motivation, willingness to oblige, design innovation, and so on*: sometimes, single sourcing works well in this connection, but there are instances of complacent and indifferent suppliers who were stimulated to make radical improvements when their monopoly was broken. On occasion, purchasers have gone to considerable trouble and some expense to build up a satisfactory second source. This suggests a fourth consideration.

■ *Effect on market structure*: will single sourcing lead to a monopoly where there is no alternative supplier left in the market?

■ The captive supplier

A related problem is the captive supplier. Procurement executives commonly consider it desirable to limit the proportion of a supplier's output which they take, and some figure from 20 per cent to a maximum of 50 per cent is often laid down in policy manuals and departmental guidelines. To take more than 50 per cent of a supplier's output makes a supplying organisation dependent on the buying organisation, limits the buyer's freedom of manoeuvre and raises unwelcome moral and social issues if a design change or a change in the product mix on the part of the buying organisation results for the supplier in a sudden loss of over half its output. Despite the general agreement that it is a risky marketing policy for the supplier to allow itself to become a vassal of one buying organisation, and questionable procurement policy for a buyer to take the greater part of a supplier's output, nevertheless the situation can deteriorate gradually unless there are periodic reviews.

■ Distributor

Goods are not necessarily bought direct from a manufacturer, and a franchisee or other intermediary may provide services. The merchant distributor is assuming greater importance in some marketing channels for a number of products – mainly because, both to end user and original maker, the distributor offers a solution to a number of problems. Increased costs of transport have led many manufacturers to re-examine their physical distribution systems and find in favour of greater use of distributors. Distributors in many cases offer additional services such as part finishing, which makes them more attractive. A further reason is the increased buying sophistication among end users who are adopting efficient routine ordering systems for the 80 per cent of their purchases that account for only 20 per cent of their budget (blanket orders, for instance).

The distributor is a middleman who usually assembles, stocks and sells a large assortment of wares to users. Some are specialists, in software for instance. Non-specialists often handle clothing, tools and equipment, supplies such as screws and switches, and maintenance, repair and operational (MRO) items such as cleaning cloths and brooms.

Their main selling point is immediate availability; the names 'stockholder' and 'stockist', which are often used, stress this point. The availability may be achieved through a location close to the customer, or through a responsive system such as that operated by RS Components, who can usually supply an item from their catalogues to anywhere in the UK the morning following the day of order. 'Responsiveness' is a key competitive factor, for most stockists and distributors.

Stockists are often used with advantage in maintaining stocks of stationery, small tools, spares and other articles in common use in perhaps a number of companies in their area. They guarantee to keep stocks to meet the various buyers' requirements and thus allow them to dispense with stocking these items themselves. The items may be called forward from the stockist as and when required, often under some monthly order arrangement, which also saves paperwork. An extension of this idea used in some places is for the stockist to maintain an area in the buyers' own stores, which is kept replenished with an agreed range of materials or parts. The prices for these parts are set in advance and those used are paid for each month against a stock check. Manufacturers are using this idea, sometimes called consignment stocking or a 'forward supply' arrangement, too, as an extension of their service. In the end, the decision to buy direct or from a stockist must be based on a comparison of the costs and benefits of the service offered with those of buying direct from the manufacturer.

■ Where?

The first reason for this is better communications generally: quicker deliveries, lower transport cost, personal knowledge of individuals on both sides, ease of contact when problems arise or something is needed urgently. It may be good business to support the local community and good politics too. However, the European Union directs through the EC directives that public sector organisations must publicise their intention to place orders of more than a certain 'threshold' value throughout the community. Local procurement should not involve paying higher prices for worse products and inferior service, and it is not to be expected that good suppliers for everything can be found in the local area.

Companies pursuing a just-in-time approach with their supplier find mutual benefit through suppliers locating close to the customer organisation, and it has become widespread practice for suppliers to set up subsidiary factories close to a customer's factory. Naturally, these factories tend to be dedicated units, geared to meet the needs of a particular customer, and with plant and equipment dedicated to the needs of the particular customer. A term which has evolved to describe this state of affairs is 'asset specificity'.

■ The contract

In any contractual relationship, amongst other things, the terms and conditions of contract need to be appropriate so as to ensure the best achievable deal for the buying concern, not just in the short run, and a fair deal for the contractor.

Irrespective of whether the contract is for the provision of goods or services, or its complexity, the terms and conditions should clearly indicate the rights and obligations of both parties. For example, the contract might contain clauses such as the following:

- An unambiguous description of the goods to be supplied or the work required to be carried out.
- The duration of the contract/specific delivery dates.
- Quality standards and acceptance criteria.
- Details of progress reports required, their scope and timing.
- The price or pricing mechanism, and what the price includes.
- Payment terms and a term to permit the recovery of any money owing.
- Terms relating to intellectual property rights, confidentiality, security, publicity, right of audit.
- Indemnity and insurance provisions.
- Terms relating to compliance with legal obligations, such as corrupt gifts and payments of commission, unlawful discrimination, health and safety, etc.
- The client's right of termination in the event of the supplier or contractor's default.
- The customer's right to break the contract, with the obligation to give written notice and pay for work done, even in the absence of any breach on the part of the contractor.
- A term to prevent the contractor from transferring the contract for completion by a third party.
- A term which describes when ownership and risk passes to the client.
- A term stipulating which law governs the contract.
- An arbitration or dispute resolution clause.

It is only natural that a supplier's standard terms and conditions are compiled to protect the position and minimise the risk of the supplier, and the client's standard terms and conditions will protect the buyer. Therefore, it is important for the buyer to ensure that the supplier's terms are treated with caution, and that where possible the buyer's own terms and conditions are those which govern the contract, and not the terms and conditions of the supplier. Care needs to be taken to ensure that during the contracting process the parties competing for the work know all the terms of the proposed contract, so that the level of risk can be determined and allowed for by the supplier. Omissions by the buying concern at this stage can be costly or impossible to rectify once a contract has been awarded and the competitive environment has passed.

■ Reciprocity

Another thorny question which many buyers, and particularly those in the manufacturing sector, have to face at some time in their careers is reciprocity. This is a problem which is probably more in evidence in times of national economic recession. One effect of recession is to reduce the volume of business available to manufacturing companies. As a result, sales organisations, anxious to maintain as large a share as possible, are urged to greater efforts. One question which is frequently asked at this time is: 'Which companies from which we make substantial purchases could utilise some of our products, but are currently buying elsewhere?' This is then followed by, 'Can we bring pressure to bear on these organisations to buy from us on the basis that we are customers of theirs?' Or the sales department may simply ask for the help of the procurement department in applying pressure to a possible customer who is a supplier.

The buyer is charged with making the best purchase possible for the company. When a selling organisation solicits business on reciprocal grounds the buyer should consider why the approach has to be made on such a basis. Does it really amount to 'even though we aren't the best source, buy from us because we're good customers of yours'? The danger in deciding reciprocal trading questions on narrow departmental grounds is sub-optimising; that is, finding an optimum solution from the viewpoint of one department or section of the organisation which is not the optimum for the organisation as a whole. Gaining sales at the expense of costly and unsatisfactory purchases could be sub-optimising from the sales angle; making the best possible purchase at a high cost in lost sales could be sub-optimising from the purchasing angle. No matter how strongly sales or procurement feel about such matters, general management in the interests of the whole company must take the decision. The task of the buyer is to assist in taking the decision by advising on the costs and benefits involved, after carefully evaluating both short-term and long-term effects on the materials budget. Some of these long-term effects are difficult to evaluate. One reason why reciprocity is not popular in purchasing circles may be that effects which are difficult to evaluate tend to get left out of consideration when decisions are taken by general management, leaving the procurement department with a frustrated feeling that their side of the case has not been given a fair crack of the whip. What happens, for instance, if one party wants to cut back on its purchases from the other? Has a reciprocal cutback to be negotiated? What does the buyer do if a new, greatly superior source is found? Normally, a buyer would be free to switch source, but when higher management on reciprocal grounds has taken the previous sourcing decision then the question will presumably have to be raised once more with general management. Is a supplier who has won the business on reciprocal grounds going to keep up a high standard of service, or will complacency and a take-it-or-leave-it attitude develop? What does reciprocal trading do to procurement department morale, to its zeal in systematically comparing and evaluating sources and materials, to its opportunities to achieve cost reductions? The better the procurement department is at its job, the better placed it is to insist that full weight be given to such considerations in deciding reciprocity questions.

■ Supplier associations

Major Japanese manufacturers have for some time encouraged the formation of and participated in 'Kyoryoku Kai' or supplier associations. Early implementations of this idea were that suppliers were assisted in getting together by the customer, but the association would then operate without the active involvement of the customer. However, it is now generally the case that suppliers and their customers participate together. The idea of supplier associations has in recent years been adopted by some American and European concerns, and seems to be paying dividends. The basic thinking is that companies with a common interest in meeting the needs of a particular customer can, through the establishment of channels of communication and regular exchanges of ideas and information, better develop effective methods of meeting customer needs, with profit for all concerned. The participants are open and co-operative with each other, and usually work on a 'self-help' basis. Figure 8.2 illustrates the principle of a supplier association, with the customer and the member suppliers freely exchanging appropriate information.

Figure 8.2
Supplier associations: known in Japan as 'Kyoryoku Kai'

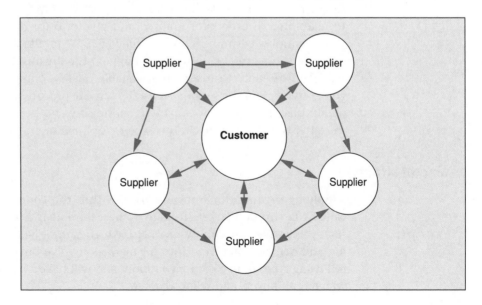

■ Intra-company purchases

Internal transactions within groups of companies can present problems similar in some respects to those raised by reciprocal trading. Different organisations lay down different policies on this.

Mini case study

Group companies should be given the opportunity to quote against our requirements when they are able to satisfy our needs. It is understood by all concerned, however, that they cannot be allowed advantage simply because they are group members. In all cases they should be treated as any other suppliers.

Buyers are reminded that companies in the group provide the following materials and services . . . please utilise these when and where possible.

. . . the use of materials and services from other group companies is encouraged. Where a group company submits a quotation which is less advantageous than a competitor, it is to be given the opportunity to meet this competition on equal terms.

Policies go from treating internal suppliers just like external suppliers, to using them when and where possible, to giving them preferential treatment. This is not necessarily a form of group philanthropy, since there may be sound policy reasons at top management level for giving temporary support to a weak group member. It does not seem efficient to compel other group companies to deal permanently with a member which cannot compete on level terms with outside suppliers. Unless there are special reasons, one would expect management either to upgrade the management of the supplier subsidiary to make it competitive on the open market, or else to divest themselves of the non-competitive operation. An internal supplier can be a great help in times of shortages, and in principle could be the ideally responsive supplier. In practice, like any organisation with a captive market, it can tend to take internal orders for granted and give priority to external customers whose business has to be won, and may be more profitable. The procurement manager should not permit this to happen: the organisational role gives the right and the duty to insist on acceptable quality, competitive prices and a good service from the supplier subsidiary. If the procurement manager fails to obtain this, in effect the company is subsidising another group company and the latter is making profits at the expense of the former.

■ Market structure

Supplying organisations operate from within the context of what is often called the supply market (though some economists insist that there is no such thing, there are simply 'markets', which cannot be other than both supply and demand markets, since all markets involve buyers and sellers). The following types of market are common, and will have a bearing on the way in which both buyers and sellers operate.

■ Monopsony, where there is a single dominant buyer, as is the case in the market for armaments in the UK where the Ministry of Defence is a monopsonistic buyer, or for certain categories of railway engineering, where Railtrack (or its successor) will be the sole UK customer.

■ Monopoly, where there is a single powerful seller, for example water companies enjoy local monopolies in the UK, though this may well change in the future.

■ Oligopoly is present where several sellers co-operate to dominate the market. The market for air passenger traffic within Europe demonstrates the characteristics of an oligopoly.

■ Price rings, cartels and restrictive practices

While collaboration between buyers through such vehicles as purchasing consortia is tolerated within the UK (though not necessarily elsewhere), collaboration between sellers comes under scrutiny through the Office of Fair Trading. That is not to say that any such co-operation is necessarily seen as a bad thing, but the OFT is concerned to see that any collaboration does not go against the public interest.

In 1994 the OFT published a booklet which gives some questions which buyers should ask in order to determine whether a cartel might exist. The questions are:

■ Does the industry or the product have characteristics which make it easier to organise, police and sustain a cartel, e.g. few sellers, homogeneous products, similar costs of production?

■ Are there factors which encourage suppliers to make a cartel agreement at a particular time, for example the development of widespread excess capacity or a recession?

■ Do prices change or behave in ways that would not be expected?

■ Do price changes over time reveal so regular and systematic a leader/follower situation as to be inexplicable without some kind of contact between suppliers?

■ Are similar phrases or explanations used in announcing price increases?

■ Are 'give away' phrases sometimes used in correspondence or conversation, for example, 'The industry has decided that margins must be increased to a more reasonable level'?

Partnering

The idea of working closely with suppliers is not new. Lord Nuffield in the pioneering days of car production in the UK worked very closely with his suppliers. He offered help in planning and organising production, and contributed to the development of components from the point of view of ease of assembly into the final product, as well as the final function. Marks & Spencer has for many years worked closely with suppliers, and other major concerns in the retailing business have established traditions in this respect. The success in world markets of Japanese manufactured goods and the increasing adoption by the Japanese companies of Britain as a manufacturing base have led to a great interest in and enthusiasm for Japanese management principles and ways of working. One of the many distinguishing characteristics of Japanese industry is the enthusiasm for working closely with their suppliers, attempting where possible to remove conflicts and tension. These ideas have been translated into English as 'partnership sourcing'.

In 1990 the Confederation of British Industry launched the 'Partnership Sourcing' initiative. The project reflected the view that traditional adversarial or confrontational attitudes towards suppliers were not conducive to the reduction of overall costs, quality improvement or innovation. With the involvement of the Department of Trade and Industry, which funds the project, energetic efforts have been made to promote the partnership sourcing ideas throughout the UK, and considerable success has been achieved. Surveys have shown that a majority (nine out of ten) of purchasing decision makers are aware of the concept, though a smaller proportion is actually employing the ideas. The CBI and DTI define partnership sourcing as follows:

> Partnership sourcing is a commitment by customers/suppliers, regardless of size, to a long-term relationship based on clear mutually agreed objectives to strive for world class capability and competitiveness.

The mission of the partnership sourcing initiative is summarised in the statement: 'To bring about a fundamental change in companies' philosophy leading to the widespread knowledge, understanding and implementation of partnership sourcing within the UK.'

A large number of influential business concerns in Britain have adopted the principles of partnership sourcing, and report considerable benefits. For example, Laing Homes, part of the Laing Construction Group, has achieved great success. Instead of keeping information about programmes close to its chest, Laing Homes shares information on where business is developing, allowing suppliers to plan production and in turn to help their own materials suppliers. Laing also reports that at one time much of the timber used on construction sites arrived in random lengths of variable quality, with 20 per cent of shipments being rejected. As a result of an improvements project involving its supplier, Palgrave Brown, and the Timber Research and Development Association, timber is now supplied to length, and of a consistent quality. Laing actually pays a higher price for timber, but the efficiency arising from the new scheme results in lower overall costs.

Another advocate of partnership sourcing is Texas Instruments (TI). At the UK headquarters and plant in Bedfordshire the US-owned company requests its customers to work with TI as closely as possible when products (integrated circuits) are being developed. This helps to reduce costs while maintaining

Figure 8.3
The principal characteristics of partnership sourcing

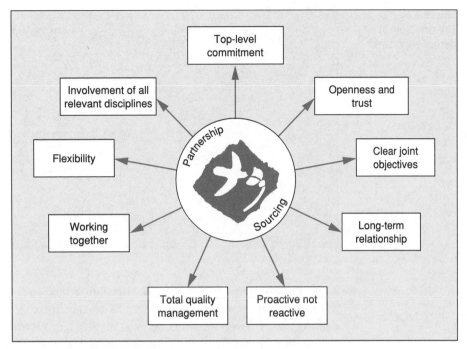

(*Source*: Courtesy Partnership Sourcing)

quality, and can reduce design-cycle times, enabling customers to beat their competitors to the market with new products. Figure 8.3 summarises the principal characteristics of partnership sourcing.

Tiering of suppliers

As is obvious from its name, this approach consists of organising supply through different 'layers' of supplier, with the immediate or direct suppliers being known as the first tier, with the second and subsequent tiers each being a stage further removed from the major manufacturer. Figure 8.4 illustrates the principle. The top tier is the final manufacturer (the original equipment maker, or OEM), the first tier suppliers provide assemblies or systems, and the second tier suppliers typically provide components.

For many years now companies have sought to reduce the number of suppliers with whom they deal. 'Reducing the vendor base' was the jargon which accompanied this movement, and for many organisations this process consisted of simply identifying the better suppliers, trying to place more business with them, and discarding the rest. Most high volume manufacturing concerns can quote impressive statistics showing how during the 1980s they reduced their number of suppliers from thousands down to a couple of hundred or so.

Figure 8.4
**The principle of
tiering suppliers**

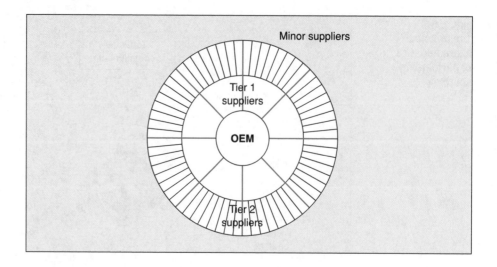

Standardisation and variety reduction are linked to the idea of vendor base reduction; a narrower range of products bought is likely, obviously, to lead to dealings with fewer suppliers, as well as other economies. As an example of this policy in action, Volkswagen targeted the avoidance of replications. Previously the group used 26 different cigarette lighters in the various vehicles; they now use five. Formerly 53 different exterior mirrors were specified; now there are seven.

It is perhaps misleading to call the first tier companies merely suppliers. Supply is what they do, of course, but as key vendors they work very closely indeed with the OEM, collaborating in a great variety of ways, and becoming risk and benefit sharing partners in the OEM's business. Nor are they simply contractors (though this might be a more appropriate description than suppliers). There is a degree of mutual commitment and dependency which places them in the position of stakeholders in the OEM's business, with the investment being commitment, development activity and, perhaps, dedicated assets, rather than financial. The dependency is, of course, two way, with the OEM heavily reliant upon the services of the first tier suppliers.

Tiering is, however, a much more complex process than simply reducing the number of direct suppliers. It involves the identification of the supplier, or groups of suppliers, that can supply the OEM with systems, such as braking, electrical, trim, etc., and empowering the key supplier to orchestrate the second tier suppliers to play their part in harmony. To some extent the second tier suppliers may be encouraged to do the same thing with their suppliers.

So, tiering is not just (or even) about reducing the vendor base. In fact it might be found that with the design and adoption of a structured, tiered supply framework, the number of suppliers to an actual OEM may increase, though of course the vast majority of suppliers will have no direct contact with the OEM. The direct vendor base can be reduced to very small numbers of contractors indeed. At the time of writing, a leading Japanese automotive company is envisaging a situation where, for a particular model of car, there will be fewer than ten suppliers directly involved.

Figure 8.5 summarises the shift in the structure of supply in the automotive and similar industries.

Figure 8.5
The shift in pattern of supply in high volume manufacturing

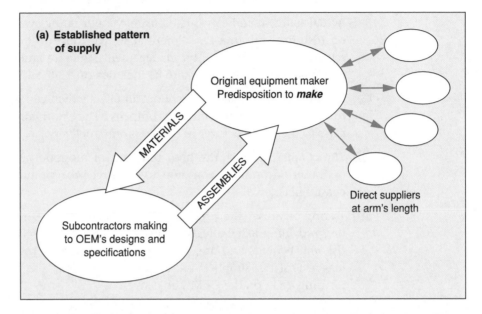

(a) **Established pattern of supply**

Original equipment maker
Predisposition to *make*

MATERIALS

ASSEMBLIES

Subcontractors making to OEM's designs and specifications

Direct suppliers at arm's length

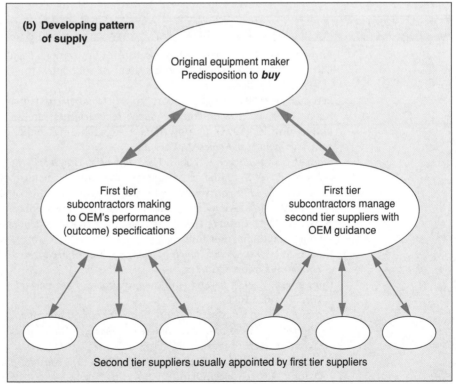

(b) **Developing pattern of supply**

Original equipment maker
Predisposition to *buy*

First tier subcontractors making to OEM's performance (outcome) specifications

First tier subcontractors manage second tier suppliers with OEM guidance

Second tier suppliers usually appointed by first tier suppliers

Summary

1 Those responsible for sourcing must have good knowledge of the market in which they are involved. Supply market research, undertaken either formally or informally, is essential. It also imparts awareness of substitute product markets.

2 Actual sources can be evaluated using vendor rating systems which are based on historical information. Potential sources have to be 'judged'. Questions regarding financial stability, management structure and order book commitments are among the criteria to be included on a site survey.

3 Just-in-time manufacturers rely on suppliers which can respond immediately to a demand from the buying company. They normally have to be located close to the manufacturer to enable prompt delivery.

4 The chapter outlines the pros and cons of monopoly supply, also the sub-optimisation problem common to both reciprocity and intra-company purchase agreements.

5 Tiering organises the precedent given to suppliers. Direct suppliers are first tier, providing assemblies/systems. They are very closely linked, sharing the risk and benefits and are, in effect, shareholders in the original equipment maker. First tier suppliers are empowered to direct the second tier suppliers, focusing them on the OEM's objectives.

References and further reading

Arminas, D (2002), 'The double advantage for innovation', *Supply Management*, October.

Barnett, H (1995), 'The Japanese system of subcontracting', *Purchasing and Supply Management*, December.

Beecham, M (1999), 'Cogent theory', *Supply Management*, January.

Birch, D (2002), 'How do you do?' *Supply Management*, March.

Butterworth, C (1995), 'Supply tiers, the purchasing challenge', *Selected Readings in Supply Chain Management*, Ascot: CIPS.

Emmett, S and Crocker, B (2006), *The Relationship Driven Supply Chain*, Aldershot: Gower.

Griffiths, F (1993), 'Alliance partnership sourcing – a major tool for strategic procurement', *Selected Readings in Purchasing and Supply*, vol. 1, Ascot: CIPS.

Heal, C (2002), 'Moving on up', *Supply Management*, September.

Hines, P (1994), *Creating World Class Suppliers, Unlocking Mutual Competitive Advantage*, London: Pitman Publishing.

Kotabe, M (1992), *Global Sourcing Strategy: R & D, Marketing and Marketing Interface*, New York and London: Quorum.

Lamming, R (1993), *Beyond Partnerships: Strategies for Innovation and Lean Supply*, New York: Prentice Hall.

Lamming, R and Cousins, P (1999), 'For richer or poorer', *Supply Management*, April.

Nishiguchi, T (1994), *Strategic Industrial Sourcing: The Japanese Advantage*, New York: Oxford University Press.

Womack, J P, Jones, D T and Roos, D (1990), *The Machine that Changed the World*, Oxford: Maxwell Macmillan.

9

Price and total cost of ownership (TCO)

Introduction

This chapter is concerned with examining how prices and costs are determined both short term and long term. As you will appreciate from previous chapters, any buying decision is affected by many factors, for example quality, delivery, responsiveness, etc., not just price.

We will look at various factors affecting the pricing and costing decision. Techniques such as cost analysis, price adjustment clauses and learning curves will be evaluated. Finally we will look more carefully at moves to reduce costs in the supply chain and the concept of strategic acquisition costs.

Objectives of this chapter

- To examine the factors influencing pricing decisions
- To compare 'price analysis' with 'cost analysis'
- To analyse the ways in which major contracts might be priced
- To explain contract price adjustment clauses
- To explain the use of incentive clauses in relation to price and cost
- To explain the effect of the 'learning curve' on the cost of production

Factors affecting pricing decisions

Four factors enter into most pricing decisions:

1 Competition and other market considerations – price mechanism.
2 Value as perceived by customers.
3 Cost of production.
4 Strategic considerations.

These factors tend to pull in different directions, as shown in Figure 9.1, and any one may be the key factor in the price decision.

Figure 9.1
Factors affecting price decisions

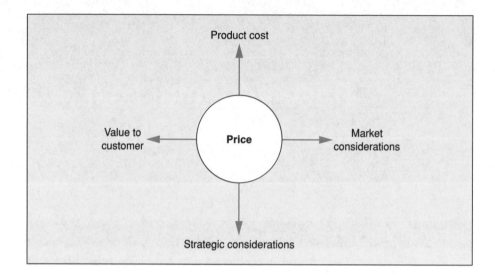

Figure 9.2
Price mechanism

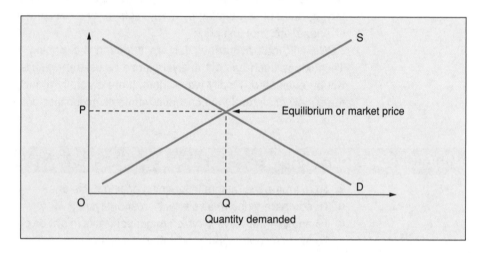

■ Supply and demand

Pricing in nearly all types of business is affected by what economists call the *price mechanism*, which is the theory of supply and demand. There is the notion of an equilibrium price, which proposes that at the equilibrium or market price exactly the same quantity is both demanded and supplied (Figure 9.2). In most free market economies the process of an equilibrium price helps to decide what is produced and what is not produced.

■ Competition and other market considerations

Organisations sell their products or services in a wide variety of market conditions ranging from perfect competition to monopoly. The characteristics of each type of market are shown in Table 9.1.

Table 9.1
**Competition
conditions**

Competition	Conditions
Monopoly	One supplier
Duopoly	Two suppliers
Monopolistic competition	Many suppliers Differentiated product
Perfect competition	Many suppliers Same product
Monopsony	One buyer Many suppliers

As you can see from Table 9.1, the extent of competition can range from one supplier in the case of monopoly to many suppliers in the case of perfect competition. In the case of monopsony, while there could be many suppliers of certain products or services, there may be only one buyer, e.g. National Health Service and drugs.

Conventional procurement thinking held the belief that monopoly was bad and competition good. Government legislation adopted a similar line and attempted through various Acts of Parliament, e.g. Monopolies and Restrictive Practices Acts of 1948, 1956 and 1964, Fair Trading Act of 1973 and Competition Act of 1980, to reduce the power of monopolies and restrictive practices. Counter-arguments, however, maintained that economies of scale more than compensated for problems associated with monopolies. More recently the European Union has increased its profile in this area.

It is generally believed today that the so-called economies of scale are not as great as was originally claimed and that responsiveness to changing demands of the customer makes it difficult for larger organisations to be as efficient as they could. Today many buyers believe that unnecessary costs can be driven out of the price if buyers and suppliers can work closely together in a partnership. Working together they can drive out unnecessary costs throughout the supply chain, both upstream and downstream (see Figure 9.3). This is achieved by such means as:

- reducing the number of suppliers in the supply chain;
- joint development of new products;
- having responsive suppliers;
- use of integrated databases;
- assisting key suppliers.

Major influential buying organisations have in recent years been more concerned with selecting suppliers committed to policies of continuous improvement and driving out unnecessary costs than the initial price of a product or service. They believe that with the right supplier partnership and by working closely together over a period of time prices can be reduced by eliminating unnecessary costs and inefficient practices. Thus while the price mechanism

Figure 9.3
Suppliers and buyers working together to drive out unnecessary costs

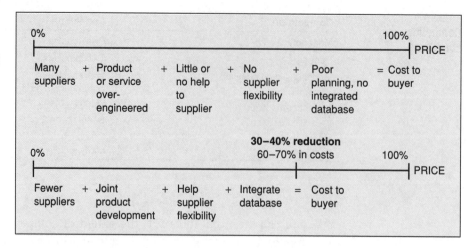

and market conditions may determine prices overall, if both buyer and supplier work closely together they can become more efficient and drive out unnecessary costs and either reduce prices or increase profits.

Product life cycle and pricing

The product life cycle is shown in Figure 9.4 (see also Chapter 2). All products tend to go through a five-phase cycle of development: introduction, growth, development, saturation and eventually decline. Pricing policy can vary dramatically depending on where in the product life cycle a product has reached.

In the early stages of the life cycle prices are often provisional and might be changed. Sales organisations may pursue policies of *skimming* in the early stages of the life cycle, meaning that because their capacity is limited supplies are relatively scarce, so they can charge high prices for the limited output. As the capacity increases and other suppliers offer similar products so they move towards much lower *penetration* pricing to increase market share. Buyers will thus notice big differences in price over the life cycles of products.

Price and the cost of production

Cost-based pricing is widely used. Buyers may be able to insist that prices are justified by cost evidence when goods are produced specifically to their requirements.

Cost-plus contracts are sometimes used when the work is difficult to cost in advance, for instance when research and development work is involved. The final contract price payable under these contracts is the actual cost incurred plus a fee, which may be an agreed percentage of cost, or an agreed amount, or a target fee with incentives as discussed later in this chapter.

Mark-up pricing, widely used in the retail trade, marks up the cost of purchase by adding a percentage to arrive at the selling price. The percentage

Figure 9.4
Product life cycle

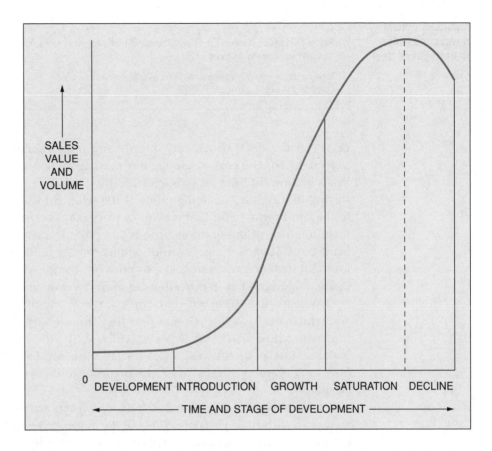

mark-up varies, fast-moving goods such as greengrocery typically having a low margin and slow-moving goods such as jewellery or furniture having a high margin.

Target pricing is also used. If for instance a firm sets itself a target of earning 20 per cent on the £30m capital employed in the business, and if total annual costs are expected to amount to £60m, then the percentage added to the cost of production to arrive at the selling price would be determined as follows:

$$\frac{\text{capital employed} \times \text{target rate of return}}{\text{annual costs}}$$

$$= \frac{30m \times 20\%}{60m}$$

$$= 10\%$$

This is not as simple as it looks, because cost of production varies with the quantity produced, which in turn depends on sales, which are affected by the price charged. An example of the costs associated with a manufactured item and its eventual price is given in Figure 9.5.

Costing cannot be an exact science, as any buyer who negotiates cost-based prices, perhaps with a cost analyst sitting in with them, becomes aware. Apart

Figure 9.5 Costs associated with a manufactured item

> Prime costs (direct materials, direct labour, direct expenses) + factory overheads (fixed and variable expenses) = works cost
>
> Works cost + administrative and sales overheads = total cost
> Total cost + profit = SALES PRICE

from variable costs, which vary directly and proportionately with the quantity produced, the cost of production must include a contribution to overheads and profit. Sales revenue must, in the long term, cover the full cost of staying in business, including profit, if the seller is to survive – even though in the short term a firm that is short of work may accept prices which do not make a full contribution to overheads and profit in order to keep people and plant busy. There are other reasons why particular products may be sold at a loss – for instance, to clear stocks, to price out competitors, to gain a toehold in a new market – but in general prices must cover overheads and profit.

Overheads are the fixed costs which a firm incurs to stay in business and which are fixed in the sense that they do not vary directly with output (e.g. rent, rates, salaries of senior executives). (In the long run all costs are variable; just as in the very short run all costs are fixed.) One problem is how to allocate overheads when the quantity to be produced is not known accurately.

For instance, if a single-product factory expects to sell 100,000 products next year, with fixed costs of £200,000, the appropriate amount to include in product cost for overhead contribution is £2. But if sales are 20 per cent below target, fixed costs will be under-recovered by £40,000, and if sales are 20 per cent above target, there will be a windfall profit of £40,000. Such calculations may be charted on break-even diagrams similar to Figure 9.6. Within limits this may average out, but if a major customer takes most of the output at a price closely based on cost, it is right that the risk should be shared. At the end of the year the buyer can check the seller's costs for labour, material and overheads and adjust the price in line with the actual level of sales. Thus, in the last example, if sales total 80,000 rather than the 100,000 expected, overhead contribution needs to be £2.50 rather than £2, and if sales were as high as 120,000, the overhead per product would fall to £1.67.

Another problem occurs when fixed costs have to be allocated to products which have different cost structures. Product X and product Y, for instance, both sell at a unit price of £100 each. But fixed costs account for 90 per cent of product cost for X and only 10 per cent for Y. Changes in selling price, and in quantity sold, will not affect profitability in the same way.

A 10 per cent price increase for product X would increase its contribution to overhead and profit by £10, an 11 per cent improvement, but a 10 per cent increase for product Y would double the contribution, from £10 to £20, a 100 per cent improvement. The profitability of product Y is thus much more sensitive to price changes than that of product X.

Figure 9.6
Break-even chart

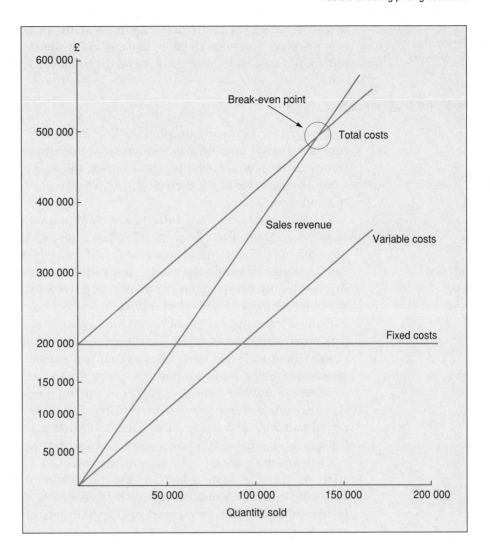

At the original price of £100, each product brings in a revenue of £10,000 a year if sales are 100 a year. A 10 per cent increase in sales volume would in each case improve revenue to £11,000 a year. In the case of product X the contribution to overhead and profit would increase from £9000 to £9900 and in the case of product Y the increase would be only one-ninth of this, from £1000 to £1100. The profitability of product X is thus much more sensitive to volume changes than that of product Y.

Capital-intensive businesses, such as train operators, hotels and airlines, can add appreciably to their profits by heavy discounting once sales at normal prices have reached the break-even point. Any sale at a price which is above direct cost will make some contribution to profit once fixed costs have been covered. This is why railways offer special fares for off-peak travel, and hotel operators offer bargain breaks or cheap rates for weekend stays. Capital-intensive manufacturers such as chemical producers are able to dump products abroad at prices which are not only below domestic prices but are actually below average cost of production, and still make a profit on such transactions if domestic sales have taken them above the break-even point.

■ Price and perceived value

Another factor in pricing decisions is how customers value the offering. A supplier's market offering may include, in addition to the product itself, such things as reliability, durability, good service and prompt delivery. Perceived value pricing is based on the customer's perception of relative value rather than on cost.

Different customers have different orders of priority and some are willing to pay more than others for a given product. This fact is exploited in the use of skimming prices for new products. A high price is set initially to recover development costs and reap the greatest benefit before competition appears. After skimming the cream off the market, as it were, price is lowered in stages to reach wider and wider market sectors.

Quite a different pricing policy sets a low price from the outset to achieve maximum market penetration. This leads to low cost of production through economies of scale and establishes a dominant market position which competitors will find difficult to attack.

These are not the only alternatives in pricing a new product. Industrial suppliers often prefer to set a price which can be held for a considerable period and will yield the required profit over that period as a whole, partly because this is what most of their customers also prefer.

Another aspect of perceived value is the extent to which changes in price affect the quantity sold. Economists use the term price elasticity of demand for a ratio which measures this sensitivity to price change. Price elasticity can be defined as the ratio of percentage change in quantity sold to percentage change in price. An alternative formula is:

$$\text{Price elasticity} = \frac{\Delta Q}{\Delta P} \times \frac{P}{Q}$$

where ΔQ = change in quantity sold
ΔP = change in price
Q = quantity sold before price change
P = price before the change

Thus, if a certain item sells 1000 a month at the price of £100 each, and a 2 per cent increase to £102 results in a 5 per cent drop in sales to 950 a month, the price elasticity would be 5 per cent divided by 2 per cent, i.e. 2.5. Alternatively, using the second formula given above, we would obtain the same result:

$$\text{Price elasticity} = \frac{50}{2} \times \frac{100}{1000} = 2.5$$

In this example, the demand would be regarded as elastic. If a 2 per cent price change resulted in a less than 2 per cent change in quantity sold, demand would be regarded as inelastic.

Sales of many consumer goods are sensitive to price changes, although there are some (e.g. salt, cigarettes and petrol) for which substantial increases in price do not greatly affect the quantity sold. Demand for industrial goods tends to be inelastic. The quantity sold is, within wide limits, not sensitive to the price charged, except when some close substitute exists to which customers can switch easily.

The main reason for this is that the demand for industrial goods is largely a *derived* demand. The demand for support or maintenance, repair and operational (MRO) items such as milling cutters and lubricants is derived from the demand for the finished products in the manufacture of which they are used. Quantities sold vary with the general level of activity in the manufacturing industries that use these items, and with sales of the particular products of individual manufacturers using them, but do not vary significantly with changes in the prices of the items. The demand for components and materials used in the manufacture of products is derived from the demand for those products. At least in the short term, the manufacturer cannot reduce the quantity purchased in response to a price increase if they are to meet sales commitment or planned production.

How buyers obtain prices

Several methods are widely used for communicating price, for example:

- A price list is made available.
- Prices are quoted on request, based on an internal price list not available to customers.
- Individual quotations based on specially prepared estimates are made on request.
- Potential suppliers submit sealed bids or tenders.
- By negotiation.
- Purchases are made at auction, or by reverse auction.

For commodities and other materials where there is an open market price the prevailing price can be obtained by reference to the market, and some prices are published in the national press. The Chartered Institute of Purchasing and Supply publishes price and cost indicators in the journal *Supply Management*, and various professional journals publish statistics relevant to their own commercial or industrial sector.

For non-standard goods, such as those made to the buyer's specification or designed by the supplier for a special purpose stated by the buyer, there can be no standard price list. Indeed final prices in the methods mentioned above may be subject to a degree of negotiation.

Price lists are available for many standard articles such as small office items, lamps and industrial fasteners. They are commonly used for goods sold through wholesalers and through industrial distributors. List prices are often subject to discounts.

Auctions

The advent of the Internet has made it practicable for buyers to post invitations to bid for supplies electronically. The idea is usually implemented by means of a reverse auction, through which suppliers meeting any criteria laid down by the buyer submit electronically their priced offers to do work or supply goods or services to the buyer's organisation.

Online bidding, as this approach has become known, is now employed for all kinds of contracts, including those of extremely high value.

Mini case study – Eutilia

In May 2002 Eutilia, a Dutch-based global marketplace for the utility sector, announced that it had successfully managed one of the largest online auctions in Europe for the utility industry. An electronic auction with a total retail value of over €23 million was held, resulting in the award of contracts to General Motors (Vauxhall) and DaimlerChrysler. The contracts were for cars, light commercial vehicles and trucks for two British utility companies – Scottish Power and United Utilities.

Heads of procurement for both client organisations identified many benefits from the exercise, including fair bidding, significant price savings, and reduced procurement costs.

Discounts

The criteria for supplier discounts are many and any attempt to identify and describe all of them would be bound to fail. Nevertheless, it might be useful to point out the main categories of discount, and some of the types in each category. Figure 9.7 provides an 'at a glance' summary, and may well be self-explanatory for many readers. It indicates the following four categories.

■ Prompt payment

Many suppliers are prepared to offer a discount if the customer does not keep them waiting for their money. These discounts may be for cash or cheque with order, or for payment within a certain specified period of time.

It is the practice of some *customers* to insist on a discount for prompt payment, even where no discount has been offered by the supplier. In large-scale retailing concerns this approach is widespread. It is, of course, arguable that a supplier who expects to be pressured in this way will price products or services in such a way that they recover the sum they require *after discount*.

Figure 9.7
Main categories of supplier discounts

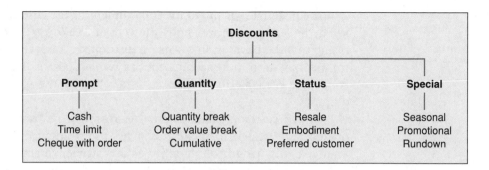

It is possibly unnecessary to point out that the buying organisation is only in a position to insist upon the supplier delivering on time and meeting the agreement to the letter when payment is made exactly as agreed. While not advocating delay in meeting obligations to the supplier, care should be taken that any discount for early payment is worth taking. In many cases the benefit is marginal, if it exists at all, and is obviously likely to be close to the cost of money in the marketplace, as evidenced by interest rates.

■ Quantity

Many suppliers use discounts as incentives to attract the customer to buy more of the product. Discounts of this kind may be very attractive and should always be considered carefully, as they may reflect more than simple economies of scale. For example, it is possible that the supplier can make additional products at a 'marginal' cost, having recovered the overheads on the initial quantity.

Of course, taking more material than is needed in the short term is risky, and can result in waste. In addition, there will be costs associated with the financing and storage of the temporary excess. As with all discounts, a balanced view is necessary.

Discounts are typically 'quantity breaks', where a lower price becomes available if more than a given amount of material is ordered. Order value may replace quantity as the threshold, and in some cases order values or quantities may be added together over a given time period to lead to a cumulative discount.

■ Status

Discounts may be offered according to the status of the buying organisation. For example, if the supplies are being acquired by an organisation acting as a stockist, agent or other intermediary, it is likely that the producer will adjust the price by means of a discount. This reflects the fact that the buyer is assisting the producer in the distribution of the product.

If the material is acquired for embodiment in the customer's product, then it may be seen as appropriate by the vendor to allow a discount, again recognising that the buyer is, in a sense, a distributor. A buyer of, say, ball bearings for incorporation in a machine tool as *manufacturer* is likely to receive a discount not available to another customer buying the parts for maintenance purposes.

Preferred customer status is another reason why discounts are sometimes offered. Entitlement to this status may arise from such factors as reciprocal arrangements, length of standing as a customer, membership of the same group of companies or a wish on the part of the supplier to expand sales in a particular market sector.

■ Special discounts

Many discounts fall within this category. It is frequently the case that seasonal discounts may be offered. Heating oil or lighting appliances may be available at a discount in the summer, the maintenance of air conditioning installations is more easily accommodated by the service provider in the winter, and discounts may be offered to attract this work.

Promotional discounts and special offers, familiar to all of us in the consumer goods market, are employed for much the same reasons where sales to organisations are concerned. A desire to increase brand or product awareness, or to increase market share may result in attractive short-term discounts becoming available.

As a final example, 'runout' discounts are widely offered. At the time of writing the Vauxhall motor company has recently replaced the 'Astra' range. Dealers, with the support of the manufacturer, are clearing stocks of the old Astra model by offering buyers very substantial discounts on the published list price. Obviously, this is very much a special discount, made available only by exceptional and temporary circumstances.

Price analysis and cost analysis

In the consideration of quotations, some form of price analysis is always used; sometimes a more specialised technique, cost analysis, is brought into play, for instance to support negotiations about cost-based pricing.

Price analysis attempts, without delving into cost details, to determine if the price offered is appropriate. It may be compared with other price offers, with prices previously paid, with the going rate if applicable, and with the prices charged for alternatives which could substitute for what is offered. Expert buyers deal with prices daily, and like their opposite numbers on the other side of the counter they acquire a ready knowledge of what is appropriate. When considering something like a building contract, which does not come up daily, they refer to prices recently quoted for comparable buildings.

When several quotations are received, some will usually be above the average and some below it. Any prices well below the norm should be examined with care.

If a supplier is short of work, a price may be quoted which covers direct labour and materials cost without making the normal contribution to overheads and profit. Accepting such an offer can be beneficial both to supplier and buyer; but it may be prudent to ask why the supplier is short of work. It can happen to anyone of course, but in this instance have customers been voting with their feet because the supplier's work is not satisfactory?

Low prices may be the result of a totally different situation: a seller may have enough work on hand to cover overheads (i.e. expected sales revenue already exceeds break-even point) and is consequently able to make a profit on any price which is above direct cost. Such offers are not necessarily repeatable; next time around, the price quoted may be higher to cover full costs.

Low prices may also be quoted as a special introductory offer to get new customers to give a fair trial to new suppliers. This may be regarded as compensation to the buying organisation for the risk incurred in switching to an untried source.

Building long-term working relationships with proven suppliers matters more than a one-off cheap price, but this does not exclude all special offers. Management may be pleased with an immediate cost reduction, but may also expect the buyer to do even better next year; this can be overcome if it is made clear that special offers cannot be made the basis for standard prices.

Low prices can also be quoted because of a mistake or incompetence. Suppliers should be allowed to correct their mistake or withdraw their offer if their bid is well outside the normal range of variation (e.g. 25 per cent below the average quoted price). Insistence on a contract at the quoted price can lead to bankrupt suppliers and unfinished contracts, and thus eventually to high costs.

High prices may be quoted as a polite alternative to refusing to make any offer by sellers with full order books. Buyers should not write off such suppliers as too expensive, since next time around they could well submit the lowest bid if conditions have changed. High prices may also be quoted because a better specification, more service, or more prompt delivery, etc., is offered. Obviously such offers should be considered with care. The best buy, not the cheapest price, is the buyer's objective.

Cost analysis examines prices in quite a different way from price analysis: it looks at one aspect only, how quoted price relates to cost of production. When large sums are involved and a considerable amount of cost analysis needs to be done, full-time estimating staff or cost analysts may be employed by the procurement department to do it. These people are as well qualified to estimate price as their opposite numbers in suppliers' sales departments are to estimate a selling price; they have the same qualifications, engineering experience and costing knowledge plus specialist knowledge of sheet metal processing, light fabrication, electronics or whatever is relevant.

Figure 9.8
Price and cost investigation tools

- Previous history of price increases.
- Competition prices – tenders/quotations – bid analysis.
- Product cost breakdown, i.e.

  Labour %
  Materials %   } Check increases against indices
  Overhead %
  Profit %

- Break-even analysis – the more business you take, the stronger your negotiating position.
- Learning curve – when labour costs are high.
- Value analysis – are costs necessary?
- Standardisation – reduce range.
- Buyer/supplier business – what percentage of business do you give?
- Payment terms – could these be improved?
- Negotiations – used in conjunction with above.

Usually suppliers are asked to include with their price quotations detailed cost breakdowns. Some are reluctant to comply, but if one supplier does, others find it hard not to follow suit. Differences between a supplier's cost breakdown and the buyer's cost analysis can then be examined one by one to arrive at a mutually agreed figure. Cost analysis is also used by procurement management to set negotiating targets for their buyers.

Cost analysis is a useful technique for keeping prices realistic in the absence of effective competition. It concentrates attention on what costs ought to be incurred before the work is done, instead of looking at what costs were actually incurred after the work is completed. This seems more likely to keep costs down, as well as less expensive to operate, than the alternative of wading through a supplier's accounting records after contract completion, probably employing professional auditors to do it.

A summary of the price and cost investigation tools is given in Figure 9.8. It starts with the bid analysis where prices and other variables are compared. Further cost reduction exercises could then be concluded depending on the likely areas for cost reduction.

■ Total acquisition cost and total cost of ownership

Today increasing concern is being directed at long-term or total acquisition cost and total cost of ownership. This approach to costing is concerned with what the price of a product or service could be in the long term if buyer and supplier worked closely together and drove out unnecessary costs in the supply chain.

When evaluating price the question may be asked, have we captured all the costs? For example, have we allowed for lead time or capacity problems with the supplier, what about extra resources and support we may have to devote to suppliers if problems arise and so on. What could look like a good price from a supplier could suddenly escalate if problems occur.

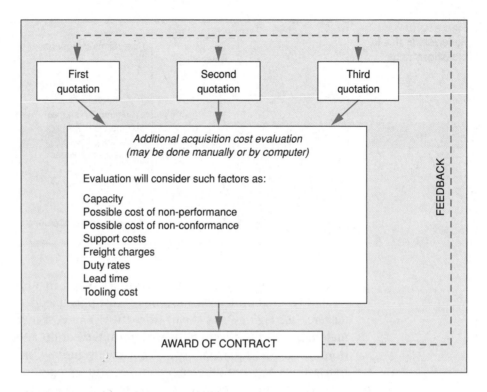

Figure 9.9
IBM procurement –
acquisition cost

Acquisition costs can be defined as all the costs involved in bringing a supplier's product to the buyer's organisation. It is made up not just of price and freight cost but any other costs in completing this activity properly, e.g. any quality or delivery problems need to be costed in. More procurement organisations than ever are now attempting to measure these costs, which are often considerably more than the price.

An example of a model by IBM for attempting to calculate true acquisition cost is given in Figure 9.9. Quotes from various suppliers are entered into a computer software package and estimates of other costs given. From this, a more accurate assessment of the price can be made.

Pricing major contracts

How to price major contracts is itself a subject on which many books have been written. Such contracts may involve any of the main engineering disciplines: civil, mechanical, electrical or chemical plant engineering – and some large contracts involve all of them.

Often large sums of money are at stake and long periods of time are involved, so there is risk. Fixed price contracts are administratively convenient to the buying organisation, but all the risk has to be taken by the seller. Cost reimbursement contracts are administratively convenient to the seller, but all the risk is taken by the buying organisation. Between these two extremes

Figure 9.10
Buyer/seller risk in major contracts

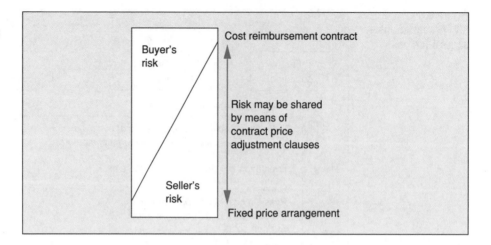

there is a whole range of varied contract types, including fixed price with escalation, target price with incentive, cost plus fixed fee, cost plus incentive fee, etc. (see Figure 9.10). Apart from the risk of cost increases for labour and materials, and the effect of government intervention and of changes in taxation and in the financial cost of borrowing money, many contracts entail transactions between different countries, and changes in the rate of exchange between the currencies involved have to be taken into account.

With fixed price contracts the buying organisation knows exactly what has to be paid and can provide for it in budgets. The seller, however, arrives at the fixed price by forecasting costs as accurately as possible and then adding a contingency allowance to cover unpredictable cost increases. It would be prudent for the seller to make this contingency allowance as large as possible, which means that the buying organisation pays a lot for the administrative convenience of a fixed price. If the seller is keen to win the contract and faces competition then the contingency allowance could be cut to a minimum. It may be cut too much, so that sellers have to appeal for *ex gratia* baling out, or alternatively cut corners to avoid losing money on the contract. In times of severe inflation, fixed price contracts may not be to the advantage of the buying organisation even if sellers are willing to sign them. When prices are stable and costs are reasonably predictable, buying organisations will prefer fixed price contracts at least for contract periods not exceeding two years.

Fixed price contracts should not be confused with lump sum contracts. In lump sum contracts a single all-in price is payable for the whole of the contract. It may be a fixed price or it could be subject to escalation. A fixed price contract would not be a lump sum contract if it fixed the prices for various classes of labour and material without finalising the amounts to be costed out at these schedules of rates in the final invoice.

In cost-plus contracts the seller is reimbursed for all costs legitimately incurred, plus either a fixed fee or a percentage fee for contribution to overhead expenses and profit. This type of contract is appropriate for research and development work, where total cost is usually impossible to predict. Close control is required.

When total cost can be estimated with enough accuracy to set a target cost, which is nevertheless capable of improvement and may also be subject to cost slippage, incentive contracts are often used. When the target cost is likely to be affected by changes in the cost of labour and materials, contract price adjustment or escalation clauses, such as the British Electrical and Allied Manufacturers Association (BEAMA) contract price adjustment system, are often used.

■ Incentive contracts

Incentive contracts are used when neither the supplier nor the customer can estimate the cost of the work covered by the contract with sufficient confidence to enable a fixed price to be agreed, but when a reasonable forecast can nevertheless be made of the actual costs of performing the work and a most likely (or target) cost can be agreed. A fee is also agreed for the profit which would be payable if the cost of the work comes out on target together with a ratio in which any under-runs or over-runs from target cost will be shared between the supplier and the customer. The supplier has a positive incentive to keep costs down because by so doing they can increase profit or avoid contributing towards an over-run on costs. The incentive thus provided motivates the supplier to act in the customer's best interests.

An example is given below of a typical incentive contract, together with details of the outcome:

Example:

Target cost	£500 000	
Profit (at target)	£40 000	

Share ratio for over- and
   under-runs, 75% customer
   25% supplier

Outcome (i.e. actual cost)	£487 495		
Fee for profit payable: Target profit		£40 000.00	
Supplier's share of under-run			
(500 000 – 487 495) × 25%		£ 3 126.25	
	Total	£43 126.25	

Thus:

Expected Price (£)			*Actual Price (£)*		
Target cost	500 000		Cost	487 495.00	
Target profit	40 000	= 8%	Fee	40 000.00	= 8.85%
			Share of u/run	3 126.25	
Total	540 000		Total	530 621.25	

Customer saved £9378.75   Supplier earned £3126.25 bonus

■ Escalation and price adjustment

Inflation is a general and persistent tendency of prices to rise, which, because it is general, is equivalent to a fall in the value (or buying power) of the currency affected. Britain suffered from several periods of severe inflation in the last century, and although not severe in the UK at the time of writing, inflation still remains a serious problem in many parts of the world. Buyers dealing on world markets, and multinational corporations, have to cope with inflation somewhere within their field of operations.

How are contracts to be priced when costs are rising by amounts that cannot be predicted with any accuracy? An option convenient for the seller is to charge the price ruling at date of despatch. Buyers reject this if they can; it gives them no contractual basis to challenge whatever price is eventually charged. Another option is to quote a fixed price which includes contingency allowances large enough to cover any cost increase which might conceivably occur. Fixed prices are convenient for the buyer, but this option cannot be to the buyer's advantage despite its convenience.

There are two better options. In both, the quoted price is based on the costs which apply at the date of tender, but the contract terms allow the price to be adjusted in line with cost increases which occur between date of tender and completion date.

In the first option, the seller is entitled to make the adjustment to the contract price considered to be justified by cost increases, and the buyer is entitled to request independent evidence that the adjustment is correct. In the second, a formula is agreed for index-linking contract price: that is, for adjusting it in line with changes in published indexes of cost which are available both to buyer and seller. Contract clauses which define these arrangements are called contract price adjustment (CPA) clauses. They are also called escalation (or escalator) clauses. Some of them are very complicated. The Osborne formula for building works lists 48 basic work categories plus five special engineering installation categories, and cost variation in each of these is separately evaluated. On the other hand, the BEAMA formula is about as simple as a CPA formula can be without becoming unrealistic, and consequently has been very widely used in all sorts of industries. BEAMA first agreed this formula many years ago on the basis that 40 per cent of a contract price could be attributed to labour costs, and 45 per cent to material costs, and these could be adjusted by reference to published indexes for labour and material costs. The remaining 15 per cent of contract price was regarded as invariable, because the intention was not to increase profits but to compensate the seller for cost increases. Subsequent alterations to these weightings have been made. A version is shown in Figure 9.11.

The BEAMA CPA Advisory Service sends monthly to subscribers notifications of labour and material cost index figures used in the formula. These are also available from government statistical offices. How these figures

Figure 9.11
Typical BEAMA clause for contract price adjustment

CONTRACT PRICE ADJUSTMENT CLAUSE AND FORMULAE FOR USE WITH HOME CONTRACTS

ELECTRICAL MACHINERY:
(for which there is no other specific Formula)

If the cost to the Contractor of performing his obligations under the Contract shall be increased or reduced by reason of any rise or fall in labour costs or in the cost of material or transport above or below such rates and costs ruling at the date of tender, or by reason of the making or amendment after the date of tender of any law or of any order, regulation, or by-law having the force of law in the United Kingdom that shall affect the Contractor in the performance of his obligations under the Contract, the amount of such increase or reduction shall be added to or deducted from the Contract Price as the case may be provided that no account shall be taken of any amount by which any cost incurred by the Contractor has been increased by the default or negligence of the Contractor. For the purposes of this clause 'the cost of material' shall be construed as including any duty or tax by whomsoever payable which is payable under or by virtue of any Act of Parliament on the import, purchase, sale, appropriation, processing or use of such material.

The operation of this clause is without prejudice to the effect if any which the imposition of Value Added Tax or any tax of a like nature may have upon the supply of goods or services under the Contract.

Variations in the cost of materials and labour shall be calculated in accordance with the following formulae:

(a) Labour

The Contract Price shall be adjusted at the rate of 0.475 per cent of the Contract Price per 1.0 per cent difference between the BEAMA Labour Cost Index published for the month in which the tender date falls and the average of the index figures published for the last two-thirds of the contract period, this difference being expressed as a percentage of the former index figure.

(b) Materials

The Contract Price shall be adjusted at the rate of 0.475 per cent of the Contract Price per 1.0 per cent difference between the Price Index figure of Materials used in the Electrical Machinery Industry last published in the Trade and Industry Journal before the date of tender and the average of the Index Figures commencing with the Index last published before the two-fifths point of the Contract Period and ending with the Index last published before the four-fifths point of the Contract Period, this difference being expressed as a percentage of the former index figure.

---

are used to make adjustments to the contract price may be seen in principle from the example in Figure 9.12.

Investment appraisal

When acquiring capital equipment the idea is that the investment made will pay back the cost over a period of time. If the investment is to be worthwhile, then the total cost of acquisition and use should be *negative*. See Chapter 14 on capital goods for notes on investment appraisal and the time value of money.

Figure 9.12
Calculating the price adjustment

BASIS OF CLAIM FOR CONTRACT PRICE ADJUSTMENT	
Customer: John Smith — Customer's Order No: 5002	
A Contract Price	£177 500
B Tender or Cost Basis Date	20 Feb 2001
C Date of order	12 March 2001
D Date when ready for despatch/taking over	2 Jan 2002
E Contract Period between C and D days	296 days
F Date at one-third of Contract Period	19 June 2001
G Date at two-fifths of Contract Period	8 July 2001
H Date at four-fifths of Contract Period	4 Nov 2001
I Labour Cost Index at tender or cost basis date	128.1
J Average of Labour Cost Indices for period F to D	139.0
K Department of Industry Index figures of Materials used in Electrical Machinery or Mechanical Engineering Industries last published before tender or cost basis date	195.9
L Average of Department of Industry Index figures commencing with index last published before date at G and ending with the Index last published before date at H	202.8

M Labour Adjustment $\quad 47.5 \times \dfrac{J-I}{I} = \dfrac{10.9}{128.1} \times 47.5 = 4.0418\%$

N Materials Adjustment $\quad 47.5 \times \dfrac{L-K}{K} = \dfrac{6.9}{195.9} \times 47.5 = 1.6730\%$

P *Total percentage Adjustment for Labour and Material* = 5.7148%

TOTAL PRICE ADJUSTMENT

$$= A \times \frac{P}{100} = £177\ 500 \times \frac{5.7148}{100} = £10\ 140$$

Learning curves and experience curves

We turn now to an empirical relationship between the cost of performing a task and the number of times it has been performed. In some instances cost decreases by a fixed percentage every time the total quantity made doubles.

Everyone knows that we can learn from experience. The first time a complicated product is built, fitters have to stop to consult drawings and work out how to do things. The second time, the work should go appreciably faster. By the time the twentieth product has been built, production time should be considerably reduced, and further reductions could well be achieved as the total quality produced increases, although at a diminishing rate.

This can be shown on a graph, as in the lower part of Figure 9.13. It can also be drawn on a log–log graph as a straight line, as in the upper part of Figure 9.13, which is easier to work with. In this example, average man-hours

Figure 9.13
Learning curve (80 per cent): (a) as usually drawn on log–log graph paper; (b) as drawn on ordinary graph paper

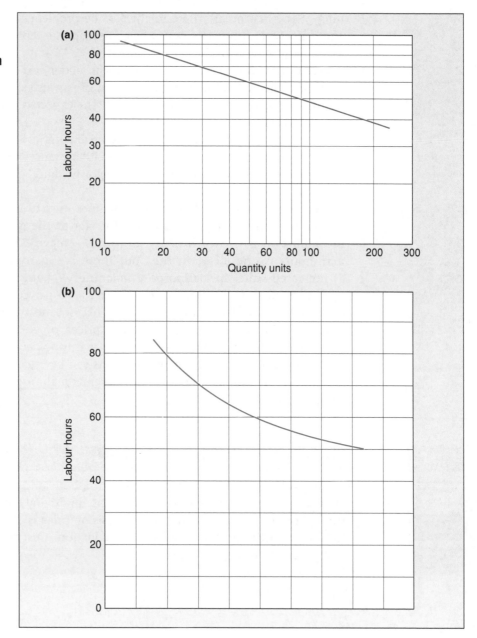

to make the product reduce by 80 per cent every time the total accumulated quantity made doubles.

Learning curves can be very useful in working out the right price when complicated products, such as aircraft (one of the earliest applications), are made in relatively small quantities. The problem for the buyer is that average cost of production for the first order placed is not a good guide for the next order because of the learning effect. Obtaining quotes from other possible suppliers is not much help either, since they would have to start from scratch and thus would be in a similar position to the existing supplier at the beginning of the first order. There might also be problems with quality, tooling and delivery. Learning curves can be a big help in establishing the right price for a repeat order with the existing supplier.

Learning curves refer to the reduction in labour cost because of reduction in the average time taken. Changes in rates of pay also affect labour cost, usually increasing it, so it is better to calculate the expected reduction in terms of time taken rather than in terms of cost.

The learning curve can be a most useful buying tool in situations of the kind to which it is relevant, and in such circumstances the buyer will find it worthwhile to spend some time acquiring a working knowledge of the tool and how to use it.

The term improvement curve is sometimes used to mean the same thing as learning curve, but it is also used to refer to the general improvement in production costs which many industries achieve. The learning effect in man-hours is one factor in this, but there are many other factors, such as increased scale, special-purpose machinery, changes in manufacturing process or product design. In recent years a 70 per cent experience curve effect has been observed in electronics. This is a most dramatic rate of cost reduction, but everyone has seen the prices of electronic watches, for instance, tumble. In power tools an 80 per cent experience curve has been seen. Knowledge of these experience effects can be useful to the buyer, but it is not a buying tool like the learning curve; its main use is in marketing and company policy.

Conclusion

In the past, the buyer has had to concentrate on price. Today, by working closely with key suppliers and concentrating on driving out unnecessary costs throughout the supply chain, the emphasis on price is considerably reduced, the focus shifting to total cost and its reduction. Cost removal rather than cost allocation is frequently pursued.

Summary

1 The chapter explains how pricing is affected by market conditions, competition levels, the product's life cycle, cost of production and perceived value.

2 The author outlines the various methods of costing and where they are most applicable – cost-based pricing for specifically built goods; mark-up pricing for retail goods, etc. All techniques aim to cover overheads and profit.

3 Discounts may be offered for prompt payment, quantity or for seasonal/promotional reasons. Stockists/agents, in assisting the producer in distribution, will also attract a discount.

4 Price analysis attempts to determine if the price offered is appropriate. The cost of alternatives and historical price may be used as a comparison. Lower prices may be offered as a way to enter a market, while a higher one may be a polite refusal or because the specification is greater than requested.

5 Price increases may be agreed by mutual consent for the duration of the contract. More commonly, escalation formulae index-linking contract prices are used.

References and further reading

De Beer, M (1998), 'A framework for total cost of ownership costing for integrated purchasing', *7th International IPSERA Conference*, London.

Ellram, L (1993), 'Total cost of ownership: elements and implementation', *International Journal of Purchasing and Materials Management*, 29 (4).

Emmanuel, C (1992), *Transfer Pricing*, London: Chartered Institute of Management Accounting.

Hubbard, R G and Weiner, R J (1992), 'Long term contracting and multiple price systems', *Journal of Business*, 65 (2), April.

Lamming, R (1993), *Beyond Partnership – Strategies for Innovation and Lean Supply*, New York: Prentice Hall.

Lamming, R, Jones, D and Nicol, D (1996), 'Cost transparency: a source of supply chain competitive advantage?' *IPSERA Conference*, April.

Sako, M (1992), *Prices, Quality and Trust: Inter-Firm Relations in Britain and Japan*, Cambridge: Cambridge University Press.

Schillewaert, N (1996), 'Total cost of acquisition as an instrument for supplier evaluation', *IPSERA Conference*, April.

10

Negotiations

Introduction

It is generally accepted that a key competence in a procurement executive is an ability to negotiate. Negotiations may involve dealing with a single issue or many. They may be conducted on a one-to-one basis or between teams of negotiators representing different interests, and may be conducted over the telephone in a matter of minutes, or take many months to complete. It is also worth mentioning that negotiations are not necessarily confined to the buyer–seller relationship; many buying negotiations take place on an intra-organisational basis, involving the reconciliation of the views of supplies staff and colleagues. In this chapter we explore the nature of negotiation, and give some practical guidance.

Objectives of this chapter

- To understand negotiating as a 'mutuality of wants, resolved by exchange'
- To identify the activities carried out during the different stages of negotiation
- To analyse the characteristics of a skilled negotiator
- To recognise the key points of discussion stage behaviour and recognise negotiating ploys
- To introduce the concept of body language and how it can be interpreted
- To view how negotiating technique is influenced by long-term interests

Negotiation

There have been many attempts to define negotiation, for example 'to confer with others in order to reach a compromise or agreement' (*Oxford Encyclopedic English Dictionary*); or 'the process by which we search for terms to obtain what we want from somebody who wants something from us' (Kennedy, 1991). The latter definition points up a key factor: that negotiation implies some mutuality of wants, resolved by exchange.

It is perhaps worth mentioning at this stage that negotiation has two other meanings, not closely related to its 'bargaining' connotation. Negotiation may be employed by a mariner or navigator to mean something like 'finding a way', whereas a banker might employ the term to mean 'exchange for value' as, for example, a cheque or bill of exchange is negotiated. Procurement and supply is certainly concerned with exchanging for value, and with finding new ways of doing business, but we confine our attention in this chapter to the more conventional usage of the term.

However defined, bargaining negotiation is seen as a process whereby agreement is sought. One should not forget that there are alternative ways of reaching agreement that do not involve negotiations and can be appropriate and effective in the right circumstances.

■ Alternatives to negotiation

Some alternatives to negotiation are:

1 *Persuade*. Encourage the other side to accept the merits of a particular case with no concessions from yourself.
2 *Give in*. Accept totally what the other side offers.
3 *Coerce*. Insist that the other side meets your demands 'or else'.
4 *Problem solve*. Remove the difference, so that there is no need to negotiate.

A vast amount of literature has emerged on the theory and practice of negotiation, and the topic continues to provide scope for a considerable amount of research and publication. The material available could generate several doctoral studies and much learned analysis and discussion at both a practical and academic level. Good theory, after all, mirrors and formalises descriptions of practice. Thus, helpful guidelines for the practising manager should have a close relationship with the theoretical findings of the academic.

We have drawn upon a considerable bank of knowledge in developing this chapter. A dilemma was to select a framework around which we might present a helpful section of the book for the diverse readership of this text. Our solution was to take our own framework and relate other work to it as pertinent. In so doing, it is our intention that the practising manager or buyer might find the discussion helpful as it relates to their day-to-day negotiations, while the student who wishes to consider the theories in greater depth would be provided with a starting point for study. It should be emphasised that in using this framework we are not claiming its excellence over others. It is presented purely to provide a structure for discussion. However, it would be surprising if we did not believe it to be a sensible basis for such discussion, having used it as a structure in helping to develop negotiating skills in many thousands of managers around the world.

It should be noted, too, that in working with these managers we have learnt a great deal from them which has helped us hone the model and the ideas which are put forward in this chapter. Like salesmen, buyers need to be

Figure 10.1
The basic phases
of negotiation

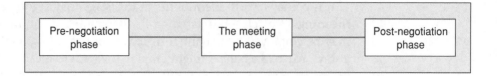

proficient in such skills as asking good questions, listening, interpreting trends in the negotiation, pre-planning a negotiation and ensuring that what is agreed is implemented. They need to be able, too, to analyse and interpret information and to be aware of the dangers of making unwarranted assumptions. Since negotiation is an interpersonal process, they need to understand something about human behaviour, needs and motivation: they need to develop interactive skills.

■ The three phases of negotiation

It is useful to consider negotiation conceptually as a three-phase process, as shown in Figure 10.1.

The first of the three phases is the preparatory stage, when the information is analysed, the objectives are set and strategies developed. The meeting phase is concerned with the process of discussion, further information collection and analysis, and with the reaching of agreement between the parties. The final stage involves the implementation of the agreement within and between the organisations represented in the previous phase.

This is a simple model; apart from the elements of the meeting phase, which will be discussed later, the process of negotiation may involve several meetings. The preparation stage may then require consideration of phased objectives. For example, it may be that the first meeting between the parties will be concerned solely with exploratory discussions: both sides may need to clarify the issues of the negotiation and there will always be the need to obtain more information.

A subsequent meeting (or meetings) might be concerned with discussions leading towards the desired agreement. In some cases, agreement may be reached in one meeting; in others the situation might necessitate further meetings to conclude the agreement. Figure 10.2 extends the model by way of illustrating such a situation.

This expanded model has applications even when the negotiation is concluded at a single meeting. Figure 10.3 illustrates the same model adapted for a single meeting.

In considering the elements of this model, some of the key skills and concepts involved will be discussed. However, it is not the intention to attempt a comprehensive treatment, for this would be outside the scope of this chapter. Nonetheless, as has been indicated, the reader, whether academic or practising manager, should be able to build from this base, perhaps in conjunction with the books and articles which are listed at the end of this chapter.

Figure 10.2
**The phases of
negotiation –
multi-meeting**

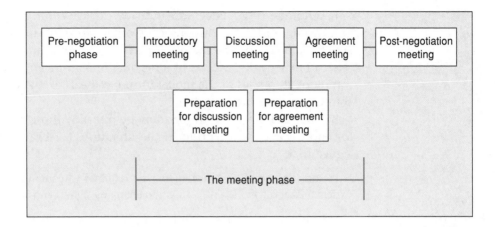

Figure 10.3
**The phases of
negotiation –
single meeting**

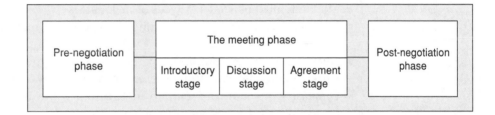

Negotiation skills

Rackham and Carlisle, who in 1978 pioneered an analytical approach to negotiating skills development, argued that there were three criteria which relate to successful negotiators:

- They should be rated as effective by both sides.
- They should have a track record of significant success.
- They should have a low incidence of implementation failures.

They emphasised behavioural and interactive factors such as 'image', integrity, status and self-actualisation. Then they stressed one of the significant findings of our own research, which is that problems frequently occur in converting agreements into action. It is this feature which appears in the foregoing model as the 'post-negotiation phase'.

These behavioural factors also relate to another important aspect of negotiation. This is that in negotiation there are two basic areas which need to be borne in mind:

- The corporate issues (those pertaining to the organisations involved in the negotiation).
- The human issues (those which relate to the individuals involved in the negotiation).

It is not that these issues are mutually exclusive; rather that concentration on one group to the exclusion of the other can result in invalid assumptions about the behaviour of the other party. A recognition of these, often inter-related but separate, aspects of a negotiation can be an extremely important feature of all phases of the model introduced earlier. In addition they have a considerable bearing on success.

Behavioural aspects of negotiation are probably those which have attracted the most academic attention in the literature. For example, Spector (1977) argued that:

> Persons, in the roles of negotiators are required to communicate positions, make demands and concessions, respond to changing signals and arrive at outcomes.

He added that the resolution of conflicting interests through negotiation is motivated by:

- The individual personality needs of negotiators.
- The personality compatibility among negotiators representing opposing parties.
- Negotiators' perceptions and expectations of the opponent – strengths and weaknesses, intentions and goals, and commitments to positions.
- Persuasive mechanisms employed to modify the bargaining positions and values of the opponent to achieve a more favourable convergence of interests.

As will be seen, these features overlie and add to those described by Rackham and Carlisle. They emphasise the complexity of the negotiation process and demonstrate the problems of the behavioural scientist in grappling with studies involving so many variables.

It follows that the skilled negotiator needs to be aware of the many variables which may be present in a negotiation. Further, that in order to be successful, the negotiator needs to be able to apply relevant skills at all phases of the negotiation process.

Preparation

A recurring finding of our own work is that the major source of difficulty for negotiators is inadequate management of the pre-negotiation phase. The implications of this finding include the fact that most managers believe they would have achieved better results had they prepared more effectively. Further, that those who are successful tend to have adequately managed the pre-negotiation phase.

Not every negotiation necessitates the same measure of preparation, and the amount of time spent will depend upon the complexity of the negotiation and its importance to the organisation concerned. The manager must decide, in each case, how long to spend on preparation. In cases involving long-term relationships (e.g. with key suppliers) it could be argued that preparation is continuous: certainly this is true of information gathering. However, the particular circumstances which apply in a given market at a given time will probably be quite different from those which were experienced a year earlier. The economic climate, competition and the company's own situation are key variables which may have changed. A negotiation at the latter date will involve careful consideration of changes in the present situation, in addition to what has occurred in the past and what is likely to occur in the future.

■ Features of preparation

Kennedy (1991) identifies three key considerations in preparation for negotiation:

1 What do we want? This question may not be as easy to answer as we might at first imagine. Our wants may not become crystal clear until we enter discussion with the other side. They may, for example, include:
   (a) a lower price;
   (b) an improved relationship;
   (c) a bigger discount;
   (d) faster delivery; and/or
   (e) changes in quality.
   The range of negotiable variables in most buyer–seller relationships or transactions is very wide.

2 How valuable is each of our 'wants' to us? Perhaps, for example:
   (a) prompt delivery = high priority;
   (b) lower price = medium priority; and
   (c) quality changes = low priority.

3 What are my entry and exit points? Your entry point is really your 'opening bid'. Once disclosed, you are unlikely to better it, so the bid obviously requires careful thought. The exit point is your 'walk away' position. It is clearly desirable that this should be identified and understood at the preparatory phase, if only to obviate the possibility of striking a bargain which may be regretted later. If your exit point and your opposite number's exit points do not overlap then the probability of achieving a deal is severely reduced, though of course an apparent gap can be closed through negotiation, and an overlap achieved.

Figure 10.4 shows, first, a situation where the buyer's and seller's ranges of possibility do not overlap and, second, a situation where the gap is replaced by overlap, and a range of mutually satisfactory outcomes are possible. Note that the overlap does not suggest a single possible outcome; there is an infinite range of possibilities between the two exit points.

Rackham and Carlisle (1978) make a useful point regarding preparation when they suggest that 'it is not the amount of planning time which makes for success, but how it is used'. This apparently obvious conclusion is worth

Figure 10.4
Ranges of possibility

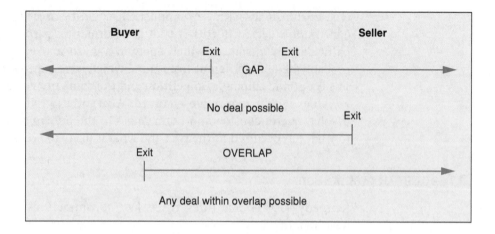

discussion for two reasons. The first is that their analysis indicates some aspects of the emphasis of the successful negotiator's pre-negotiation behaviour. The second is that those who are less successful may need, initially at least, to spend more time in preparation in order to cover the same ground. As with most areas of human activity, a major aspect of expertise is the ability to focus on the important issues and deal with them effectively in a given circumstance. Or, as it has been put, doing the right things as well as doing things right.

Rackham and Carlisle suggest, for example, that the skilled negotiator considers a wider range of outcomes or options for action than their average counterpart. They show that the former typically considers twice as many outcomes/options per issue, both which they might introduce, and which might be raised by the other party. They emphasise that this wider-ranging analysis provides a major preparation for exploring every opportunity to obtain 'a better deal for both parties' (Karrass, 1972) during the actual negotiation.

Another of their findings relates to the time spent in preparation on areas of agreement as against those of potential conflict. They found that successful negotiators, while spending as much time on conflict areas, gave three times as much attention to common ground aspects as did average negotiators. They imply from this that concentration on 'common ground' areas may be the key to 'building a satisfactory climate'. Our own conclusion that the negotiator should build from a platform of known agreement supports this finding, though it will be clear that such an emphasis should not be confined to the preparation stage. Indeed, for best effect, it will extend through all the phases of negotiation suggested by Figure 10.3.

Our own observations suggest another important feature of preparation, that is the necessity to differentiate between 'facts' and 'assumptions'. Many problems stem from the negotiator's inability to recognise whether the data available are factual or not. Clearly, if objectives and strategies are based upon invalid assumptions, the negotiator will be in difficulty during the negotiation itself. A sound procedure which we have noted, used by successful negotiators, involves:

- specifying the key assumptions which are implied at the preparation stage;
- giving them some weight of probability, which helps signal the level of necessity to develop alternatives; and
- testing these assumptions, particularly in the introductory stage of the negotiation.

Among the advantages of this approach is the fact that negotiators may be forced to develop alternatives if the bases of their thinking are challenged. In other words, negotiators will be obliged to consider more options as a result of questioning. One consequence of this is that they will align themselves with the pattern of behaviour of the successful negotiators discussed earlier.

A further aspect of preparation which we have noted as resulting in negotiators being less effective in negotiations than they might have been is their perception of the strength of their position vis-à-vis the other party. Generally speaking, we have found that negotiators understate their own strengths, while overstating those of the other party. There is a tendency, too, to understate the weaknesses of the other party's position while overemphasising their own. Not surprisingly, more successful negotiators are better at analysing both aspects.

It could be argued that the successful negotiator has learned:

- to increase the level of perception of the strengths of their position; and
- to influence the views of the other party in line with their own.

Clearly, perceptions associated with relative strengths and weaknesses in negotiation have a great deal to do with assumptions. Thus this implies a further advantage for the negotiator in questioning the key assumptions. It also emphasises the need to consider such questions as: 'What do we believe to be the views of the other party on relative strengths and weaknesses?' 'What are our own?' 'Can we influence their views to our advantage?' and 'How might we do this?'

It is important in this analysis to recognise that 'strengths and weaknesses' do not simply refer to the negotiating positions of both parties. As will be seen from Table 10.1 a wide variety of variables may impinge upon a negotiation, including, for example, information, time and tenacity.

■ Collecting information

The information required in order to prepare for any negotiation will be unique to that situation. The manager concerned has to make a judgement as to the quality of the information which is collected. Quite apart from these considerations, there will also be a time constraint on the collection of the data. In part, this will result from the resources allocated to the task and

**Table 10.1
Some 'personnel'
factors in
negotiation**

Ability to:	Influence control; avoid conflict; deal with conflict creatively; interpret non-verbal signs; analyse other party's position; form and use questions; listen; use verbal skills; maintain concentration and control discussion; persuade.
Traits:	Risk-taking propensity; level of commitment; level of loyalty; level of self-esteem.
Background:	Intelligence; fitness; age; race; sex; class; ethics.
Experience:	Of negotiation; of type of negotiation; of other party's company; of other party.
Approach:	Negotiating style; management style.
Status:	Personal conception of other party.

partly from the length of time available to the negotiation. Even the type of information which is collected in order to prepare will depend upon the circumstances surrounding the negotiation. Nonetheless, the following questions are typical of those which the negotiator might ask in a buying negotiation.

**The current
agreement
(where one exists)**

- What is the duration of the current agreement?
- What is the financial history regarding part transactions (e.g. pricing history)?
- What cost data are available?
- What has the supplier's delivery performance record been like?
- What has their quality record been like?
- What disputes have arisen over the period of the contract? Are they pertinent as far as the coming negotiation is concerned?
- By what date should agreement be reached?
- With whom will we be negotiating (e.g. name the individuals; what is known about them)?

**Some specification
issues**

- Has the supplier been given the opportunity to improve the value in the specification?
- What aspects of it are critical?
- Which can be varied to achieve the same function?
- How is conformity with specification to be measured?
- Who will do that measurement and where?
- If the item is a special item, is it possible to replace it with a standard?

**Some delivery
issues**

- How frequently do we wish the supplier to deliver?
- In what quantities?
- How will the material/components be delivered?
- Who is responsible for packaging/pallets/containers?
- Which is the delivery address?
- Are there restrictions there (e.g. timing of delivery, size of lorry)?
- If the purchases are to be delivered in a container/rail truck, what is the position regarding demurrage?

Some financial issues

- In what currency is the transaction to be made?
- If a foreign currency, what rate of exchange is to be agreed?
- What dates are important in this respect?
- What credit terms apply?
- What are the general terms of payment (e.g. against letter of credit, free on board)?
- Does the supplier require stage payments?
- If so, are these terms negotiable?
- Is there a set discount for early payment?
- How could this be improved?

Some contractual issues

- Who is responsible for insurance?
- What is the level of cover? For what?
- Under which country's law is the contract made (in the case of a purchase from a foreign supplier)?
- Are customs requirements clearly stated?
- Has the method of transportation been agreed satisfactorily?
- Do the contract terms clearly delineate responsibility for elements of purchase cost?
- Has the offer been accepted by the supplier in a manner which ensures a valid contract?
- Have your administrative requirements been clearly stated and understood?

Some personnel issues

- With whom are you going to negotiate (individuals)?
- What do you know about them?
- If a team is to be involved, what will it comprise?
- Do these people have the authority to come to an agreement?
- Which of these people will be responsible for ensuring that what is agreed is implemented?
- Which people at the supplier's factory/office are to be the key contacts?
- What should our team comprise?
- Who is to lead?

Some general issues

- What are our strengths and weaknesses?
- What are those of the other party?
- What is the duration of the agreement to be negotiated?
- What published data are available?
- What is the current contractual position?
- By what date should agreement be reached?
- What are the major issues?
- What key assumptions have been made?
- What information do we need to verify those assumptions?

Having assembled and analysed the relevant information it is then necessary to:

1 set objectives for the coming negotiation(s);
2 develop strategies/tactics in order to achieve those objectives;
3 prepare relevant data for easy reference;
4 if more than one person is to be involved in the negotiation, to develop a method of working which is understood and agreed by all concerned;
5 make the necessary arrangements for the meeting phase.

■ Objectives

Meaningful objectives are essential to successful negotiating, yet the authors' experience in working in negotiating training over many years is that rarely are objectives meaningful and clearly defined. This failure has proved to be particularly damaging in team negotiations where ambiguity has led to confusion, the disruption of team solidarity or the failure of a particular tactical approach. It can help to write down the agreed objective(s) for the coming negotiation. If they have been properly thought through, they will be the culmination of the manager's appraisal of the situation in hand, and writing them down will serve to ensure that those involved know:

■ what is to be achieved; and
■ upon what assumptions those objectives have been based.

It is important to recognise that the objectives which are set will be based upon an assessment of the situation given existing information. If some of the information proves to be faulty, then it may be necessary to change the stated objectives and probably the methods by which they are to be achieved. This is why the introductory stage of the meeting phase is important; the negotiators should seek to verify at least the data upon which they have based their tactics and objectives. Our own experience confirms that of Karrass (1972) as to the way skilled negotiators develop objectives. They tend to set upper and lower limits to a derived target, rather than simply stating a single point. In addition they tend to have higher aspirations.

The reasons for this behaviour stem from the problems associated with the validity of information at the preparation stage, which were discussed earlier.

Since negotiators deal with a mixture of fact and assumption, they cannot *know* that an objective is valid at the pre-negotiation stage. Thus they provide themselves with a range within which they work. Karrass argues that this often enhances the aspiration levels of the negotiators. It also allows them to calculate the various implications of maximum and minimum positions in their preparation. The effects of movement in either direction can then be monitored more easily during the negotiation proper.

Best alternative to a negotiated agreement (BATNA) In 1982 a very important book on the subject of negotiation was published, entitled *Getting to Yes* and sub-titled *Negotiating Agreement Without Giving In*. The book is still in print, albeit in much expanded and revised form, and continues to be one of the better selling and more influential texts on its subject.

The authors, Roger Fisher and William Ury, were, at the time of the book's creation, associated with Harvard University.

One of the important concepts highlighted in this book is that of the BATNA. The authors explain that in a situation where the other side has more power than you do, it is unlikely that you will gain all you might hope from the negotiation. You are almost bound to make concessions of some kind. They explain that in response to power, the most that any approach to negotiation might achieve is that you do not make an agreement you later regret, and that you do make the most of any assets that you do have in order to satisfy your interests to as great a degree as possible.

The idea of the BATNA has gained wide attention, and is now routinely employed as a more appropriate basis for the determination of the walk-away position than the more traditional 'bottom line' approach. In other words, the use of a BATNA is a better way of deciding when to say 'no'. Quite often, negotiators will make a decision as to what the 'bottom line' figure is, based on a subjective assessment of the situation through personal perceptions of value or worth. This tendency might well be even stronger if a group of individuals are involved in planning the negotiation. A statement along the lines of 'I don't think it's worth paying more than $1000' might well be supported by another member of the team adding 'I agree, the bottom line should be less if anything'. In a sense these views indicate a sound view of negotiation. They are likely to lead to a stretching and measurable 'last resort' objective. However, 'bottom line' figures of this kind are not necessarily realistic or attainable. They tend to represent ambition and sentiment, and not analysis of true costs and benefits associated with the negotiation. The result is that negotiations are often concluded without agreement, even though the reality was that there was scope for an outcome of the 'win–win' kind. What happens is that one (or both) sides in the negotiation do not, in planning the negotiation, look at the true costs of the course of action that must be taken in the light of the absence of negotiated agreement. If the costs of the necessary course of action exceed those associated with a negotiable outcome, then some form of loss occurs.

So, the advice is 'know your BATNA'. Work out in advance what the most attractive course of action will be if you fail to make agreement in the negotiation. This might be a difficult and relatively expensive thing to do, but it should be done. If you do not know what the real BATNA is, then you cannot place any real value on what is 'on offer' in the negotiation. That is not to say, of course, that you should readily concede until you reach a situation where you are close to taking recourse to your BATNA. The BATNA represents the limit of your negotiation range, and as such you should, if possible, stay clear of this position. It is sometimes appropriate to devise and embody in your planning a 'tripwire' figure, some way short of your final BATNA position, to serve as a kind of warning that you are approaching your true limit.

Realistically, both parties to a negotiation are likely to have a BATNA position, and the scope for negotiation is the distance between the two positions.

Least acceptable agreement (LAA)

The concept of the least acceptable agreement (LAA) has some relevance when discussing the BATNA, as does the expression 'the bottom line'. Traditional negotiating practice and theory involves participants in deciding in advance the extent to which they will move. Obviously, there will be a point at which the negotiator can concede no more; it is in their best interest to say, one hopes politely, 'no deal' and to stop negotiating. The difference between the BATNA limit and these ideas is that applying BATNA thinking compels the negotiator to think outside the negotiation, and to really consider and quantify alternatives. The limit position has a meaning determined not by questions such as 'What is fair?' or 'What is desirable or attractive?' but by facts and analysis. Through BATNA we derive power, and we know when to say no.

Most favoured position (MFP) or most desired outcome (MDO)

It is a good idea to determine in the planning phase of negotiation what the ideal outcome would be. Realistically it is probable that a position falling short of this outcome will be achieved, but it is important to think carefully about this before bargaining. This analysis will be beneficial in determining the objectives in negotiation.

■ Issues

To conclude this section of the chapter, the important aspect of issues should be noted. In every negotiation there is a series of issues which needs to be resolved. The weight of these issues in the eyes of either party will depend upon a mixture of their perceptions as well as real pressures which are being applied. Thus, an understanding of what is at issue as perceived by the negotiator, and the negotiator's belief of what is accepted by the other party, are vital elements in preparation.

Rackham and Carlisle (1978), in illustrating how effective negotiators deal with issues which they perceive to be important, add a further element to this discussion. They note that skilled negotiators do not assume that they will be able to deal with issues in a sequential way according to their own plans. They see a propensity to plan around each issue in a manner which is independent of sequence. They argue that this approach provides the negotiator with greater flexibility. It also prevents the assumption that the other party will be prepared to deal with issues in the negotiator's preferred sequence. Thus it increases the options which emerge for consideration.

The introductory stage

Successful negotiators in the introductory stage (see Figure 10.3) tend to expend considerable effort in:

- Establishing an atmosphere conducive to agreement. This may include: social interchange; giving an impression of wishing to work to a mutually advantageous goal; the physical arrangements of the site; and restating the areas of agreement while avoiding irritators.

■ Validating assumptions.
■ Testing the other party's position, willingness to collaborate or propensity to oppose.
■ Clarifying issues and the weight given to them by the other party.
■ Trying to ascertain whether any new information will be introduced by the other party.

From our own experience, working with more than 7000 managers in small groups over the years, some prescriptive points may be made:

■ *Be on time.* Being late necessitates an apology, signals a lack of organisation and results in the negotiator having to go into the negotiation hurriedly.
■ *Emphasise the positive.* As suggested earlier, build from a base of known agreement, change 'but' to 'and' whenever qualifying a statement from the other party.
■ *Make brief opening statements.* Listen, and be seen to be listening, to the other party.
■ *Do not make quick decisions.*

In this, and indeed in all three stages of the meeting phase, the three skills used to the greatest effect by skilled negotiators are questioning, listening and observing.

Discussion stage

Most of the actual negotiation time after preparation is spent on the debate stage. At this stage we are, amongst other things, endeavouring to test our assumptions and find out what the other side wants.

In the course of the debate stage there will be discussion and argument. Ideally one should attempt to keep this as objective as possible. There are a number of important points to remember here:

■ Debate, while promoting the negotiation process, can also, if not handled correctly, hinder or deadlock deals.
■ You cannot negotiate arguments. No matter how often you argue and disagree with the other side it does not help move forward the negotiation. We would advocate making proposals to overcome arguments. In other words, suggest a solution that could overcome the problem.
■ Avoid destructive debate attacking/blaming the other side.
■ Regular summarising during this stage helps to avoid later confusion.
■ If the other side does not have an agenda, you could suggest one.
■ Try to establish a rapport quickly with the other side – watch for the signals or body language that are indicative of how the other side feels and wishes to proceed.

■ Bargaining

During discussions we move on to the bargaining stage. This is the point when we convey the specific terms on which we would settle; for example: 'If you reduce your price by 3 per cent we will increase our order by 10 per cent.' Both the condition and offer are specific. Even at this stage, however, offers might not be accepted; there could be problems that take the two sides back into the preparation stage.

■ Ploys in negotiation

During discussions negotiators will from time to time be faced with one side using a ploy or tactic to try to gain advantage over the other.

Roy Webb of Negotiate plc, one of the better known negotiating trainers in the UK, believes that such ploys are of limited value in long-term relationships. He comments as follows:

- All ploys have counters that a seasoned negotiator would be aware of.
- Reliance on ploys can often ruin a long-term relationship.
- Ploys, when recognised, can be disarmed.
- While a knowledge of ploys assists the negotiation, reliance on them exclusively should be avoided.

■ Examples of ploys

Nice guy/hard guy   You are faced by two people, one difficult to deal with and aggressive, the other softer and conciliatory. The idea is that you become so afraid of the 'hard guy' that you make concessions to the softer negotiator.

Add ons   Basic deal only is negotiated. Everything else costs more money.

Deadlines   Telling the other side the deal has to be completed by a certain time otherwise it is off, the idea being to pressurise the other side into making a quick rather than the correct decision.

Russian front   Two choices are offered, of which one is so bad that you choose the second, less awful, option.

Empty larder   Attempting to convince the other side by lying that you have little to offer so that they will reduce their demands.

Approval from a higher authority   Telling the other side that anything you agree to over a certain amount will also have to be agreed back at base, the idea being to get the other side to agree to deals that do not require approval from a higher authority.

These are some of a large number of ploys that are used in negotiations and for which you should be prepared.

Table 10.2
**Manipulative
techniques and
ploys**

Negotiation ploys	Methods of dealing with ploys
Nice guy/hard guy	Either match style or adopt contrast style
Add ons	Carefully check what you are getting for your money before agreement
Deadlines	Avoid revealing what time you have to finish. Agree to meet another time
Russian front	Do not accept poor deals. What is your best alternative to a negotiated agreement?
Empty larder	Ask for an explanation of any constraints in a deal. Offer what you can within those constraints
Approval from a higher authority	Establish opposite number's full authority before negotiation

As one moves, however, towards building up long-term relationships with suppliers there is far less reliance and indeed positive avoidance of such tactics in an effort to enhance a strategic relationship between buyer and supplier.

Professor Gavin Kennedy (1991) argues that all ploys can be neutralised by the other side provided they have the necessary experience. Table 10.2 gives examples to illustrate.

Agreement stage

If a bargain is accepted we have agreement and the negotiations are concluded. Once there is agreement it is advisable to record full details of what has been agreed and to circulate these details to interested parties.

The post-negotiation stage

The final stage in our model follows the negotiation itself. Like Rackham and Carlisle (1978), we have found that successful negotiators work to ensure that agreements are implemented. Less successful negotiators pay insufficient attention to this. It might be said that no negotiation is complete until what has been agreed is enacted.

Typically, skilled negotiators confirm with the other party what has been agreed. They also specify who is to do what, and by when, not only as between them and the other party, but also in their own organisation. Failure to perform will always have an adverse effect on relationships between the parties. It will, for example, result in a lack of trust or of belief in the other party's abilities or authority. Consequently, if there is another negotiation (and many buying transactions involve long-standing partners), this will have a bearing on the behaviour of both parties. The reader need only consider their own feelings at being let down on a delivery promise by a supplier. How should the next negotiation with that party be approached?

Our prescriptive guidelines for the post-negotiation phase include:

- Produce the first draft agreement. Despite the fact that you are reporting, honestly, what you believe to have been agreed, it will be your version, developed from your viewpoint. In addition, the other party will be freed from doing the initial draft – a fact which will be appreciated by most people. Clearly, the draft should be sent to the other party with a request for comments and agreement. A sound piece of work can do much for ongoing relationships.
- Ensure the commitment of people in your organisation to making the agreement work.
- Prepare official contracts in line with the agreement.
- Remember no negotiation is successful until what has been negotiated is done.
- Find time to evaluate performance, first in negotiation, and second in enactment.

Competition and co-operation in negotiation

When a negotiation takes place it is usually assumed that there is some conflict of interest between the parties involved. The logic stemming from this is that because of this conflict the parties involved will oppose each other in order to achieve their preferred ends. The word 'opponent' is then placed in a 'game' context where one side will 'win' over the other, and their gain will result from the other's loss. Yet the appeal of this thinking is bounded by a simplistic assumption that negotiation is a 'zero sum' process. That is, that there is a 'cake' of x units which is to be shared between the parties. In a buying context, for example, A wishes to sell to B 10,000 components at £x each, whereas B wishes to pay £x minus 10 per cent. An outcome in which B is obliged to pay £x for the items then places A as the 'winner'. However, the price of the components may be only one of the points at issue. For example, the rate of delivery, batch size and point of storage could all change the 'shape' of the cost package from the point of view of both parties. Thus, by examining the many variables involved, the negotiators might be able to arrive at a more creative solution in which both parties gain.

It is, of course, a moot point whether one side will gain more than the other even then, and in a strictly quantitative sense have a larger share of the perceived 'cake'; however, the psychological drive of a negotiator seeking (and being seen to be seeking) mutually advantageous solutions can be considerable. This does not imply that either side should be 'soft' with the other. Rather it suggests that they may each gain greater advantage by collaborating rather than competing. Figure 10.5 contrasts the 'zero sum' perspective with the collaborative approach.

It is reasonable to argue that in some circumstances it will be difficult, perhaps incorrect, to follow this approach. For example, the behaviour (past or

Figure 10.5
**Two views of the
negotiation process**

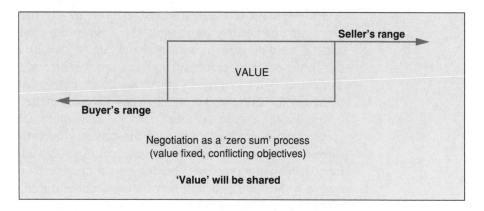

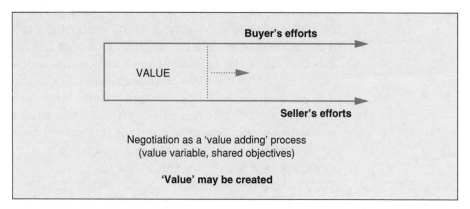

present) of the other party, or environmental pressures, may suggest more aggressive/competitive behaviour. However, it is worthwhile making a further point which may influence the negotiator's behaviour in such circumstances. Most major buyer–seller negotiations tend to result in longer-term relationships being developed or extended. Thus a 'win' for either party when circumstances favour their position will tend to the converse when, for example, the market position changes. Consequently, immediate benefits need to be weighed against those pertaining to the longer term, and to the level of motivation of both parties to perform against agreed norms. There is, too, the important issue of trust.

■ Zero sum or positive sum?

Most negotiations will include both elements that are adversarial and those that are collaborative. Remember that one of the definitions includes the words 'bargain' and 'confer'. Bargaining implies that both sides are seeking to maximise benefit for themselves. This will often require concessions to be made and received. Conferring means exchanging views, and has a rather more 'warm' feel to it than bargaining.

An important question to consider prior to any negotiation is, 'Is this a zero sum, or a positive sum negotiation?' A zero sum negotiation exists where there is a single issue to be negotiated, and a gain for one side represents a loss to the other. A frequently used example of the zero sum scenario is where two children are sharing an apple pie. If one child receives a bigger piece of pie, then the other gets a smaller one. Each allocation of value is to somebody's benefit, and to the other party's disadvantage. On the face of it, many commercial negotiations fall into the category of 'zero sum', meaning that there is no value other than the price paid or received. We are probably all familiar with the process of buying or selling a house or a used car. On the face of it these are zero sum negotiations, a pound into one side's pocket is a pound out of the other's. In reality, even these apparently straightforward negotiations can be turned into 'positive sum' exchanges, where some additional value is added. Imagine that you are buying a car, and you are anxious that it should be given a full mechanical service before you drive it. Imagine also that the seller is keen to keep the car for another week because the replacement does not arrive until then. The seller might reduce the price a bit if he can keep the car for a while, and you, the buyer, might pay a little more if it receives a service. There is potentially additional value in the negotiation if it can be discovered. If the seller keeps the car for a few days, and during that time has it serviced, he gets a better deal, and so do you. Part of the skill of the negotiator is in discovering this additional value.

Many negotiations between buyer and seller in the business context take place where there are complementary assets. Neither party can achieve what is desired without the other. Staying with apple pies: if one person in a block of flats has the ingredients and the skill as a cook to make pies, but no kitchen, and another has a kitchen but no materials or skill, then the implication is obvious. There are great benefits to be achieved through getting together and combining resources, which are of little value on their own. This is a classic positive sum scenario. Value is created or realised through negotiation. The apple pie example is an extreme one, but it is commonly the case that a commercial buyer needs the products or services of a particular supplier, and the supplier has, in turn, a strong need or desire to do business with that particular customer. They have complementary assets. In other words, the investments made by the seller in getting into business can only be realised with the involvement of the buyer. The buyer is in an equivalent, if opposite, position.

■ Positional bargaining or principled bargaining?

In their best-selling negotiation text *Getting to Yes*, Fisher and Ury discuss positional bargaining, which can be characterised as a process whereby the participants each adopt positions such as 'I want £1000 for this machine' or 'Your machine is not worth much more than £500'. And then an exchange takes place, each party talking then listening in turns and changing their

Table 10.3 **Principled bargaining contrasted with positional bargaining**	Positional bargaining: which game should you play?		Change the game: negotiate on the merits
	SOFT	HARD	PRINCIPLED
	Participants are friends	Participants are adversaries	Participants are problem solvers
	The goal is agreement	The goal is victory	The goal is a wise outcome reached efficiently and amicably
	Make concessions to cultivate the relationship	Demand concessions as a condition of the relationship	Separate the people from the problem
	Be soft on the people and the problem	Be hard on the problem and the people	Be soft on the people, hard on the problem
	Trust others	Distrust others	Proceed independent of trust
	Change your position easily	Dig in to your position	Focus on interests, not positions
	Make offers	Make threats	Explore interests
	Disclose your bottom line	Mislead as to your bottom line	Avoid having a bottom line
	Accept one-sided losses to reach agreement	Demand one-sided gains as the price of agreement	Invent options for mutual gain
	Search for the single answer: the one *they* will accept	Search for the single answer: the one you will accept	Develop multiple options to choose from; decide later
	Insist on agreement	Insist on your position	Insist on using objective criteria
	Try to avoid a contest of will	Try to win a contest of will	Try to reach a result based on standards independent of will
	Yield to pressure	Apply pressure	Reason and be open to reason; yield to principle, not pressure

(*Source*: Fisher and Ury, 1982)

position somewhat. Agreement might ensue; it might not. A danger is that the parties will entrench themselves, so that no further movement is easily possible, even though it might be desirable.

Positional bargaining can be undertaken by using a 'soft' or a 'hard' style, although it is argued that whichever style is used the approach has many disadvantages. Fisher and Ury advocate 'principled' bargaining. The ideas underpinning this approach are given in Table 10.3.

Body language

While over the centuries people have become more articulate, they have also developed an ability to hide how they really feel in situations. Thus as negotiators you may consider that the other side is being honest and open, but this may not be true. Although you may feel the other side is happy, this also may not be the case.

As a negotiator you must watch for the body language. No matter what people *say*, how they really *feel* can often be picked up from their body positions and gestures during the negotiations. It is not our intention in this

Table 10.4
The interpretation of postures

Posture	Possible meaning
Leaning forward when making a point	Interested; wants to emphasise a point
Avoiding eye contact	May be embarrassed; not telling the truth
Arms folded; body turned away from you	Defensive; no compromise. Not interested
Body turned towards you leaning forward	Interested; warming towards your comments
Looking away at watch or at a window	Wants to leave or avoid any further discussion
Hands supporting head and leaning back in chair	Confidence
Stroking nose regularly with a finger – avoiding eye contact	May be lying
Good eye contact; fingers stroking face	Interested in what you are saying

general text to go into any great detail in this area but Table 10.4 lists a number of postures and what they might indicate.

One should, of course, be very careful in interpreting body language. You can get it wrong. Experienced negotiators, however, over a period of time get to understand the body language of the other side, which can contribute to increased effectiveness. A good negotiator must also be attuned to the way people answer and ask questions. From the other side's tone you can quickly pick up signals such as anger, impatience, annoyance and agreement.

Negotiation strategies

How buyers negotiate with suppliers will be affected by their long-term interests. In the case of long-term strategic suppliers it is far more likely they will consider their negotiating approach in terms of:

- How it will affect future negotiations – e.g. a short-term manipulative or tactical strategy at the supplier's expense could jeopardise a long-term partnership agreement.
- Developing a supplier – a major buying organisation may well make considerable concessions to influence suppliers in order to encourage their development. However, with other suppliers a more aggressive negotiation stance may be taken.
- Reducing the supplier base – the preferred supplier may be given totally different treatment from others.

Negotiation mix

As you will now begin to appreciate, negotiations can take on different styles e.g. aggressive, assertive or submissive, or may be dominated by a manipulative as opposed to an assertive phased approach. During the negotiations body language will be studied. One cannot say definitely which is the best way to negotiate or which is the best style, much will depend on existing relationships and objectives. It is, however, argued by experienced negotiators that a purely short-term manipulative approach to negotiations based on *I win – you lose* leads to long-term problems. These days, particularly with a view to longer-term negotiation objectives, one finds a move towards more of a *win–win* approach based on trading wants and using a phased approach to reach a settlement.

Conclusion

Early in this chapter, three criteria to differentiate the successful negotiator were introduced. In conclusion, we put forward a more comprehensive list, which itself is far from definitive. Negotiation is a complex, fascinating subject which, since it involves people, contains many variables. This list and the related discussion are meant only to indicate the areas which we and other writers have noted as pertaining to successful negotiation. Those who negotiate successfully:

- Plan well.
- Can deal with pressure.
- Listen well.
- Understand people well.
- Observe well.
- Can handle confrontation.
- Have sound business judgement.
- Avoid excesses.
- Are creative thinkers.
- Are committed to their cause once established.
- Are skilled at dealing with risk.
- Are skilled at asking questions.
- Have higher aspirations.
- Can handle time effectively.

Finally, we complete this chapter with some practical hints derived from the experiences of major negotiators:

- Negotiation is concerned with trading not conceding.
- Always trade something for something.
- Remember if you help me, then I'll help you.
- Attempt to educate the other side by putting a price on their demands.
- Listen to what they say.
- Avoid interrupting a proposal.
- Entry terms can influence the other side's expectations, therefore open credibly, trade concessions and do not fear deadlock.

- Good preparation is a must for successful negotiations.
- Don't tell lies, but there is no need to tell the other side about things that will give them an advantage.
- Avoid too many arguments, remember only proposals can be negotiated.
- Remember which phase you are in and act appropriately.
- Avoid sarcasm, blaming or point scoring.
- Agree an agenda.
- Avoid accepting the first offer.
- Test assumptions.
- Do not change the price, change the deal.
- Find out your best alternative to a negotiated agreement. It helps you to decide whether to agree or walk away.
- Value every 'tradable' in the other negotiator's terms.
- Identify your strategic objectives.
- Use ploys carefully and in a limited way. Remember if the other side feels on reflection after the negotiations that they have got a bad deal it may ruin future deals.
- At the end of negotiations write down what has been agreed and show it to the other side for approval.

Mini case study

A UK engineering group received a price increase notification from a key US supplier. It was felt that this was possibly unjustified. Working with a local university, the buying company studied the economics of the situation fully, and also paid attention to the practice of negotiation, including the use of role-playing exercises to sharpen skills. Thus prepared, the buying team met with representatives of the US supplier and achieved, instead of the sought increase in prices, an actual price reduction.

Summary

1 Negotiation may not always be the appropriate way to reach an agreement – persuasion, complete acceptance, coercion or problem solving may prove sound alternatives.

2 The authors outline three broad phases in the negotiation process: *preparatory* – analysing information, setting of objectives, and developing strategies; *meeting* – introductions, clarification and the reaching of an agreement, and *final* – implementation of the agreement.

3 The chapter emphasises the importance of pre-negotiation preparation – evaluating the objectives, entry and exit points.

4 A skilled negotiator considers a wide range of options; gives a great deal of attention to common ground aspects; is flexible dealing with issues as they arise. They confirm what has been agreed in a 'first draft' agreement which is then confirmed/commented upon by the other party.

5 Negotiation style depends on the objective to be achieved – short-term gain may use an aggressive, assertive style. This approach tends to lead to long-term problems. A longer term 'win–win' approach based on trading wants is far more likely to reap reward – while one party may concede on price, it may be gaining on delivery or payment terms.

References and further reading

Beasor, T and Steele, P (1999), *Business Negotiations*, Aldershot: Gower.

Crampton, P C *et al.* (2002), 'Promoting honesty in negotiation', *Journal of Business Ethics*.

Fisher, R and Ury, W (1982), *Getting to Yes: Negotiating Agreement Without Giving In*, New York: Penguin.

Fortganf, F *et al.* (2002), 'Negotiating the spirit of the deal', *Harvard Business Review*, February.

Johnson, R (2000), 'Body talk', *Supply Management*, November.

Karrass, C L (1972), *The Negotiating Game*, New York: World Books.

Kennedy, G (1991), *Everything is Negotiable*, London: Arrow Books.

Nielson, R P (1990), 'Generic win–win negotiating solutions', *Long Range Planning*, 22 (5).

Pease, A (1993), *Body Language*, New York: Sheldon Press.

Rackham, N and Carlisle, J (1978), 'The effective negotiator, parts I and II', *Journal of European Industrial Training*, 2 (6 and 7).

Roberts, G (2000), 'Striking accord', *Supply Management*, December.

Spector, B I (1977), 'Negotiation as a psychological process', *Journal of Conflict Resolution*, 21 (4).

Part 3

Applications

Chapter 11   Project procurement

Chapter 12   Procurement of commodities

Chapter 13   International and global sourcing

Chapter 14   Capital procurement

Chapter 15   Retail procurement and efficient consumer response (ECR)

Chapter 16   Services procurement

Chapter 17   Corporate social responsibility

11

Project procurement

Introduction

This chapter will explore the characteristics of projects and project procurement, identifying the range of approaches in project contracting and procurement. It will indicate how procurement can contribute to meeting the project's objectives. Comparisons will be made between differing approaches using recent examples of the Scottish Parliament Building, Wembley Stadium and the project for the construction of the Terminal 5 building at Heathrow Airport in London.

Objectives of this chapter

- To outline the key features of projects
- To understand how procurement adds value in project management
- To examine various success factors and how these impact on the procurement activity
- To examine the issues of project planning
- To appreciate the importance of procurement within project control
- To consider the various types of contract for major projects such as Wembley football stadium and the Terminal 5 Building at Heathrow Airport
- To appreciate the issues involved in subcontracting
- To outline network analysis

Introduction to projects

A project is a set of activities which:

- Has a defined start point.
- Has a defined end state.
- Pursues a defined goal.
- Uses a defined set of resources.

■ All projects have common elements

- An objective – definable end result, output or product.
- Complexity – large number of different tasks.
- Uniqueness – projects are usually 'one-offs'.
- Uncertainty – projects are planned before they are executed, hence they carry an element of risk.
- Temporary nature – defined beginning and end.
- Life cycle – resources needs change during the life of the project.

Projects can be categorised according to:

1 Their complexity – in terms of size, value and the number of people involved in the project. Complex projects are not necessarily difficult to plan, but they can be difficult to control because of the large number of activities they involve.
2 Their uncertainty – in terms of achieving the project objectives of cost, time and quality. Uncertainty makes projects difficult to plan because it makes it difficult to define and set realistic objectives.
3 Project management is the process of managing the activities within a project by planning the work, executing it and co-ordinating the contribution of the staff and organisations that have an interest in the project.

Successful project management depends upon various factors:

- Clearly defined goals.
- Competent project manager.
- Top management support.
- Competent project team members.
- Sufficient resource allocation.
- Adequate communication.
- Control mechanisms.
- Feedback capabilities.
- Responsiveness to clients.
- Trouble shooting mechanisms.
- Project staff continuity.

Project management and control consists of five stages:

1 Understanding the project environment – the internal and external factors which may influence the project. Procurement has a vital contribution in terms of knowledge of the marketplace and risk management.
2 Defining the project – setting the objectives, scope and strategy for the project.
3 Project planning – deciding how the project will be executed. This involves five stages.
   - Identifying the activities within a project – work breakdown structure. The work project breakdown structure helps as projects are often too

complex to be controlled unless they are broken down into manageable portions. This is done by building a family tree which specifies the major tasks or sub-projects. Once this top level family tree has been built, the major tasks are subdivided until a manageable 'work package' is ultimately defined. Once defined each work package is allocated its own objectives in terms of time, cost and quality.

- Estimating times and resources for activities – essential to monitor contactor's progress.
- Identifying the relationships and dependencies between the activities – network analysis.
- Identifying the schedule constraints – resources and time.
- Fixing the schedule.

4 Technical execution – performing the technical aspects of the project.

5 Project control – ensuring the project is carried out according to the plan.

These stages are iterative, rather than sequential.

Project planning

Project planning is particularly important where complexity of the project is high. The interrelationship between activities, resources and times in most projects, especially complex ones, is such that unless they are carefully planned, resources can become seriously overloaded at times during the operation. The involvement of procurement throughout is imperative as indicated by the mini case studies in this chapter.

What techniques can be used for project planning

Network planning and Gantt charts are the most common techniques. The former is particularly useful for assessing the total duration of a project and the degree of flexibility or float of the individual activities within the project. The most common method of network planning is called Critical Path Method (CPM). The logic inherent in a network diagram can be changed by resource constraints. Network planning models can also be used to assess the total cost of shortening a project where individual activities are shortened.

What is project control and how is it done?

The process of project control involves three sets of decisions:

- How to monitor the project – check its progress.
- How to assess the performance of the project by comparing monitored progress to the project plan.
- How to intervene in the project in order to make the changes to bring it back to plan.

Earned value control assesses the performance of the project by combining cost and time together. It involves plotting the actual expenditure on the project against the value of the work completed, both in the form of what was planned and what is actually happening. Both cost and schedule variances can then be detected.

Project control

It is essential to monitor the project in order to check on its progress. The main objectives of any project are usually defined in terms of cost, quality and time. Hence these are the things that need to be measured. In the case studies in this chapter the level of control varied and contributed to massive cost and time overruns.

■ How to assess the performance of the project by comparing progress with the project plan

Time can be monitored by comparing progress to plan. The planned times can be found on the project schedule.

Expected costs can also be estimated using the schedule. Normally few activities can be started immediately as most are dependent on other activities being completed. As the project progresses, more and more activities can be started. Then, towards the end of the project, fewer and fewer activities remain to be undertaken.

■ Project management via earned value

The concept of 'earned value' can be very useful in controlling large, expensive projects.

What is earned value (EV)?

The simplest way to think of EV is to equate it with physical progress. As the term implies, it is gained through some effort. In project management, this value is earned as activities are completed. EV is also a measure of progress and has three main attributes.

■ It is a common and consistent unit of measurement for progress on a project or any sub-element of the project.
■ It provides a consistent technique for analysis of project performance.
■ It forms a basis for comparing cost performance across projects or sub-elements.

EV uses the units of time and money. It provides the basis for cost performance analysis. It is necessary to know the planned cost at any time and the cost of work completed to date.

How is EV used? There are four steps to the setting up of an EV control system for a project and four steps in its subsequent use. To set up the EV system:

1 Establish a work breakdown structure (WBS) that divides the project into its component activities (or simply into manageable portions).
2 Estimate and allocate a cost to each activity.
3 Schedule the activities over time.
4 Construct a schedule for the overall project to confirm that the plan is acceptable.

To use EV as a control process:

1 Calculate how much physical or intellectual work has been scheduled to be completed as the point of measurement. What was the budgeted value of the work scheduled?
2 Calculate how much of the scheduled work has actually been accomplished. What is the budgeted value of the work actually performed?
3 Calculate the costs which have actually been spent and/or incurred.
4 Finally calculate the 'schedule variance' which in earned value is the difference between our planned value scheduled and our earned value achieved, and the 'cost variances'.

Earned value Rather than measuring progress in terms of days of work completed, earned value control measures the value of work done. There are three important measures associated with earned value control.

- The budgeted cost of work scheduled (BCWS) – this is the amount of work which should have been completed by a particular time.
- The budgeted cost of work performed (BCWP) – this is the actual amount of work which has been completed by a particular time.
- The actual cost of work performed (ACWP) – this is the actual expenditure which has been incurred as a result of the work completed by a particular time.

From these three measures, two variances which indicate deviation from plan can be calculated:

- Schedule variance (SV) = BCWP minus BCWS.
- Cost variance (CV) = BCWP minus ACWP.

It is essential to intervene in the project in order to make the changes which will bring it back to plan. When intervening in the project it is important to be aware of interactions, and/or the knock-on effects of any interactions. Figure 11.1 outlines earned value.

For partnering to be successful, it must be based on a sound contract and both parties must understand their responsibilities.

Valid claims at the end of the contract should be a thing of the past. For this to happen, the contract needs to provide for the contractor to be able to request a variation. The monthly reporting procedure also needs to provide for

Figure 11.1
Earned value

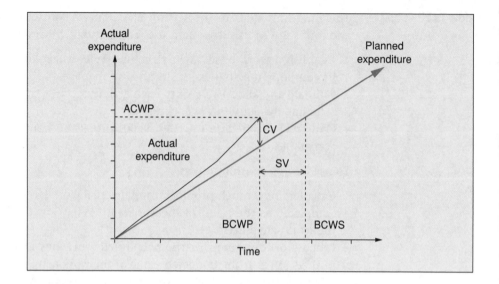

the contractor to keep the client informed of the cost of any variations that have not been approved. With this procedure, valid claims at the end of the contract should only result from the client's refusal to recognise the validity of the contractor's request for a variation at the time of the event. Therefore, the contract must establish a recognised 'variation to contract form'.

These techniques should not be regarded as being solely preventative measures and should encourage co-operation and assist in sustaining a partnering relationship.

■ Administration instructions

The use of administration instructions should be one of the key elements in claims avoidance strategy. The contract should require the contractor to provide a monthly report that addresses predetermined issues including;

- highlights – problems, solutions, key events;
- volumes to date and forecast;
- financial information – variations priced and agreed, the estimated value of variations issued but not agreed and, crucially, the estimated value of requested variations considered to be outstanding;
- performance – in line with the basis of reporting stated in the contract;
- resource information;
- health and safety information.

It is difficult for the contractor to make a claim at the end of the contract if no relevant mention has been made in the monthly report during the contract. However, if concerns are raised and the client has not taken appropriate action, the monthly report will be used in support of the claim.

The correct use of the monthly report and monthly meetings, together with the prompt issuing of variations, goes a long way to reducing the need for endless point scoring correspondence. The mini case study of the Scottish Parliament demonstrates how projects which are not effectively managed can result in the original project objectives of time and cost vastly exceeding budget.

Mini case study – Scottish Parliament: the £431m question

Scotland's new parliament building cost more than 10 times the original estimate and opened three years behind schedule.

Official cost estimates changed 10 times and ballooned from the initial £40 million estimate to a final £431 million.

The procurement model chosen for Holyrood in early 1998 has emerged as the root of the problem. A fast-track contracting method known as construction management was used to build the parliament. It works by splitting a large building job into numerous smaller packages that are designed, tendered and let independently of one another.

Its main advantage is to speed up construction, because the overall design does not have to be complete before basic building work can begin.

It does not allow a client to know the total cost of a project until well after work has begun. It is considered risky for the client, which is responsible for running each individual package – in this case more than 60.

The project cost escalated from about £40 million in 1997 to £109 million in 1999, £241 million in 2001 and £294 million in 2002, and finally £431 million in February 2004.

There were 18,000 design change orders over the five years of construction, combining to form a three-year delay. Requests for design freezes on three occasions were ignored.

The reality is that construction management was the only contract option for a client wanting to make an early start on a project that was still at the design concept stage.

It is also clear that this was a classic case of procurement expertise being bypassed. The procurement department at the Scottish Office was not involved in the project. It was not consulted over the procurement model.

There is nothing wrong with construction management as a procurement route. It is best suited to high quality, potentially high cost projects, where the client is fully engaged, has a clear goal and works closely with the supply side team.

Some estimates put the money lost to delays and backtracking over design changes at as much as £100 million. If one trade contractor has a problem, it tends to ripple through all the others and cause delay and changes. The contracts are with the client, so the client picks up the cost of that.

However, between the extremes of fixed speedy construction management, a host of options exist under the heading of 'conventional' procurement. Their structures affect the risk and control over the final design that falls to the client.

The 'design and build' route would have seen the project management team drawing up a detailed design brief, which the main contractor then builds. It leaves the contractor footing the bill for cost overruns, but freezes the design as well.

A middle-of-the-road option, prime contracting, keeps design more open, but cuts the risk of costs going up if things go wrong. This is because a contractor joins the client's project management team, and brings its entire supply chain of proven builders and suppliers along.

Then there is management contracting, where the client retains the design brief fully and splits up the project into small packages to be individually let, as in construction management. However, a professional intermediary runs all of the contractors on a daily basis, although they are still contracted to the client, which pays for design alterations.

Management contracting may, it seems, have given a more stable framework to the project by introducing an industry expert to run the many contractors.

Construction management was not the most suitable procurement vehicle. Sir Michael Latham, whose influential 1994 report, 'Constructing the Team', called on the construction industry to move towards partnering in the supply chain, says that full partnering should have been used to share the risk between client and contractor.

The following case study examines the project to build the new Wembley stadium in the UK. It is a prime example of adversarial procurement and project management which Latham was recommending should be replaced by a partnering approach.

Mini case study – Wembley Stadium

The completion of the £757 million Wembley stadium project faced many delays after claims by main contractor Multiplex that client Wembley National Stadium Ltd (WNSL) had not begun some of the works required to achieve practical completion.

The delays by WNSL meant that Multiplex was unable to sign off the works for approval and reach practical completion.

Wembley Stadium firmly rejected Multiplex's statement and refuted any claims made against them.

WNSL appeared to blame Multiplex 100 per cent for the delays.

Multiplex strongly disputed the claims and replied that design changes from the client were partly to blame.

Multiplex believed that the changes justified an extension of time.

Terminal 5 London Heathrow

Stage one of the new £4.2 billion fifth terminal at London Heathrow Airport opens in 2008 and will boost Heathrow's passenger capacity by around 50 per cent to more than 90 million annually. Unlike so many comparable high-profile construction projects, however, T5 is on time and to budget. In a sector where huge delays and vast overspends are commonplace (the recently opened £40 million Scottish Parliament building was years late and cost 10 times the original estimate), this is uncommon.

Suppliers were partners and were involved at a much earlier stage than is normally the case; usually there is a complete break between the consultants who design and the contractors who build – there is no meeting of minds.

'By integrating the design-and-build processes with their requirements, BAA, the British airports authority, have avoided any adversarial approach . . . BAA's new way of working is the contract which tells them what to do to make things go right.' Perhaps the most singular aspect of it is the fact that BAA shoulders all the risk. It is a bold move that runs counter to standard procedure – partnership deals usually involve shared risk – but has worked. Freed of concerns over who takes all the risk, contractors can concentrate instead on doing a quality job.

This document is called the T5 Agreement. Instead of concentrating on apportioning blame and compensation after problems arise, the T5 Agreement aims instead to encourage effective co-operation. The contractors have elected to work in partnership, using the same offices, sharing information and resources, and, crucially, any savings or overruns. Contractors are paid on a cost-reimbursable basis, with performance encouraged by offering bonuses for beating target costs and completion dates.

It is a more proactive approach, working together with their contractors and solving the problem rather than apportioning the blame. Suppliers work as part of an integrated team to mitigate potential risk and drive exceptional achievement.

The contract actually states that they want different behaviours. Basically they behave with their suppliers as they would want them to behave with them, and create a problem-solving environment rather than a blame culture.

The whole T5 strategy has been distilled into four statements: to build T5 on time, on budget, to high quality standards and to do it all safely.

'The Contract'

The T5 Agreement is BAA's response to a project whose sheer size and complexity defy traditional construction management techniques. Legally binding, in essence it is a contract in reverse. Instead of specifying what redress can be taken in the event of things going wrong, it aims to stop problems happening in the first place. This is done by fostering constructive behaviour and a recrimination-free environment. Key features include:

Ownership of risk

In contrast to most so-called partnership deals, risk is not shared between client and contractors. BAA carries it all, allowing contractors to concentrate on delivering results. The focus is on managing out the cause of problems, not their effects if they do happen.

Complexity management

The task of building T5 is split into 16 main projects, plus 147 sub-projects of between £30 million and £150 million each. The agreement binds BAA and its 60 key first-tier suppliers only, these suppliers are themselves responsible for the appointment and management of second- and third-tier suppliers, who must also work within the spirit of the agreement.

Close supplier involvement

To avoid the traditional and potentially damaging demarcation between design and build, key suppliers were brought on board at a much earlier stage in the planning process than is usual. This enabled potential hitches to be spotted before designs were finalised and construction began.

Integrated teamwork

Both within and across teams, the concentration has been on proactive problem solving rather than the avoidance of litigation.

Shared values

Common induction programmes and regular communication initiatives help to ensure that all of the 6000 workers from 400 supplier companies who can be involved at any given time share the same values and objectives, which include being proud of working on T5 and delivering the project on time, on budget, to quality and safely.

There are two key innovations. This first is an 'incentive fund' which aims to provide a financial reward for getting things right in the first place. If time and cost targets are met, the fund is divided between the suppliers involved, so it is in everyone's interests to work together to solve problems before they start costing money. Conversely, if a supplier fails to perform, everyone suffers because the incentive fund pays out to put things right and there is less at the end of the day for the suppliers to share.

> Second, the working arrangements have been structured to encourage co-operation between suppliers. Suppliers work together to targets agreed with the client.
>
> A further benefit of the co-operation at the heart of the project is that it gives suppliers opportunities to work together to reduce costs through aggregated spending. Low voltage electrical switchgear, for example, which would normally have cost about £22 million, ended up at £15 million. Lighting came in at £9.5 million against the £12 million it would have cost if bought separately by several suppliers. Typically, savings were 10–20 per cent.
>
> BAA fundamentally changed the relationship between clients and suppliers.

One of the key critical success factors in project procurement is the effective management of subcontractors.

Subcontracting

Organisations of all kinds subcontract aspects of their activity, and subcontracting is often viewed as a means of augmenting limited resources and skills while enabling the contractor to concentrate on their main area of expertise. A main contractor in project engineering normally assigns part of the contract work to subcontractors, who are legally responsible to the contractor rather than the client even when the client has stipulated which subcontractor is to be used. The specialised subcontractor is better positioned to secure and maintain a grip at the leading edge of technological change and innovation (see Figure 11.2).

■ Selecting a subcontractor

Key questions in major subcontractor selection include:

- What is the company's major specialisation? For example, are they general machinists, or are they capable of working to close tolerances?
- For whom have they worked? How long have they worked for these companies?
- What part of their capacity is on subcontract work? Can it be established whether the resources allocated to subcontracting will fluctuate in accordance with other sales?
- What is their capacity in terms of plant and output devoted to subcontract work?
- Have they a permanent and well-trained labour force?
- Are their quality-control procedures adequate?
- Are their engineering standards, procedures and controls adequate? How reliable is their forecast of availability of capacity?
- Are their production-control procedures adequate?
- Are they adequately financed?
- What is the state of their order book, current and projected?

Figure 11.2
Subcontracting

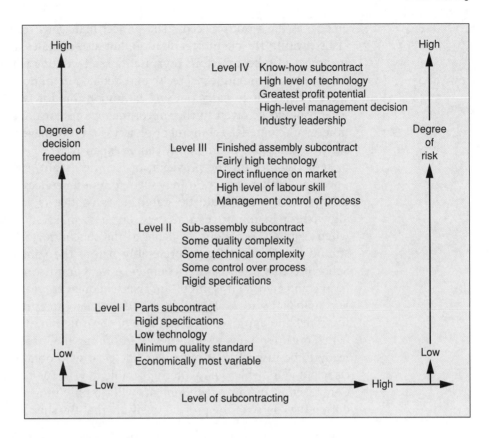

- If tooling is required, can they make the tools themselves?
- Do they own their own transport? Is it reliable? If they use a carrier, which will be used? Is it reliable?
- In higher levels of subcontracting, does the company itself employ subcontractors?
- What tools and skills are required for the contract?
- What tools will be provided by the subcontractor?

Construction projects are often very complex in nature and the contractual arrangements usually reflect and amplify the complexity. A very complex construction project is often divided into phases which represent the major categories of work; for example, phase one would be ground preparation and foundations, and so on. The client may appoint one main contractor for the project or one for each phase. Sometimes the client nominates a particular subcontractor to complete one element of the project; in other cases the client issues a list of approved subcontractors. If the contractor seeks to appoint a subcontractor not included on the approved list, they will need to obtain the approval of the client. The client will appoint a project manager to supervise the project to ensure timely completion to cost and specification. Large-scale construction projects are notoriously difficult to manage. In spite of careful preliminary investigation and planning, many exigencies often emerge as the work proceeds. The project manager's team incorporates specialists within the client organisation, but also includes members of the contractor's and subcontractor's organisations, all working within a common aim of completing the project. Precise and detailed definition of the work which the contractor is to carry out and be responsible for is necessary. Particular regard should be given to the subcontractor's responsibility for making good other work, materials, equipment or access ways damaged in carrying out the services; omissions or ambiguity can be expensive.

Responsibility for the provision of facilities, plant, storage and receiving, power and other services (often such common services are provided by the main contractor) should be stated. If assistance is given, this should be allowed for in the price, and steps taken to make such facilities available when required. Locations available to the subcontractor for storage or work should be clearly defined, preferably before the subcontract is awarded. Subcontractors often cannot commence work until some previous stage has been completed, so it is important that schedules are realistic (part of the project manager's role). If building and civil engineering work needs to be inspected and approved in the course of construction, it should be laid down which organisation is responsible for informing the inspector that the work is ready to be inspected. It must be made clear who obtains the permission to carry out work which may interrupt traffic flow or the passage of pedestrians. Care taken in defining requirements will simplify supervision and inspection during the course of the project, to ensure that the subcontractor:

- works in accordance with the specification as regards materials and practice;
- does not use any material, equipment or facility without authority;
- observes safety regulations; and
- makes progress in accordance with the negotiated time and leaves the site or workplace cleared or ready for the next stage.

It is important to define the subcontractor's liability for damage to persons and property. The extent to which the main contractor is indemnified in respect of claims must be stated. Care must be taken that the main contractor's insurance policy provides adequate cover for the subcontract operation, particularly as regards third party liability. Careful records should be kept by all parties in relation to activities on site covering relevant factors such as: interruption of works – duration and reasons; exceptional weather conditions; hazardous occurrences; variations to the contract. These records may prove valuable in respect of a dispute or variations claim for additional payment.

Network analysis

A group of techniques known as network analysis is often used to assist in the planning and control of certain types of project. Essentially, these are ways to organise and present certain information, such as what activities constitute the project, how these activities are related logically, their duration and cost, and the demand they make on resources. Critical path analysis is the network analysis technique which determines minimum project duration, and this is the one we shall consider.

This technique can be applied to any collection of related activities which has a definite beginning and a definite end. In the classroom, for purposes of explanation, it can be applied to such simple 'projects' as making a cup of tea or dressing in the morning. In the real world, it is applied only to complicated projects, for example:

- constructing and equipping a new factory;
- launching a new product;
- setting up a new department;
- building and civil engineering contracts, for example, a new motorway, a new department store, a new town;
- major overhaul of a chemical plant or a blast furnace.

The word 'new' occurs frequently in these examples. Network analysis has notched up most of its successes on new projects rather than on the replanning of operations which have been carried out for a considerable time. One of the first successful applications to be described was, in fact, a very large-scale procurement project which was in several ways unprecedented. This was the design, development, construction, equipping, staffing and getting into operation of the first fleet of nuclear submarines armed with Polaris missiles by the United States navy. Much as the existence of these frightful weapons may be deplored, and still more their proliferation, a detached view can still be taken of the way this gigantic project was planned and controlled. It was actually completed ahead of time.

Network analysis calls for the production of a visual representation of the project in the form of a network of arrows which show the activities. Consecutive arrows stand for activities which must be carried out in sequence; parallel ones show activities which can be carried out simultaneously. Following this, the calculation of timing and, for certain applications, such other matters as cost, resource allocation, etc. is done. This part can be handled on a computer.

The following are the usual steps in the preparation of a critical path analysis of a project:

1 List the activities or jobs which have to be done to complete the project. Careful thought is needed as to what has to be done and how best to do it. A decision is also needed as to the level of detail to be shown. (Sometimes an outline network is prepared for top management, with detailed networks for operational use.)

2 Sketch a rough arrow diagram on rough paper or a blackboard. For each activity ask: Which activities must be completed before this starts? Which ones cannot start until this is complete? Arrows start and finish in junction

points shown as circles or ellipses and known as nodes or events. Every activity shown by an arrow going into an event must be complete before any activity shown by an arrow coming out of that event can start. Consequently an event is defined as: 'A state in the progress of a project after the completion of all preceding activities but before the start of any succeeding activity.'

3 Find out how long each activity will take to complete and write its duration on the diagram.

4 Time the network, determining minimum project duration and critical path.

5 Re-draw the network, producing a neat version for circulation. Avoid crossed arrows and backward pointing arrows if possible. Earliest and latest dates can be shown in the event circles, which should also be numbered.

6 Re-plan if necessary to speed things up or to balance the use of scarce resources.

We illustrate this by the following example.

■ Project X: example of critical path analysis

An order has been received to make a batch of equipment. This involves preparation of detailed drawings and works orders, buying out parts and materials, machining components, assembling, testing and shipping. Activities involved and their durations in weeks are:

Detailed drawings and works order	3
Purchase castings	5
Purchase forgings	6
Purchase assembly parts	2
Purchase crates and packing	4
Draw bar stock from stores	0.2
Machine castings	3
Machine forgings	3
Machine bar	1
Assemble	2
Test	1
Pack and ship	

Questions

1 Draw the network for the above.

2 If start time is week 0, what is the latest time at which castings could be issued for machining if the whole batch is to be completed on time?

3 In week 6 a serious fire at the crate manufacturer's works destroys work in progress and means the procurement department have to find a new source for the crates. How much time have they got to get the crates in?

4 Draw a Gantt or other bar chart for the events and activities on the network.

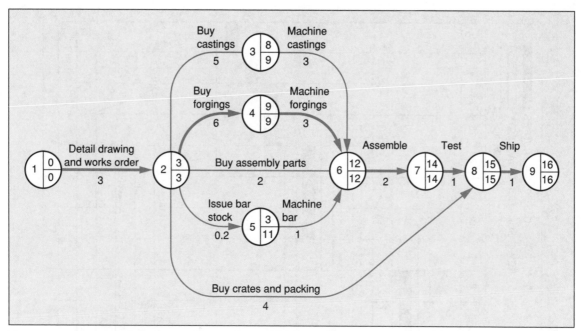

Figure 11.3 Arrow diagram for project X

Solution

Figure 11.3 shows the diagram as it exists on completion of step 5. The initial activity, preparation of detailed drawings and works order, is shown by the first arrow, referred to as 1–2 because it connects event number 1 to event number 2. On completion of this activity, a number of others can be started: activities 2–3, 2–4, 2–5, 2–6 and 2–8. Event 9 is the completion of the whole project.

Conventionally, the start date is at first shown as time 0. Since the first activity, 1–2, has a duration of 3 weeks, the earliest date for event 2, that is to say the earliest date at which activities 2–3, 2–4, 2–5, 2–6 and 2–8 can start, is the end of week 3, and this is shown in the top right-hand quadrant of the circle known as event 2. Since activity 2–4 cannot start until week 3, and has a duration of 6 weeks the earliest date for event 4 is 3 + 6, that is, the end of week 9, as shown in the top right-hand quadrant of the corresponding event circle. Proceeding in this fashion we reach event 9 and find the project minimum duration to be 16 weeks.

In most cases, the minimum duration is also the maximum duration since completion is required as soon as possible. We have found the earliest date for event 9 to be week 16; we now say that this is also the latest date for event 9. The latest date is written in the lower right-hand quadrant. Activity 8–9 has a duration of 1 week. Since the latest date for its completion is week 16, the latest start date for it is week 15, which therefore becomes the latest completion date for event 8.

The critical path is the sequence of activities which determines minimum project duration because its total duration is longer than that of any other sequence of activities in the network. Here it is activities 1–2, 2–4, 4–6, 6–7,

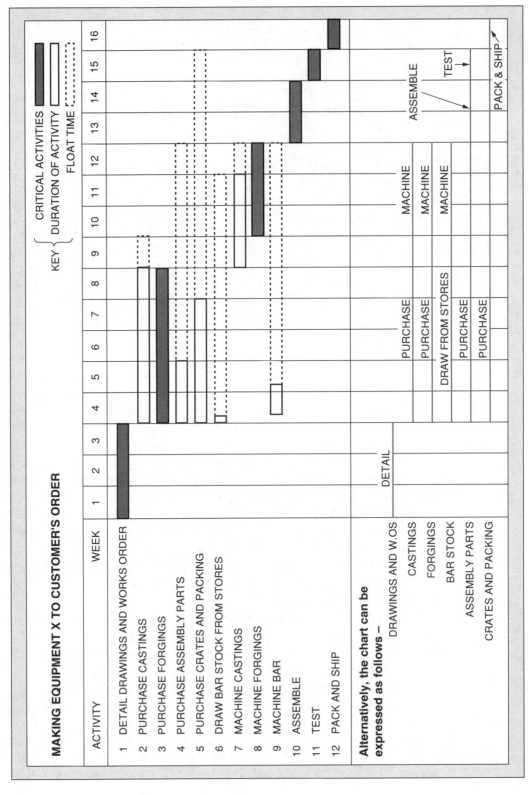

Figure 11.4 Bar charts for project X

7–8 and 8–9. In all the events on this sequence, earliest date is the same as latest date, and the duration of each activity in the sequence is the same as the difference between dates for predecessor and successor events. The critical path is marked out by a heavy line.

Some activities, however, are not on the critical path, for instance 2–3 and 3–6 which have a week of 'slack' or spare time between them. In answer to question 2, we can therefore say that the latest date at which castings could be issued for machining is week 9, as shown in the lower right-hand quadrant of event number 3. This is because the machining takes 3 weeks and must be complete by week 12, the latest date for event 6. The answer to question 3 is also clear from the diagram. The crate purchase is shown as arrow 2–8, which has a latest completion date of week 15. The fire occurred in week 6, leaving 9 weeks to locate a new source and obtain the crates.

Two versions of the Gantt chart called for in question 4 are shown in Figure 11.4. Gantt and other bar charts are often drawn for ordinary time-only networks at the stage where the critical path network is converted into a detailed work plan. These charts show the expected duration of jobs by horizontal lines drawn against vertical divisions which represent time intervals; actual time taken is shown by differently coloured lines. They are useful for controlling relatively simple projects, but they become less useful as the project gets more complex, because they cannot easily show the relationship between the various jobs in a work package or project.

Another network application is to combine time data with cost data.

PERT/COST (PERT stands for Production Evaluation Review Technique) was developed not long after PERT/TIME and has been used for years on big US defence contracts. Costed networks can be used right through a large contract from tendering stage to final payment. Costs can be attached to individual jobs, but it is usual to attach them to groups of jobs or work packages. Builders now request progress payments based on completed sections of networks, and this is said to be easier for the client to check as well as enabling job progressing and collecting payments, both to be done by the same method. Costed networks usually show:

- actual costs incurred to date;
- budget estimates for rest of project; and
- commitments for further expenditure, i.e. purchase orders outstanding.

Summary

1 Project management is the process of managing the activities within a project by planning the work, executing it and co-ordinating the contribution of the staff and organisations that have an interest in the project.

2 Project planning is particularly important where complexity of the project is high. The interrelationship between activities, resources and times in most projects, especially complex ones, is such that unless they are carefully planned, resources can become seriously overloaded at times during the operation. The involvement of procurement throughout is imperative.

3 Project planning – network planning and Gantt charts are the most common techniques. The former is particularly useful for assessing the total duration of a project and the degree of flexibility or float of the individual activities within the project.

- The most common method of network planning is called Critical Path Method (CPM).
- The logic inherent in a network diagram can be changed by resource constraints.
- Network planning models can also be used to assess the total cost of shortening a project where individual activities are shortened.

4 The concept of 'earned value' can be very useful in controlling large, expensive projects. Rather than measuring progress in terms of days of work completed, earned value control measures the value of work done. There are three important measures associated with earned value control.

- The budgeted cost of work scheduled (BCWS) – this is the amount of work which should have been completed by a particular time.
- The budgeted cost of work performed (BCWP) – this is the actual amount of work which has been completed by a particular time.
- The actual cost of work performed (ACWP) – this is the actual expenditure which has been incurred as a result of the work completed by a particular time.

5 Case studies of the Scottish Parliament, Wembley stadium and Terminal 5 for London Heathrow airport are included to demonstrate the varying approaches towards project procurement involving adversarial and partnership approaches.

6 Organisations of all kinds subcontract aspects of their activity, and subcontracting is often viewed as a means of augmenting limited resources and skills while enabling the contractor to concentrate on their main area of expertise. A main contractor in project engineering normally assigns part of the contract work to subcontractors, who are legally responsible to the contractor rather than the client even when the client has stipulated which subcontractor is to be used.

7 A group of techniques known as network analysis is often used to assist in the planning and control of certain types of project. Essentially, these are ways to organise and present certain information, such as what activities constitute the project, how these activities are related logically, their duration and cost, and the demand they make on resources. Critical path analysis is the network analysis technique which determines minimum project duration, and is the one this chapter considers. This technique can be applied to any collection of related activities which has a definite beginning and a definite end.

References and further reading

Burt, D (1994), *Proactive Procurement*, New York: Prentice-Hall.

Broome, J (2003), *Procurement Routes for Partnering: A Practical Guide*, New York: Thomas Telford.

Drake, M (1999), 'Signed and sealed', *Supply Management*, March.

Fortescue, S (2004), '431 million pound question', *Supply Management*, October.

Hines, P and Samuel, D (1993), 'The economic importance and evaluation of subcontracting', Paper presented at 2nd IPSERG Conference, Bath University.

Hossack, D (1994), 'The 10 per cent that gets the best from the other 90 per cent', *Purchasing and Supply Management*, April.

Latham, M. (1994), *Constructing the Team*, London: HMSO.

Lockyer, K and Gordon, J (1991), *Critical Path Analysis and Other Project Network Techniques*, 5th edn, London: Pitman.

Marsh, P D V (2000), *Contracting for Engineering and Construction Projects*, Aldershot: Gower.

Pearman, R (2006), 'Wembley plagued by more setbacks', *Contract Journal*, 434, May.

Pearman, R (2006), 'Wembley Stadium', *Contract Journal*, 432, May.

Raby, M (2000), 'Project management via earned value', *Work Study*, 49 (1).

Whitehead, M (2005), 'At the terminal velocity', *Supply Management*, January.

Wolstenholme, S (2004), 'Terminal velocity', *Human Resources*, November.

Wright, G and Goodwin, P (eds) (1998), *Forecasting and Judgement*, Chichester: Wiley.

12

Procurement of commodities

Introduction

The primary commodities are natural products rather than manufactured products. This affects the prices at which they are sold even though they normally enter into trade in processed or partly manufactured form rather than just as harvested or mined. Cocoa, coffee and sugar, for instance, are processed before they reach the market. Many primary commodities are bought and sold locally without entering into world trade. This chapter is mainly concerned with those primary commodities which are in worldwide demand, and are traded worldwide, so that organised commodity markets have developed to facilitate that trade.

Objectives of this chapter

- To identify the different soft and hard commodities and their impact on the material costs of producers incorporating them
- To evaluate the different short-term and long-term price stabilisation techniques
- To consider the risks of speculation and measures undertaken to reduce them
- To appreciate that modern futures markets trade only in titles or rights to commodities rather than actual goods
- To consider various procurement techniques
- To demonstrate the 'price of indifference'
- To show how to insure against fluctuating prices by placing call and put options

The main procurement problem in buying commodities is the large fluctuations in price which occur, often in short time periods. Coping with this price variability presents a real challenge to any purchaser needing large quantities of commodities to support production in factories whose products are sold at prices which cannot be varied in the same way. It can also have serious effects on the material costs of producers using secondary products which incorporate price-variable primary commodities.

For instance, cable manufacturers buy copper; chocolate manufacturers buy cocoa; some carpet manufacturers buy wool; tyre manufacturers buy rubber;

battery manufacturers buy lead; and some food-container manufacturers buy tin. All these materials – copper, cocoa, wool, rubber, lead and tin – are traded on organised commodity markets which offer facilities for hedging by means of futures contracts. Specialist commodity buyers are experts in these markets. Other buyers, however, who are not specialists and do not have the opportunity to become experts still have to make occasional purchases in these markets, or buy products at prices which are affected by the cost of the commodities used in their manufacture. They also need to understand why commodity prices fluctuate and to have some appreciation of the buying strategies which can be used in such conditions.

The principal commodities

Aluminium

This metal has been traded as a commodity since 1978 when the London Metal Exchange (LME) introduced aluminium contracts. The rather recent introduction of aluminium contracts is probably due to the fact that production is controlled by a few companies – Alcan, Kaiser, Reynolds and Alcoa. The tonnage of aluminium produced overtook the production of copper by the late 1970s.

Cocoa

A very volatile commodity, with frosts, disease and other factors having a fairly unpredictable effect on the supply and hence prices. Main producing countries are Brazil, Ivory Coast and Ghana. The main cocoa markets are in New York and London, though Ivory Coast cocoa is traded in Paris.

Coffee

Coffee is produced in many tropical countries, though Brazil is by far the biggest producer, with Colombia some way behind. As with cocoa, the two main markets are in New York and London.

Copper

The London Metal Exchange is the most important copper market, and its prices are adopted as the world reference price. Only a very small proportion of the world's copper is handled through LME trading, but producers and consumers often use the LME price as their basis for direct contracts. The Commodity Exchange (COMEX) in New York is the major pricing influence in the United States though in practice prices on all exchanges are closely related.

Cotton

Cotton provides half of the world's textile requirements, and is traded in Hong Kong, Liverpool, London and New York.

Gas oil

Gas oil is a generic term covering a fraction of the products resulting from refining crude oil. In the United States it is often called heating oil, and in Europe diesel is the usual name. It is traded on the New York Mineral Exchange (NYMEX) and the International Petroleum Exchange (IPE) in London.

Gold
Until the 1960s gold prices were fixed by governments on an international basis. This practice was abandoned in the 1960s and in 1982 the London gold futures market was established.

Grains
Wheat, barley, corn (maize), rye and oats are the important cereals, and the trade in these commodities is dominated by North America. The main exchanges are in Kansas City, Minneapolis, Winnepeg and Chicago.

Lead
Today the main application of lead is in the manufacture of batteries, and, to a lesser extent, it is used in the construction industry. Former important applications, such as plumbing, in pigments (as an oxide) and as a fuel additive, are all declining. Supplies are relatively plentiful, and much lead is recycled. Because of this, price movements tend to be limited.

Nickel
Introduced on the London Metal Exchange in 1979, nickel is mainly used in the production of stainless steel. Prices have changed dramatically in recent years.

Rubber
Rubber is an interesting commodity in that there is a synthetic substitute interchangeable with natural rubber for most applications. By far the greatest market is for the manufacture of tyres. Though traded in several places, the most important market for rubber is the Malaysian Rubber Exchange in Kuala Lumpur.

Silver
The price of silver can be erratic because it is both an industrial metal and a medium for investment. Industrial materials tend to attract fewer buyers when the price is rising, but the opposite is true if the purchase is for investment. The London Metal Exchange is a market for silver, but the COMEX in New York occupies the key position.

Soya beans
There has been a good deal of speculation in soya beans in the past, though by the early 1980s the market had become rather more stable. The main markets are as foodstuffs (soya bean oil for cooking and margarine manufacture) and as animal feeds (soya bean meal). Soya bean meal is 47 per cent protein, and hence a very high-value commodity.

The prices of these commodities are reported widely. Figure 12.1 is an extract from the 'Prices and Cost Indicators' pages in the journal *Supply Management*, published by the Chartered Institute of Purchasing and Supply.

Why do commodity prices fluctuate?

Anyone who buys food for a household or a restaurant is familiar with the way prices change for farm products. In Britain, the first new potatoes, Jersey Royals perhaps, appear in spring at very high prices. Potato prices fall as the

Figure 12.1
Commodity prices, 2002 and 2003

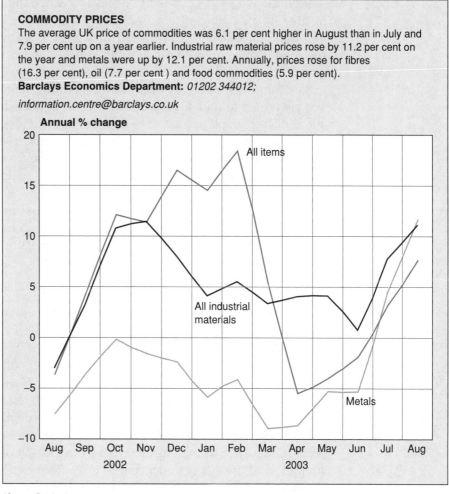

COMMODITY PRICES
The average UK price of commodities was 6.1 per cent higher in August than in July and 7.9 per cent up on a year earlier. Industrial raw material prices rose by 11.2 per cent on the year and metals were up by 12.1 per cent. Annually, prices rose for fibres (16.3 per cent), oil (7.7 per cent) and food commodities (5.9 per cent).
Barclays Economics Department: *01202 344012;*

information.centre@barclays.co.uk

(*Source*: Barclays)

months pass and keep lowering as the main crop of potatoes reaches the market, until by autumn old potatoes are selling for less than a tenth of the price of the first new potatoes in spring. The first asparagus reaches the market at astronomical prices; there is not a lot to sell, but at those prices there are not many who are willing to buy. Supply and demand are brought into equilibrium by means of these price changes. Price also changes from year to year; in some years potato prices stay high all year because the weather or some other reason has resulted in a major shortfall in supply.

These factors affect the prices at which 'soft' commodities trade on commodity exchanges, but there are additional considerations. As well as producers and consumers, participants in these markets include speculators, dealers and jobbers. Prices react continually to expectations of present and future supply, of present and future demand, of stock situations, etc.

Even though some commodity prices stay much the same for long periods of time, many commodity prices change by much larger amounts, and in much shorter periods of time, than the prices of manufactured goods. Also commodity prices move down as well as up, unlike most manufactured goods prices.

Soft commodities (agricultural raw materials) often fluctuate in price by 100 per cent, and sometimes by 500 per cent, in just one season. Price fluctuations of such amplitude are unwelcome both to consumers and to producers. A major cocoa consumer had to confess in the mid 1970s that procurement staff had made 'transactions in the company's name on the cocoa terminal market which were not disclosed to the Board' – and which led to trading losses of £32.5m.

Hard commodities such as copper can also increase in price by 300 per cent in a year, only to be cut in half in a few months. Consumers and producers would both prefer more stable prices. This is generally agreed, although the actual level of price may not be so easy to agree. Price stability, however desirable, has not in practice proved easy to achieve.

Flood, drought, plant disease and crop failure can result in a shortfall of agricultural produce, while exceptionally good harvests can produce a glut on the market, and the natural outcomes are high prices and low prices respectively. Wars, strikes, revolutions and changes in government policy have also had serious repercussions on the supply of commodities. Changes in economic activity in the industrialised countries, which are the main customers, have immediate effects on demand, and changes in taste or technology or the availability of substitutes have long-term effects on demand.

In the case of many commodities, the effect on price of any changes which occur in supply or demand is increased by the length of time it takes for any attempt to adjust supply to demand to take effect. Newly planted coffee, rubber and cocoa trees take years to come into full production. Small changes in metal output can be made with existing facilities, but a large increase in output might require a lengthy process of reopening old mines, or digging new mines and providing housing, transport and shipping facilities to exploit them. A large reduction in output is equally difficult to achieve because of the serious effects on employment and export revenue which would result.

Price stabilisation schemes

It might at first appear easy for producer and consumer to agree on a stable price if this is what both parties want. There is considerable use by large manufacturers of direct contracts with the producer, the producer's agent or the shipper. Although the commodity markets provide a medium for hedging and speculation, a means for buying and selling commodities, and a consensus of trading views on market conditions, reflected in market price, the fact is that a large part of the world trade does not pass through these markets.

If both buyer and seller prefer a stable price, surely they are free to negotiate a fixed-price contract?

In practice, however, if a price gets too much out of line with world prices it becomes almost impossible to resist the pressure to renegotiate. Prices payable under direct contracts between producer and consumer are usually referred to the basis price set by the commodity markets for this reason. Prices for major individual contracts can be stabilised in general only if the world market price can also be stabilised.

A number of schemes have been successful in damping down short-term price fluctuations on commodity markets, although long-term changes are a different matter. Short-term fluctuations tend to occur about a mean, until a change in the supply/demand ratio triggers off an upwards or downwards trend.

A typical scheme would be administered by a governing body, such as a producer cartel, or possibly a council with representatives appointed by consumers as well as producers. This governing body would appoint and finance a buffer stock manager and fix floor and ceiling prices between which to operate. The buffer stock manager buys for stock when price tends to fall, and sells from stock when price tends to rise; and if operating on sufficient scale the result is to stabilise market price. Such market operations have worked well for appreciable periods of time; but they break down once a definite upward or downward trend develops. They cease to work in the case of rising price when the warehouses are empty and the buffer stock manager has no more to sell and in the case of falling price when the financial reserves are exhausted and there is no money to buy.

For long-term price stabilisation to be successful the governing body needs also to monitor world demand and to make appropriate changes in output in order to keep the tonnage which reaches the market in line with market requirements. This is much more difficult to achieve than short-term buffer stock operations, because output is affected by unplanned events. Planned changes cannot in many cases be implemented quickly, and governments of some producer countries may feel that a change which is agreed to be in the general interest does not advance their own particular interest.

The role of the speculator

All futures markets offer opportunities for speculation, which is, of course, a very high-risk activity. Speculation will not normally be entered into by the producers or consumers of commodities, although there have been some spectacular windfall gains and unplanned losses made through the speculative activities of individual buying decision makers, sometimes without the knowledge or consent of top management. Most manufacturing and service organisations claim that speculation is at least discouraged, and is often forbidden, and it is common to find that procedures or policy manuals contain guidance to this effect.

However, professional investors or institutions may well have a proportion of their capital which they are prepared to put at risk in the hope of a very high return. The contribution of these speculators is *essential* for the smooth operation of the commodity markets. The speculators help to ensure the liquidity of the market, and ensure that the risks which the hedger is seeking to avoid are taken up.

Hedging with futures contracts

Both consumers and suppliers of commodities thus find themselves exposed to serious risk of loss (as well as of windfall profit) because of unpredictable changes in price. It is the sort of risk which might be insured against, in the same way as insurance is taken out against the risk of loss through fire, theft or flood, if this were feasible. Unfortunately, it is not feasible. Insurance is based on the fact that only a small statistically predictable minority of those at risk will actually suffer loss in a given period. Consequently, compensation can be paid to them from a fund which is provided by premiums collected from all those insured and calculated according to the degree of risk. Fire insurance is feasible because only a few of the buildings insured actually catch fire in a given period, but market changes affect all those trading in the market, not just a small minority.

Although normal insurance is not available, a different form of risk reduction technique is possible because, while price changes affect all traders, they affect some adversely and others favourably. Some stand to lose and others gain if the price rises, for instance; and those who stand to gain if it rises are also at risk of loss if the price falls. In either case the risk can be reduced by hedging, which in this context means balancing a trading position by making compensating transactions in futures contracts.

Futures contracts should not be confused with, for instance, a construction contract to be completed in two years' time, or an order for castings to be delivered two months in the future. They are a special kind of commodity contract which originated in the nineteenth century as world trade expanded and the markets developed arrangements whereby traders could agree on the sale or purchase of standard quantities of goods to standard descriptions for completion at a stated future date and at a fixed price. These contracts were made alongside the physical transactions in which actual goods were sold by sample and description for immediate delivery and constituted a facility whereby traders were able to reduce the risk of trading loss. Modern futures markets trade in titles or rights to commodities rather than actual goods (known as actuals, physicals, spot or cash). Futures contracts do not normally lead to actual deliveries of goods (although this is technically possible on some markets); they are closed out before completion by means of a reverse transaction.

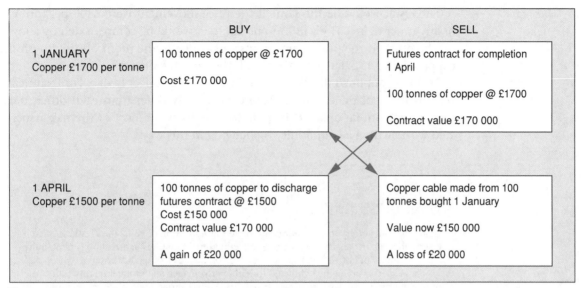

Figure 12.2 **A simple 'buyer's hedge': the two transactions made on 1 January compensate each other**

How this works may best be seen by example. Suppose that, on 1 January, a copper cable manufacturer sells a quantity of cable containing 100 tonnes of copper and agrees that the price paid by the customer will be based upon the prevailing value of copper at the time of delivery of the cable to the customer. It will take three months actually to manufacture the cable, so on 1 January the manufacturer has to buy 100 tonnes of copper in order to start manufacturer work. The pays £1700 per tonne for this copper, the prevailing LME price on 1 January.

If the manufacturer does not take precautions, there is now the risk of the copper losing value because of the changing market price. If the market price goes down it will not be possible for the manufacturer to recover what was paid for the commodity. The price could, of course, go up. However, the company is in business to make cable, not to speculate, so it decides to hedge. On 1 January, as well as *buying* 100 tonnes of copper for production, it *sells* a commitment to deliver 100 tonnes on 1 April (a three-month futures contract). It does not yet own this copper, and does not need to. It will be sufficient to get hold of the copper on 1 April in time to make delivery.

Figure 12.2 shows what happens if the price goes down to £1500 per tonne. The company will lose £20,000 on the physical copper. It paid £170,000 for it, and it is now worth only £150,000. The hedged position saves the company though. On 1 April it can buy 100 tonnes of copper for £150,000 to meet its obligations under the futures contract. Receipts under that contract are £170,000, so the compensating gain here is £20,000.

The result would be the same if the price movement were £300 per tonne, or any other figure. The gain on one contract would be compensated by a loss on the other. If the price went up instead of down, the profit on the physical copper would be balanced by a loss on the futures contract.

This is a simplified illustration, and as such is a perfect hedge. For technical reasons the spot price and the futures price may differ from each other, but they are seldom far apart. It is quite feasible to avoid most of the risk associated with owning a commodity by hedging in this way.

Mini case study

Using the tools of cryopreservation and rapid multiplication of cells, the Nestlé Research Centre in Tours (France) is building a collection of cell cultures and seedlings containing a large number of coffee plant species selected on the basis of quality criteria.

These species are being evaluated for field performance and product quality traits. The promising clones will be distributed to farmers to improve their planting materials for Arabica coffees in Thailand and China, and for Robusta coffees in Mexico, Thailand, the Philippines and Malaysia.

Some buying techniques

Time budgeting or averaging is a cautious policy which ensures that the cost of commodities consumed is the same as the market price. No expert knowledge is required and no risks are taken. The exact quantity required is purchased at the time of requirement and no stocks are held. If stocks have to be held, as is often the case, this simple policy cannot be used.

An ingenious formula approach, known as £-cost averaging or budget buying, does even better by ensuring that the cost of commodities consumed is less than market price, provided that average market price can be predicted successfully and that actual prices fluctuate in random fashion about this average. The idea is to spend a standard sum based on the average price at regular intervals of time. This 'budget' amount buys a larger amount when actual price is below average and a smaller amount when price is above average. Let us suppose that 1 tonne a week is required of a commodity of which the average market price is £100 a tonne, and that in three successive weeks, actual market price is £150, £50 and £100. With the back-to-back or averaging policy, 1 tonne would have been bought each week; but with the budget-buying policy £100 would be spent each week, the budget amount to obtain 1 tonne at the average market price. In the first week, £100 would buy two-thirds of a tonne at £150 a tonne. In the second week, it would buy 2 tonnes at £50. In the third week, it would buy 1 tonne. Over the three-week period, budgeted buying would have resulted in 3.66 tonnes being bought for £300,

Table 12.1
Actual market prices

Weeks	Weekly prices in £/tonne				
1–5	277	265	220	209	280
6–10	234	246	202	205	204
11–15	215	240	206	287	288
16–20	217	218	277	266	214
21–25	268	227	285	211	217
26–30	226	295	268	297	273
31–35	275	264	227	245	201
36–40	287	220	202	219	236
41–45	245	242	296	272	298
46–50	278	281	252	231	288

at an average cost below the average market price. The averaging policy would have resulted in 3 tonnes being bought for £300, at cost equal to the average market price.

A more sophisticated approach developed by operations research workers is known as dynamic programming. To illustrate this technique, let us suppose that 100 tonnes a week are required of a commodity the price of which fluctuates randomly between £200 and £300 a tonne, and that the buyer is authorised to purchase up to 10 weeks' supply (1000 tonnes). We will also assume that futures contracts are not available. Having found a method of determining each week how much to buy, we will then reconsider these simplifying assumptions.

In order to establish a yardstick by which we can measure how well the dynamic programming technique works, let us first see how well we could buy if we knew in advance what the market price would be each week. Over a 50-week period, let us assume that prices each week are going to be as shown in Table 12.1.

Assuming we start with no stock, we must buy 100 tonnes in the first week to meet the first week's requirements, but as price is falling we buy only one week's supply. The same applies in weeks 2 and 3, but in week 4 the price of £209 is the lowest until week 8, so we buy 400 tonnes to last until week 8. In week 8 the price of £202 is the lowest which is going to apply for a considerable time, so we buy 10 weeks' supply, the maximum authorised. Each week we look 10 weeks ahead and buy as little as necessary to meet requirements until we can stock up at a low price. With the advantage of advance knowledge of price we would be able to supply the 50-week requirement at an average price of just below £210 a tonne, as shown in Table 12.2.

If, on the other hand, we took no chances and had no advance knowledge, and simply bought 100 tonnes a week at the going price, the average cost would be £248 a tonne.

Table 12.2
Actual cost

Week number	Opening stock	Price paid	Amount bought	Total expense
1	Nil	277	100	27 700
2	Nil	265	100	26 500
3	Nil	220	100	22 000
4	Nil	209	400	83 600
8	Nil	202	1000	202 000
10	800	204	200	40 800
13	700	206	300	61 800
20	300	214	100	21 400
24	Nil	211	1000	211 000
25	900	217	100	21 700
35	Nil	201	1000	201 000
38	700	202	300	60 600
39	900	219	100	21 900
49	Nil	231	200	46 200
	Totals		5000 tonnes	£1 048 200

Average price paid = £209.64/tonne

Indifference prices

In order to decide a buying rule for the practical situation in which advance knowledge of market prices is not available, the procedure is to determine a *price of indifference* at which it does not matter if an order is placed or not. If market price is above the price of indifference, no order will be placed, and if it is below the price of indifference, we make a further calculation to decide how much to buy. Clearly the price of indifference is affected by the amount of stock in hand; with nil stock we cannot afford to be indifferent but must buy whatever the price. We will denote the prices of indifference by P_0, P_1, P_2 ... P_{10}, where the subscript denotes the number of weeks' stock in hand. These prices can easily be calculated on the simple assumptions we have made; that:

1 demand is 100 tonnes a week;
2 orders are for multiples of 100 tonnes;
3 maximum stock is 1000 tonnes; and
4 price varies randomly and evenly from £200 to £300 a tonne.

With nil stock we must buy whatever the price; but as price will not exceed £300, P_0 is £300.

With one week's stock, the price of indifference is determined by the fact that we must buy next week if we do not buy this week. Next week's price we do not know, but on the average will tend to be halfway between £200 and £300, so we should buy this week if the actual price is below £250; and this gives the value of P_1 as £250.

With two weeks' stock, the situation is more complicated. If we do not buy this week, next week we will be down to one week's stock and $P_1 = £250$. The chances are even that next week's price will be below £250, and if it is on the average it will be £225. Consequently,

$$P_2 = \text{(probability of price being below } P_1) \times \text{(expected price if it is)}$$
$$\qquad + \text{(probability of price being above } P_1) \times P_1$$
$$\qquad = 0.5 \times 225 + 0.5 \times 250$$
$$\qquad = £237.5$$

With three weeks' stock, a similar calculation can be made:

$$P_3 = \text{(probability of price being below } P_2) \times \text{(expected price)}$$
$$\qquad + \text{(probability of price being above } P_2) \times P_2$$

Since prices are assumed to be evenly distributed, if the price is below P_2 it will on the average be halfway between £237.5 and £200, so:

$$P_3 = 0.375 \times 218.75 + 0.625 \times 237.5$$
$$\qquad = £230.5$$

Proceeding in this way we obtain the following prices of indifference:

$P_0 = £300$
$P_1 = £250$
$P_2 = £237.5$
$P_3 = £230.5$
$P_4 = £225.8$
$P_5 = £222.5$
$P_6 = £220.0$
$P_7 = £218.0$
$P_8 = £216.4$
$P_9 = £215.0$
$P_{10} = £214.0$

These are shown in graphical form in Figure 12.3.

Now we can work through the 50 weeks' prices previously given once more. In week 1, with nil stocks, P_1 applies and we must buy. The quantity to buy is also derived from the above list; if market price was £218, equivalent to P_7, we should buy enough to supply seven weeks' requirements. But in week 1, market price is £277.5, higher than P_2, so we buy just one week's supply. In week 2 we again buy just 100 tonnes. But in week 3, price is £220, corresponding to P_6, so we buy six weeks' supply, in addition to our requirement for the current week. Proceeding in this way, by the end of the year our buying record is shown in Table 12.3.

It can be seen that the 5000-tonne requirement would have been bought for an average price of £214 a tonne. This is much better than the average market price of £248, which is the best that could have been achieved by the risk-reducing policy of averaging, or in this case buying 100 tonnes a week.

Figure 12.3
Indifference prices

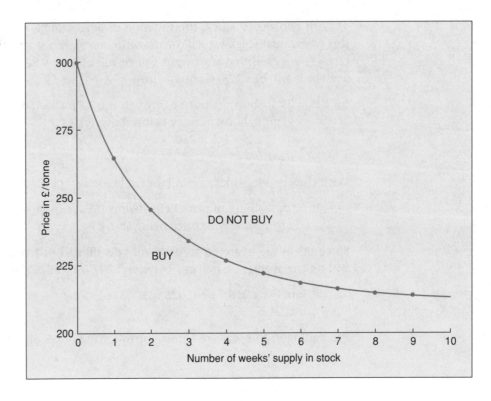

Table 12.3
Buying record

Week number	Opening stock	Price paid	Amount bought	Total expense
1	Nil	277	100	27 700
2	Nil	265	100	26 500
3	Nil	220	700	154 000
4	600	209	400	83 600
8	600	202	400	80 800
9	900	205	100	20 500
10	900	204	100	20 400
13	700	206	300	61 800
16	700	217	100	21 700
20	400	214	500	107 000
24	500	211	500	105 500
33	100	227	300	68 100
35	200	201	800	160 800
38	700	202	300	60 600
48	Nil	252	100	25 200
49	Nil	231	200	46 200
	Total		5000 tonnes	£1 070 400

Although it is not quite as good as the average price of £210, which is the best obtainable with complete advance knowledge, it really is quite close to it.

It may be objected that anyone can set up a simplified illustration and devise a winning strategy; how applicable is this to the real world? Well, the simplifying assumptions that demand was a fixed 100 tonnes a week, and that prices varied once a week, and that buy decisions were made in multiples of 100 tonnes are made only for ease of explanation and can be relaxed without affecting practice. The assumption that a maximum of ten weeks' supply could be bought reflects the fact that in reality some limit must always be set to the buyer's discretion and that authority must be sought from higher management if it seems that commitments can with advantage be made beyond that limit. Finally, it was assumed that price distribution was rectangular, or flat between the two limits stated. In practice a price forecast with its likely error distribution could be used instead. Kingsman (1975) has given a fuller account of this technique, which he says can also allow for futures contracts as a less expensive alternative to holding stock.

Traded options

One way in which a buying organisation may protect itself against fluctuating commodity prices is by means of traded options. These are, in essence, insurance policies. The party requiring insurance cover pays a premium to another party who is willing to provide the cover. In this process the buyer of an option acquires a right (but not an obligation) to buy or sell a commodity under certain conditions in exchange for a premium. It follows that the holder of the option may or may not exercise the right, though the seller of the option *must* meet his or her obligations if called upon to do so by the buyer.

An option conferring the right to buy is known as a 'call' option; a 'put' option is one which confers the right to sell. It is sometimes erroneously said that 'put' and 'call' options are opposite sides of the same transaction. This is not the case – the markets for the two kinds of option are entirely separate from each other. A 'put' option provides protection against declining prices; a 'call' option protects against rising prices.

The use of options may provide protection for a manufacturer whose raw materials are commodities, and who has to quote prices for their manufactured goods, but knows neither whether they will be awarded a contract, nor the price they will have to pay for the raw materials should their bid be accepted. Hedging will not be appropriate in these circumstances, as it requires the manufacturer to take delivery of the physical commodity, though they are, as yet, unaware as to whether their bid will be accepted. The problem can be overcome by using a traded option. The company should purchase call options, which confer the right to buy. If the offer is accepted by the customer, the company can take up the option and enter into a standard futures hedge, but if the offer is declined or rejected, the company either will simply not take up the option, or may trade against it and possibly make a profit from doing that. In short, options allow those employing them to delay making a commitment to the actual acquisition of a commodity until it is appropriate to so do.

We conclude with a brief glossary of commodity market terminology.

Glossary

Arbitrage Buying in one market, e.g. London, and selling in another, e.g. New York, in order to profit from price anomalies. This in fact smoothes out the anomalies.

Backwardation Exists when the futures price is *lower* than the spot price.

Basis Difference between cash price and futures price.

Bear One who speculates for a fall in price.

Bear market A market in which the price is falling.

Broker One who buys or sells for others in return for a commission.

Bull One who speculates for a rise in price.

Bull market One in which price is rising.

Call option An option which confers the right to purchase a particular futures contract at a specific price.

Commission Charge made by a broker for buying or selling contracts; rates of commission are fixed by market authorities, and brokers are not allowed to depart from them.

Contango When the spot price is lower than the futures price.

Forwardation Same as *contango*.

Long Owning physical commodities or futures contracts which are not fully hedged.

Put option An option which confers the right to sell a particular futures contract at a specific price.

Premium The 'price' of the option; the amount of money transferred between buyer and seller for the benefits and rights conferred by the option. The premium represents the maximum amount that the option buyer can lose.

Prompt date The day on which delivery against a declared option contract must be made.

Short Selling physical commodities or futures in excess of what is owned.

Summary

1 Soft commodity prices can fluctuate by 100–500 per cent in one season due to weather conditions. Commodity price is also affected by speculators; dealers and jobbers; expectations of present and future supply and demand.

2 Supply is affected by drought, flood, strike, war and revolution, while demand can change with economic activity, changes in taste and the advances of technology bringing alternative materials to the market.

3 Suppliers and buyers may agree to a direct contract in order to stabilise price, avoiding the commodity market. This will work if the price is in line with the market price. In the short term, producer cartels can control price by administering a 'buffer stock'. This works until there is a definite upward or downward price trend, in which case the stock or the money to service it is exhausted. Long-term price stabilisation requires the monitoring of world demand and the alignment of output to meet it.

4 The chapter illustrates various buying techniques – time budgeting (no risk and no stock), cost averaging/budget buying (undercutting market price) and dynamic programming (complex operational research approach).

5 Traded options incur a premium to insure against fluctuating prices. A 'put' option protects the supplier against declining prices and a 'call' option protects the buyer against rising prices. Manufacturers bidding for work use this technique of conferring the right to buy should their bid win the tender. (Hedging would not be an appropriate strategy at the bid stage.)

References and further reading

Buckley, J (1986), *A Guide to World Commodity Markets: Physical, Futures and Options Trading*, 5th edn, London: Kogan Page.

Gibson-Jarvig, R (1989), *The London Metal Exchange: A Commodity Market*, Cambridge: Woodhead Faulkner.

Kingsman, B G (1975), in D H Farmer and B Taylor (eds), *Corporate Planning and Procurement*, London: Heinemann.

Kingsman, B G (1986), *Raw Materials Purchasing: An Operational Research Approach*, Oxford: Pergamon Press.

Seidel, A D and Ginsberg, P M (1983), *Commodities Trading: Foundation, Analysis and Operations*, Upper Saddle River, NJ: Prentice Hall.

13

International and global sourcing

Introduction

A substantial amount of goods are imported into the UK every year, and as more companies decide to outsource manufacturing this trend continues to grow. The same value for money objectives are pursued and much the same range of methods and systems are employed in this pursuit. Exactly the same problems need to be thought about and overcome, though, of course, additional problems also need to be dealt with, and these form the main theme of this chapter.

Objectives of this chapter

- To define international and global sourcing
- To appreciate why it is necessary or preferable to source internationally
- To outline the stages of international sourcing development
- To highlight the growth in international sourcing
- To consider the problems associated with international sourcing
- To provide a briefing on 'Incoterms'
- To explain countertrade as a form of barter
- To outline the role of the European Union

Global sourcing and international procurement

Global sourcing (sometimes called global procurement) and international procurement are similar concepts and can be distinguished as follows:

■ Global sourcing/procurement

Global sourcing is often used when what is meant is international procurement/sourcing. Some textbooks whose titles include such expressions as 'global purchasing' or 'global sourcing' have subtitles which indicate that they really mean international purchasing and that is often the majority of the content.

Global sourcing is more of an approach born of the globalisation of large multinational conglomerates within a range of industries and services. Due to the globalisation of corporations, phrases such as 'global purchasing' or 'global sourcing' have become common but they are, as yet, without a totally clear definition. There have been various suggestions such as:

- Using local suppliers, controlled locally, but under the wider direction of a central corporate structure.
- Using local suppliers controlled from a central corporate site.
- A contract between multinational organisations to service the needs of the contract worldwide on a local basis.

A clear definition comes from John Stevens (1995): 'Global Sourcing is the integration and coordination of procurement requirements across the world-wide business units, looking at common items, processes, technologies and suppliers.'

It is only practised by large corporations as they have the need and leverage to gain competitiveness from global sourcing, and also the facilities around the globe to enable them to apply the process. They are usually contractually bound to other large corporations who have the ability to supply products to the globally located sites of the multinational purchaser. A good example of this is the agreement Volvo has with Meritor Automotive Inc. to supply axles to all Volvo plants.

■ International procurement

International procurement is the purchasing, from another country, of the products and/or services required for the organisation. In other words it is importing.

All organisations can practise international purchasing. What it does not require or involve is the global integration and co-ordination of the buying organisation's demand with the supplier's global ability to supply.

It would seem therefore that global procurement requires a globally located purchaser and a globally located supplier. There often needs to be a strong element of co-location, i.e. both supplier and purchaser often need to be located in the same place or at least in the same region. Figures 13.1 and 13.2 summarise the key differences.

Figure 13.3 depicts the development of international sourcing into global sourcing. It portrays the stages which companies move through as they become more involved in international and global sourcing. However, it is by no means the natural order that all companies will become truly global in their sourcing, as it is only multinationals that can achieve this. Moreover, as the next case study demonstrates, even multinationals find that they have to be selective with their global strategies.

**Figure 13.1
Definitions of
international and
global sourcing**

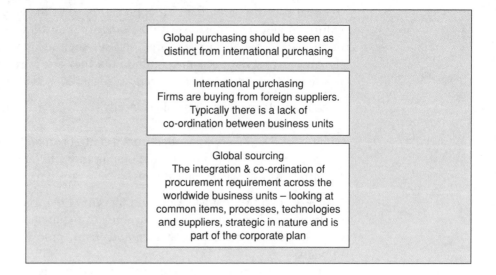

**Figure 13.2
Global sourcing**

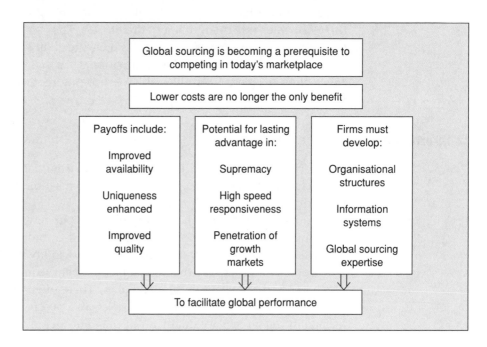

Mini case study – Diageo/EMI

International drinks company Diageo is scaling back its global procurement group and refocusing on more regional buying.

The main driver is a recognition that global deals for things like facilities management have not worked. This raises two key issues. How is a global strategy defined? And does the organisation have purchasers with enough experience to put one into effect and manage the complex relationships between different countries and cultures?

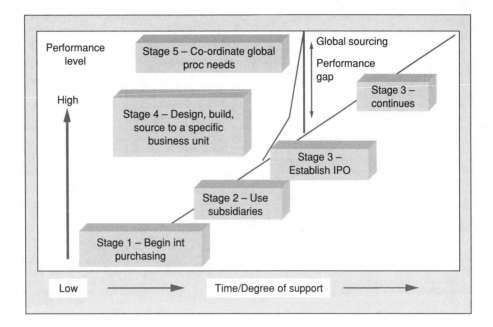

**Figure 13.3
International v
global sourcing**

On the first issue, defining a global strategy is where many problems start, according to several heads of global procurement. By definition, the strategy does not mean buyers at central office to hammer out deals for their company's regions and territories.

The central organisation is mostly contract management, general due diligence that allows local or regional purchasers to negotiate deals. This set-up may not be called a true global procurement function, simply a central contracting resource.

EMI Recorded Music agrees that a global procurement department at head office need not be the deal maker for a series of worldwide contracts.

A global strategy is not necessarily about one supplier in a given area taking care of your needs worldwide – EMI has found there are probably no more than eight to ten categories that are truly global.

EMI has centralised globally its key production materials such as polycarbonate and plastics components, for which there is a global supply base. The company buys from regional suppliers but deals with purchasing in a co-ordinated way.

Why source internationally?

The principle of comparative advantage is of relevance here. The basic idea is that if one country has an advantage, for whatever reason, as an efficient producer of one good, and another country has an advantage in a different good, then it is in their interests to trade. Exchanging these goods leads to greater efficiency for both. As an example of this, consider the relationship between the UK and Saudi Arabia. Saudi Arabia produces oil at a lower cost than Britain can from the North Sea. Britain has advanced manufacturing capabilities; Saudi Arabia is developing in this area. While both countries could pursue

**Figure 13.4
GATT/WTO**

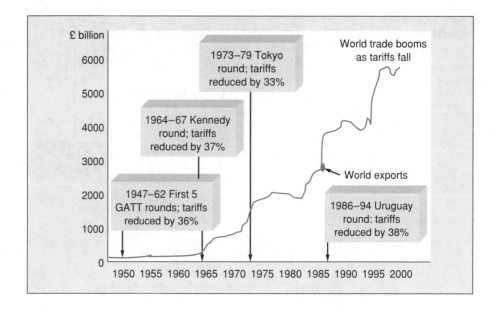

self-sufficiency, it is beneficial to both to export those items for which they are efficient producers, and import those where they are less efficient.

So why has international trade increased dramatically? Figure 13.4 depicts the considerable increase in international trade globally as GATT/WTO rounds of tariff reductions encouraged trade and reduced protectionism.

In addition to the initiatives by those organisations to boost international trade, reasons for the growth in international sourcing include the following:

1 The buyer may be compelled to go abroad to get what is required. Many raw materials are not produced at all in the UK: for instance cocoa, coffee, cobalt. The UK traditionally imported raw materials and exported manufactured goods. Some countries, on the other hand, export raw materials and import manufactured products that are not produced by their domestic industries.

2 The buyer may prefer to purchase from a foreign source which offers features not available on domestically produced goods of a similar type. Technological innovation occurs all round the world.

3 Although goods of the type required are produced domestically, domestic capacity may not be enough to meet demand, so the gap has to be filled from abroad.

4 There may be strategic reasons for international purchases, for instance to improve supply security by having a second source in another country.

5 It may be possible to buy equivalent goods more cheaply abroad, because of larger quantities, lower wages, better productivity, better plant, or the rate of exchange (China is a good example).

6 Countertrade may compel your firm to buy abroad. Sometimes it is not possible to win an export order without agreeing to a reciprocal import order.

Problems with international sourcing

The main problems associated with international sourcing are as follows.

■ Communication problems

These arise not just because of language difficulties, but also because of time differences between countries, and differing meanings attaching to trading terminology and technical vocabulary. *Consensus ad idem*, agreement on the same thing, is fundamental to a valid contract. It is therefore important to ensure that understanding is mutual. Even though both parties may be employing English or some other shared language in conducting their business, it is possible that if one party is less familiar with the language than the other then differing meanings may be attached to words or contract terms. Difficulties arise in connection with interpretation when contracts are entirely domestic; the probability of problems of this kind arising is much increased in international contracts.

■ Currency differences

The conversion of one currency into another does not, of itself, pose any great difficulty if the currencies are 'convertible', but it does cost money for the conversion to take place. More importantly, the extent to which exchange rates fluctuate does cause considerable problems. The risk and uncertainty associated with the change in relative values between the exporter's and the importer's currencies have to be taken into account and managed. This is not an easy task. The rate at which one currency exchanges for another tends to change continuously because of changes in the demand for and supply of each currency. These exchange rate fluctuations can and do affect international transactions in the same way as price changes.

For instance, suppose a British firm buys an American machine tool on three months' delivery for $10,000. The rate of exchange is $1.50 = £1 when the purchase is made, so the customer sees the price as about £6666. During the three-month delivery period, the exchange rate alters to $1.60 = £1, and so the amount payable becomes £6250. This looks like a price reduction to the purchaser, although the seller still gets the price in dollars as quoted. If the rate altered the other way, the buyer would suffer the equivalent of a price increase, although the seller would not benefit from it.

It may be possible for the buyer to eliminate this uncertainty as to the amount payable by stating the contract price in the buyer's currency. This puts all the uncertainty on the seller. The buyer knows exactly what will have to be paid, but the seller does not know how much will be received. Naturally, there may well be reluctance on the part of sellers to contract in this way.

Sometimes contracts are negotiated in which the risk is shared equally; for instance, a clause might be included such as this:

The amount payable will be calculated by converting the agreed dollar price to sterling according to the formula:

$$£1 = (\$x + \$y)/2$$

where $\$x$ is the dollar value of £1 at the date of the contract, and $\$y$ is the dollar value of £1 at the date payment is due.

Prices can also be stated in a third currency, acceptable to both parties.

The standard way purchasers cope with currency risks is to make a forward purchase of the amount of foreign currency required to settle the bill. The banks provide a marketplace in which these purchases can be made. On a large scale, currency futures are traded in the same way as commodity futures (discussed in Chapter 12). They are even sometimes traded in the same markets, such as the Chicago Board of Trade, perhaps the biggest marketplace in the world for transactions of this kind. Forward rates are quoted in the newspapers. Whether forward rates are at a premium or at a discount against spot rates, once the purchaser has made the forward currency purchase the amount payable is certain.

A multinational business which buys components in Singapore and Japan to manufacture goods in the UK for sale in Germany and is controlled financially from the USA is exposed to a combination of exchange risks, which might best be handled by a small central group of foreign exchange experts.

■ Payment

The international transfer of funds poses its own difficulties, and a third party, usually a bank, will probably need to be involved to facilitate this process. Of course, this service will cost money, a cost not applicable in domestic sourcing. Most transactions in the domestic market are on open account (credit terms). Typically the customer is allowed a month from the invoice date, or the date of delivery, whichever is the later, to settle the account. More precisely, *net monthly account* terms mean that the account must be settled by the end of the month following the month of delivery or invoicing, whereas *net cash 30 days* means that the account needs to be settled within 30 days of delivery or invoicing.

Trade within the EU is frequently conducted on open account, although sometimes the delay and expense associated with international cheque payments make it preferable to use telegraphic transfers, mail transfers, banker's drafts or international money orders to settle the account. Telegraphic transfer is an instruction by telegraph from the buyer's bank to the seller's bank to transfer to the seller's account a stated sum of money. Mail transfer is a similar instruction sent by post. Banker's drafts are issued in any currency by banks, and the seller can usually pay them into an account at a local bank. International money orders are useful for small amounts.

Major international transactions outside the domestic market of the EU are frequently settled by bill of exchange or letter of credit. There is a basic conflict of interest between seller and buyer, which assumes greater significance when the relationship is an international one. Basically the problem is that the seller will not wish to release their goods to the buyer until payment has been made, or they are certain that payment will be made. The buyer, of course, is in a similar position. It is unlikely that the buyer will release funds until in possession of the goods, or at least a guarantee of their delivery. Because of these conflicting interests the contracting parties will usually employ the services of an intermediary, usually a bank, which will make payment only when evidence of performance is produced, but can be relied on actually to make the payment under such circumstances. The essential difference between a bill of exchange and a letter of credit is that in the case of a bill of exchange the bank is looking after the interests of the exporter, whereas in the case of a letter of credit the importer has the greater protection from the bank.

A bill of exchange is 'an unconditional order in writing addressed by one person to another signed by the person giving it requiring the person to whom it is addressed to pay on demand, or at a fixed and determinable future time a sum certain in money to, or to the order of, a specified person or to bearer'. There are two principal types of bills of exchange:

1 *Documents against acceptance (DA)*, meaning that the importer accepts the documents giving title to the goods and signs a bill of exchange drawn on them which is to be met at a given future date. With this form of bill of exchange a certain amount of deferment can be attached to payment, while making as certain as possible the fact that the importer will pay.

2 *Documents against payment (DP)*, which means that the importer is obliged to pay *before* the documents are released.

■ Letters of credit

A documentary letter of credit is a promise in writing by a bank to an exporter that the goods will be paid for providing that the exporter complies exactly with the terms and conditions laid down. The promise is, of course, made on behalf of the importer. The bank will naturally need to be sure that the importer has the necessary funds (see Figure 13.5).

There are three types of letter of credit, namely:

1 A *revocable* letter of credit, which means that the importer may instruct their bank to revoke it at any time prior to payment becoming due. Such letters are rarely used these days, as the degree of trust necessary between the two parties would mean that a direct payment might be made.

2 An *irrevocable* letter. Once one of these has been raised it cannot be withdrawn under any circumstances. If the exporter performs their obligations they are virtually certain of payment.

3 A *confirmed irrevocable* credit provides dual protection. A bank in the exporter's country agrees to pay if the importer's bank fails to do so (see Figure 13.6).

Figure 13.7 outlines the flow of the letter of credit procedure.

Figure 13.5
Documentary letters of credit

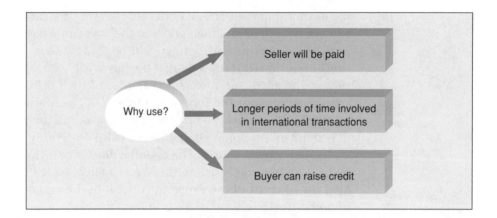

Figure 13.6
Three main types of letters of credit

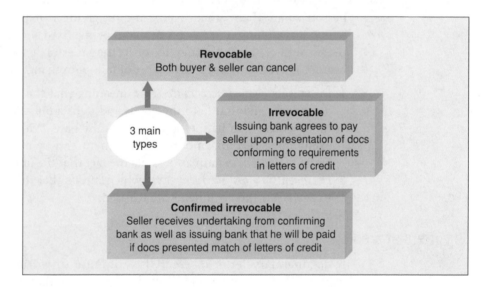

■ Differing legal systems

When purchasing internationally it is important to establish whether the courts of the exporter's country, those of the importer's, or the courts of a third country have jurisdiction in the event of a dispute. In the case of a contract made in England or Wales, and in the absence of an express term to the contrary in the contract, the English courts will normally assume jurisdiction.

There remains, however, the question as to which law is the proper law of the contract. If the law of another country is relevant, then the applicable rules will have to be established by an expert witness. It is quite possible to have a situation where matters relating to the *form* of the contract may be liable to be decided by the legal system of one country, and matters to do with *performance* fall to be decided by the legal system of another.

The proper law of the contract is the law which the parties stipulate. Under English law the parties are free to stipulate in their contract the legal system

**Figure 13.7
Letters of credit
procedure**

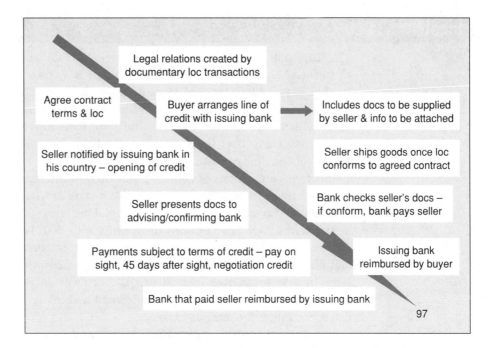

which is to be applied. Sometimes the legal system of a country not connected with either contracting party is specified, for example because the goods are likely to pass through several owners in the course of trade, and a particular legal system is the generally accepted one in that particular trade.

It is sometimes the case that parties neglect to stipulate their intention as to which law shall be applied. When this is the case then the courts will infer the proper law from the contract and the circumstances surrounding it.

Consider the not unlikely scenario of a consignment of goods of Japanese design, manufactured in Malaysia and shipped from Singapore. The goods are sold by a British agent to a customer in France, and are to be shipped in a Norwegian-owned ship, registered in Liberia. The goods are to be paid for in US dollars. Obviously, the questions of jurisdiction and the prevailing law can be quite complex.

Of course, most buyers from overseas will buy through agents, and even where direct purchases are made the buyer is likely to employ an appropriate specialist to advise on or, more likely, organise such matters as shipment, insurance, handling, clearance, payment and other related matters.

Mini case study – Courts UK

Courts UK plc is a large furniture and furnishings distributor, with retail outlets in Singapore, Malaysia, five other Far Eastern countries and 11 Caribbean islands. Courts has 'leveraged' purchasing by working with just a small number of global suppliers. The company distributes outside the UK through two hubs, one in Singapore, the other in Miami.

Incoterms 2000

The International Chamber of Commerce (ICC) publishes *International Commercial Terms* (*Incoterms*). This document is a valuable aid to negotiators in that it provides standard terminology, clarifying the responsibilities of buyer and seller in international trade. The parties need to negotiate and agree which term to use, of course, but their meanings are clearly explained. There have been, over the years, several editions of this document; the one current at the time of writing is *Incoterms 2000*.

Incoterms are a series of defined terms used in international trade. The ICC designed them in an attempt to establish a standardised language for buyers and sellers who are conducting international business.

The terms have not yet been universally accepted. For example, FOB and CIF are routinely (if improperly) used for airfreight consignments; the abbreviation C&F (Cost and Freight) is still widely used instead of CFR; and FIS (Free Into Store) is used instead of DDU or DDP. In the United States and Canada, FOB does not mean 'free on board a ship' as it does elsewhere – it can mean much the same as Ex Works.

The current terms are explained below and summarised in Table 13.1. Readers should not rely on these notes when taking, or refraining from taking, action in relation to international or any other form of trade. The notes are given for general guidance only, and do not constitute a full explanation of the terms. Practitioners are referred to the ICC publications.

EXW: Ex Works

Ex Works means the sellers' only responsibility is to make the goods available at their premises. They are not responsible for loading them on vehicles provided by buyers or clearing them for export. Buyers bear the full costs and risks of taking goods from sellers' works to their destination. This is the minimum obligation of sellers.

Table 13.1
A summary of current Incoterms

Term	Description	Transport mode applicable
EXW	Ex Works	All modes
FCA	Free Carrier (named place)	All modes
FAS	Free Alongside Ship	Water
FOB	Free On Board	Water
CFR	Cost and Freight	Water
CIF	Cost, Insurance and Freight	Water
CPT	Carriage Paid To (named place)	All modes
CIP	Carriage, Insurance Paid To (named place)	All modes
DAF	Delivered At Frontier (named place)	Land
DES	Delivered Ex Ship	Water
DEQ	Delivered Ex Quay	Water
DDU	Delivered Duty Unpaid (named place)	All modes
DDP	Delivered Duty Paid (named place)	All modes

FCA: Free Carrier (named place)

This can be used with any form of transport (air, sea, rail, truck or multimode). The 'carriers' are the transporters, including any freight forwarders that buyers have designated to receive the goods. Sellers must hand the goods, cleared for export, over to the carriers at the place indicated in the shipping terms. This can involve sellers paying for some transport from the factory to the carrier. Where delivery takes place at the seller's premises, the seller is responsible for loading. If delivery occurs at any other place, the seller is no longer responsible for loading. Sellers may, and commonly do, act as buyers' agents in arranging transport, which buyers pay for.

FAS: Free Alongside Ship

This term is properly used only for ocean or inland water transport. Sellers are responsible for placing the goods alongside the ship on the quay or in lighters, at the place named in the quotation. 'Alongside' means within reach of the carrying ship's tackle. From that moment, buyers bear all costs and risks of loss or damage to the goods. Sellers are responsible for clearing the goods for export.

FOB: Free On Board

Again, this is properly used only for ocean or inland water transport. Once sellers place the goods, cleared for export, on board a ship at the port named in the sales contract, their obligations end. Buyers assume the risk of loss or damage to the goods once they pass the ship's rail. In other modes of transport, or if the ship's rails are not the point at which the seller transfers ownership to the buyer – such as with container, roll-on/roll-off cargo – FCA is the closest equivalent term.

CFR: Cost and Freight

Sellers must clear the goods for export and pay the costs and freight necessary to bring them to the named destination. However, buyers assume the risk of loss or damage to the goods, and any cost increases, once the goods pass the ship's rail in the port of shipment. This is another term properly used only for transport by water (sea or inland). In other modes of transport, or if the ship's rails are not the point at which the seller transfers ownership to the buyer – such as with container, roll-on/roll-off cargo – CPT is the closest equivalent term.

CIF: Cost, Insurance and Freight

This term is similar to CFR, but sellers must also buy marine insurance for the buyers. Sellers contract with the insurers and pay the premiums, but buyers assume the risk of loss from the time the goods pass the ship's rail in the port of shipment. This term also applies only to transport by water (sea or inland). CIP is the closest equivalent term for other transport modes.

CPT: Carriage Paid To (named place)

This can be used with any form of transport (air, sea, rail, truck or multimode). Sellers must clear the goods for export and pay the costs and freight necessary to bring them to the named destination. However, buyers assume the risk of loss or damage to the goods, and any cost increases, once the first carrier has received the goods.

CIP: Carriage, Insurance Paid To (named place)	As for CPT, but the seller must also contract with the insurers and pay the premiums.
DAF: Delivered At Frontier (named place)	Sellers fulfil their obligations once the goods, cleared for export, are made available at the named point, which will be before the destination customs border. Buyers must clear the goods through customs. The frontier can be the export country's frontier, so it is very important to specify exactly where the delivery point is, as seller bears all costs and risks to that point. This term is designed for rail or road transport, but can be used when goods are shipped by any method. It is useful when shipping to a bonded customs warehouse or a free trade zone.
DES: Delivered Ex Ship	This term is normally used for commodity shipments by sea. Buyers assume risks and costs once the ship reaches the named destination, but before the goods are cleared for import.
DEQ: Delivered Ex Quay	This is also normally used for commodity shipments by sea. Buyers assume risks and costs on the quay at the named destination. Sellers are responsible for discharge costs and buyers for import clearance.
DDU: Delivered Duty Unpaid (named place)	Under this term sellers handle everything necessary to deliver the goods to the stipulated place – usually the buyer's own place – except customs clearance at the country of destination. Buyers pay duties and taxes.
DDP: Delivered Duty Paid (named place)	This means sellers handle everything, including customs clearance, to deliver the goods to the stipulated place. Since the stipulated place is usually the buyer's own place, sellers arrange and pay for every step in the process. A common alternative is 'DDP exclusive of duty and taxes'. This oxymoron is not the same as DDU, because sellers are responsible for clearance, but not for paying duties and taxes.

Arbitration

Litigation between buyer and seller is generally a complicated and expensive business, and is to be avoided if at all possible. This is particularly true in the case of international transactions. Fortunately, there is an alternative in the form of *arbitration*. This is relatively inexpensive and much quicker, and involves a panel of independent arbitrators examining the case with a view to finding a solution which reflects the rights and interests of both parties. The International Chamber of Commerce in Paris is the leading body for the provision of arbitration services in connection with international trade, and has a set of rules for conciliation and arbitration. Arbitrators can be appointed for any country by the court of arbitration in Paris. The London Court of

Arbitration of the London Chamber of Commerce and Industry also offers arbitration services, as do some other chambers of commerce. Panels of expert arbitrators are maintained and advice is available on arbitration clauses suitable for use in international contracts.

Importing

Importing involves a more distant supplier with extended transit lead times. As lead times are one of the critical components when deciding how much to order from suppliers, knowledge and control of this lead time are necessary.

However, what often happens is that many UK buyers decide to import on CIF or C&F terms and their organisation leaves to the supplier the organisation of the transit. Effectively, therefore, the associated lead time is also externalised. Importing companies will then often spend time expediting and checking where the goods are and when they will arrive.

Delays in transit times can also cause potential product shortages, with many impacts, for example customer service levels and not satisfying customer requirements. With regular repeat orders, any delayed transit times will inevitably add to increasing stockholding, as the buying company will have to hold stocks to protect against the uncertainty of the supplier's lead time.

Benefits of changing to EXW/FOB terms

It is possible to better control the imports by switching to Ex Works (EXW) or Free on Board (FOB) terms. By doing this the following benefits will be realised:

- Control and knowledge of exactly what is happening; management needs to recall here that the management cycle not only involves planning, organising and directing but also controlling.
- Visibility and knowledge of exactly where the products are during the transit, as the transit is now in your control.
- Cheaper freight costs as your company is now paying them directly. Importers and buyers need to understand that suppliers are more than likely to have a margin on the actual freight costs they have paid.

How to change

Starting out

A useful place to start is to understand some of the aspects of total supply chain management, for example:

- What are your costs of holding inventory?
- What supply lead time is required?
- What part of the supply lead time is the transit lead time?
- What would be the effects of reliable and consistent on-time in-full receipts and how does this compare to your current situation?

Answers to these questions are always revealing and show how, often, the internal structure is fragmented and unorganised to undertake effective importing. Answers will also provide the basis for accessing the benefits of changing.

The next steps

- Ask for the supplier's EXW price.
- Negotiate freight terms, possibly by going out to tender.
- Check on the track/trace system to be used. This can be a simple key point reporting with spreadsheet recording, or an instant on-demand access to a carrier's system.
- Assess the risk of changing, for example, possibly extra management costs, insurance cover and freight variation rate exposures. It is important to ensure a like for like comparison with the current methods as many of the current costs may well be hidden.
- Compare and contrast.
- If deciding to change, and effectively changing the buying strategy, then please ensure that the internal structure supports the changes.

What others have done

There is much evidence to support that the changes detailed above are worthwhile.

A major food retailer had spending of £1200 million on imports via third party wholesalers and £500 million on direct imports. For example, home and leisure products were ordered through UK agents who arranged everything to DDP. Meanwhile, beers, wines and spirits were bought EXW works or FOB with freight arranged through various forwarders. A change in management identified that the company had:

- no systems;
- no cost visibility;
- no economy of scale;
- poor product availability;
- an internal fragmented structure; for example,
    trading on product selection, negotiations, selection of suppliers, and ordering;
    finance on letters of credit, payments;
    logistics on order quantity and phasing into supply chain.

The company tendered and then outsourced to one forwarder but maintained and determined carrier selection when appropriate. The reported results were:

- freight costs fell by 8 per cent;
- duty charges reduced by 10 per cent;
- fuller visibility of supply chain;
- reduced stock levels.

The previously fragmented internal control was centralised as a new structure following the new strategy.

A major clothes retailer with nearly 200 stores had 70 per cent of products imported, mainly from the Far East. It identified the following problems:

- no accurate data therefore no visibility;
- orders arrive 'unexpectedly';
- 40 per cent of time spent checking;

- paid high demurrage/rent port costs;
- restricted on buying currency forward;
- poor quality control.

The solution was to:

- change from C&F to FOB and use one UK forwarder;
- set up a simple database tracking on transfer points: PO, confirmed, tariff heading, cargo booked, authorise shipment, confirm shipment, documents banked, documents received, arrival time, clearance time, arrival at DC, QC checked, released/available;
- integrate all internal systems.

The benefits reported were:

- lower demurrage costs;
- improved warehouse efficiency due to scheduled arrivals;
- improved finance due to forward currency buying;
- quicker customs clearances;
- better product availability.

Transport

All five basic modes of freight transport – road, rail, air, water and pipeline – are used in international transactions. More than one mode may be used in delivering goods: a consignment may make part of the journey by road and the next part by air. The Channel Tunnel now provides more choice and competition in road and rail haulage to and from Britain. Severe delays occur in the transport arrangements for some international transactions. Strikes and congestion at ports in the Middle East and in Africa have led to ships queuing for months to be unloaded. One way to counteract these delays is to hold stocks in the country of import. This can be expensive. A big selling point of airfreight is that buffer stocks can be low because of the 'lead time economics' of air travel: fast delivery, in effect.

Customs

Import and export procedures between countries which are members of the EU are being considerably simplified with the single market and the abolition of import taxes. For purchases from countries outside the EU, however, careful administration is needed to avoid unnecessary expense.

It is important to reduce the length of time goods are in customs. Every day's delay can add to costs. Inaccurate, incomplete or incorrect information on documents such as invoices, waybills, import licences and letters of credit causes delay. Sometimes information must be given in connection with consignments of goods from different sources combined for one destination. Consolidation is the term used for airfreight; groupage for overland transport.

A major air forwarder may have as many as 100 consolidation routes to airports around the world, with agents meeting consignments on arrival and breaking them down into packages for delivery to individual addresses. Consolidation enables customers to benefit from bulk rates, with up to 50 per cent reduction in cost. Airlines also benefit from these arrangements, and over 80 per cent of UK airfreight is handled by forwarders.

Groupage is used in overland transport to enable several consignors to share the journey cost. Consignments from several sources, which are going to the same destination, are collected together to make a unit load. This can delay things while the load is being accumulated, although it does reduce transport costs. Substantial differences occur between the prices quoted, so buyers would be well advised to obtain several quotations. In one instance five quotations were obtained for transport, insurance and documentation of a consignment of 2500 lb ball valves door to door from Perth to Hamburg. The highest quote was 64 per cent above the average while the lowest was 51 per cent below the average. Of course, price is not the only thing to consider, but when price differentials are as large as this, non-price differences must be considered with care.

Countertrade

Countertrade is a form of barter. It takes place whenever goods are traded internationally, not in exchange for cash or currency, but for other goods. Countertrade is widely practised in international business, and facilitates transactions with countries which are unable or unwilling to export in a more conventional manner, perhaps for one or more of the following reasons:

- One or both trading partners has no (or limited) foreign exchange.
- A country wishes to promote exports, and is prepared to accept goods rather than hard currency in payment to facilitate this.
- There may be political pressure to balance trade between two countries.

The most straightforward form of countertrade is the full compensation arrangement, where a single contract is established between two parties, and goods are exchanged for other goods. Of course, it is unlikely that a coincidence of wants will be experienced in practice, and one party to the transaction is likely to need to sell the goods received under the contract. When British Aerospace supplies military aircraft to Saudi Arabia in exchange for oil from that country, or a European car maker sends vehicles to a South American country in exchange for sheepskins, it does not mean that the supplying company is likely to have a use for the materials exchanged. What happens under a full compensation arrangement is that the goods are valued in money, and the party that wishes to liquidate the materials received will do so by arranging for the sale of goods, usually with the assistance of an experienced third party.

Counter-purchase arrangements, where two separate contracts are formed simultaneously, are also widely employed. A company in country A agrees with a company in country B to ship goods from country A to country B in exchange for money. At the same time agreement is made that country B will ship goods to country A, also in exchange for money. Although the two contracts balance each other, so that the net effect is simply that an exchange of goods has taken place, it is easier to manage two conventional contracts, to assign rights and responsibilities, to arrange insurance and so on.

There are, in practice, many kinds of arrangement under which countertrade exchanges may be made, some of them extremely complex. The arrangements have in common the fact that the outcome results in one of the parties discharging some or all of their obligations by supplying goods or services rather than by paying money (see Figures 13.8–13.13).

Figure 13.8
Countertrade

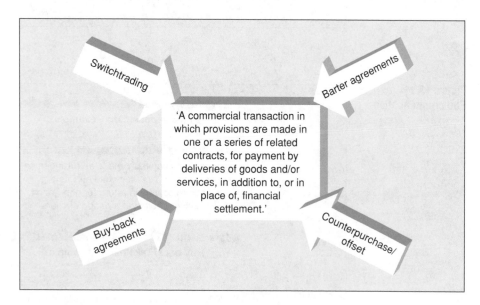

Figure 13.9
Barter trade

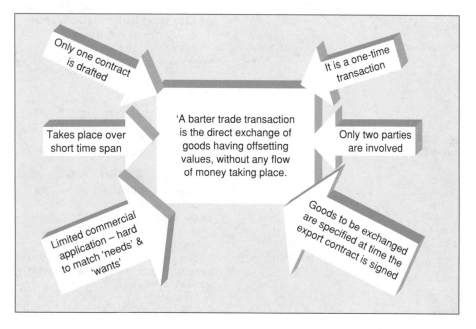

Figure 13.10
Switchtrading

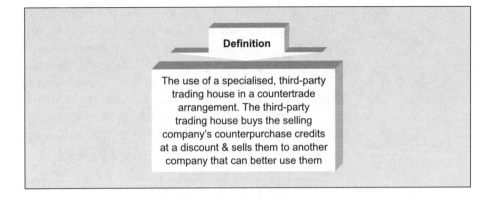

> **Definition**
>
> The use of a specialised, third-party trading house in a countertrade arrangement. The third-party trading house buys the selling company's counterpurchase credits at a discount & sells them to another company that can better use them

Figure 13.11
Full compensation

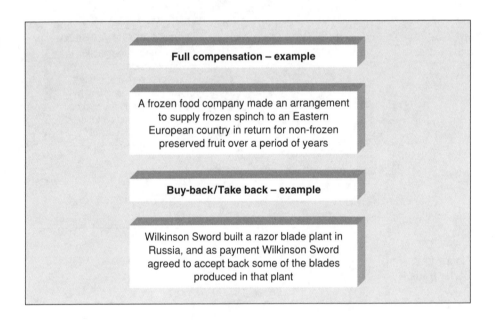

> **Full compensation – example**
>
> A frozen food company made an arrangement to supply frozen spinch to an Eastern European country in return for non-frozen preserved fruit over a period of years
>
> **Buy-back/Take back – example**
>
> Wilkinson Sword built a razor blade plant in Russia, and as payment Wilkinson Sword agreed to accept back some of the blades produced in that plant

Figure 13.12
Compensation with buy-back

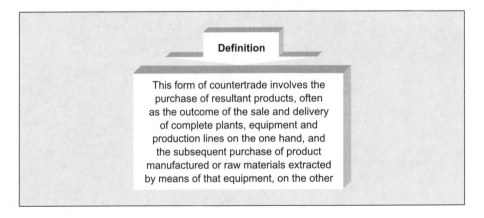

> **Definition**
>
> This form of countertrade involves the purchase of resultant products, often as the outcome of the sale and delivery of complete plants, equipment and production lines on the one hand, and the subsequent purchase of product manufactured or raw materials extracted by means of that equipment, on the other

**Figure13.13
(a) Counter
purchase and
(b) offset**

(a)

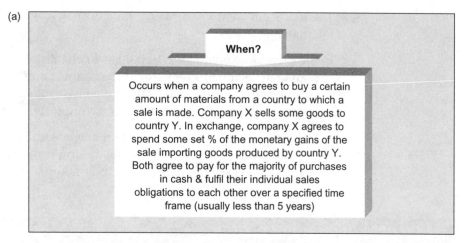

When?

Occurs when a company agrees to buy a certain amount of materials from a country to which a sale is made. Company X sells some goods to country Y. In exchange, company X agrees to spend some set % of the monetary gains of the sale importing goods produced by country Y. Both agree to pay for the majority of purchases in cash & fulfil their individual sales obligations to each other over a specified time frame (usually less than 5 years)

(b)

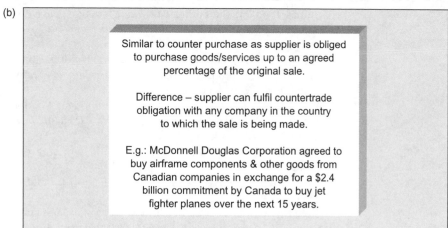

Similar to counter purchase as supplier is obliged to purchase goods/services up to an agreed percentage of the original sale.

Difference – supplier can fulfil countertrade obligation with any company in the country to which the sale is being made.

E.g.: McDonnell Douglas Corporation agreed to buy airframe components & other goods from Canadian companies in exchange for a $2.4 billion commitment by Canada to buy jet fighter planes over the next 15 years.

Summary

1 Communication problems (language, time difference, interpretation) complicate foreign trade. Exchange rate fluctuations can be dealt with by making a forward purchase of the amount needed in the same way as a commodity.

2 International payment may take several forms. Within the European Union, payment will normally involve the transfer of funds by telegraphic means, mail, banker's draft or international money orders. Outside the EU, bills of exchange or letters of credit, which require an intermediary, are used.

3 There are two types of bills of exchange – documents against acceptance (allowing deferment of payment) and documents against payment (importer is obliged to pay before the release of the documentation). The three types of letters of credit are revocable, irrevocable and confirmed irrevocable.

4 The use of Incoterms can reduce the possibility of conflict or confusion in international trading.

5 In the event of a dispute, it is important to establish which court has jurisdiction. Matters relating to the form of the contract and matters relating to performance may be decided by separate courts (sometimes the court is of a country not connected with either contracting party).

6 Countertrade may be a straightforward single contract between two parties 'swapping' goods or it may be performed using two separate contracts simultaneously, each assigning rights and responsibilities.

References and further reading

Arminas, D (2003), 'End of the worldwide function', *Supply Management*, July.

Branch, A (2001), *International Purchasing and Management*, London: Thomson Learning.

Branch, A E (1990), *Elements of Import Practice*, London: Chapman & Hall.

Bugg, R and Whitehead, G (1990), *Elements of Transportation Documentation*, Cambridge: Woodhead Faulkner.

Butler, J (1994), *The Importer's Handbook*, Cambridge: Woodhead Faulkner.

Emmett, S (2006), *Logistics Freight Transport – Domestic and International*, Cambridge: Cambridge Academic Press.

Evans, K and Grossman, S (2002), 'Should you stay or should you go?', *Supply Management*, February.

Foster, D (2002), *The Global Etiquette Guide to Africa and the Middle East*, New York: Wiley.

Galbraith, J (2001), *Designing the Global Corporation*, San Francisco: Jossey-Bass.

Moncza, R M and Trent, R J (1991), 'Global sourcing: a development approach', *International Journal of Purchasing and Materials Management*, 27, Spring.

Nolan, A (1990), 'On top of the world', *Supply Management*, February.

Rugman, A (2000), *The End of Globalization*, London: Random Business Books.

Stevens, J (1995), 'Global purchasing in the supply chain', *CIPS Purchasing and Supply Management*, January.

14

Capital procurement

Introduction

Some organisations have historically appeared to believe that in the acquisition of capital equipment they need not involve their procurement professionals. In such cases engineers and production staff have tended to be closely involved. Procurement staff were drawn in simply to sign the contract or get a discount. Yet the commercial implications of capital purchases are as important as the commercial implications of production materials or components. The main emphasis of this chapter, therefore, is on explaining the role of procurement.

Objectives of this chapter

- To identify procurement's contribution to the acquisition of capital equipment
- To outline the differences between the procurement of capital and non-capital goods
- To appreciate leasing and hiring as a means of employing capital goods
- To appreciate the importance of 'performance' specifications and how dealing with them can be simplified by tabulation
- To involve procurement from the earliest stage of identifying a need through the process of supplier selection, commercial input into contract clauses and appraisal of after-sales service
- To discuss the concept of lifetime cost
- To assess the various methods of investment appraisal

The acquisition of capital equipment

It is evident that operators, and production and finance staff, need to be involved in making buying decisions concerned with capital equipment. Depending upon the type of capital purchase, each may have a significant part to play in, for example, identifying the type of equipment required, examining the alternative sources which may be able to provide that equipment, and in

Table 14.1
The role and contribution of purchasing

The acquisition of capital equipment – procurement's contribution
• Location of sources
• Vetting of suppliers
• Negotiating (active role/consultancy)
• Cost–benefit analyses
• Life-cycle costing
• Advice on residual values
• Organisation of product trials
• Establishment of total supply cost
• Lease/hire/buy comparison
• Contract drafting
• Contract management
• Provisioning of support materials
• Co-ordination of procurement team

specifying the performance specification and budget factors that are involved. However, in our experience, decisions made by such a group without purchasing/commercial input frequently lead to contractual difficulties; for example, the equipment does not function to the level which the supplier's specification promised. In many such cases the buying company is obliged to seek compensation from the supplier with little commercial leverage other than, say, 10 per cent of purchase price retention. In our view, proper participation of the buying professional would help to ensure that such circumstances were avoided. Even where the outcome is the same, effective pre-contract negotiation can ensure that the buyer is protected, at least to some degree.

We are sometimes asked for advice from purchasing personnel who feel that it is necessary to convince users that the purchasing function can contribute to the making of appropriate decisions in relation to the acquisition of capital equipment. In this respect, Table 14.1 is used to stimulate discussion on the role and contribution of purchasing.

This chapter comments on the role that the buying professional has to play in buying capital equipment or in making other types of capital purchase. Procurement executives who aim to make a useful and constructive contribution to the capital expenditure decision, and one which will be recognised as such by other members of the decision-making unit, need diplomacy as well as top management backing. Alternative assets differ in their features, and technical assessment of these features is required. This technical assessment, followed by a financial assessment – Will it pay? Can we afford it now? – is usually the main part of the investigation, but examination of commercial aspects can also be very rewarding, and here astute procurement people can make a real contribution.

Because the equipment will have a working life of several years, it is important to consider such matters as product support, availability of spares, after-sales service, the financial soundness and management stability of the supplier. Cost of use after service is important, and is affected by reliability and the possibility of downtime.

Contract price is negotiable, as are payment terms. In addition it does not necessarily follow that a request by the supplier for stage payments needs to be accepted. It may well be the normal terms of trade of a particular manufacturer to charge X per cent with order, Y per cent when ready for despatch, Z per cent upon delivery, with the balance being paid a stated number of months after commissioning. However, depending upon, for example, the state of the order book, the supplier may well be prepared to forgo any payment prior to commissioning. Indeed we have been involved with one company in the printing industry where a Swiss supplier agreed to give the buyer 18 months' credit against a 10 per cent deposit. This is not to say that such arrangements can always be negotiated. Rather it is to emphasise that such negotiations should be undertaken in a manner which seeks the best commercial and technical outcome from the buyer's viewpoint. Frequently this involves challenging the apparent 'givens' of a tender for capital equipment.

The buyer should always seek some level of retention; for example, 10 per cent of the purchase price may be retained by the buyer until, say, one month after the equipment has been demonstrated on a production run as meeting its specified performance level. Contract terms of this kind can be negotiated by purchasing in the more straightforward cases. In more complicated cases (e.g. involving trade-offs between technical alternatives as well as commercial and financial alternatives) negotiating teams are set up with representatives of the various specialist functions.

What are capital items?

Buying capital goods, such as buildings, plant and machinery, and computers, differs in several ways from the purchase of non-capital goods. Unlike merchandise, production materials or office supplies, capital goods are not bought for current needs, to be used up in a short time, but are bought for long-term requirements, to be used for the production of goods or services. Capital goods have, as a rule of thumb, working lives longer than one year.

Capital expenditure is treated differently for taxation purposes and in accounting. Special tax allowances or cash grants may be available for investment in new equipment or for factories in certain areas of the country. Consequently, tax considerations, usually ignored in non-capital purchases, can be significant in capital purchase decisions; they can affect timing, they can make a big difference to the expected return, and they can be crucial in deciding whether to go ahead with the purchase.

Often the initial price is high, so that commitment to one capital project means that rival proposals have to be rejected. Even if initial price is not high compared with current expenditure, capital goods tend to be highly specific so that the cost of a wrong decision could be much higher than for current expenditure items. Alternative uses of a high-bay automatic warehouse, a crankshaft transfer line or a special-purpose machine tool may be negligible. If stocks are built up to meet increasing sales which fail to occur then stocks can be run down by selling back to suppliers or by deferring further purchases; but if specialised plant is procured to cope with the sales increase, it will not be so easy to dispose of it.

Most capital expenditure is postponable. Individual consumers would not last long if they stopped their intake of food and drink, and manufacturing organisations which stopped acquiring parts and material for production would soon be out of business. Individual consumers can, however, postpone the replacement of consumer durables such as a car or refrigerator with no great loss of amenity so long as the existing equipment works, and manufacturers in the same way can defer the replacement of old plant until prospects look brighter or the financial situation improves. This has unfortunate consequences for capital equipment suppliers; their order books alternate between feast and famine. When their customers experience a minor recession they suffer a major recession; the business cycle hits them in amplified form, with some time lag.

Leasing and hiring of capital equipment

Leasing and hiring can be taken together, in that they are closely related approaches employed where the ownership of an item, usually a piece of capital equipment, remains with another organisation, and in exchange for payment the client organisation enjoys possession and use. The two terms are frequently employed as though they are synonyms, but there is, strictly speaking, a difference. Normally, equipment is hired from a business which exists to supply that class of material to those who wish to use it from time to time. We might hire a chain saw or cultivating machine from a local tool hire company if the need arises; the same kind of thing might be done by a business requiring a crane or piece of earth-moving machinery for a short time. The hire company will gladly take the equipment back into their possession on completion of the period of hire, and will then be able to lend it to another customer on similar terms. Leasing is normally a financial transaction, and usually what happens is that the user organisation enters into a contract with a finance company, and agrees an arrangement whereby the finance company assists in the purchase and provides the using company with the relevant equipment. Ownership is retained by the leasing company, but the reason for this is rather similar to the reasons why a bank may wish to retain security for a loan. The leasing company does not wish to possess physically or have custody of the asset, merely to own it. The benefits which can be gained from leasing or hiring include the fact that if an item is required for a short time only it may well be cheaper to hire than to buy, cash flow might be conserved, and there is more business flexibility inherent in a situation where nothing is owned. It may surprise some students to learn that many of the word's leading airlines lease a proportion of their fleet of aircraft.

Capital requisitions

Because of their high costs, special procedures are commonly used for capital purchases. In small or medium-sized organisations all capital expenditure has to be authorised by the board. In larger organisations, authority to approve capital expenditure up to a specified cash limit is delegated to local directors, division or area managers, profit centre managers, or others below main board level; but above this limit the projects which make large demands on organisation finance, or affect capacity and method of working for a long time, are still referred to the main board even in large organisations.

Most capital decisions will be influenced by a range of interests. Figure 14.1 suggests some of the interests which may contribute to the acquisition of a fork-lift truck.

Delay in obtaining authorisation for capital expenditure resulting from such procedures can lead to excessive haste to get on with the work once authorisation is forthcoming. The requisitioner may have been waiting months for approval, and as soon as it is obtained may telephone the chosen supplier with the good news, chivvy purchasing to get the order off before contractual details are finalised, and generally ignore commercial aspects in the natural zeal to get the equipment installed.

In such circumstances the buyer is forced to negotiate from a disadvantageous position. The seller, having been told that the order is theirs and that delivery is required as a matter of urgency, is in an extremely strong position

Figure 14.1
Contributors to capital equipment decisions

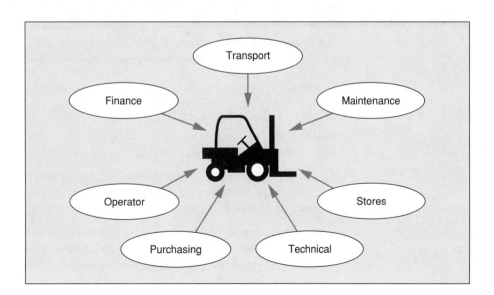

from which to negotiate. The professional buyer should seek to ensure that company procedures are in place to obviate such difficulty. It is our view that their involvement should begin at the earliest stage when a need is defined, and that, in conjunction with their technical and financial colleagues, they should undertake the market search for qualified suppliers and suitable equipment. After all, commercial as well as technical negotiations commence in those early stages and while engineering colleagues would be primarily focused upon technical issues the buyer would be concerned with the many commercial issues as they unfold.

The purchase department needs to insist that enough time be allowed to negotiate contract details. Where possible it is better for purchasing to participate at an earlier stage so that commercial as well as technical aspects are agreed and are included in the proposal put up for approval.

As an example of difficulties which can be encountered if these things are neglected, a case occurred in which a company ordered a new design of production equipment costing over £1 million. Engineers in the buying company had been assured that the equipment would be fully installed and operational in six weeks and would reach target output by week 8. Nine months after delivery, actual output was less than half of target output, which caused embarrassment with customers whose orders were held up. The company had inserted a 5 per cent retention clause in the contract, but apart from that was unable to obtain compensation from the equipment supplier. When negotiating a contract for production equipment which is wanted because of its indicated performance, it is necessary to include performance criteria in the contract and to relate payment, at least in part, to achievement of the agreed output norms.

Specification of capital equipment

In an article in *Purchasing and Supply Management*, Nigel Moore (1993), writing on the theme of specification of capital items, said:

Sometimes specifications are improved by being split into a general requirements section that is changed infrequently and a particular requirements section that is customised to each individual order or contract. [The particular requirements section forms the basis of the tabular format specification shown in part in Figure 14.2 and comprises three main sub-sections]:

1. section on the **required equipment, services or works**.
    The entries are kept short and must be read in conjunction with the information in the vertical columns, Table A, Table B and Inspection.

    Table A   This is completed by the specifier to show what is required.
    Table B   This is completed by the vendor to show what is being offered.
    Inspection   This is completed at the time an inspection of the works or equipment is carried out.

2. A **site details** section (not shown). Relevant details and factors about the location that could affect the design and performance of the plant, equipment, services or works.
3. A section on **additional information** that is required from the vendor (not shown).

The general or 'wordy' specification can remain to support this particular requirements specification. It could be updated to provide further clarification of terms and to ensure that they cannot be misinterpreted. The tabular format can have wide application as the contractual and specified requirements are not changing. The only departure from the traditional is the way the information is presented. It can be used for supply of equipment or services and scope of works on site. Usually the information is presented in a logical order of importance. Often this is based on the cost and difficulty for the vendor to comply with as part of fulfilling the subsequent contract. Typically this could include:

- Scope of supply including any extra items (for example, tests).
- Overall performance requirements.
- Any specific design requirements.

The detail can be made as comprehensive as desired or kept to the minimum. Consequently the specification can comply with EN 29000 by stating functional or performance requirements.

Table A is pre-printed to show the standard practice. The specifier needs only to complete the remainder and he or she is prompted on what information to provide. This can entail, for example, filling in a blank line or crossing out the options that do not apply. Consequently his or her job is made easier. Often all the vendor has to do is enter a 'Yes' to confirm compliance, although data can be written in where appropriate.

When the completed documents are returned from potential vendors, it is a simple task to compare their offers with the specification. The bid tabulation merely requires lining up the Table Bs. It takes little extra time to compare offers even if there is a large number of tenderers or alternatives. Possible copying errors or difficulties extracting information from the vendors' offers are removed.

At the tender evaluation stage, differences are highlighted and can be resolved before the order is placed. Even meetings with vendors are made easier as the specification forms a convenient agenda and when photocopied on to a larger sheet can be used to record the minutes. The process of issuing enquiries, evaluating tenders and placing orders is consequently speeded up.

The vendor also benefits. There is much less paperwork to look through and try to understand. The major part of the vendor's price and costs can be worked out by just examining a few sheets, instead of reading many pages. This is especially useful as tendering departments are often overworked and tender submissions are against tight time limits. Alternative offers can be submitted with greater confidence that they will be seriously evaluated.

Perhaps the greatest advantage to both specifier and vendor is that when the order is placed, there are markedly fewer opportunities for extra costs through copying errors, mistakes, misunderstandings and omissions. They also have a simple document to refer to during the contract and the last column can be used at any time by the specifier or the vendor to check that what has been agreed is actually being provided. Typical uses are for drawing checks and final inspection before despatch or handover.

Figure 14.2
Format of a particular requirements section of a specification

BATTERY AND CHARGER REQUIREMENTS			
1.0 EXTENT OF CONTRACT	**Table A**	**Table B**	**Inspection**
1.1 Supply, Design, Testing, Delivery site/~~FOB~~ At site installation, commission (a) Delivery: date req'd/length of time in months (b) Quantity:	Yes Yes/~~No~~ *10 weeks* *Two*	*Yes* *Yes* *15 wks* *2*	
1.2 Testing to EN/IEC (incl. tolerances) **1.2.1.** All equipment previously type tested **1.2.2.** Witness tests at work by purchaser	 Yes Yes	 *No* *Yes*	
2.0 OVERALL PERFORMANCE REQUIREMENTS			
2.1 Supply standing load and recharge battery (a) Time to recharge battery.......................hours	Yes *10*	*Yes* *8*	
2.2 Battery only supply standing load curve (a) At rated min./max. ambient temp. degrees C (b) Min. Battery terminal volts...........................V	Yes 20/30 *45*	*Yes* *20/30* *45*	
2.3 Equipment suitable for specified location (a) IP Number external during normal operation	Yes 32 min.	*Yes* *45*	
2.4 Design life min...years (a) Battery expected service life min.............years	25 3/~~10~~......	*Yes* *5*	
2.5 Packed for transport to site (a) Suitable 6 months min. indoor/outdoor storage	Yes Yes/~~VTA~~	*Yes* *Yes*	
3.0 GENERAL REQUIREMENTS			
3.1 Spares + consumables required for ....years (a) List of spares + future availability + prices	2 RWT	*Yes* *Yes*	
3.2 Finish (colour/RAL/vendor's std)	*Grey*	*Yes*	
4.0 DOCUMENTATION			
4.1 Quality Assurance, Quality Plan to BS 5750-1	RWT/~~No~~	*Yes*	
4.2 Manual copies: ....*5*............Loose leaf, A4 size	Yes	*2*	

Note: Table A lists specified requirements. The information provided in Table B forms the basis of the vendor's technical offer. Comments in brackets provide clarifications of information required.

Abbreviations: RWT = Return with Tender; VTA = Vendor to Advise; incl = including the following; m = minute; min = minimum value; max = maximum value.

(*Source*: Adapted from Moore, 1933)

The project approach

Whatever the size of the company, any purchasing professional worth their salt ought to be seeking to make an effective contribution to the control and management of capital purchases as suggested earlier. The person concerned should be the one who searches the market to locate suitable sources for the equipment. This presupposes that the requisitioner has developed a preliminary specification. Too often this is not written in sufficient detail to allow proper research to be done. The specification should indicate desirable performance criteria and delivery date as well as any special requirements such as safety and other legal requirements in the country where the equipment is to be used. The buyer could then:

1 Draw up a list of potential sources – worldwide if appropriate.
2 Obtain relevant data about sources.
3 Get names of current users of the suppliers' products for possible use as referees.
4 Obtain prices for alternative equipment, including ex-works price, transport and installation cost.
5 Find out lead-time details – ex works, delivered, installed, operational, and up-to-target output.
6 Establish expected equipment life, recommended spares and maintenance schedules.
7 Obtain statements of operating costs and performance criteria.
8 Find out what after-sales service suppliers are prepared to provide.

Next, the team can consider available alternatives and where feasible draw up a shortlist of companies able to meet technical and commercial requirements. Each company will be appraised individually, as well as being made aware of the terms and conditions applicable. Detailed discussions with shortlisted sources may be necessary to ensure that they understand what is required, when and how it will be done, and what criteria will be used to assess performance. Suppliers and referee customers may be visited in this stage.

Finally, one supplier is selected and the contract is negotiated. It should state the responsibilities of both parties and the procedures to follow in commissioning the equipment. It may well be the whole team which negotiates, but the purchasing professional, whether or not designated as team leader, should play the key role in commercial and contractual matters, and in communication between customer and supplier about the contract.

In these negotiations many issues need to be covered. Among the commercial issues the most obvious is price. What does the price include, what is excluded? Is it a delivered price or an installed one? If there are to be extras, what is the means by which their value will be calculated? In what currency is the purchase to be made? If a stage payment agreement has been made it is necessary to specify under what circumstances the price may be varied. If there is a long lead time and the supplier wishes to be protected in an inflationary period, it may be necessary to negotiate the application of a formula, for example, BEAMA.

As far as specification is concerned, leading companies are moving towards a functional rather than product specification; for example, that a particular machine should be capable of producing N widgets every minute over a period of Y hours' continuous running. Where that is the case, many buyers are seeking to agree contracts where the buyer retains a substantial percentage of the purchase price until the equipment performs as specified. Others agree payment against a performance bond where money is held, as it were, in trust until the equipment meets the specified output figures.

Other important areas for consideration include warranty terms and a clear understanding as to when title passes. Also, given the assumption that title does not pass until satisfactory commissioning, who is responsible for insurance relating to associated risks and liabilities until that time.

Time, of course, is always an element and in some major capital negotiations can be of fundamental importance. Suppose a retail organisation decides to refurbish one of its stores; each day which passes without trading results in lost sales. Consequently time becomes a major focus given the extent of the opportunity costs associated with the store not trading.

Spares provision, training of operators, a clear understanding of what facilities (e.g. electricity, water, cranage) are to be provided by the buyer, safety and arbitration arrangements are further considerations.

Lifetime costs

It should be remembered that capital items are likely to be employed over a substantial period of time, and that cost implications arise at the main lifetime stages of specification, price, purchasing, installation, operation and disposal (see Figure 14.3).

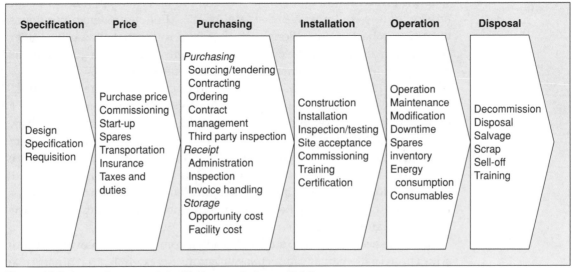

Figure 14.3 Some elements of the lifetime cost of a capital item

Investment appraisal

In a sense, almost any expenditure can be seen as an investment: the immediate expenditure procures a return which is not entirely immediate but extends some way into the future. A comparison can be made between what is likely to happen if the expenditure is made; and what is likely to happen if it is not made: if, for instance, the money is spent on something else. Such 'appraisals' are more important when the amount to be spent is larger because, in committing a larger proportion of available resources, the expenditure cuts down the options which remain open. The individual consumer is likely to give more thought to the purchase of a house or a car than to the purchase of a shirt or a drink for this very reason.

Capital expenditure of the sort we are considering is concerned with the acquisition of permanent physical assets used in the production of goods or services, and thus very definitely represents an investment. To appraise properly the costs and benefits associated with a particular proposal requires the life-cycle cost approach referred to above. The standard procedure is to prepare a detailed statement of the net cash flow per period throughout the life cycle (which may be the end of the project or asset life, or else up to a planning horizon). Net cash flow is the difference between cash received and cash paid. Positive cash flows, which increase available cash, may include payments from customers, savings in operating costs, reductions in the tax bill and tax refunds. Negative cash flows, which reduce available cash, may include payments to suppliers and employees' wages and salaries, interest on loans and repayment of loans, and tax on profits attributable to the project. The sequence of net cash flows for the life cycle is the earnings profile – a term used particularly when there are substantial differences between earnings (or profits, or savings) in different parts of the life cycle.

Complete accuracy is unattainable even for the simplest proposal, such as the replacement of worn-out machinery. For more complicated projects such as launching new products or opening up world markets, great uncertainties exist in estimating the future streams of costs and benefits which constitute the earnings profile. Nevertheless, the attempt must be made, since without some figures to work on most investment decisions would just be leaps in the dark.

Once the cost–benefit analysis or earnings profile has been prepared, a decision has to be taken as to whether to go ahead with the project. Even if it looks likely to be profitable, most organisations have many calls on available resources. A number of other paying proposals may be put forward, some of which have to be turned down because resources (financial, human, management) are limited. The process of calculating or estimating earnings profiles for investment proposals and applying various criteria to assess their profitability is known as investment appraisal.

The criteria applied to assess investment projects include payback period, average rate of return and discounted cash flow methods, of which the two most widely used are net present value (NPV) and discounted cash flow (DCF) yield or internal rate of return. Since the procurement executive who is involved in the capital expenditure decision may encounter any of these, we will explain them all with the aid of examples which may point to the short-comings of some of them. In most of the examples there is no specific reference to tax because this is the province of the accountant – not because it is unimportant. Taxation incentives in a development area could treble the expected yield of an investment in plant and machinery; taxation is also an important factor in deciding whether to buy or lease a facility.

Investment appraisal criteria

The payback criterion, popular because of its simplicity, consists of calculating how long the investment will take to pay for itself: the time taken for savings or profits (net positive cash flow) to accumulate to an amount equal to the initial outlay (negative cash flow). Its disadvantage can be seen from an example. Suppose the choice is between Project A and Project B, both requiring an initial outlay of £3000. Project A earns £1000 a year for three years, £600 in the fourth year and nil after that. Project B earns £750 a year for eight years. The payback criterion would prefer A, which pays for itself in three years, to B, which takes four years to pay for itself, even though B continues to earn money for twice as long as A.

The crude 'rate of return' criterion is applied in several ways. Typically, the average annual earnings are calculated and then expressed as a percentage of the capital invested. For instance, Project A has total earnings of £3600 over four years; therefore the average annual return is £900; as a percentage of the capital invested, £3000, this is a 30 per cent rate of return. Project B earns £750 a year, a 25 per cent rate of return. This criterion would also prefer A because B gives a lower rate of return. The fact that it earns it for a longer period is left out of account.

More accurate appraisal techniques take account of the fact that a pound received today is worth more than a pound which will not be received for two years. The present value of money receivable in the future can be calculated quite simply. The procedure is the inverse of the compound-interest calculation by which the future value of money invested today can be worked out.

For instance, if £100 is invested for three years at say 10 per cent interest, it will amount to £100 + 10 per cent at the end of the first year, i.e. £110. At the end of the second year it will amount to £110 + 10 per cent, i.e. £121. By the end of the third year it will be worth £121 + 10 per cent, i.e. £133.10. Now if we can say that £100 invested today at 10 per cent interest will be worth £133.10 at the end of three years, we can also say that if £133.10 is due three years from now, it must be worth £100 today, using a discount rate of 10 per cent.

Published tables show interest factors: we could have looked up 10 per cent for three years and found the factor of 1.331. Multiplying £100 by this factor would immediately have given the future value of £133.10 which we worked

Table 14.2 Discount factors for DCF calculations
(This table shows the present value of 1 discounted for various numbers of years at various rates of discount)

Rate of discount	5%	6%	7%	8%	9%	10%	11%	12%	13%	14%	15%	16%	17%	18%	19%	20%
Year																
0	1.000	1.000	1.000	1.000	1.000	1.000	1.000	1.000	1.000	1.000	1.000	1.000	1.000	1.000	1.000	1.000
1	0.952	0.943	0.935	0.926	0.917	0.909	0.901	0.893	0.885	0.877	0.870	0.862	0.855	0.847	0.840	0.833
2	0.907	0.890	0.873	0.857	0.842	0.826	0.812	0.797	0.783	0.769	0.756	0.743	0.731	0.718	0.706	0.694
3	0.864	0.840	0.816	0.794	0.772	0.751	0.731	0.712	0.693	0.675	0.658	0.641	0.624	0.609	0.593	0.579
4	0.823	0.792	0.763	0.735	0.708	0.683	0.659	0.636	0.613	0.592	0.572	0.552	0.534	0.516	0.499	0.482
5	0.784	0.747	0.713	0.681	0.650	0.621	0.593	0.567	0.543	0.519	0.497	0.476	0.456	0.437	0.419	0.402
6	0.746	0.705	0.666	0.630	0.596	0.564	0.535	0.507	0.480	0.456	0.432	0.410	0.390	0.370	0.352	0.335
7	0.711	0.665	0.623	0.583	0.547	0.513	0.482	0.452	0.425	0.400	0.376	0.354	0.333	0.314	0.296	0.279
8	0.677	0.627	0.582	0.540	0.502	0.467	0.434	0.404	0.376	0.351	0.327	0.305	0.285	0.266	0.249	0.233
9	0.645	0.592	0.544	0.500	0.460	0.424	0.391	0.361	0.333	0.308	0.284	0.263	0.243	0.225	0.209	0.194
10	0.614	0.558	0.508	0.463	0.422	0.386	0.352	0.322	0.295	0.270	0.247	0.227	0.208	0.191	0.176	0.162
11	0.585	0.527	0.475	0.429	0.388	0.350	0.317	0.287	0.261	0.237	0.215	0.195	0.178	0.162	0.148	0.135
12	0.557	0.497	0.444	0.397	0.356	0.319	0.286	0.257	0.231	0.208	0.187	0.168	0.152	0.137	0.124	0.112
13	0.530	0.469	0.415	0.368	0.326	0.290	0.258	0.229	0.204	0.182	0.163	0.145	0.130	0.116	0.104	0.093
14	0.505	0.442	0.388	0.340	0.299	0.263	0.232	0.205	0.181	0.160	0.141	0.125	0.111	0.099	0.088	0.078
15	0.481	0.417	0.362	0.315	0.275	0.239	0.209	0.183	0.160	0.140	0.123	0.108	0.095	0.084	0.074	0.065
16	0.458	0.394	0.339	0.292	0.252	0.218	0.188	0.163	0.141	0.123	0.107	0.093	0.081	0.071	0.062	0.054
17	0.436	0.371	0.317	0.270	0.231	0.198	0.170	0.146	0.125	0.108	0.093	0.080	0.069	0.060	0.052	0.045
18	0.416	0.350	0.296	0.250	0.212	0.180	0.153	0.130	0.111	0.095	0.081	0.069	0.059	0.051	0.044	0.038
19	0.396	0.331	0.277	0.232	0.194	0.164	0.138	0.116	0.098	0.083	0.070	0.060	0.051	0.043	0.037	0.031
20	0.377	0.312	0.258	0.215	0.178	0.149	0.124	0.104	0.087	0.073	0.061	0.051	0.043	0.037	0.031	0.026
21	0.359	0.294	0.242	0.199	0.164	0.135	0.112	0.093	0.077	0.064	0.053	0.044	0.037	0.031	0.026	0.022
22	0.342	0.278	0.226	0.184	0.150	0.123	0.101	0.083	0.068	0.056	0.046	0.038	0.032	0.026	0.022	0.018
23	0.326	0.262	0.211	0.170	0.138	0.112	0.091	0.074	0.060	0.049	0.040	0.033	0.027	0.022	0.018	0.015
24	0.310	0.247	0.197	0.158	0.126	0.102	0.082	0.066	0.053	0.043	0.035	0.028	0.023	0.019	0.015	0.013
25	0.295	0.233	0.184	0.146	0.116	0.092	0.074	0.059	0.047	0.038	0.030	0.024	0.020	0.016	0.013	0.010

out longhand. Similar tables are published for discount factors: $1/1.331 = 0.751$, the discount factor for three years at 10 per cent. If the future value of £133.10 is multiplied by this factor of 0.751, we have the present value of £100. Table 14.2 gives such factors.

■ Some problems on present value (ignoring inflation)

Example 1

Would you rather be given £100 now or £200 in five years' time, given that the current interest on a safe investment is 10 per cent?

The present value of £200 in five years' time is $0.62 \times 200 = £124$.
The present value of £200 in five years' time is greater than £100, and if present value were the only consideration I would rather have £200 in five years' time.

Example 2

Capex Ltd is trying to decide whether to replace an old machine. The purchase price of a new one is £10,000 and it is estimated that it will result in a saving of £3000 per year for five years in operating costs. Should Capex Ltd go ahead with the purchase? Use a discount factor of 10 per cent.

Year	Cash flow (£)	Present value (£) (discounted at 10%)
0	−10 000	
1	+3 000	+2 727
2	+3 000	+2 478
3	+3 000	+2 253
4	+3 000	+2 049
5	+3 000	+1 863
		+11 370

In present value terms, the new machine will save £11,370 in operating costs over the next five years. Purchase of a new machine at a price of £10,000 is justified.

Example 3

To pass its annual inspection, Mr. Jones's old car will need repairs costing an estimated £200. He has been offered a 10-year-old Volvo (with a new MOT) for £500. He estimates that the 'new' car will save him £80 a year for five years in fuel and repair costs. He could sell his old vehicle for £80. Should he buy the 'new' car if he can borrow the money he will need this year at an interest rate of 12 per cent?

	£	
Purchase price of new car	−500	
Selling price of old car	+80	
Cost of repairs for MOT	+200	(saved by purchase of new car)
Net cost of purchase	−220	

Year	Net cash flow (£)	Present value (£) (discounted at 12%)
0		
1	+80	+72
2	+80	+64
3	+80	+56
4	+80	+50
5	+80	+46
		+288

By purchasing the new car, Mr. Jones would save £68 on present value terms.

Example 4

Project A can now be compared with Project B on a more rigorous basis. Using a 10 per cent discount rate we obtain the following figures:

Year	Project A			Project B	
	Cash flow (£)		Present value (£)	Cash flow (£)	Present value (£)
0	−3000			−3000	
1		+1000	909		+750	682
2		+1000	826		+750	619
3		+1000	751		+750	563
4		+ 600	410		+750	516
5					+750	466
6					+750	423
7					+750	385
8					+750	350
	−3000		2896	−3000	4004

Project B is obviously much more profitable than Project A. This was not shown by the payback and crude rate of return criteria applied earlier, which indeed suggested the opposite.

Example 5

In fact, in the last example, Project A is not profitable, since the present value of the earnings, £2896, is less than the initial outlay to obtain the earnings, £3000. One factor in determining the present value of the earnings is the discount rate: if a lower discount rate were applied, the present value would be higher. What discount rate would show Project A as breaking even?

As we have only four figures to consider, the effect of various discount factors can easily be calculated. The one which comes nearest to breaking even is 8 per cent:

Year	Cash flow (£)	Present value at 8% (£)
1	+1000	926
2	+1000	857
3	+1000	794
4	+ 600	441
		3018

Would Project B still be the more profitable at this lower discount rate?

Example 6

Project C and Project D each require an initial investment of £2600 and each has a three-year life. While C produces earnings of £2000 by the end of the first year, £1000 by the end of the second year, and £200 by the end of the third year, D has quite a different earnings profile: £200 in the first year, £1000 in the second, and £2000 in the third year. After the third year there are no cash earnings either for Project C or for Project D.

On the payback criterion, C is preferable since it pays for itself sooner. On the crude rate of return criterion, there is nothing to choose between them since they both produce average earnings of £1066 a year, or 41 per cent. If present value is created at a discount rate of 10 per cent, we see that D actually loses money:

Year	Discount factor	Project C earnings (£)	PV (£)	Product D earnings (£)	PV (£)
1	0.909	2000	1818	200	182
2	0.826	1000	826	1000	826
3	0.751	200	150	2000	1502
			2794		2510

The net present value, when the initial investment of £2600 has been deducted from the PV of the earnings, is minus £90 for Project D, and plus £194 for C.

■ The discount rate

The present value of future payments depends on how much they will amount to, how far away in time they are located, and the discount rate which is used. The amount and the timing of the payments are estimates of facts, but the discount rate is not factual in this sense; it is a matter for decision.

Financial experts see it as a technical decision, at least as complicated as such technical questions as the life of electronic components or the strength of embankments. It may sometimes be the cost of capital finance, although this is multi-valued; firms raise finance from several sources at various costs. Risky projects may be thought of as calling for risk capital while virtually risk-free projects can be funded at safe rates.

The two most popular DCF criteria for investment appraisal are: net present value (NPV), and internal rate of return (IRR) or DCF yield. In example 2 above, the gross present value of the savings of £3000 a year is £11,370, a positive cash flow; the negative cash flow required to buy the machine is £10,000. Consequently, the net PV, the difference between the two, is £1370. Similarly, in example 3, the NPV of the car purchase is £68.

The IRR criterion is to find what discount rate would make the NPV equal to zero. In example 5, we saw that a discount rate of just over 8 per cent would make the present value of the earnings equal to the initial outlay, giving a zero NPV. This is the rate of return which the investment will actually earn. It can thus be seen as a more rigorous version of the crude 'rate of return' criterion used by some firms. It can also be regarded as showing the actual cost of capital finance at which the project would break even; for instance, if Project A in example 5 could be financed by a loan at 7 per cent, it would show a small profit. The method of finding this discount rate, which will determine the DCF yield by making the NPV zero, is basically trial and error, but short-cut methods have been developed which reduce it to a quick and simple routine.

A common reaction to DCF methods is that they are too complicated; they lend a spurious appearance of precision to estimates which are basically far from precise. As the economist J M Keynes wrote in the 1930s, 'the outstanding fact is the extreme precariousness of the basis of knowledge on which our estimates of prospective yield have to be made'. The contemporary economist Paul Samuelson writes: 'The world as it is today was predicted by nobody' – so how can we expect to succeed in our life-cycle costing exercises? What is the point of taking our earnings profiles, riddled as they must be with assumptions, pious hopes and power ploys, and putting them through the DCF calculation process?

The point is very simple. It is that DCF methods, which are theoretically sound, do not increase whatever error is in the data. Unsound criteria such as payback (if used uncritically) make the data even more misleading. Admittedly, it will hardly be economic to apply procedures to small routine replacement investments such as typewriters, and it may not be practical to apply them to major non-routine decisions such as diversification, or to investments which must be undertaken because of legislation or other compelling cause; but between these two extremes extends a great range of 'middle management' investment proposals for which DCF criteria are now considered normal.

This elementary introduction to investment appraisal has referred only in passing to such matters as sensitivity analysis, taxation, and the comparison of proposals which have different life cycles or differently shaped earnings profiles. Readers wishing to find out more about these matters should study some of the excellent books available.

Conclusion

Contracting for a North Sea oil rig, a new hotel, a major computer installation or a replacement machine tool would in each case have its own special set of problems. In buying capital goods each case is likely to be different, but in each case the purchasing department has an important part to play.

Market and source information can be obtained for the project team. Help can be provided in evaluating available alternatives. Good communications should be established with preferred suppliers. Time scales should be made known to all parties. Performance criteria, and who is responsible for what, need to be spelled out.

Perhaps the most important of the purchasing department's duties is to ensure that all important aspects of the contract are considered and agreed, and what is agreed is written into the contract and that the supplier performs against the terms of the contract.

Summary

1 The chapter outlines the differences between the purchase of capital goods and non-capital goods. Capital goods are bought to meet long-term needs; are normally highly specific and highly priced (thus the cost of a wrong decision could be critical). Most capital expenditure is postponable.

2 Performance specifications are widely used in the acquisition of capital goods. Once this is complete, the buyer can shortlist potential sources, obtaining the relevant data including lead times, expected equipment life, recommended spares and maintenance schedules.

3 With high levels of investment, decisions are normally referred to the main board, which may take some time to reach an agreement. It is imperative that no hasty actions are taken by the requisitioner once approval has been obtained – full regard must be given to the commercial implications. By being involved from the earliest opportunity, purchasing will be able to input sound commercial and contractual knowledge throughout the project.

4 Investment appraisal serves to assess the costs and benefits associated with a proposal. The life-cycle approach profiles the net cash flow. The chapter also outlines the methodology behind the following approaches: payback period, average rate of return and discounted cash flow.

References and further reading

Barker, J (1993), 'How to achieve more effective purchasing through activity-based costing', *2nd PSERG Conference*, University of Bath.

Freeman, M and Freeman, K (1993), 'Consider the time value of money in break-even analysis', *Management Accounting*, 17 (1), January.

Keynes, J M (1936), *General Theory of Employment, Interest and Money*, New York: Harcourt, Brace and Co.

Moore, N (1993), in *Purchasing and Supply Management*, July.

Morgan, M (1993), 'How the Japanese account for long-term risk: some lessons for western companies', *Multinational Business* (MTN), Issue 4, Winter.

Samuelson, P A and Nordhaus, W D (2001), *Economics*, New York: McGraw Hill.

Turner, J R (1999), *The Handbook of Project-based Management*, New York: McGraw-Hill.

15

Retail procurement and efficient consumer response (ECR)

Introduction

Buying merchandise for resale while having much in common with other types of buying also has some major differences. Buyers in other sectors of the economy can learn much from studying some of the good practices found in the retail sector. Buyers in major retail organisations such as Marks & Spencer or Tesco are likely to be far more involved with their supply chains and customers than in other sectors of the community.

Objectives of this chapter

- To analyse the role of the retail buyer and their involvement with the supply chain
- To differentiate between selector, buyer and merchandiser
- To understand retailing research and the different methods of collecting data
- To define all the aspects involved in merchandising
- To appreciate the value of brand names and how they compete with 'own brand' labels and generics
- To understand the concept of efficient consumer response

Decisions have to be made in terms of what to buy, quantities, prices, delivery terms, and mode and timing of payment. In addition, there may be negotiations covering training of retailer's staff by the seller, sale or return, sales promotion deals, and so on.

There are, however, differences. What retailers, wholesalers or other members of the distributive sector buy, they also sell. The 'what to buy' decision must be taken with a strong feeling for what will sell. There is a much greater overlap between the marketing/selling activities and buying than any other sector. Almost certainly a trained buyer in Marks & Spencer or Tesco would have spent a considerable time on the sales side prior to becoming a buyer. This chapter concentrates on the distinguishing characteristics of buying for resale.

Retailing

It is interesting to note that a small proportion of retailers account for most of retail sales. Chain stores – for example, Tesco, Sainsbury's, Asda, Marks & Spencer, the Co-op – account for about 70 per cent of total food and drink retailing in the UK. The rest is made up of smaller independents and multiple independents (e.g. Spar).

Tesco is renowned as an example of a retailer utilising its buying power effectively to give it advantage in the high street. It is interesting to note that the policies and strategies of the company from its beginning included procurement as a fundamental key.

Other successful retailers in the UK and Europe which have tended to dominate food retailing in recent years have also laid great store by procurement. Clearly the food retailer that works with relatively tight margins has to maximise profit by moving the goods more quickly through the store. It is not uncommon for the more effective retailers to turn their stock over 52 times a year. Suppliers in such circumstances find that what the economists call non-price variables are seen to be extremely important. Date/time scheduling is now common, for example with the supplier being required to deliver on a stated day at a stated time. The majority of the buying for the larger organisations is centralised. Tesco and Sainsbury's each employ hundreds of buyers backed by teams of agronomists, technologists, quality controllers and researchers. 'Buying is the glamour job in retailing', according to one expert. 'Store sizes are going up, and they need to find more lines to fill them. So they're constantly searching.' The pressure is on the buyers to come up with more innovative and upmarket 'niche' products. Certainly, the range and quality of food products on offer in the supermarkets have greatly improved in recent years. This should be good for consumers and it should be the key to success for those retailers that manage to stock what consumers want, at prices they can afford, which is also the key to success for small specialist outlets.

Marks & Spencer employs a range of specialists involved in the buying activity who, while they all work together, each have specific roles. To take clothing as an example, the selectors are responsible for identifying suitable lines for sale in Marks & Spencer's stores. They visit fashion shows and other influential events. This may involve travelling widely, identifying appropriate merchandise. Buyers determine the budgets/estimates and, working closely with selectors, decide whether or not lines will sell. Buyers have the final say in any decision, and also have some involvement in identifying appropriate merchandise. Once a line has been selected buyers require the supplier to produce samples for examination, trials and testing by various technologists. Finally, the merchandiser will decide on levels of stock to hold in the stores and which stores will carry various lines. These three activities – selector, buyer and merchandiser – which do overlap from time to time, are co-ordinated by HQ in Baker Street.

Most large retailers are organised in broadly the same way. In smaller organisations and department stores the buyer may be responsible for selecting, buying and certain merchandising functions as well.

Retailing research

In deciding what to buy, the buyer's intuition and feel for the market are considered especially important in connection with fashion goods, the demand for which is very hard to predict. There is always some scope for intuition and feel for the market, but marketing research is intended to provide a factual basis for rational decisions, especially for such relatively standard lines as food and drink. Marketing research has been defined as: 'the systematic gathering, recording and analysing of data about problems in marketing goods and services'.

An early version of retailing research was the retail audit which Nielsen invented in the United States. A representative group of shops is selected – representative of chemists, groceries, off-licences, or whatever is the research subject – and checks are made at regular intervals, usually twice a month, of what stock is on the shelves and in the storeroom. Sales for each item audited are calculated from the figures for this and the previous stock check and from quantities invoiced in the period between the two. Increasingly, electronic data capture at checkouts makes this sort of information immediately available to retailers for their own merchandise sales and this is leading to new forms of retail audit.

Supply chains in retailing

In many types of retail distribution, but particularly in the grocery business, the main retailers stock the goods of most, if not all, of the major manufacturers. The consumers are free to visit the retailer of their choice in the knowledge that the product they seek, whatever the brand, will be likely to be available. This situation is depicted schematically in Figure 15.1, but of course the true situation is considerably more complex. Unlike the situation in most supply chains, in retailing of this kind there is a very wide range of possible routes from the manufacturer to the consumer. This is especially true in respect of branded items such as canned food, detergents, coffee, sweets and confectionery and so on. The major retailers compete on price and on aspects of customer service and satisfaction in an attempt to increase market share, but of course market share is of no great value unless it is profitable for them. Profitability comes from efficiency, and there is a considerable difference in profitability between those retailers that are able to manage their complex supply chains well.

Figure 15.1
**Supply chains
in retailing**

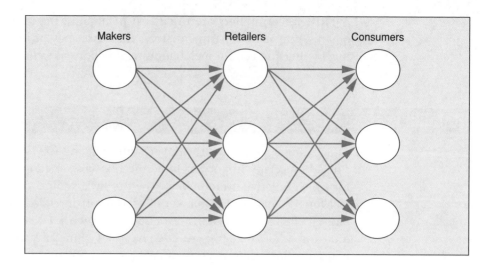

Mini case study – Sainsbury's

Sainsbury's, formerly the UK's largest supermarket chain in terms of sales value, was overtaken in the 1990s by Tesco, and later by Asda. In a determined bid to regain its lost status, Sainsbury's looked closely at the logistics and distribution side of its business. Today the company moves 2.5 million cases of goods from approximately 2000 suppliers to 500 outlets. In order to achieve this movement efficiently, Sainsbury's, working with suppliers and logistics service providers, has undertaken what it calls a 'business transformation programme'. It now has in place a highly automated supply system, and a company spokesman has said of the firm's supply chain strategy, 'There is a need to eliminate everything that doesn't add value, such as checking and counting deliveries'.

Electronic point of sale (EPOS)

Bar-coding enables a situation where every stock line can be uniquely identified. 'Bar codes' – the familiar panels containing numbers printed as a series of narrow and wide lines and spaces – are used to identify merchandise. These codes can be read quickly and accurately by sensors at the checkout or till, and numbers matched with a computer file, enabling the description, current price (not encoded, but 'looked up' by computer), and other details of the product specification to be accessed. Compared with checking by hand, scanning is three or four times faster. We can update information on sales as changes occur, in terms of dates and times, amounts bought, prices paid and so on. This system greatly facilitates data collection compared with traditional methods.

'Real time' information is available on patterns of store traffic, sales, and profitability on every line carried. This information can be passed on to the suppliers of the merchandise concerned. Electronic point of sale (EPOS) is

Figure 15.2
Schematic representation of an EDI system

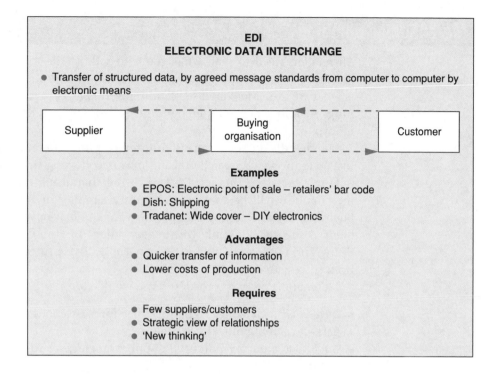

EDI
ELECTRONIC DATA INTERCHANGE

- Transfer of structured data, by agreed message standards from computer to computer by electronic means

Supplier → Buying organisation → Customer

Examples
- EPOS: Electronic point of sale – retailers' bar code
- Dish: Shipping
- Tradanet: Wide cover – DIY electronics

Advantages
- Quicker transfer of information
- Lower costs of production

Requires
- Few suppliers/customers
- Strategic view of relationships
- 'New thinking'

an example of electronic data interchange (EDI): that is, the transfer of structured data by agreed message standards from computer to computer by electronic means. As goods are sold, information is transferred directly to major suppliers via the buying organisation, in this case the retailer. There is no need for huge amounts of paper documentation, and savings are considerable. Figure 15.2 is a schematic representation of an EDI system.

Probably the most developed EDI systems are those used by retailers in connection with EPOS. Indeed, this usage has been seen by many manufacturing organisations as a benchmark against which to judge their own development in this field.

Much of the information generated from retailers' EPOS systems can provide valuable real-time information to suppliers selling merchandise to the retailer. Such information includes:

- how well a product is selling;
- the effects of promotional activity from the supplier;
- shelf space allocations;
- the effects of other merchandise changes; and
- the effects of price increase or decrease.

It can quickly be fed back to suppliers for decision-making purposes. This type of information is often only made available to suppliers as part of a negotiated 'deal', i.e. they pay for it.

Merchandise planning

All retailers need to plan what goods to sell. At the top level, merchandise planning is about the nature and purpose of the business: 'what we sell is what we are'. Merchandise planning at this level is part of corporate planning. At a lower level, merchandise planning is about what to order next month.

Merchandising is a term used differently by different organisations. For instance, in Firm A merchandising means collecting the information which buying needs to do its job. In Firm B merchandising means deciding what merchandise will be sold, deciding on a supplier or suppliers, negotiating buying prices and setting selling prices for the first buys, the buying department as such dealing only with repeat orders. In Firm C the terms merchandising and buying are used interchangeably. These three examples are taken from three actual firms.

Merchandising in its broadest sense would comprise:

- *Merchandise planning*. Preparing sales forecasts, setting merchandise budgets, developing model stock plans.
- *Buying*. Evaluating potential suppliers, selecting suppliers, negotiation, ordering.
- *Distribution*. External transport arrangements, receiving goods, marking, internal transport.
- *Control*. Stock-turn rate, financial control, unit control, and other measures.

Corporate objectives normally include targets in all of these, and strategies will be devised in most areas.

A retailer develops a product mix: that is to say, a particular combination of products to meet the needs of one or more target markets. This is not a once-and-for-all process. The right mix for today might not be the right mix next year. New products appear on the market, old products sometimes lose their appeal, consumers' preferences alter. The target market is itself subject to change.

The product mix includes ranges of merchandise. A product line or range of merchandise is a group of related products. Products can be related in several ways to form a range of merchandise, for instance, various kinds of canned soup, or children's clothing, or wallpaper. In developing a range of merchandise, retailers consider such questions as:

- Is this product suitable for our store image?
- Is it appropriate for our target markets?
- What is the likely demand?
- Who are the suppliers?
- How readily is it available?
- On what terms could we buy it?

■ Model stock plans

A model stock plan specifies the stock of the articles which the retailer intends to be available off the shelf. In planning the stock, retailers consider assortment, variety, width and depth.

Assortment

Every retailer has to decide what combination of goods and services to offer for sale. The assortment may be exclusive, like a camera shop that sells only Kodak cameras; wide, like a shop that sells cameras alongside many other lines related in some way, for instance leisure activities; deep, like a camera shop which stocks many different makes of accessories; or scrambled, stocking many unrelated lines. The assortment a retailer chooses is related to the target customers at which the retailer is aiming.

Variety

Variety is the number of lines carried by a shop. A fish-and-chip shop does not offer the variety offered by a Chinese takeaway, for instance. Variety has two aspects: width and depth:

1 *Width* refers to the level of specialisation; it measures the number of different product groups or lines offered.
2 *Depth* refers to the level of choice; it measures the number of items in each product group or line, size, colour, style, price.

A narrow and deep assortment would be appropriate for a product specialist, for instance a shoe shop. A wide and shallow assortment might suit a variety store.

■ Logistics and retailing

Huge amounts of money have been spent by the larger retailing concerns to find more efficient methods of moving merchandise from suppliers to their various stores up and down the country. Considerable savings have been achieved by using third-party carriers. Larger retailers such as Tesco, Sainsbury's and Marks & Spencer have led the way in establishing a more efficient approach to the total logistics problem of getting the merchandise to the customer at the lowest cost, through employing specialist logistics concerns to contribute to efficiency.

Stock analysis and sales analysis

Stock can be analysed in many ways – for instance, into fast movers and slow movers. For a retailer this is a form of sales analysis: which lines sell best? As one retailer said: 'There are some types of merchandise in which we do very well, for example newspapers and magazines where the turn round is measurable in hours rather than weeks. On the other hand, some of our slower selling lines such as the less familiar book titles are held for much longer periods, but this is essential for maintaining a service to our customers.'

Pareto or ABC analysis is a very useful method of stock analysis. This groups stock items into high demand value items, which tend to be few in number, medium demand value items, and low demand value items, of which there are many. According to one retail chain store:

> We organise our stock control on ABC lines; that is, the A lines are the top 1 per cent accounting for 30 per cent of the volume, the C lines are 85 per cent lines accounting for 20 per cent of the volume, and the B lines are somewhere in between. The figures are not precise. Our A lines, the top 1 per cent, are partly controlled by a top seller's system. Branches report the stock level of each of these lines at weekly intervals and from this we calculate rates of sale. The system has been highly successful in keeping stock levels down to very acceptable figures while maintaining service levels to the branches in the region of 94 per cent. Our books are mainly C items in stock control terms, that is they are 85 per cent of the lines which account for 20 per cent of the volume. For example, we hold 31,000 lines at our main warehouse of which 25,000 are books.

Unit stock control is the term used in the retail trade for procedures intended to ensure that the quantity available in the shop of each article on sale is not too little or too much to meet sales targets profitably. What is controlled is the physical quantity, or number of units, available as stock-in-trade. Financial stock control on the other hand aims to control the amount of money committed to stock-in-trade. Since these two kinds of stock control have different aims, it makes sense to use both of them.

The traditional basis of unit stock control is counting the stock. The simplest version, sometimes called 'eyeballing', is the periodic visual check, unsupported by records. This can work well in a small shop if the shopkeeper knows the stock well enough to keep a suitable assortment without records, and can predict demand without records, especially if the merchandise is not costly and can be obtained quickly. Millions of shops around the world use systems of this kind. 'Two-bin' systems are sometimes used. For example, two cases of an item are bought. One is put on the sales floor and the other in storage. When the case on the sales floor is empty, the other case is brought out of storage and one more is ordered.

Periodic actual count gives tighter control. Different classes of merchandise could be counted at different intervals of time: daily, weekly, or monthly, for instance. Count records plus order records enable demand for each item in stock to be calculated, providing a basis for forecasting future demand for it.

Perpetual inventory shows what is in stock at any time of any item. Electronic data capture at checkouts and the use of computers have finally made this feasible. Point-of-sale devices have become much more than cash registers; they can carry a complete stock record, analyse sales, work out order levels and reorder automatically.

Just-in-time also affects retailing probably more often than the average manufacturing organisation. At one time, most retailing organisations allocated huge areas to hold stock not actually on the shop floor. Today, very few retail organisations can afford to lose selling space by holding reserve stock. What you see on the shelves and counters is frequently what the store holds as stocks. It is therefore imperative that suppliers resupply stock exactly when it is required. Failure to supply on time means lost sales and profit. Flexibility is essential and EPOS provides the way ahead, linking customer demand with deliveries.

Brands

Brand names can be valuable property, and can account for hundreds of millions of pounds in corporate asset statements.

For a small shop, the national advertising and reputation which attract customers to well-known brands on sale can be very useful. A larger retailer wishing to establish its own distinctive image may prefer to sell exclusive brands which are not available from any other retailer. For instance, a distributor such as Currys may negotiate with a producer such as Hotpoint for a special version of their latest model to be sold only through Currys, which thus benefits from Hotpoint's well-advertised brand name while still being able to offer a unique product.

For a major chain there are advantages in selling goods under its own brand name. Marks & Spencer probably invented own brands in 1928, when Simon Marks registered St Michael as the Marks & Spencer brand name. He picked this name partly because St Margaret was the brand name used by Corah, which had just been persuaded to sell direct to M & S instead of through wholesalers, partly because Michael was his father's first name, and partly because the archangel Michael was the guardian angel of the Jews.

In a typical Sainsbury's supermarket, 5000 out of 6500 lines may be own brands. Many BHS goods are own brands, Tesco has its own brand of lager, and there are plenty of other examples.

There are two versions of 'own branding'. In one, the manufacturer supplies standard production line goods, but with the retailer's brand label rather than the manufacturer's. In the other, the retailer draws up a specification and finds a manufacturer to make goods to it.

The advantage to the manufacturer of the first version is getting a large order for goods which are being produced anyway, without incurring any expense in advertising or sales promotion. The advantage to the retailer is the lower price this makes possible, enabling their own brand to be stocked next to the manufacturer's brand on the shelves – identical goods at lower prices.

The second version of own branding is specification buying. Major retailers like this because as well as improving margins it helps to establish the retailer's image. Specifications can be very detailed, covering everything from what pesticides a farmer can use to how often packers must wash their hands. Not only the dimensions of the product, but the raw materials, the production processes and the quality control methods are specified. Specifications may even list the suppliers' suppliers from which raw materials can be obtained.

■ Generic brands

This is where one uses the basic product – for example, corn flakes can be sold for considerably less than Kellogg's Corn Flakes, which are branded. Similarly with pharmaceuticals – for example, aspirin may cost a fraction of the price compared with a brand name drug, although both may offer the same benefits. There is a considerable movement to provide more generic products as well as the brand equivalents. This enables retailers to tap the lower spectrum of the market.

Supplier selection

Standard criteria for supplier selection are quality, price, terms, delivery and service, together with actual performance on previous orders. These are discussed elsewhere in this text, since they apply to most buying decisions taken by an organisation. Additional criteria which may be taken into account by retailers include merchandise criteria and promotion criteria.

Merchandise criteria include the suitability of the merchandise for the store's requirements, how well it fits the store's image and the needs of its target customers; its availability – whether it can be delivered in the quantities, to the locations, at the times required; and perhaps adaptability, whether the supplier is willing to meet any special needs, such as supplying exclusive brands or own brands.

Promotion criteria include the type and amount of promotional support which a supplier provides. Apart from the support given by the supplier's national or local advertising, there may be an advertising allowance or joint advertising by producer and retailer. In-store demonstrations, display materials and other consumer inducements may also be provided.

In specification buying, the role of the buyer (or 'selector', as Marks & Spencer call them) is rather different from the traditional retail buyer's role of selecting from lines offered by competing suppliers. It is much closer to the industrial buyer's role. Indeed, Marks & Spencer has been called a 'manufacturer without factories'. As one supplier said: 'they don't buy products from us, they buy production capacity'. A typical buying office at Marks & Spencer includes the selector and assistant selector (buyers); the merchandise manager and merchandiser; the technical manager, technologist and quality controller; plus secretary, admin assistant and clerk. This is the buying team, all next to each other in the same office, not in separate departments.

Developments in the retail sector

The following is a brief summary of some of the issues facing the retail buyer and likely consequences.

Greater concentration of retail outlets

The trend towards bigger out-of-town retail establishments is growing. Often the effect of this is that an even greater range of products and services will have to be offered to the customer. The buyer's traditional breadth and depth of merchandise is likely to increase as a result, requiring more back-up services to assist the buyer.

Moves towards own brands

The majority of Marks & Spencer merchandise is own label. The growth of own-label brands puts even greater pressure on the retail buyer to expand in this area. Along with this is an associated problem referred to as 'passing off'. This occurs when a retailer produces a branded product with similar labelling and package design to an existing product so as to cause confusion in the customer's mind, the effect being to increase sales of the new branded copy product at the expense of the genuine article.

E-commerce

More routine buying decisions are being taken by the computer and EPOS system in terms of routine buying. This should give the retail buyer more time to spend on supplier development, negotiations and customer care.

Direct ordering by the customer from their own computer systems gives the retail buyer more time to carry out market research on new merchandise.

Efficient consumer response

What is efficient consumer response (ECR)?

Over several years, the authors have received numerous definitions of ECR from a multitude of retailers. The following are just a small selection.

'ECR is a grocery industry strategy in which distributors, suppliers jointly commit to work closely together to bring greater value to the grocery consumer.'

'Efficient consumer response – a strategy in which the grocery retailer, distributor and supplier trading partners work closely together to eliminate excess cost from the grocery supply chain whilst improving customer value.'

'Efficient consumer response is a "strategic initiative" working to overcome traditional barriers between trading partners, thus eliminating internal barriers, that result in costs and time that add little or no value to consumers.'

'Efficient consumer response is a commitment to the belief that sustained business success stems only from providing consumers with products and services that consistently meet or surpass their demands and expectations.'

It is a holistic approach that addresses the entire value chain of a manufacturer/retailer relationship, building on and utilising previous concepts such as:

- just-in-time;
- lean supply;
- quick response (QR);
- manufacturing resource planning (MRPII).

It also incorporates electronic point of sale (EPOS) and electronic data interchange (EDI) in a way that seeks to optimise the whole supply chain.

It implies trust and sharing of information and ECR provides a common language that enables different trading partners to work together.

■ Barriers to the successful implementation of ECR

- Traditional barriers between trading partners.
- Barriers within companies, between internal departments.
- Unwillingness to share information.
- Conflicts with other priorities.
- Inflexible information systems.
- Inadequate training.
- Unwillingness to make the necessary organisational changes.

■ Implementation issues

- Adopting the ECR philosophy is often more difficult than anticipated.
- Companies must dedicate time, training, investment in both people and infrastructure to achieve the change in attitude and mentality.
- Access to detailed internal information by partnership companies is often a source of disputes.
- Full benefits are not realised until a critical mass of suppliers/retailers start using ECR concepts e.g. EDI and continuous replenishment (CRP).
- Promotions can cause havoc in CRP because
  1 Peaks in demand are difficult to accurately predict.
  2 Multiplication in the number of SKUs

Efficient consumer response (ECR) offers major savings through improving the whole supply and promises to spell an end to the adversarial relationships which still dominate the grocery business.

As its name implies, ECR basically aims to fulfil consumer demands more efficiently and faster at lower cost. ECR takes a total supply chain perspective, considering packaging and ingredient suppliers, manufacturers, wholesalers, retailers and consumers.

■ Key prerequisites for successful ECR

For ECR to be successful, however, some long-held beliefs and attitudes have to change. Relationships between retailers and manufacturers need to become 'more honest and more open'. A shared vision is called for, with trading partners rewarded on their true contribution to creating consumer value.

The following aspects of ECR are assessed as of such fundamental importance that little can be achieved unless they are in place:

- high scanning accuracy;
- automated store ordering;
- optimising promotions;
- assortment planning;
- reliable operations;
- synchronised production;
- integrated suppliers.

The 'key to success' for reaching the ECR goal therefore seems to be closely related to the integrated partnership management of the information flow.

ECR is a logistical partnership between retailers and manufacturers in the grocery industry with enormous saving potentials. Within the ECR channel, no inefficiencies prevail. Each step of the channel concentrates on its very own core competences and reduces non-value-adding activities. The savings potential results from a total-chain reduction of inventory by speeding up cycle-time (see Figure 15.3).

Figure 15.3 ECR grocery supply chain

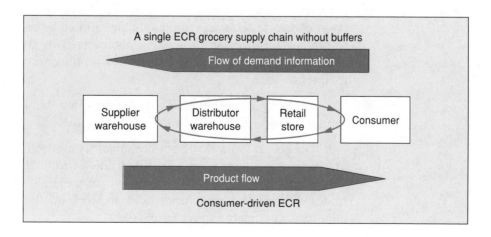

A single ECR grocery supply chain without buffers
Flow of demand information
Supplier warehouse — Distributor warehouse — Retail store — Consumer
Product flow
Consumer-driven ECR

■ ECR savings

Area	Savings potential through
Production (cost of goods)	Better capacity utilisation by reduced product losses owing to better packaging expenses, more efficient raw material procurement, reduced damaged rates
Marketing	Reduced trade and consumer promotion administration expense, fewer product introduction failures
Purchasing (selling/buying)	Simplified administration by automated ordering systems
Logistics	Efficient utilisation of warehouses and trucks, cross-dock flow through distribution
Administration	Reduced clerical and accounting staff
Store operations	Higher sales by square foot by automated ordering systems

Conclusion

Buying in the retail sector has many of the characteristics found in most buying jobs. The major difference is likely to be found in the scope of the buyer's role. Retail buyers are far more involved in the running of the retail organisation, the customer and the supplier base than the average buyer in other non-retailing organisations. Some of the best procurement practices can be found in large retail organisations in terms of EPOS, supplier development, supply chain management and the customer/buyer interface.

Summary

1 The 'what to buy' decision is directly related to what will sell. This decision may be taken by a team comprising selectors, buyers and merchandisers (in large organisations) or by an individual buyer who is responsible for all three aspects.

2 Bar-coding means that every stock line can be uniquely identified. Electronic point of sale systems scan product codes and collect real-time data relating to product turnover, stock levels, profitability. This greatly aids the retailer and the supplier by providing information on the effect of promotional activities, etc.

3 Merchandising comprises four aspects: planning; buying; distribution; and control. Targets set in each of these areas form the basis of corporate objectives.

4 *Unit stock control* looks at the physical quantity available as stock-in-trade and uses various methods from 'eyeballing' to electronic data capture. *Financial stock control* aims to control the amount of money committed to stock-in-trade. Most retail organisations hold all stock on the shelves – hence the importance of timely and accurate restocking.

5 When undertaking a supplier appraisal, merchandise and promotion criteria are also assessed. Is the supplier adaptable? What type of promotional support will they offer?

6 Efficient consumer response is a 'strategic initiative' working to overcome traditional barriers between trading partners, thus eliminating internal barriers, that result in costs and time that add little or no value to consumers.

References and further reading

Baily, P J H (1991), *Purchasing and Supply Management*, 6th edn, London: Chapman & Hall.

Barry, A (1996), 'Efficient consumer response – will they deliver the goods?', *Supply Management*, May.

Cox, J and Brittain, A (2000), *Retail Management*, London: McGraw-Hill.

Elliot, F and Morpeth, J (2000), *Retail Buying Techniques*, Washington: Management Books.

Foster, A and Thomas, B (1990), *The Retail Handbook*, London: McGraw-Hill.

James, R (1996), 'Winning promotions', *Supply Management*, August.

Kotler, P (1992), 'Silent satisfaction', *Marketing Business*, Issue 6.

McRae, C (1991), *World Class Brands*, Wokingham: Addison-Wesley.

Sinfield, R, Gassenheimer, W and Kelley, D (1992), 'Co-operation in supplier–dealer relations', *Journal of Retailing*, 68 (2).

Swindley, D (1992), 'The rise of the buyer in UK multiple retailing', *International Journal of Retail and Distribution Management*, 20 (2), March/April.

Williams, G (1996), 'Store wars', *Supply Management*, May.

16

Services procurement

Introduction

The acquisition of services is an important part of procurement and supply work, so much so that many organisations spend a greater amount with service providers than with suppliers of goods. Service supply is further gaining in importance as more and more organisations 'contract out' non-core aspects of their work. This contracting out may arise from a wish to concentrate more closely on the main business, and hence focus on the specialist skills that give rise to competitive advantage. Alternatively, and particularly in public sector concerns, the pressure to contract out services arises from the need not only to be efficient, but to demonstrate that open and competitive buying methods are employed. The practice of 'market testing' to ensure that work performed by organisations is undertaken at least as efficiently as would be the case if contractors or other providers were employed has given rise to a considerable increase in the external sourcing of services. Compulsory competitive tendering required by local and central governments in many parts of the world has resulted in a greater emphasis on the acquisition of services from external providers, services formerly supplied by 'in-house' supply. This chapter is concerned with the acquisition of services inasmuch as such acquisition processes differ from those for goods.

Objectives of this chapter

- To assess the differences between buying services as opposed to tangibles
- To outline a range of approaches to the procurement of services such as advertising, marketing, PR and legal services
- To highlight the main features of relevant EU directives
- To indicate some features of relevant legislation

What is meant by 'services'?

A service is any kind of supply where the main component is a task of some kind, rather than the provision of some tangible good or material. A service is a performance of some act of value, which, unlike the situation where goods are sold, does not result in the customer's ownership of anything. Almost any kind of service might be required. The list which follows is only a representative sample of some of the more commonly bought services; a complete list would be impossibly long:

Accountancy	Decorating	Logistics
Advertising	Design	Maintenance
Arbitration	Freight forwarding	Medical
Banking	Grounds maintenance	Research
Catering	Importation	Security
Cleaning	Insurance	Training
Computing	Legal advice	Transportation
Consultancy		

Special factors

There are a number of factors which differentiate services from tangibles, and which give rise to particular difficulties associated with their acquisition.

■ Impracticability of storage

By their nature, services cannot be stored. This means that they must be provided at a time that exactly coincides with the need. It is neither possible for a supplier to stockpile them in anticipation of a need arising, nor for a user to carry inventories to protect against uncertain supply or demand. Of course, not all services are time critical. It will probably not matter too much whether the windows are cleaned on Monday morning or Tuesday afternoon. Other services, while not 'storable', are provided continuously (e.g. insurance services, power and other utilities) and pose no significant scheduling problems for the user.

Nonetheless, the majority of services are likely to be the subject of careful planning and programming to ensure that they are provided at the right time and to the right location, with any failure giving rise to significant consequences. As an example, consider the design of a timetable in a school or college. The matching of tutors, appropriate groups of students from a range of courses, in suitable accommodation at mutually available times is a puzzle that taxes hundreds of academic minds at the start of each academic year, and which has, as yet, defied attempts to formalise and render it completely susceptible to a software-based solution.

If the requirement for a service is not steady, or is difficult to predict, the challenges associated with its provision are enormous, and normally require a very great investment in standby resources. The armed forces provide an excellent example of this type of situation.

Inspectability

Tangible materials can be measured, weighed, tested and inspected in any number of ways in order to ensure that they conform to the agreed specification. This is not so with services, which are generally rather more difficult to test for quality. Quality may be specified in 'conformance' terms, by saying things like 'the consultant shall be on the client's premises until 3 p.m. on Friday', or 'the work shall be completed and recommendations made by such and such a date'. More appropriately though, at least in most cases, 'performance' specifications are employed. Examples might be 'at the end of the training programme participants shall be competent to operate a 1 tonne counterbalance fork-lift truck', or 'vehicles maintained under this contract shall be capable of travelling safely at 70 mph and returning 25 mpg'.

A most important characteristic of services is that the results cannot be seen prior to buying, so preliminary assessment will tend to focus more strongly on the service provider, rather than the product.

Do or buy?

This question is related to the make-or-buy decision, which may be made when tangibles are being acquired. However, though the question occurs occasionally with tangibles, usually there is no real alternative to buying the material. In the case of services, the do-or-buy question is more commonly posed, and may frequently be reduced to a consideration of the pros and cons of employing persons with the necessary competencies to undertake the work in question, or contracting with an external organisation to perform the activity. The decision is often a difficult one, with the economic considerations becoming quite complex, and in turn overlaid by questions relating to corporate policy, and in some cases to government policy.

Contractual arrangements

When goods are to be bought, it is usually relatively easy to ascertain when a contract comes into existence, and when it has been completed, usually on payment for goods supplied according to the buyer's specification. In the supply of services the situation is often less clear-cut. Suppose an architect is commissioned to design a suite of offices according to a specification laid down in terms of accommodation required, within budget figures determined by the client. The architect supplies proposals that meet the criteria, but are not to the client's aesthetic taste. The client requires an alternative design.

Who pays? 'Not enough information' will be the correct response to this question, which nevertheless illustrates the type of difficulty which easily arises in arrangements for the supply of services.

■ Provision

Many services can only be acquired through the physical presence of the service provider or the employee. Gardening, or the servicing of a computer installation requires the appropriate personnel to be 'on-site'. However, banking or insurance services, for example, can be organised and provided remotely.

■ Complexity of acquisitions

While it is useful to look at the supply of services separately from the supply of goods, and to deal with such supplies in this chapter, it is the case that few contracts are purely for the supply of goods, and, equally, few are for services alone.

Figure 16.1 contains a list of nine different but typical organisational requirements, arranged in order with an item which is plainly 'goods' at the top, and a clear 'service' at the bottom. However, the supply of parts made to a customer's specification is not entirely a supply of goods. The parts will need to be shipped from supplier to customer, and there are other intangible considerations such as inspection and transfer of ownership (as opposed to possession) to take into account.

At the other end of the list, consultancy is, obviously, a service. Nevertheless it is difficult to envisage any kind of consultancy where no materials of any kind are involved. The consultant will usually hand over drawings, plans or other documents. Even when an oral presentation is to be made the physical resources for this to take place must be provided.

Figure 16.1
List of typical organisational requirements

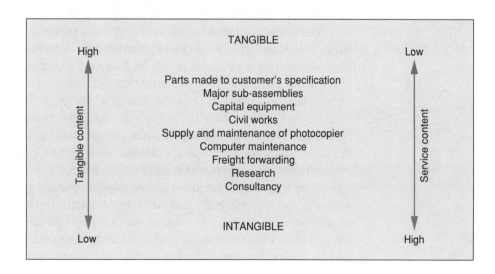

367

There are, of course, many supply arrangements that are clearly for both goods and services. A restaurant meal would provide a good example for the domestic buyer; the contract hire of a fleet of motor vehicles would be an organisational example.

■ Resale

Unlike goods, services cannot normally be resold. This means, of course, that the relationship between the service provider and the user of the service is a direct one. Intermediaries are not usually involved.

■ Variability

People, of course, provide services, and people are individually unique. Standardisation, homogeneity and repeatability may be challenging requirements where goods are concerned. In the provision of services complete uniformity would be a goal verging on the impossible.

We should mention that the exclusion of outsourcing in this chapter on 'services' could be somewhat misleading, as it is entirely possible that manufacturing capability might be outsourced, for example by an aircraft engine manufacturer outsourcing the fabrication of nacelles, or an engineering company divesting itself of its foundry business. The subject of outsourcing has been discussed in full detail in Chapter 4.

■ Approaches to the provision of services

A basic distinction to be made when considering the provision of services is that between 'provider present' and 'provider not present' services. For many organisations the provision of everyday services such as catering, cleaning and security involves the presence of the service provider's staff on the premises of the client concern. This, of course, adds another set of issues to be contemplated and determined connected with such matters as supervision, safety, confidentiality, access and the 'host–guest' relationship. Some services, for example banking, insurance or credit rating, will be undertaken at the provider's place of business, and some, such as transportation, will involve the presence of the provider for only some of the time during which the service is provided.

Occasionally there may be a choice as to whether the service provider will be present or not. For example, some companies, in entering into arrangements with travel agents, have agreed with the service provider that the agency maintains an office at the client's location.

Services may be provided on an occasional 'one-off' purchase, such as, for example, the development and delivery of a training programme to meet a specific need. In other circumstances call-off arrangements are sometimes entered into, where the service provider and client arrange a scale of charges, and in return for the commitment of the client not to buy outside the arrangement preferential terms are offered. Contracts for repair services are commonly arranged on this basis. Such arrangements are most common in larger organisations with a range of locations at which the service might be required. Frequently, services are provided on a regular, planned and programmed basis, and some form of medium to long-term agreement is entered into between provider and client. Routine cleaning services are generally provided in this way. Where this is the case it is desirable that some form of continuous assessment and improvement initiative is established and maintained, along the lines suggested by Figure 16.2. Below are case study examples of the procurement of a variety of services.

How to buy advertising and marketing services

The three most critical parts of the buying process are

- Agency selection.
- Contract negotiation.
- Continuing evaluation of the agency's performance.

Selection

Agency selection involves two parallel assessments, creative and commercial. Short-listed agencies that appear likely to have the appropriate skills and resources are asked to respond to an invitation to tender. It should include a detailed written brief.

This will outline the scope and purpose of the campaign, marketing messages and objectives, target audiences, timing and delivery, proposed methods for evaluating effectiveness and so on. The brief also needs to make clear whether the client is looking for a broad strategic proposal or a detailed creative 'pitch' – bearing in mind that the latter is a costly and time-consuming exercise.

When it comes to assessing an agency, a team combining marketing and procurement people should be involved. Clearly the marketers will take the lead in assessing creative and strategic issues, but procurement managers need a good enough understanding of these to be able to assess the commercial value of the proposals.

Negotiation

Creative issues cannot be commoditised to a tight specification, production and delivery issues certainly can and here procurement can add significant value. Procurement's role also includes creating clear lines of accountability in a complex supply situation.

When an agency is regularly employed on an account, a retainer may be suitable. A fixed fee may be paid for the delivery of a specific campaign. Alternatively, a percentage commission may be payable, based on their party and media costs, or a combination of these methods may be used.

Evaluation

The most problematic issue is evaluation. In direct marketing, for example, and continuing or repetitive work in general, performance can be measured fairly rigorously – how many mailshots reach the agreed target market and the response rate, for example. At the other end of the scale, the effectiveness of PR activity may be unquantifiable, except in a damage limitation crisis.

Overall, the message is that performance must be assessed where it can be, on cost control, response and delivery times, but there will generally be a large area of performance that can only be judged subjectively.

Figure 16.2
The service cycle

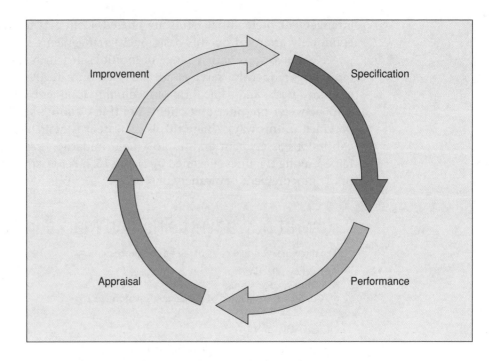

Prerequisites for success

- Choose the right agency: creativity and cost are important, but so is the ability to work with your marketing staff.
- Brief the agency well: tell it about the specific product or brand and the wider corporate strategy and culture.
- Work as a team: internally and with the agency and its key subcontractors.
- Go for a win–win deal: explore partnerships and methods of sharing risk and reward. The negotiations will affect the ability of the agency to attract and retain the staff you want on your account.
- Be proactive and creative: the agency doesn't have a monopoly on good ideas.
- Advertising and marketing are complex and fascinating supply chains and buyers can make a real difference.

Get the confidence and trust of the marketing people = they may see buying as old school, but they need to recognise that purchasing has moved on. We can help marketing become better practitioners. (Procurement Manager, major FMCG Company)

What would be the effect of applying procurement principles to this area? Procurement has strengths that any business unit will welcome, including negotiation expertise, policy and compliance advice, project management experience and strategic sourcing and market knowledge. Procurement can contribute to contract negotiation and agreement, terms and conditions discussions, commercial relationship responsibility to procurement. It can result in better management information, clearer costs and improved campaign management performance.

Therefore, although marketing and advertising colleagues often perceive a threat that procurement involvement will prolong negotiations and delay the reaching of contract agreements and therefore of service delivery, the opposite is in fact the case.

Mini case study – BA

Organisations such as BA have led the way in setting up specialised procurement teams to work with their marketing functions.

Their approach is that they are not buying a commodity, but are paying for creativity, time and the desire of a client to work with this organisation. Obtaining the cheapest option will not produce the best value it they cannot work hand-in-glove with a supplier.

Procurement's role is to facilitate this relationship by helping to identify critical suppliers and cementing partnerships. So why has marketing services remained outside procurement's remit for so long?

Marketing people have tended to have a perception of what a procurement department does – buy things cheaper – and many will have no idea of the creative element of procurement's work.

The issue of cost versus value highlights one of the difficulties of exerting influence over marketing services: measuring effectiveness.

Supplier relationships is another important area of potential added value from procurement.

Despite the increased pressure professional procurement can bring, suppliers generally welcome the benefits of improved processes, in terms of more definable specifications and performance targets, making disputes less likely. Suppliers want contracts which motivate them and incentivise them. They want to feel more involved in the business and have longer-term relationships.

The following is a 'pitch guide' from the Incorporated Society of British Advertisers. It clearly demonstrates areas where procurement expertise will add value.

The pitch

Where prospective agencies present to the client for a particular job is in some ways similar to any other contracting process. However, there are important differences for procurement professionals.

- Prepare background information (outline brief, profile of type of agency required, research from trade press) and make informal approaches to agencies that match your criteria. Invite up to three agencies to pitch (four if incumbent is included).
- Prepare a thorough brief, making clear all the judging criteria. It should be made clear whether strategic proposals alone are required or whether creative input is expected. Proposed remuneration and contract terms should also be outlined.
- Prepare a firm timetable for responses. At least four weeks is suggested for work to a full creative pitch.
- Be prepared to share confidential data with agencies and allow their staff access to company people they would work with in the future.
- Establish an objective evaluation system for pitches. All decision makers should be fully briefed on the process and present at all pitches. Ensure that agency presentation teams include those who will actually work on the contract.

Procuring public relations (PR)

Procurement may find itself involved in buying publicity for the goods or services for which a department or division wants to attract internal or external customers.

■ What does PR encompass?

PR may include at least the following:

- press releases and 'advertorials';
- features;
- articles;
- leaflets;
- in-house journals;
- marketing literature;
- financial presentations;
- opinion polling;
- sponsorships;
- road shows;
- videos/DVDs;
- conferences;
- exhibitions;
- radio and television;
- product launches;
- lobbying.

■ What are you procuring when you buy PR?

- Images and perceptions – not necessarily reality.
- Improved corporate commercial positioning.
- Heightened public respectability.
- Damage limitation when needed.
- Potential influence with top decision makers.
- Access to powerful opinion-forming groups.
- Mechanisms to best push your message.

Let us look at some of these areas.

In-house journals, leaflets and literature

Procurement will need to be involved only in the external buying in of services where required to facilitate production of in-house journals and general promotional literature.

Marketing literature and financial presentations

When a buyer has to buy in directly the design and production of marketing literature and financial presentations a range of key issues should be considered, such as:

- ability of PR outsourcers to successfully wrap up key business issues;
- succinctness of presentation as demonstrated in existing work;
- use of graphics, illustrations, *aides-mémoire*, colour;
- impact of the artwork and creative concepts;
- quality of the documentation, handouts, and card inserts;

- quality of paper used (e.g. fine art papers used for image projection);
- clarity of arguments and logical development of themes;
- effective motivating conclusions in other briefs prepared;
- environmentally friendly production of the presentation material.

All of these will enable the buyer to set some benchmarks in evaluating the forward direction and the worth of a PR consultancy for projecting his company's business.

The Public Relations Consultants Association (PRCA) and the four key trade and consultative bodies for the advertising and marketing industries – the Direct Marketing Association, Institute of Practitioners in Advertising, the Marketing Communications Consultants Association, the Incorporated Society of British Advertisers and its procurement directors group Compaq – have collaborated on guidelines that provide direction for clients selecting consultancies. To examine 'The Guide', visit the PRCA website at www.prca.org.uk.

How to buy legal services

The procurement of legal services starts with identifying a problem. The team will look at the problem in the light of the risk it poses to the company, its similarity to previous problems, how far the 'ideal' solution differs from the realistically likely outcome, and whether it is likely to be a 'one off' or a recurring difficulty.

An adviser recommended for success in employment law may not be ideal if the issue is really one of health and safety.

■ Five pieces of legal advice

- Functional managers are not expected to be legal experts, but they should be required to keep abreast of changes in those parts of the law that affect their operations.
- It is always cheaper to seek and take legal advice before a problem arises than it is to brief lawyers afterwards.
- See the most appropriate advisers for a given issue. They will not necessarily be solicitors and barristers.
- Always explore non-litigious methods of dispute resolution, such as arbitration.
- Legal costs can be controlled by accurate briefing, focused negotiation and structured monitoring.

Selection could depend on many factors from geographical proximity to current clients, but costs, quality and personal relationships will be paramount. Quality may be indicated by the Lexcel mark, a voluntary, independent scheme awarded by the Law Society.

Costs consists of several elements, typically an hourly expense rate covering salaries and overheads plus a mark-up, sometimes called 'care and conduct' or 'uplift' which is commonly around 50 per cent, and representing the solicitor's commercial profit. In some areas, such as property transactions, there may be a third *ad valorem* element, based on the value of the property being transferred. There is no set scale of charges for commercial matters, so there is plenty of scope for negotiation. There could be a fixed fee for straightforward non-contentious work, and/or fixed costs per interview, phone call and so on. In many civil cases, conditional or contingency fees are now allowable.

Mini case study – BT

BT treats its external legal provider in the same way as it would any other service provider, by producing a proper written brief and understanding what they are trying to achieve. In that way it ensures that it will get value for money.

European Union Public Contracts Directive

The following notes are intended to highlight the main features of the directive. There are many matters of detail that are omitted, and the reader should not rely upon what follows as either a complete or an authoritative statement.

Council Directive 92/50/EEC relates to the co-ordination of procedures for the award of public service contracts. For the purposes of the directive, public service contracts means 'contracts for a pecuniary interest concluded in writing between a service provider and a contracting authority'. Provision is made, however, for a range of exclusions, including:

- rent of land, existing buildings or other immovable property;
- development of programme material by broadcasters;
- contracts for broadcasting time;
- contracts for certain telecommunications;
- contracts for arbitration and conciliation services;
- central bank services;
- certain other financial services contracts;
- employment contracts;
- certain research and development service contracts.

Contracting authorities are state, regional or local authorities, bodies governed by public law, associations formed by one or more authorities or bodies governed by public law. 'Service provider' means any natural or legal person, including a public body that offers services.

The directive applies to public service contracts, the estimated value of which, net of VAT, is not less than the current threshold. This is expressed in euros, and is adjusted from time to time. Where services are subdivided into lots, the value of each lot must be taken into account, and for contracts which do not specify a total price, the basis for calculating the estimated value is either the total contract value for the duration, or, if the duration exceeds 48 months, the monthly instalment multiplied by 48. In the case of contracts which are regular, or of contracts which are to be renewed within a given time, the contract value may be established on either the basis of the actual aggregate cost of similar contracts over the previous year, or the estimated aggregate cost during the 22 months following the first service performed.

A contracting authority in selecting a service provider may be required to do so under the following procedures:

- Open procedures under which any interested provider may submit a tender.
- Restricted procedures whereby only those providers who have been invited may submit a tender.
- Negotiated procedures where selected provider(s) are approached directly.
- Design contests where selection is based on a competition between providers, with the selection being undertaken by a jury.

Contracting authorities may elect to award the contract either on the basis of the lowest price, or the economically most advantageous tender, although in the latter case the criteria adopted must be made known to candidates or tenderers.

A requirement of the directive is that common advertising rules should apply. Contracting authorities are to make known their intended total procurement of certain categories of services, and also how they wish to award the contract. Moreover, it is a requirement that the results of the award procedure should be notified to the Office of Official Publications of the European Communities, which they will then make public.

Management in service provision

As has been said, it is possible to express service requirements by means of a conformance specification or a performance one. Where conformance specifications are employed it is often the case that the specifications for even an apparently straightforward service are extremely long. For example, specifications for cleaning services, grounds maintenance or similar activities may run to very many pages and represent weeks of preparation time. The tasks and activities required to be performed must be explained in precise and unambiguous detail. To illustrate this point, the relatively small part of a grounds maintenance specification used by the Civil Service concerned with upkeep of soil borders includes a subsection on pruning and caring for roses which is in itself a fairly comprehensive guide to this branch of horticulture. The principal benefit arising from the use of performance specifications is, of course, that it can usually be readily seen whether the contractor has provided the service as agreed.

Frequently the situation is that the client is unable to produce a conformance specification, often because the reason the service is being acquired from outside is that the client does not possess the time, knowledge or skill to do the work 'in-house'. When this is the case more attention will be paid to desired outcomes than to the manner in which the contract is to be performed. A contract for consultancy services will provide a good example of a situation in which this is likely to be the case. It may not be possible to prescribe exactly what it is that the consultant is expected to do, but it is reasonable to agree ground rules which govern aspects of the relationship. For example, questions such as working hours, observation of regulations, ownership of intellectual property arising from the work, terms of payment and so on can be formalised and agreed by the contracting parties.

Sometimes services are provided simply on the basis of an agreement between the parties based on a presumed joint understanding that a certain outcome is desired by the client and that the provider possesses the requisite competencies to undertake the work. Assumptions are frequently made, and these assumptions are often incorrect. The client expects work of sound quality, undertaken in a reasonable time, and at a fair price. The problem is, of course, that few people will agree on the exact meaning of these expressions. There are many stories told by clients of service providers treating them unfairly, and it is not unusual to hear service providers complaining about the unrealistic expectations of their customers.

While this text does not attempt to explain the legal aspects of purchasing and supply in general, it will be useful at this point to mention the 1982 Goods and Services Act and to highlight one or two features of that legislation. The first, obvious, point is that it does apply to services. Much of the legislation relating to trading is concerned solely with goods. The Act also applies to all situations where services are being provided. It is not a piece of 'consumer' legislation in that it protects all kinds of customers, including business or commercial organisations.

Some of the main provisions of the Act where it relates to services may be summarised as follows, though it should be remembered that this summary is not intended to convey anything other than an indication of the nature of the legislation: 'In a contract for the supply of service where the supplier is acting in the course of a business, there is an implied term that the supplier will carry out the service with reasonable care and skill.' Another implied term is: 'The supplier will carry out the service within a reasonable time.' Usually, though, the time will be agreed when the contract is made. The Act limits the recipient's obligation to pay for services to 'a reasonable charge'. Of course, the above provisions do not, in themselves, indicate just what the word 'reasonable' should be taken to mean, and neither do they indicate what remedy is available to the recipient if the provider is deemed not to have been reasonable. We would probably need to turn to a member of the legal profession if, in practice, we felt that a service supplier was providing less than a 'reasonable' standard.

Summary

1 The purchase of services differs from goods in that the customer does not become the owner of a tangible good. Services cannot be stored and cannot normally be resold.

2 Usually, results cannot be seen prior to the purchase of a service. Often it is the actual service provider who is assessed. As people provide services, and people are individuals, there can be no standardisation or 'repeat' purchase as for goods.

3 Outsourcing is widely practised in connection with non-core services. This policy requires a systematic approach, and has important long-term implications.

4 Service level agreements quantify the minimum acceptable service to the customer and are agreed between the client and the service supplier. They are normally written into the contract.

5 'Provider present' services involve the provider's staff being on the client's premises. Access, supervision, confidentiality and safety matters must be addressed. 'Provider not present' services include banking and insurance where the service is provided remotely.

6 Systematic approaches to the procurement of services in the areas of marketing, advertising, PR and legal services have demonstrated the role of procurement in the acquisition of such services.

7 The European Union Public Contracts Directive applies to public service contracts over the threshold value. The contracting authority may select a service provider using open procedures; restricted procedures; negotiated procedures or a design contest. The results of the award are published by the Office of Official Publications of the European Communities.

References and further reading

Beauchamp, M (1995), 'Procuring persuasive PR', *Purchasing and Supply Management*, January.

Boyle, E (1993), 'Managing organisational networks – defining the core', *Management Decision*, 31 (7).

Casey, T (2005), 'Influence over sales and marketing', *Supply Management*, September.

Edward, N (1997), 'Buying for selling', *Supply Management*, February.

Hiles, A (1993), *Service Level Agreements*, London: Chapman & Hall.

Lancaster, G (2003), 'How to buy public relations services', *Supply Management*, October.

Pagnoncelli, D (1993), 'Managed outsourcing: a strategy for a competitive company in the 1990s', *Management Decision*, 31 (7).

Takal, P F (1993), 'Outsourcing technology', *Management Decision*, 31 (7).

Tulip, S (2001), 'How to buy advertising and marketing services', *Supply Management*, April.

Tulip, S (2001), 'How to buy legal services', *Supply Management*, August.

White, R and James, B (1996), *The Outsourcing Manual*, Aldershot: Gower.

17

Corporate social responsibility

Introduction

The concept of corporate social responsibility has several common strands:

- The degree to which a company minimises its negative impact on the communities in which it operates.
- The positive benefits it brings to the community and to society in general. This extends beyond its product/service ranges to include such areas as charities, sponsorships and education.
- As the environment is inextricably linked to perceptions of corporate citizenship, a company cannot be considered a good corporate socially responsible entity unless its activities are environmentally friendly, unless it is seen to be taking positive steps to minimise the environmental impact of its operations.
- The way in which a company treats its employees and the extent to which it prevents them from harm.
- A company should have an ethics code, such as that provided by the CIPS.

As procurement is responsible for a large percentage of the total costs of an organisation, the contribution to corporate social responsibility of an ethical and green supply chain cannot be ignored.

Objectives of this chapter

- To understand the concept of corporate social responsibility and how it relates to the organisation as a whole
- To examine various best practice structures and how these impact on the procurement activity
- To examine the issues of compliance and business drivers for CSR
- To appreciate the importance of organisations such as the Ethical Trading Initiative, Fairtrade and the International Labour Organization
- To consider the Social Accountability Standards

Corporate social responsibility (CSR)

What is CSR?

Corporate Social Responsibility is the continuing commitment by business to behave ethically and contribute to economic development while improving the quality of life of the workforce and their families as well as of the local community and society at large. (World Business Council for Sustainable Development)

What is involved in CSR?

Carroll (1996) offers a fourfold obligation:

- Economic
- Legal
- Ethical
- Philanthropic

See Figure 17.1 for the hierarchy of CSR responsibilities.

What do corporations mean by corporate social responsibility?

- British Airways sees it as ethical behaviour within business and the environment.
- BSkyB sees five distinct areas:
  1 Customers.
  2 Employees.
  3 Community.
  4 Suppliers.
  5 Environment.

Figure 17.1
Hierarchy of CSR responsibilities

(*Source*: After Carroll, 1996)

- Traidcraft sees three distinct areas:
  1 Economic impact.
  2 Social impact.
  3 Environmental impact.
- BT sees that as well as just looking at trading standards in the supply chain, it's about how the company relates to its suppliers, how it manages those relationships and working in an ethical way.

The CSR issue should just be part of the adjudication criteria and be considered as part of the whole life cost.

What CIPS says

Certainly CIPS, which represents purchasing and supply management professionals in the UK and elsewhere, believes its members can take the social responsibility agenda further.

The institute's 'Ethical practices in purchasing and supply' draws on various codes, including the UK government-backed Ethical Trading Initiative, the core conventions of the International Labour Organization and the UN Declaration on Human Rights. It says buyers should work with suppliers to make sure that:

- Employees are free to work for their employer or not.
- Employees should be given a clear contract, including how much they will be paid.
- Suppliers should not discourage or prevent employees from joining trade unions.
- Wages and benefits should at least meet industry benchmarks or national legal standards.
- Employees should not be expected to work more than 48 hours a week regularly.
- Suppliers should not abuse or intimidate employees.
- Suppliers should always work within the laws of their country.
- Suppliers must uphold health and safety requirements.

They aim to eradicate child labour, but in the meantime make sure children and young people are not made to work in dangerous conditions or at night, and that they have access to education.

Corporate social responsibility brings with it enormous business benefits, from enhanced reputation to real cost savings, from higher staff morale to greater customer loyalty. CSR is good business.

Price is only one factor when selecting suppliers. Reputation is vital in today's critical world. Any company that wants to stay in business in the long term must treat social issues as paramount.

CSR incorporates initiatives in the local community, the workplace and the environment. Examples include: Barclays Bank has a scheme to make use of business suits that it no longer needs; Tesco computers for schools project.

BOC has backed the UN Global Compact, a code aimed at fostering 'corporate citizenship' among companies, based on the principles of the Universal

Declaration of Human Rights, the International Labour Organization's Declaration on Fundamental Principles and Rights at Work and the Rio Principles on Environment and Development.

Mini case study – Diageo cures audit fatigue

Diageo assesses new suppliers with a questionnaire to make sure they are acting sustainably.

Mini case study – Top Shop

Top Shop has a buying executive dedicated to sourcing ethical clothing, and has signed a deal to sell Fairtrade cotton lines.

The shift presents buyers with several challenges. They need to develop the core competences of supply chain professionals to include ethical considerations in buying activities. They also need to develop the capacity of the supply base. Research shows that manufacturers often do not operate to international labour standards, so buyers need to work with suppliers to ensure improvements are made across the board.

Public accountability

Back in the early 1990s global brands and retailers were under attack. Scandals swept through supplier's overseas factories exposing child labour, low wages and horrific working conditions. Many brands signed up to codes of conduct.

Companies have relied on these codes and on-site audits, safe in the belief they are doing the best they can to improve conditions for workers in their supply chains.

Research from the Institute of Development Studies (IDS), commissioned by the Ethical Trading Initiative (ETI) to assess the impact of its base code, is used by companies including Marks & Spencer, Tesco and Gap. The researchers interviewed more than 400 workers in 23 supplier sites across the world, as well as retailers, manufacturers, agents, managers, trade unions, and non-governmental organisations (NGOs).

On the plus side, researchers found children at work in only one of the sites visited. In addition, health and safety measures were of a higher standard in most factories as a result of the implementation of the base code. Regular and overtime working hours had also fallen.

But in other areas the code had made little or no impact. No increase in union membership was seen, and women were still subject to basic inequalities. There was no impact in terms of ensuring workers received a living wage. For example, some workers in some Bangladeshi factories are paid just 5p an hour to produce clothes for retailers including Tesco, Asda and Primark. All three have signed the ETI's code of labour practice.

The quality of auditing in general is very poor either because of lack of training, lack of understanding, laziness or sometimes downright corruption. Strategies comprising education, communication and support need to complement audits for more challenging issues such as freedom of association and discrimination.

Buyers need to examine their price, lead time and product cycle and 'review the impact of that on their suppliers' ability to meet their standards'.

Mini case study – Wal-Mart

Wal-Mart announced targets for reducing greenhouse gas emissions and cutting waste. The company also committed itself to working with its suppliers to promote good environmental practices.

Best practice – what buyers can do to improve labour conditions

- Avoid putting undue pressure on suppliers that might impact on workers – for example, changing an order at the last minute or shortening lead times could mean workers are forced to do overtime.
- Think about the effect of the prices you set – insist suppliers comply with the ETI base code.
- Give reasonable time scales for suppliers to address areas of non-compliance and provide support to help them improve, such as education and training.
- Help your major suppliers to share good practice by developing benchmarking groups where they can get together to exchange ideas about how to overcome specific issues in their region or industry.

Mini case study – FTSE4GOOD

In 2004 FTSE4GOOD, part of the FTSE Group, announced the introduction of the FTSE4GOOD standards for assessing human rights in supply chains.

The standards set out a timetable for companies to introduce a policy, a system for monitoring and a reporting methodology on issues ranging from equality and discrimination to forced and child labour and worker representation. The labour standards also consider working hours, wages and disciplinary procedures.

Procurement staff can take the lead in ensuring that their companies and their suppliers understand what is involved in being a good corporate citizen.

◼ Compliance

Businesses can only insist their suppliers are CSR compliant if they are willing to pay more and work with them to enable improvements.

Company buying practices and management of production schedules have a major influence on suppliers' ability to comply with CSR and labour standards. Businesses should review their own buying practices to ensure they do not put undue pressure on suppliers and workers.

Companies should work with suppliers to make realistic improvements over time, rather than demanding immediate compliance. For example:

- M & S – 'As part of this we will train our buyers to further understand the part they play in helping suppliers maintain labour standards in the production of our goods'.
- The Co-operative Group operates a 'sound sourcing code of conduct' for suppliers. 'Our aim is to develop an effective working partnership with our suppliers to secure safe and decent working and living conditions for anybody involved in the production of own brand products.'
- The Co-op audits suppliers to check CSR compliance. It also equips them with a self-assessment workbook, which enables suppliers to carry out their own site assessment, implement action plans and provide evidence of continuous improvement. This allows the supplier to learn what issues the buyer may have, and is given the chance to raise concerns or ask for clarification.

■ Six steps to responsible buying

1 Establish good relationships with suppliers to ensure long-term, stable, risk-sharing connections.
2 Make sure your communications are clear and timely, so suppliers know the terms of the trade, have information about expectations and are able to give feedback.
3 Establish sustainable pricing so the supplier, buyer and those further down the chain benefit from the relationship.
4 Give clear lead times and payments.
5 Show respect for human rights in the supply chain. Buyers should give preference to suppliers who demonstrate they are improving social and environmental conditions.
6 Offer continued support for small-scale producers and home workers. Buyers should find out who their suppliers are and if they include smallholders, home workers and those in disadvantaged areas, they should be careful not to change that.

If you want to be sure of conditions you need to know the extended supply chain. The Ethical Trading Initiative, a CSR pressure group, suggests that a sound approach has been started in which buyers are addressing the problem by developing longer-term and deeper relationships with fewer suppliers. ETI stipulated that buyers have got to become much more involved and have got to support their suppliers and not just look for compliance.

Mini case study – Tesco and CSR

Tesco monitors and assesses overall company performance towards CSR with the following range of KPIs:

- Economic – local sourcing: 7000 local products
- Environment
- Energy efficiency – year on year percentage reduction of usage
- Water consumption
- Vehicle efficiency
- Recycling
- Social – 'computer for schools': increase value of computers donated
- Charitable donations – 1%
- Employee retention and training
- Supply chain labour standards – training staff and suppliers (including SA8000)

Source: Tesco website (2004)

Business drivers for socially responsible procurement

Productivity and quality improvements

- Yield, consistency and absolute quality.
- TQM and other concepts which are concerned with eliminating waste and the more efficient use of resources are totally aligned with the environmental concerns. By eliminating waste costs are reduced at the same time as the achievement of more environmentally friendly practices.

Risk and reputational management

- To brand and business reputation. Many consumers will avoid products which are receiving negative publicity for their environmentally damaging actions.
- Conversely positive PR surrounding proactive CSR policies can be used by companies to improve their image and promote sales.

Shareholder and ethical investment pressure

- Shareholders pressurising organisations.
- CSR seen as increasingly important in investment management.
- Consumer concern growing.
- Increasing consumer and campaigning concerns relating to activities of producers and retailers.
- Buyers looking to set up corporate social responsibility strategies in their supply chains can now seek help from an advisory body.

The Corporate Social Responsibility Academy has been set up by the Department of Trade and Industry and the private sector as a central source of information for the training and development of staff.

Recent research shows the application of CSR issues in supplier selection and monitoring is at best patchy, and at worst non-existent. There was little perceived link between procurement and CSR. Corporate targets and measures were all based around compliance with operational requirements, with no explicit or implied reference to supply chain management.

Poor procurement practices continue to undermine corporate social responsibility (CSR) programmes and audits are ineffective. The Institute of Business Ethics suggests that some companies are still failing to tackle poor labour standards in supply chains. Often procurement procedures are not in line with the rest of the company's CSR programme.

Ethical coffee producer Union Coffee Roasters recommends that audits have an important role for buyers seeking better supply chains.

CSR is a growing issue and has been pursued by increasingly influential campaign groups with huge public support and governments intent on more regulation of corporate behaviour. Pressure for change is bearing down through both legislation and the actions of non-governmental organisations campaigning effectively against much corporate activity. Many organisations have recognised the risks and implemented an environmental procurement policy. Nike's purchasers still feel the pain of the revelation that some suppliers were employing children.

BOC has a global policy on contractors' working conditions that subscribes to the United Nations' Universal Declaration of Human Rights. It demands that suppliers respect health and safety standards, and do not intimidate, abuse or exploit their workers. Many such companies realise the business case for CSR and are using this to influence their suppliers across the supply chain.

Reducing risk, motivating the team, developing a good public image and improving performance in investors' eyes can all be as strong an attraction as bigger profits, and this is the message which is slowly influencing companies to develop stronger relationships in order to improve their CSR credentials and to use discussions with suppliers to find out how they can help to improve CSR performance.

By managing their supply chain, investing in energy efficiency, reducing demand and changing specifications to use less and call on sustainable or recycled resources, as well as developing a process for recycling waste, companies can not only improve their CSR record but can also reduce costs and become leaner.

Mini case study – O_2

Mobile telecoms company O_2 has developed a process for effectively recycling handsets in response to the Waste Electrical and Electronic Equipment Directive.

From a purely procurement and supply perspective, the key areas of CSR are ethics in the supply chain and environmental management. Ethical sourcing is concerned with not dealing with suppliers that have unacceptable employment practices. These include employing child labour or forced labour, inadequate health and safety, low wages, long working hours, using discrimination and intimidation, poor working conditions or not allowing trade unions or collective bargaining. To ensure that suppliers are ethical sources, companies will need to audit them. Companies should ask suppliers to become approved against one of the social accountability standards, such as SA8000.

Mini case study – TR Fastenings

TR Fastenings invests a lot of time in investigating and visiting existing and potential suppliers.

Whether they are in the UK, Europe or Asia, the same criteria are applied:

- Do they provide fair conditions for workers?
- Do they protect the environment?
- Do they exhibit reasonable, ethical corporate behaviour?

TR has a regulatory framework which is easy to understand and which conveys the standards which the company requires.

In several instances where the above have not been adequate but the companies are interested in improving, TR has agreed a contract at a price slightly higher than the norm in order to allow the companies to fund the necessary improvements. In this way, TR sees that it can meet its CSR obligations and remain competitive, and it gets a committed supplier that will work well with TR and look after its employees.

Social Accountability 8000 (SA8000)

■ Purpose and scope

This international standard specifies requirements for social accountability to enable a company to:

1 Develop, maintain and enforce policies and procedures in order to manage those issues which it can control or influence.
2 Demonstrate to interested parties that policies, procedures and practices are in conformity with the requirements of this standard.
3 The requirements of this standard shall apply universally with regard to geographic location, industry sector and company size.

The company shall also respect the principles of the following international instruments such as:

- Universal Declaration of Human Rights.
- The United Nations Convention on the Rights of the Child.

In summary, social accountability requirements cover:

- child labour;
- forced labour;
- health and safety;
- freedom of association and right to collective bargaining;
- discrimination;
- disciplinary practices;
- working hours;
- compensation;
- management systems;
- control of suppliers –

    'The company shall establish and maintain appropriate procedures to evaluate and select suppliers based on their ability to meet the requirements of this standard.'

    'The company shall maintain reasonable evidence that the requirements of this standard are being met by suppliers and subcontractors.'

Other social accountability standards and codes of practice are: Ethical Trading Initiative, International Labour Organization conventions, the ISO14000 series and Fairtrade.

■ The Ethical Trading Initiative (ETI)

The Ethical Trading Initiative (ETI) is an alliance of companies, trade unions, development and campaigning groups which works to improve the lives of workers in global supply chains.

The Ethical Trading Initiative base code includes:

- Employment is freely chosen.
- Freedom to join unions.
- Safe clear conditions.
- No child labour.
- Living wages to be paid.
- Fair working hours.
- No discrimination.
- No harsh or inhumane treatment.

Mini case study – Marks & Spencer

Marks & Spencer is going down this route. It is taking part in the ETI's Purchasing Practices project, which encourages the training of buying teams to increase their awareness of how their buying practices affect suppliers and their employees.

■ The International Labour Organization (ILO)

The International Labour Organization (ILO) has three major tasks, the first of which is the adoption of international labour standards, called Conventions and Recommendations, for implementation by member states. The Conventions and Recommendations contain guidelines on child labour, protection of women workers, hours of work, rest and holidays with pay, labour inspection, vocational guidance and training, social security protection, workers' housing, occupational health and safety, conditions of work at sea, and protection of migrant workers.

They also cover questions of basic human rights, among them, freedom of association, collective bargaining, the abolition of forced labour, the elimination of discrimination in employment, and the promotion of full employment.

ISO14001 is an international standard for environmental management.

■ Fairtrade

Fairtrade is a system monitored and operated by the Fairtrade Labelling Organisation, which sets working and social standards that must be complied with before companies are awarded a Fairtrade mark. It aims to change the way we trade, creating fairer working conditions, greater opportunities in the marketplace and social development for producer partners.

Sourcing principles from Fair Trade are:

- Engage with stakeholders.
- Understand the supplier country context.
- Transparent communication.
- Price to cover cost of labour and capital employed.
- Develop partnering relationships.
- Integrate social objectives with other buying functions.

Mini case study – Dell considers linking buyers to new standards

Computer firm Dell is considering measuring its buyers' performance by linking it to new supplier labour and environmental standards set by the electronics industry.

Dell, HP and IBM agreed to adopt a common set of supplier assessment standards from the Electronics Industry Code of Conduct, which aims to improve workers' rights and sustainability.

The firms will use a single auditor and create a database to share and track supplier information.

Summary

1 'Corporate social responsibility is the continuing commitment by business to behave ethically and contribute to economic development while improving the quality of life of the workforce and their families as well as of the local community and society at large' (World Business Council for Sustainable Development).

2 The Ethical Trading Initiative, a CSR pressure group, suggests that a sound approach has been started in which buyers are addressing the problem by developing longer-term and deeper relationships with fewer suppliers.

3 ETI stipulated that buyers have got to become much more involved and have got to support their suppliers and not just look for compliance.

4 Companies should ask suppliers to become approved against one of the social accountability standards, such as SA8000.

5 The International Labour Organization (ILO) has three major tasks, the first of which is the adoption of international labour standards, called Conventions and Recommendations, for implementation by member states.

6 Fairtrade is a system monitored and operated by the Fairtrade Labelling Organisation, which sets working and social standards that must be complied with before companies are awarded a Fairtrade mark. It aims to change the way we trade, creating fairer working conditions, greater opportunities in the marketplace and social development for producer partners.

References and further reading

Arminas, D (2004), 'Corporate social responsibility – supply chain CSR criteria unveiled', *Supply Management*, December.

Birchall, J (2006), 'Corporate responsibility', *Financial Times*, February.

Blackburn, A (2004), 'Audits ineffective against irresponsible purchasing', *Supply Management*, July.

Blackburn, A (2004), 'CSR Academy is open for business', *Supply Management*, July.

Carroll, A B (1996) *Business and Society: Ethics and Stakeholder Management*, Cincinnati, OH: South-Western College Publishing.

Clarke, E (2007), 'Purer source', *Supply Management*, January.

CSR Section (2006), 'Dell considers linking buyers to new standards', *Supply Management*, April.

Dearing, D (2004), 'Ethical traders', *Supply Management*, November.

Gilbert, H (2006), 'Ethical supply chains – sourcing good CSR', *Supply Management*, March.

Greenwood, M (2005), 'The nuts and bolts of CSR', *Supply Management*, February.

Gooch, F (2003), 'Socially responsible international purchasing: the why and how', Traidcraft Exchange UK CIPS Regional Event.

Hurst, R (2006), 'Ethics and the purchaser', *Supply Management*, March.

John, G (2004), 'CSR roundtable – beyond the greenwash', *Supply Management*, July.

Mosco, L (2004), 'Lip service won't suffice', *Supply Management*, September.

O'Brien, L (2005), 'Charity case rings an ethical warning', *Supply Management*, June.

Riley, H (2002), 'Yes, we have ethical bananas', *Supply Management*, March.

Snell, P (2007), 'Diageo cures audit fatigue', *Supply Management*, March.

Taylor, I (2005), 'The time for excuses is over', *Supply Management*, March.

Whitehead, M (2002), 'Corporate social responsibility', *Supply Management*, March.

Part 4

E-procurement systems and contract management

Chapter 18   E-procurement systems

Chapter 19   Contract management and performance measurement

18

E-procurement systems

Introduction

Procurement and supply is an activity that has usually generated and employed large quantities of paperwork. This paperwork was necessary to communicate information from one function to another in order to facilitate action, to indicate requirements to suppliers, and to obtain the necessary goods and services on time and to specification.

The advent of information technology and more integrated software systems has radically changed matters. Although the paperless office may still be in the future, and indeed may never come about, simple transactions are today seldom paper based. The Internet has provided further opportunities for electronic procurement, and has made new approaches possible in the last few years with the almost universal acceptance of e-procurement,

Companies are realising that they have opportunities to reduce their procurement processing costs and acquisition costs by revising their internal procurement policies and by fully leveraging their buying power by using the Internet. This chapter will explore some of the electronic applications which make up e-procurement.

Objectives of this chapter

- To introduce the concept of e-procurement
- To highlight some of the applications of e-procurement
- To evaluate the benefits and added value aspects of e-procurement
- To highlight potential barriers to the successful adoption of e-procurement
- To outline best practice implementation of e-procurement
- To outline relevant legislation

What is e-procurement?

E-procurement is the term used to describe the use of electronic methods in every stage of the buying process from identification of requirement through to payment, and potentially to contract management. Or, alternatively, e-procurement includes a range of technologies that apply the speed of computer processing and the connectivity of the Internet to accelerate and streamline the processes of:

- identifying and selecting suppliers of goods and services;
- placing, receiving and paying for orders;
- assuring compliance with procurement procedures;
- consolidating purchases to achieve leverage;
- providing visibility of information between collaborative partners.

In most e-procurement models there can be found the following key processes:

- e-sourcing – for contractual processes. Tools include e-tendering, e-RFQs (request for quotations) and e-auctions;
- e-procurement – for transactional processes. Tools include marketplaces using techniques such as e-catalogues;
- e-payment – tools include virtual or embedded PC (procurement cards), e-invoicing and self-billing.

The CIPS definition of e-procurement is:

'e-procurement is using the Internet to operate the transactional aspects of requisitioning, authorising, ordering, receipting and payment processes for the required services or products.'

One of the keys goals of e-procurement is to devolve buying to local users and covers the requisition against contract, authorisation, order, receipt and payment.

There is confusion about what is covered by e-sourcing and how this differs from e-procurement. The CIPS definition of e-sourcing is:

'e-Sourcing is using the Internet to make decisions and form strategies regarding how and where services or products are obtained.'

It covers the parts in the buying process which are at the discretion of the specialist buyers, which include knowledge, specification, request for quotation/e-tender/e-auction and evaluation/negotiation of contract.

If e-sourcing is to be implemented, good e-sourcing practice is essential to making e-procurement work. If you do not make the correct strategic decisions you will create a poor operational process. E-sourcing and e-procurement are parts of the e-purchasing cycle.

E-sourcing provides a platform for delivering on promises of social responsibility; it provides accountability and visibility on why a company makes a decision to source products from their chosen suppliers. E-sourcing systems should enable the sourcing team to:

- effortlessly analyse and model complex decisions in real time;
- automate the contract life-cycle management including awards, rejections, amendments and renewals;

Figure 18.1
**E-procurement
cycle (Gattorna)**

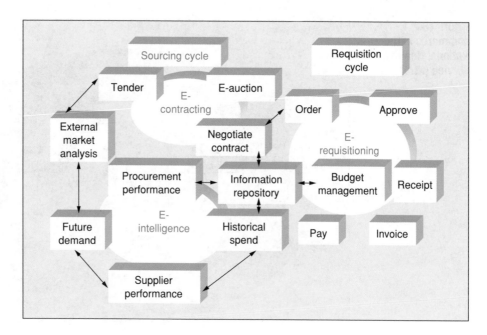

- collaborate with the supplier; using a central system enables people to collaborate easily.

E-sourcing should deliver the following visible benefits:

- Real-time information – the sourcing team get visibility on contracts and spending patterns. Any planned improvement must ensure reliable up-to-date information for analysis purposes. A system can provide pre-qualified information about suppliers.
- Integrated process automation – taking time out of the sourcing process by reducing the amount of paper involved in the system. Typically such systems can distribute all requirements electronically.

Another model of e-procurement is provided by Berger and Gattorna (2001) in Figure 18.1. This model breaks e-procurement into three distinctive processes, namely:

- e-sourcing, which includes contracting, via e-auctions;
- e-requisitioning;
- e-intelligence, which is concerned with the collation of performance management information.

This approach is being adopted currently by the NHS as shown in Figure 18.2. This e-procurement model contains:

- e-sourcing;
- e-ordering/e-requisitioning;
- e-analysis (e-intelligence).

Figure 18.2 E-commerce in the National Health Service (NHS)

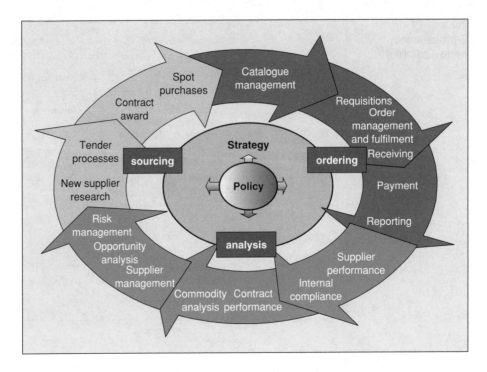

The benefits of e-procurement

The benefits can be seen as follows:

- reducing purchasing cycle time;
- enhancing budgetary control;
- eliminating administrative errors;
- increasing buyers' productivity;
- lowering prices through product standardisation and consolidation of purchasing power;
- better information management.

That is, it enables the procurement process to be redesigned, taking out the slow, costly transactional work, resulting in faster cycle times. As can be seen in Figure 18.3, many non-value-added transactions have been eliminated, thus reducing the cycle times by several days. This provides companies with enormous efficiency improvements (the way people work). It allows staff to concentrate their efforts on more strategic aspects of value-added procurement. The improvements in information flow, especially improved sharing of sensitive information, allows for improved commercial relationships with suppliers.

The public sector has also been incorporating e-procurement, as shown in the following case study.

Figure 18.3
Empowerment of users – changes in workflow

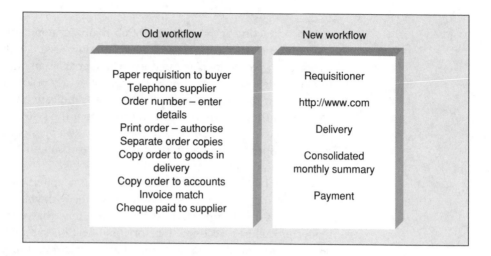

Old workflow	New workflow
Paper requisition to buyer	Requisitioner
Telephone supplier	
Order number – enter details	http://www.com
Print order – authorise	Delivery
Separate order copies	
Copy order to goods in delivery	Consolidated monthly summary
Copy order to accounts	
Invoice match	Payment
Cheque paid to supplier	

Case study – public procurement update

Recent reforms give public sector purchasers wider scope to use E–procurement

New EU procurement rules were recently implemented in the UK by the Public Contracts Regulations 2006, extending the scope of e-procurement. Contracting authorities may now purchase services, supplies and works under a number of e-tendering processes such as e-auctions and the more excitingly named 'dynamic purchasing systems' (DPS) for common purchases. The new rules also allow for framework contracts to be tendered with such systems.

Over the past few years there has been an increasing emphasis on e-procurement from the European Commission and the Office of Government Commerce, starting with the option for online tender submission, followed by online *Official Journal of the Economic Union* (OJEU) notices.

The incentives for contracting authorities to use e-tendering methods include faster tender processes and more streamlined procurement, particularly for straightforward tenders where face-to-face contact with bidders is not paramount.

E-auctions can also be used in a DPS or mini competitions in a framework contract. The auction process starts with the publications of an OJEU notice, under the open or restricted procedures, and the purchasing authority setting out its specification requirements online.

The contracting authority will invite initial bids and, after it has evaluated them against predetermined criteria, will then ask pre-qualified bidders to submit new prices. The e-auction can take place over a number of phases, and at each stage bidders will be able to see their relative ranking and the number (but not names) of other bidders participating in the auction at that time. Bids may be adjusted until the closing date.

For contracting authorities, the other main development is the DPS. This is simply an electronic framework for commonly used purchases.

The open procedure is mandatory, which enables any interested suppliers to bid. Bidders can apply to join the system at any point in its duration (as published in the OJEU notice). Bidders make indicative bids, which can be changed (if they are still compliant) throughout the system's lifetime.

When a contracting authority wishes to make a purchase it will notify the bidders of specific contracts, for which they can submit their offer. Bids are then evaluated and a contract awarded.

As a purchaser, you need to make sure your suppliers have considered the new regime because it can affect how they trade with you.

First, they must understand the rules and how they differ from previous tender procedures. Second, their pre-qualification submissions and tender responses will need to be streamlined and focused and to exactly meet the online requirements. Third, suppliers will need to speed up response times.

By using e-procurement, contracting authorities can run the process more quickly than before, so suppliers need to note the key dates.

Lastly, IT systems and software will need to be secure and compatible with submission requirements.

Complex procurement

E-procurement programmes have been successfully implemented to handle many indirect/MRO commodities. There are also opportunities for savings in the areas of direct materials and those commodities with more complex procurement processes. But the spend in these commodities can be high, with poor compliance to purchasing contracts on many previous occasions. Figure 18.4 shows a typical profile of e-procurement application across the four categories in the Kraljic Procurement Targeting Tool.

There appears to be no consensus across industries about the correct application of e-procurement to commodity groups. Some companies say that it is too risky to use e-auctions for critical and complex items. Others state that they will use many of the applications for all of their commodity groups including bottleneck and critical items, making it possible by robust specifications and processes.

Reverse auctions

Many buying organisations conduct auctions online in a quest to find the lowest price. These auctions are usually conducted as reverse auctions, with competing suppliers seeking to win the business through placing a lower bid

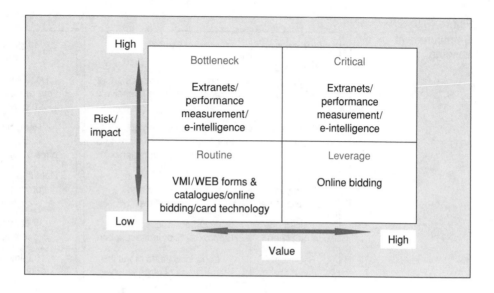

**Figure 18.4
Application of
e-procurement?**

than their competitors. Normally the bid prices are visible to all competitors, but the origin of the bids is, of course, confidential. A variation is the ranked auction, where bidders are told of their relative position, but are not informed of the actual amounts submitted by their competitors. Buying by this method might be appropriate where the items, materials or services to be acquired are available from a wider range of potential suppliers who are willing to compete with each other in this way. The items should be identical or interchangeable with each other; in other words, ideally, the only important variable must be price, or perhaps delivered cost. If there are other variables to be considered then these must be readily capable of being quantified and compared objectively. In employing this approach to acquisition purchasers will need to make clear to potential bidders the rules of the auction and the criteria for bid analysis.

Bidding rules should be established, making it clear who is qualified to bid, what the bid decrements should be and the time limits to be applied to the procedure. The submitter of the most attractive bid must expect to be contractually bound by acceptance of their offer, as must the buyer.

There are numerous organisations whose business is to facilitate online bidding, providing an electronic marketplace through which buyers and sellers might interact, fulfilling much the same role as the traditional auctioneer.

Figure 18.5 demonstrates the many ways in which companies can benefit from the application of e-procurement.

The following case study is an example of the application of e-procurement in the public sector.

Figure 18.5
E-procurement benefits

Value drivers	Pain points	Mitigation/savings estimate
Improved process efficiency	Long lead times from manual processing, time-intensive	Requisition processing time reduction of 70–80%, e.g. a week faster
Reduced costs	High transaction costs, long supplier negotiations and non-contract compliance drive up price	Requisition process reduction up to 73%, price of goods 5–10% less
Improved compliance	Fragmented and inaccurate	Data improved via contract compliance improves leverage
Reduced off-contract spend	Off-contract spend (approx 27% of indirect spend)	Off-contract spending decreases by 50%
Reduced inventory	Long lead times result in purchase of large safety stocks	Inventory expense reduction by 25%–50%

Case study – Police procurement

@UK PLC has further widened its customer base within public sector buying organisations by being selected to provide an e-procurement and e-invoicing systems to Thames Valley Police (TVP).

TVP is one of the largest non-metropolitan police forces in the country, covering 2200 square miles of Berkshire, Buckinghamshire and Oxfordshire and serving a population of 2.2 million people. The TVP area is policed by around 4140 police officers, 350 special constables, 370 volunteers and 2860 other police staff. The total spend by TVP on goods and services is over £400 million per annum.

The @UK Supplier Management Systems (SMS) will enhance existing TVP procurement systems by providing a mechanism to send electronic purchase orders to, and receive electronic invoices from all their suppliers, no matter what their size or existing electronic trading capability. Stage one of the project will be creating a link between the @UK supplier network and TVP back office systems. This builds on wide base of experience by @UK in linking to similar financial systems in other areas of the public service. Over the next three months it is intended that the @UK PLC system will then be rolled out to the majority of the force's 1500 suppliers.

TVP believe that the @UK system offers TVP an ideal infrastructure on which to build their future procurement strategy. It provides both TVP and their suppliers the ability to achieve real efficiency and process savings, eliminating time and the potential for effort right through the supply chain. The @UK e-invoicing capability for all of their suppliers is an especially important part of this.

It establishes an ideal mechanism for TVP to achieve huge efficiencies in their backend processes. It is also a way for suppliers to reduce their costs significantly in dealing with TVP, with the ability for both parties to share those benefits.

The current state of e-procurement initiatives

Successful e-procurement initiatives generally occur in two areas.

1 Procurement of office equipment and supplies using stand-alone desktop requisitioning tools.

This category was driven by the technology-focused office equipment suppliers and expanded into online ordering for simple services like business card printing, with basic integration into finance and HR systems. The focus has been on simple, indirect materials sometimes called MRO goods (maintenance, repair and operations) but in reality most initiatives have looked only at the operations elements rather than maintenance and repairs and generally start with the 'create requisition' function. They have often failed to integrate with the supply chain and do not enable supply to be matched precisely to demand.

2 Strategic sourcing using e-requests for quotation and e-requests for proposal (often jointly known as eRFX) as well as online auction tools.

This is the second wave that followed the initial e-procurement introduction. Most large organisations are using online auctions and e-tendering systems to significantly lower the input cost of goods and services and the procurement process costs. The key requirement here is that the goods and services can be uniquely defined and categorised. These tools are being used for both direct and indirect material procurement and in the final stages of complex procurements after a detailed specification had been prepared. Only now are companies seeing the use of tools such as e-intelligence (which provides tailored management and market information – such as category-level analysis – to expedite sourcing, collaboration and forecasting) in the sourcing phases.

Procurement departments in most large organisations have also evolved the process of developing global functions and strategies for procurement of key commodities. The direct contribution of an effective procurement strategy to the organisation's financial results can be extremely important, particularly in those sectors where revenue growth is flat or declining.

In the early days of e-procurement, organisations focused on internal and external transaction costs. In many cases, the business case was based on cutting the cost of producing a purchase order. Although some improvements were made in many cases, suppliers found that their costs went up due to the expense of creating and maintaining catalogue content and marketplace transactional fees – but this was necessary if they wanted to continue to do business. Marketplaces put additional contract implications in place and this, coupled with the higher level of costs needed via this medium, put some suppliers off using this route.

In a global survey, conducted by AT Kearney (2002), it was found that 96 per cent of survey respondents used electronically enabled supply management (often referred to as 'eSupply'), but covered only 11 per cent of their spend base. Despite this limited spend coverage, eSupply management delivered measurable benefits – 10 per cent cost savings, up to 41 per cent cycle time improvement and up to 10 per cent head count reduction.

So, there is clearly scope for most organisations to generate additional significant bottom line savings from e-procurement. For those leading organisations it is now time to expand their programmes into new categories. For those who have not yet started or have had limited success with their e-procurement projects now is the time to re-examine the business case.

Total cost of ownership, rather than simply process and purchase costs, becomes more important and sophisticated than for 'simple' commodities. The total cost model, however, needs to be understood if full benefit is to be derived. This should take into account not just the procurement costs but also, where relevant, maintenance, disposal, cost of managing the assets, cost of money, etc.

Whilst the scope for cost savings in complex procurement is large, it is more difficult to obtain than the simpler picking of the 'low-hanging fruit' of IT, office stationery and similar MRO categories. Careful planning is required and the payback period may well be longer. However, the ultimate value of savings can be greater.

Case study – Leeds hospital goes live

Leeds Teaching Hospital, the largest such establishment in Europe, is now live for the transmission of orders to suppliers and receipt of the equivalent e-invoices after a successful integration between the @UK supplier network and the ITH Oracle purchasing system.

Procurement staff were recently celebrating the safe receipt of their first order. This was from the hospital Sterile Services Department to contracted supplier Westfield Medical. As ever, the @UK network automatically presented the client with the appropriate range and contract prices so as to generate a requisition, to be approved within Oracle Purchasing.

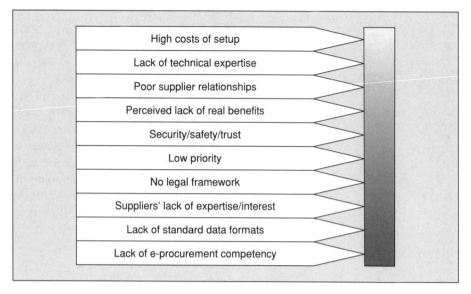

Figure 18.6
Obstacles to conducting business online

Although e-procurement is growing in terms of supplier adoption, research has shown that there are still obstacles to its acceptance (Figure 18.6).

Case study – Lewisham gets its suppliers on-board

The London Borough of Lewisham is making good progress in the recruitment of suppliers to its e-procurement programme. Over 1200 of its suppliers have completed the first stage of the process by registering their details on the @UK website, a fifth of their whole target supplier vase. Each of these businesses will be contacted by one of @UK's 20-strong supplier advisory team to identify the most appropriate solution for them. This solution will differ according to the nature of goods and services offered: whether the firm has a website already and if this site is able to receive orders and send e-invoices, although all options can be accommodated. The system will be fully integrated into Oracle iProcurement for the transmission of electronic purchase orders and electronic invoices.

Lewisham want the maximum available choice of firms able to trade with them in a way that will cut costs. They are also giving every supplier the chance to, for example, receive 'Requests for Price' for their services. This fits in with the latest guidance from the EU stressing equal opportunities for suppliers. At the same time, there are important local economic benefits as businesses linked to the @UK network are then able to trade with many other councils, schools, other firms and even individual consumers.

LB Lewisham has used the standard @UK supplier recruitment process, sending out its own tailored letter to each of its suppliers. Included in each letter is an individual reference code giving each firm access to their unique record within the @UK national supplier database.

The letter to suppliers made it clear what the mutual benefits of e-procurement were and why suppliers were warmly invited to participate. LB Lewisham has been happy to explain to suppliers what the rationale was for this change, and exactly how both parties will benefit. They are finding the whole process of supplier recruitment getting easier as the number of buying authorities taking part increases. Of course, as some businesses are getting letters now from several of their local authority/hospital clients they are beginning to understand that this is a process that the public sector is committed to.

The barriers

■ Potential high cost of integrating e-procurement tools with enterprise resource planning (ERP) systems

Companies should try to choose software tools that are already integrated with their existing systems or which have configurable and quick to implement XML-based interfaces to enable linkages to demand and inventory management. Where possible, companies should avoid stand-alone solutions which need bespoke integration work. Where appropriate, companies should look to integrate with the computer aided design (CAD) and product data manager (PDM) software systems used to design complex products and with project management and collaborative working systems including suppliers' designs and configuration tools.

■ Difficulty of building a solid business case for another e-procurement project

When companies look beyond the transaction or purchase order cost for savings, this is the moment they begin to appreciate the full potential savings and benefits from the implementation of e-procurement. By producing an end-to-end value map of the supply chain for complex goods and services in their operations, they can begin to look for opportunities to reduce the total cost of ownership such as reductions in inventory, reductions in demand and supply lead time and elimination of waste throughout the supply chain. Companies can also look for potential savings in the costs of goods and services by internal aggregation of demand, the reduction of maverick, off-contract spend and simplification of the supplier base.

■ Current spend by some of the commodities groups is unknown

The current spend metric is an essential one if a company is to source effectively. Extending product classification definitions to cover all commodities, including services, ensures that all relevant spend can be measured. This process can start with spend by supplier and this can then be further broken down to identify the goods and services which are mission critical together with major suppliers and frequency of purchase. This aim is to take an 80/20 approach rather than trying to tackle all items within a particular commodity. Historically one cannot underestimate the difficulties in getting usefully accurate information, but such vital information is of paramount importance.

Measuring the benefits of e-procurement

As the first generation of e-procurement projects have been starting to deliver measurable savings, the picture of the real extent and value of these savings is still unclear. One explanation for this is that whilst project progress has been measured in terms of milestone achievement, relatively few organisations are accurately monitoring the real benefits achieved as the projects progress.

What to measure

The principal metrics that will demonstrate a return on investment in e-procurement are the hard (directly measurable) benefits:

- price savings;
- process cost reduction (head count);
- reductions in cycle times (days/weeks);
- consequent reductions in inventory holdings (value/stock turnover ratios).

There are soft (indirectly measurable) benefits such as an increase in individual time freed up through more efficient processes, enabling staff to spend more time on value-added aspects of procurement such as:

- supplier development;
- contract management.

Soft benefits also provide important indicators of progress towards improvements in a measure that is beneficial and should not be ignored just because they are subjective or difficult to track.

Additionally there are a number of intangible benefits such as cultural change and broader staff efficiency savings delivered through training. These benefits are difficult to measure, but may provide valuable support for a business case.

Figure 18.7
Summary of the five main savings drivers for e-procurement

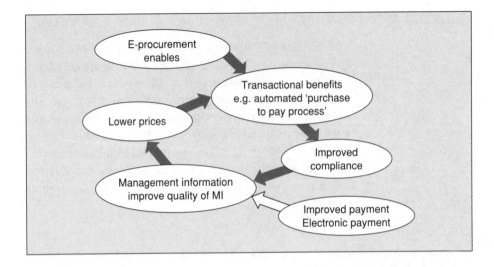

In order to identify e-procurement cost savings as distinct from those achieved through other procurement best practice, the measurement system needs to discriminate between 'business as usual' type savings and those directly attributable to the implementation of the e-procurement system. A summary of the five main savings drivers for e-procurement is shown in Figure 18.7. Note that they are interdependent, as illustrated.

Case study

@UK is the largest e-procurement marketplace servicing the UK public sector, offering 100% electronic options

A free financial model has been constructed by @UK so that buying organisations can quantify their savings from implementing 100 per cent electronic ordering and/or invoicing – both of which are now achievable using the latest @UK developments. The model combines the conclusions of organisations such as the National eProcurement Project (NEPP), @UK's own experiences with a number of clients and the expectations/situation of the particular buying organisation under examination. The model forecasts expected savings and return on investment (ROI) for any local authority, central government department, health authority or corporate body implementing e-procurement completing any of the following stages:

Stage 1 – client has their back office finance system (or P2P system if present) linked to the @UK national supplier network and uses it to route all orders to suppliers electronically (with a request for price option for services).

Stage 2 – all supplier invoices are received for processing in electronic format by implementing the @UK '@invoice' programme.

Stage 3 – client uses the @UK supplier recruitment programme to establish direct links for ordering and e-invoicing to all significant suppliers, with correct terms applied to every order.

Stage 4 – client implements a change management programme internally to roll out full e-procurement to all departments (with or without @UK implementation programme assistance).

Stage 5 – client adopts 'strategic procurement' including, e.g., buyer-neutral coding for all items, e-auctions and e-tendering, supplier pre-qualification, etc., as appropriate.

@UK believes that most organisations have now gone way beyond the stage of thinking e-procurement is some alien technology irrelevant to them. The company knows that its staff are confident buying from websites, so that 'ultimate user' is not a problem. It is the detailed implementation at procurement/finance department level so as to achieve bankable savings that is the issue now.

Electronic auctions (e-auctions)

E-auctions initiated by the buyer use the Internet to share communications, providing both buyers and suppliers with visibility of bid status in real time and allowing an instant response. If conducted properly, with adequate participant training, it creates a more level playing field for suppliers through increased transparency. An e-auction allows for a bid on price and/or quantitative attributes such as carriage charge, quantity discounts, and quality.

E-auctions should be considered as a tool in the buyer's e-sourcing toolkit. They can be used to renew existing contracts or offer consolidated spend opportunities. They can also be used to negotiate significant spot purchases and to receive pricing on frequently tendered communications or service.

■ Types of e-auctions

Electronic reverse auctions (ERAs) allow buyers to seek competitive pricing by inviting pre-qualified suppliers to participate in a real-time dynamic online event. Usually the internet-based auction begins with the buyer posting a requirement for a product or service on an internet site; a reserve price (a price which suppliers must meet in order to be considered) is usually set. The buyer then invites suppliers to bid against each other.

The term 'reverse' simply refers to the bidding process as the participating suppliers submit successively lower priced bids during a specified time period. The key difference between an internet-enabled auction and a traditional purchasing process is that all the suppliers can usually see their bid along with the current lowest bid, as well as having the opportunity to re-bid as many times as they wish.

If other quantitative attributes are included then the auction will be classed as a weighted multi-variable auction. In the same way as an auction based on price alone, suppliers know which rank their own bid is, and can usually view the other bids, but not the identity of the other suppliers. In this case, however, all bids are adjusted in real time from a range of variables from other attributes, which allows buyers to view a figure which makes up the total cost of ownership. Other attributes may include carriage, discounts in price for quantities or for successive years, packaging, payment periods, quality, or guarantee periods. Switching costs could be included in the non-incumbent supplier's calculations.

There are several types of reverse auctions. For example it is not uncommon for buyers to use the terms 'a bundled bid', or 'cherry picked' or a 'scorecard auction'.

In the case of a bundled auction the buyer usually bundles his requirements together into a single lot. Suppliers then bid for the total package. Usually they will submit a bid for each item, but these will be totalled up and one supplier usually wins the whole bid.

A cherry picked auction is slightly different. As the name suggests, suppliers have the opportunity to 'cherry pick' certain lines from an auction and only bid for these. A buyer can then choose to award the contract to several different suppliers for different lots, or award to one supplier.

A scorecard auction is slightly more complicated in that the buyer can assign an internal scorecard to each potential supplier. Each bid a supplier submits is then recalculated against the values assigned by the value on the scorecard to produce a weighted bid. The buyer may choose to share the scorecard information with the suppliers, which may improve their performance, as they will know what they are up against and where they need to improve. This type is sometimes referred to as a 'transformation reverse auction' (Figure 18.8). There are three bidders initially, but after an initial period of time one drops out to leave the two remaining to battle it out.

Clearly, the main difference between traditional tendering in which closed bids are received and the reverse auction is that the same bidders are allowed to enter many consecutive bids in a reverse auction until the closing time of the event. The event has an agreed duration, which can be, for example, 30/60 minutes, and then can be extended by discrete periods of time if the bidding is intense around the original closing time. There is an agreed start price for the bidding, in order to avoid unnecessary time-wasting bids before realistic bids can be obtained. Suppliers will obviously know which is their price on the screen, but they will not know the owners of the competing bids. An alternative method is to simply rank the bids and again the identity of the others in the ranking is not known. Clearly it is important for procurement to ensure that they do not allow themselves to accept a bid which is too low, in that it would cause requests for price variations and/or quality degradation at a later date.

Figure 18.8
**Typical reverse
auction event**

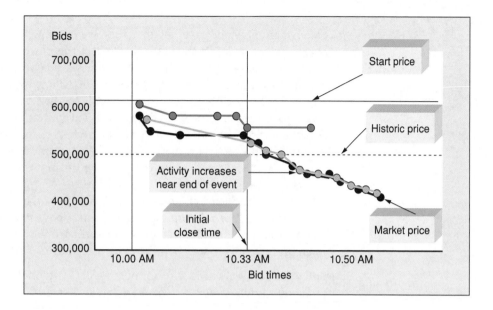

The following research from BP reveals prerequisites for effective online auctions.

Online auctions: prerequisites – best practice

- Buyers must have a thorough knowledge of the supply chain
- Pre-qualification of invited suppliers essential
- Greater onus on buying organisation to ensure clear comprehensive specifications communicated
- Acknowledge that prices can go up
- Misuse of RAS may result in a move away from understanding total costs to a focus on price
- Effect on supplier relationship must be considered
- Reversing the trend towards supply base reductions

Case study – Schools to benefit from local, regional and national savings

Schools will soon be able to benefit from a whole range of savings arranged across all types of goods and services. These will be available online and may have been set up nationally by the schools' own local authority working with other neighbouring authorities or in some cases more local still.

Ina Taylor, Director of the FfES's new Centre for Procurement Performance, said:

Many schools may have felt that they were struggling alone and have been crying out for better deals that reflect the purchasing power of the whole education system. This now becomes a practical possibility, using technology that is commonly available. The CPP is working closely with those local authorities which have schools in their remit. First of all we want to ensure that the good deals which authorities or the local government consortia may already have set up are freely accessible to schools in a way which works with the schools' local administration systems, so the process is efficient and paper free. On top of this, we, the CPP and our procurement partners from local authorities, the consortia and from Universities and Further Education Colleges are working together to identify opportunities to combine our spending power to negotiate better terms from suppliers that can directly benefit schools. We expect real and significant results to start benefiting schools budgets during 2006.

Dudley George, Marketing Director of @UK PLC, a pioneer in this area with its @Schools online network, took up a similar theme:

Our company objective is to cut the cost of commerce for buyers and suppliers. If we cut out the waste that is created for all parties by unnecessary paperwork, high levels of returns through errors and by delays in orders getting to suppliers, this allows everyone to benefit. Some arrangements, such as for instance plumbing, coach trips or grounds maintenance will probably be best set up at a local level, maybe a Local Authority on behalf of all or some of its schools, maybe by the schools themselves. Our organisation specialises in providing the facilities, to that even the smallest of suppliers can take part.

Other arrangements can be made at the level of groups of authorities, such as various Devon Procurement Partnership contracts now rolling out through that county. In other cases of course the CPP may well be able to negotiate on behalf of all UK schools. This is not the end, because even when schools have had special arrangements negotiated, they may still want to put their high value and unique service needs out for quotation, for example using our 'RFP' (Request for Price) facility. The same written specification, plus any plans, schedules can then pass securely online to 3 or more possible providers. Replies are then all available for comparison and stored as electronic records should any audit issue arise, so no need for filing cabinets of old quotes.

■ Why organisations should be aware of e-auctions

**The benefits
to buyers**

Aberdeen Group research (2001) supports the assertion that the Internet provides a low-cost and efficient mechanism for communications and negotiations between buyers and suppliers. Electronic auctions exploit technology to achieve real-time market pricing, which generally results in significant savings for the buying organisation. Overall savings of 10–20 per cent are commonly reported using the reverse auction process. Other benefits include a reduction in the sourcing cycle time (once the process is established), improved specification of requirements and increased transparency.

The IAdapt research found, using an auction to establish a new contract, the change in the five key performances factors as follows:

- Flexibility (i.e. changing order quantities at the last minute) +22%.
- Quality of the product or service +20%.
- Delivery/reliability +12%.
- Dependability (keeping promises) +11%.
- Account or customer support +8%.

There was an expectation that there would be at least no change or a reduction in at least one or two key factors; in particular it was expected that the 'soft' factors of flexibility, dependability and account management would deteriorate as the reduced supplier's margins led to a reduction in the level of support provided to their customers. It was surprising to see that this was not the case.

This may be because the supplier wants to please the buyer so as to avoid going through the e-auction process again at the end of the contract, or to factor in an increase in switching costs against other suppliers if the e-auction process is repeated at the end of the contract.

Motivation for using e-auctions

IAdapt asked buyers what motivated them to choose an e-auction as part of their purchasing process. The reasons for choosing an e-auction are:

- To improve the cost of your product/service – 86%.
- As a trial or a plot (to experience the outcome of an e-auction event) – 69%.
- Process improvement (including time/speed) – 67%.
- Your strategy for auctions is long term – 64%.
- To ascertain current market conditions – 50%.
- Told by management – 33%.
- Competitors are using it – 22%.
- Moving to a less personal approach to sourcing – 19%.

Unsurprisingly the key reason for choosing an auction was to reduce cost supported by a need to reduce the process time.

Success criteria

Buyers were also asked what criteria they used to decide whether an auction was a success. The following are the results for the success criteria:

- To obtain the best market pricing – 91%.
- Enabling software works satisfactorily – 94%.
- Suppliers are able to bid satisfactorily – 89%.
- Learnt from activity – 89%.
- Time taken for negotiation significantly reduced – 69%.
- Easy to repeat with other products – 63%.
- Significant numbers of suppliers agreed to participate – 63%.
- Suppliers agree to participate in future auctions – 60%.

Obtaining the best pricing was the top criterion, followed by the software working satisfactorily for both the buyer and the supplier.

■ Supplier management initiatives

When buyers were asked what specific supplier management initiatives they were using in their e-auction based procurement process, the following results were found:

- Developing supplier relationships – 90%.
- Using a supplier reduction programme – 70%.
- Employing joint technological development – 53%.
- Employing price as a primarily factor in your supplier selection – 33%.

These results are surprising as auctions have not generally been perceived as encouraging the development of supplier relationships, yet this was recorded as a major objective.

■ Other benefits to buyers

E-auctions generally encourage:

- Competitive behaviour amongst suppliers.
- Quick, efficient and paperless way of requesting pricing.
- Use for catalogue items or spot shortages.
- Identification of new sources of supply.

■ Enablers and inhibitors

Buyers found the top six key enablers to be:

- Comprehensive specification for product/service.
- Supplier auction training.
- Sound supplier pre-qualifying process.
- Selecting suitable commodity.
- Enabling software.
- Clear auction objectives.

Generally the e-auction process seems to encourage buyers to be more rigorous and thorough in the purchasing process.

The top barriers to successful e-auctions were found to be:

- Lack of supplier participation – there is a community of suppliers who have a policy not to enter e-auctions, even though it may mean losing contracts to their competitors.
- Unsuitable commodity/service – this might be an item where there is no competition in the marketplace, or that is too complicated or cannot be largely specified.
- Lack of competitive supply base – if a product or service does not have at least three suitable suppliers then the e-auction process is not generally suitable.
- Poor training of buyer/supplier – getting things right first time is imperative to build trust amongst suppliers in your organisation's e-auction process.
- Auction timing – if you are inviting suppliers to participate from different countries and time zones, take into account if the timing chosen to run the auction is convenient to those suppliers, and also consider company shutdowns in the UK.

Supplier adoption – SMEs

Small businesses are missing out on lucrative public and private sector contracts by failing to do business online. CIPS has found that:

- Fewer than four in 10 small businesses (37 per cent) tender for contracts online.
- Online users cite speed, savings, reduced paperwork, increased customer satisfaction and increased productivity as benefits.

However, research shows motivations for online trading as seen in Figure 18.9, while a CIPS study indicates that many organisations share the same criteria for measuring the success of e-auctions (Figure 18.10).

Mini case study – Shell

Shell International's website states:

> When spending billions of dollars a year on materials and services getting the best deal is essential. By combining the needs of individual operating units worldwide greater purchasing power has led to discounts as high as 55% over previous prices. Internet-based purchasing (e-procurement) is also increasingly leading to significant cost savings. A combination of approaches has saved some $500 million in 2000 in Exploration and Production alone.

Figure 18.9
E-auction – why buyers choose e-auctions

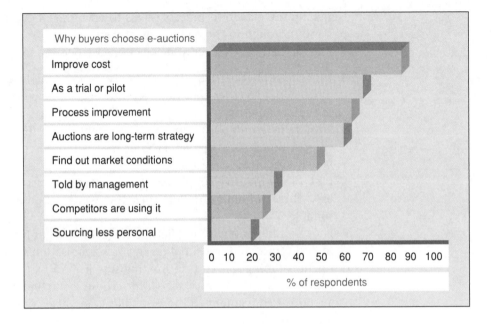

Figure 18.10
E-auctions – criteria for successful e-auctions

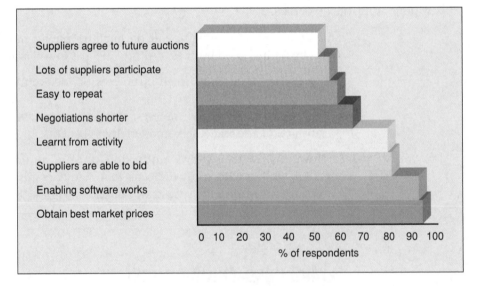

Mini case study – IBM

IBM encourages suppliers to use the Internet. The majority of purchasing transactions are conducted electronically. Suppliers must check that all their electronic transactions are correct; if so, payment is automatic and avoids payment delays. Late payment will only occur if the supplier's electronic documentation is not completed satisfactorily.

Mini case study – Powerlink

Powerlink, an Australian power company, saved 41 per cent of the originally projected cost of more than $2 million for fibre optic cable in an e-bidding event involving suppliers from four countries.

It can be argued that the use of reverse auctions is seen as a price-focused approach to buying, and that other aspects of total cost of acquisition and/or ownership are placed in the background when suppliers are being selected, only to emerge later. The approach is attractive, in that it provides a very rapid and powerful way of meeting short-term price objectives and thereby providing apparent shareholder value. However, the approach is inimical to the development of long-term alliances and relationships, and does not fit well with lean, agile and similar supply philosophies where buyer and seller work together to drive out cost.

Perhaps the approach is not the panacea that some advocates claim, but a useful addition to the range of methods available to the corporate buyer.

The Electronic Commerce (EC Directive) Regulations 2002

These regulations may apply to organisations within the UK if they:

- sell goods or services to businesses or consumers on the Internet or by e-mail;
- advertise on the Internet or by e-mail; or
- convey or store electronic content for customers or provide access to a communication network.

The key features of the regulations are:

- Online selling and advertising is subject to the laws of the UK if the trader is established here. Online services provided from other member states may not be restricted. There are exceptions, particularly for contracts with consumers and the freedom of parties to choose the applicable law.
- Recipients of online services must be given clear information about the trader, the nature of commercial communications and how to complete an online transaction.
- Online service providers are exempt from liability for the content that they convey or store in specified circumstances.
- Changes to the powers of enforcement authorities such as Trading Standards Departments and the Office of Fair Trading.

(This information is taken from A Guide for Business to the Electronic Commerce (EC Directive) Regulations 2002, published by the Department of Trade and Industry.)

Conclusions

There is overwhelming evidence from research that effective implementation of e-procurement, which actively involves all of the stakeholders, can make a positive contribution to not only lowering total costs of ownership, but also to improvements in customer service and availability. It is therefore essential to sustaining competitive advantage.

Summary

1 This chapter explores the concept of e-procurement, explaining the various tools available.

2 We have considered the benefits of e-procurement such as the reduction of non-value added manual transactions and the reduction in cycle times.

3 Several case studies have indicated the increasing application of e-procurement in the public sector.

4 The applicability of e-procurement tools and techniques across the procurement targeting tool has been explored.

5 E-auctions have been discussed and best practice implementation of e-auctions has been considered.

6 Enablers and inhibitors of supplier adoption of e-procurement have been outlined.

7 EU-directives for e-commerce have been outlined.

References and further reading

@UK (2006), E-procurement update, www.uk-plc.net.

Aberdeen Group (2001), 'E-sourcing-negotiating value in a volatile economy', www.aberdeen.com.

Abbiati, P (2001), 'Virtual agreement', *Supply Management*, March.

Berger, A J and Gattorna, J (2001), *Supply Chain Cybermastery: Building High Performance Supply Chains of the Future*, Aldershot: Gower.

Burnett, K (2001), 'Electronic rules', *Supply Management*, February.

Ellinor, R (2006), 'SMEs lack skills for online business', *Supply Management*, March.

Emmett, S and Crocker, B (2006), *The Relationship Driven Supply Chain*, Aldershot: Gower.

Guinipero, L C and Sawchuk, C (2000), *E-Purchasing Plus*, New Jersey: JGC Enterprise.

Heinritz, S, Farrell, P, Giunipero, L and Kolchin, M (1993), *Purchasing, Principles and Applications*, 8th edn, Upper Saddle River, NJ: Prentice Hall.

Kearney, A T (2002), 'Global survey of e-procurement', www.buyitnet.org.

Mukhopadhyay, T and Sunder, K (2002), 'Strategic and operational benefits of electronic integration in B2B procurement processes', *Management Science*, 48 (10), October.

Norris, M, West, S and Ganghan, K, eds (2000), *eBusiness Essentials: Technology and Network for the Electronic Marketplace*, Chichester: Wiley.

Parker, G (2001), 'Money for something', *Supply Management*, March.

Pasrija, R (2004), 'Benefits of e-procurement', IBM India.

Reason, M and Evans, E (2001), *Implementing E-Procurement*, Cambridge: Hawksmere.

Wheatley, M (2000), 'World order', *Supply Management*, September.

Wheatley, M (2003), 'How to know if e-procurement is for you?', *cio.com*.

19

Contract management and performance measurement

Introduction

In procurement, the calculation of the number of requisitions dealt with by a buyer in any one day may tell us something about their efficiency at processing work. The number of items received on time and the number of items which fail to meet the specification will also be of benefit in that regard. However, their effectiveness may be more concerned with establishing vendors who have the potential to supply for many years to come – competitively. Also with, for example, reducing the number of these suppliers so that co-makership and just-in-time approaches may be managed to the best effect. Therefore post-contract performance measurement, commonly referred to as contract management, is vitally important if companies wish to improve value-added and minimise total costs of ownership. These ideas are developed in this chapter.

Objectives of this chapter

- To examine approaches to the measurement of performance efficiency in procurement in relation to its stage of evolution
- To consider the mechanisms of contract management
- To relate procurement performance to the stage of development
- To consider the benefits of measuring performance
- To consider the role of procurement as the intelligent customer
- To analyse the basic questions in 'best practice' benchmarking
- To evaluate reporting systems and the information that should be included
- To consider service level agreements
- To consider the role of risk management

Contract management

Contract management can be defined as:

> 'The activities of a buyer during a contract period to ensure that all parties to the contract fulfil their contractual obligations.'

An important aspect of this is managing the relationships between all parties in the most effective way so as to ensure the contract meets the optimum combination of cost, time and quality. Contract activities can be split into two distinct but interdependent phases: 'upstream' (pre-award), 'downstream' (post-award). Contract management is a downstream activity but can only be effective if upstream activities are properly carried out.

Contract management applies to the whole of procurements from a simple order to a complex construction or service contract.

CIPS believes the most important measurement of effective purchasing and supply management is that the purchasing and supply management strategy precisely and continually aligns and integrates with the organisation's corporate plan, business unit and functional strategies. Contract management performance measures should reflect the objectives.

A performance measurement system therefore plays an important role in managing a business as it provides the information necessary for decision making and actions. CIPS advocates a balanced scorecard approach.

In summary, the balanced scorecard approach puts the company vision and values at the centre and classifies measures under headings of Finance/ Shareholders: People; Processes; and Customers. In a purchasing supply management context suppliers may be included within the 'customers' category. Typical measures could include:

Finance/ shareholders

- Cost savings.
- Percentage of corporate spend covered by contracts managed by procurement.
- Number of suppliers.

People

- Staff training and development, e.g. training of end-user buyers.

Processes

- Time/cost to process purchase orders.
- Implementation of effective IT systems, e.g. e-procurement.
- Performance against SLAs agreed with internal customers.

Customers/ suppliers

- Supplier payment performance.
- Supplier quality performance measures.
- Feedback from staff survey reports, i.e. customer satisfaction surveys.

There are examples of other objectives. The aim should be for continuous improvement.

■ Benefits of contract management

Post-contract management is vital. If the agreement is not regularly reviewed then the true benefits and improvements contained in the contract will not be fully realised.

The London Fire and Emergency Planning Authority (LFEPA) states:

Once you sign a contract, you have three to five years to reap the benefits. If you don't have continuity from procurement, then you don't get those benefits . . .

Potential savings, benefits and efficiencies are worked out and presented with satisfaction. But these are only really meaningful once the contract starts and the 'real' value is achieved.

■ Whose responsibility?

Contract management is important but is not always given the full attention it deserves. Companies often struggle with the question of who should be responsible for ensuring the supplier delivers the promised goods and continues to deliver innovative solutions. This depends a lot on who owns the relationship with the supplier.

There is often a lot of tension between procurement and other functions over who manages the contract. This results in a lack of co-operation. Recent estimates suggest that up to 20 per cent of companies do not involve procurement in the contract management phase, nor do they have an effective contract management strategy. Accordingly, service levels previously agreed are not met and clients fail to reap the benefits they negotiated.

Mini case study – BA

Once a year a mini business plan is created for each spend category and is shared with suppliers. It analyses supply market dynamics, what BA wants to achieve, and how to get the best value from their major interests.

The key is to align the supplier with the buyer's objectives. And that has introduced a discipline never there before.

For each of BA's 80 most strategic suppliers, which accounts for 80 per cent of its spend, a detailed account plan is prepared to improve communication between procurement, contracting departments and the supplier.

It is visible to all the people in the business that deal with that supplier. Within it there is a page dedicated to supplier relationship management which lists the key people responsible for managing the relationship.

BA thinks that buyers should not get involved in the day-to-day relationship. They do not and should not have the time or resources as it is the commercial lead that should come from procurement.

Other organisations believe procurement should work with other departments to extract the most value out of their contracts. Successful companies are those that align procurement and finance to co-ordinate policies for measuring contract compliance.

Mini case study – HMPS

Procurement at HM Prison Service (HMPS) has three staff wholly dedicated to contract management, to ensure the department gets the most value from its deals.

Buyers need to push suppliers for continuous improvement, something managers chiefly concerned with the day-to-day running of the business fail to do. Companies should ask themselves what they are doing to build up trust with the supplier. And how can they build communication between all parties in the absence of effective contract management? Penalising contractors for minor slippages will result in poor relationships – it is better to help manage and improve the performance of the contract throughout its life. Procurement needs to be involved in contract management to a greater or lesser extent, depending on their organisational model and culture.

Mini case study – O_2

At O_2, procurement is involved in two elements of contract management. Procurement must initially take care of the 'hygiene factor' (the basics) before it can tackle vendor management.

The first is transactional. It's about making sure you are getting what you thought you would be getting.

Back to basics

Major contracts are given 'hygiene' checks every six weeks by procurement. Every six months for less strategic deals. Once this is done, procurement takes it further.

At that stage they are talking about vendor management, where they work with the vendor rather than the contract. This is followed by reviewing, redefining and developing the relationship.

Often, such important activities are neglected when companies have multifaceted relationships with a supplier and where vendor management is diluted.

Examples of performance metrics

Strategic
- Total supply chain cycle time.
- Order lead times.
- Supplier lead time against industry norm.
- Level of supplier's defect-free deliveries.
- Delivery lead time.
- Delivery performance.

Tactical
- Purchase order cycle time.
- Supplier ability to respond to quality problems.

■ Supplier cost-saving initiatives.
■ Delivery reliability.

Operational

■ Total inventory.
■ Supplier rejection rate.
■ Quality of delivery documentation.
■ Quality of delivered goods.

Pitfalls of traditional performance measurement

There are three basic steps companies should take in the design and implementation of their performance measurement system:

1 Defining the business objectives.
2 Designing the performance measures.
3 Managing through measurement.

The concept of a balanced performance measurement system emerged in the late 1980s and early 1990s as a reaction against the increasing focus on purely financial measures. Some have criticised financial performance measures for:

■ Focusing on external financial reporting needs rather than the needs of managing the business.
■ Encouraging emphasis on the short term.
■ Being backward looking.
■ Being internally focused, concentrating attention on internal efficiencies.
■ Encouraging minimisation of variance rather than continuous improvement.

Many activities are much better measured in non-financial terms (e.g. productivity, speed of response, quality, and variability).

Setting business objectives by itself is not enough, even when these are quantified. An important second step is to define the measure in such a way that it reinforces the achievement of the business objective. It is useful to define the measure precisely otherwise the resulting behaviour may well not match what is expected.

■ Why are we measuring this?
■ To which top-level objective does this relate?
■ What is the target level of performance to be achieved and by when?
■ How is the measure to be calculated?
■ How often is this measured and reviewed?
■ Who is responsible for measuring?
■ What is the data source?
■ Who is responsible for action on this measure?
■ What action should they take?

Defining a performance measure in this way enables the company to stimulate action through identifying who should act and what should be done and should influence behaviour. Measuring performance explicitly focuses attention. This influences behaviour.

- What behaviour will result from the introduction of this measure?
- Is this behaviour desirable?

Performance measurement only really works if it is seen to be important to the running of the business. This requires procedures to be put in place so that the measures are collected, analysed, reviewed and acted upon on a regular basis over a sustained period of time. This involves arranging regular review meetings where the measures are discussed, the performance reviewed and action taken. Displaying the measures throughout the organisation makes the performance visible.

Performance measurement: effectiveness

So the function needs a robust method of measuring its performance to show how it adds value as a strategic resource. There might be process measures such as transactions per person, value of purchases per member of the function, accuracy, proportion of time spent with suppliers, percentage of e-procurement, or the proportion of spend under the function. Cost and competence measures are about input, not performance.

First the performance of the function must be clearly connected to the organisation's objectives and constraints by:

- getting away from cost and process and putting the focus on outcomes, which signals that performance is about delivery;
- setting targets at levels defined by the organisation's objectives and customers, e.g. response times for queries;
- adopting the latest techniques;
- improving the quality of feedback to and from procurement. Getting proper feedback on customer perceptions and educating them about the role of procurement is important;
- trading off quality against on-time delivery.

■ SLAs

When drawing up contracts for services, it is crucial for buyers to define clearly what they expect of suppliers. This is often addressed in a service level agreement (SLA), which sets out what the service includes and the required standards. When drafting these types of contracts, you should cover these areas.

Service requirements

Key performance indicators (KPIs) cover the level of the service provided. They should be chosen and set at levels so that if they are all met, the buyer will receive the services it requires.

Credits

The supplier may give the purchaser credits if it fails to meet defined KPIs.

Company buy-in

Dispute resolution measures should be in place. Typically, there will be provisions in the SLA so that problems are escalated within set periods if they cannot be resolved by the staff working on the project on a day-to-day basis. Provisions relating to mediation (for example, using the Centre for Effective Dispute Resolution methods), binding arbitration or going to court may also be in the SLA.

Get external advice

You should certainly consider using external advisors if:

- Either party is unfamiliar with all of the concepts involved in SLAs.
- The services covered are high value.
- The services covered are business critical, such as IT systems.

Keep it simple

Agreements that are complicated or hard to follow are likely to fail. In addition, because SLAs are likely to change over the course of time to meet the parties' changing business requirements, there should also be built-in change control mechanisms to ensure that the SLA is flexible enough to cope:

- SLA
- Services
- Service levels
- Regular performance reports

It is also essential that the contract contains a tailored mechanism that incentivises performance. The most successful long-term service contracts contain not only disincentives against poor performance but also incentives to improve it.

There should be a robust contract management structure. This will provide a framework for regular communication between the parties.

The agreement should also provide a mechanism for regular reviews of the service, price and strategy, and should cover purchaser's termination rights: with termination for cause, the purchaser should specifically identify those types of behaviours that will count as a material or persistent breach. Basic exit provisions include the preparation of an exit plan during the early part of the contract.

In much of the literature concerning procurement, the measures of performance which are discussed relate primarily to operational activities. Yet effective procurement must involve activities, objectives and measurement relating to both tactical and strategic issues. As Herb Simon (1996) argued, we should ask 'Are we doing the right things?' before we ask 'Are we doing them right?'

Nevertheless, we still need to be concerned with the measurement of operational action. Indeed, in that respect measurement can be one of the major influences for improvement. One problem in measuring procurement's performance is that it is difficult to isolate responsibility: quality failure may be due to poor tooling provided by the buying company as much as to poor source selection; delivery failure may result from production control changing schedules frequently, or from late requisitioning; poor supplier performance might stem from the buying company being slow payers. The point is that many functions are involved in one way or another with the buying process. They may influence supplier performance in a variety of ways by their actions, yet the complex interrelationships make it difficult to segregate the effect of that influence. This is one of the arguments for management by objectives where corporate objectives are supported by a network of interconnected sub-objectives. It is also a basic thrust behind the growing interest in what might be termed 'collective' approaches – materials management, logistics management, physical distribution management, and materials administration. These all aim to group authority and responsibilities in ways which allow control and measurement. A department which indents for materials, stores them, purchases those materials and schedules supplies to production can be held responsible for total material performance. Such approaches may be conceptually and administratively attractive, but it is still desirable for management to gauge how well the function is performing.

Measuring procurement performance

One can examine efficiency in procurement in relation to its stage of evolution. At very early stages of development, procurement invariably has a low status and is reactive in operation. Its effectiveness or otherwise is seen in terms of its ability to handle transactions. While it is important that transactions are handled efficiently, achieving strategic procurement objectives can often assist in simplifying or reducing them.

Measurement that centres on the generation of transactional activities in itself often perpetuates the view that procurement is essentially a reactive clerical function. One might find, for example, that procurement in an organisation is subordinate to the Finance Director. This person's view of procurement may be that the function should:

- encourage competition by placing numerous enquiries;
- change suppliers regularly;
- pay the lowest price; and
- delay paying suppliers for as long as possible.

These objectives could in turn lead to the following results:

- Too many suppliers offering materials at the lowest price, with no incentive to look at longer-term aspects that could lead to strategic savings.

■ An enormous amount of expediting time could be spent by the buyer because suppliers are not paid on time.

■ Too many short-duration orders again increasing administrative effort rather than longer-term arrangements that could perhaps cover a number of years.

■ Buyers wastefully involved in routine ordering rather than the computer scheduling supplies when required.

More advanced buying organisations would argue that the buyers' time is much better spent on such tasks as negotiation, supplier development, cost reduction, and internal interface development than on routine administrative activity.

■ Measurement criteria

Table 19.1 shows the likely measurement criteria as the procurement and supply function develops. The table illustrates how, as the focus of the buying activity changes, so the methods used to evaluate performance also change. Initially measurement is clerically orientated and superficial; as the function develops, measurement criteria become more tactically and strategically based, and the range of measurement criteria increases.

Table 19.1 Measurement criteria for the procurement and supply function

Position of procurement	Status	Procurement performance measurement	Focus on
Fragmented purchasing carried out mainly by functional areas; small clerical purchasing function	Low	Very few; staying within agreed budgets	Getting the goods in
Purchasing function established; mainly clerical; functional area still involved in buying	Low but improving; reporting via other function to top management	Mainly measuring clerical efficiency of the function, i.e. orders and requisitions outstanding	Clerical efficiency
Procurement function commercial	Recognised function with procurement manager reporting to functional head, e.g. Finance Director; all buying carried out by procurement department	Clerical buying efficiency: i.e. savings, cost reduction, negotiating efficiency	Clerical buying efficiency
Procurement function commercial, but elements of strategic involvement	Reporting directly to MD; procurement manager	As above, plus supplier development and intra-organisational interface development	As above, plus beginning to measure overall effectiveness on a longer-term basis
Procurement is a strategic business function	Reporting to MD/Board; procurement director heads function	As above, but concerned with strategic development, JIT, etc.; measurement of 'total costs of supply'	Strategic effectiveness

This framework of criteria is based on work undertaken by Van Weel (1985) and allows for five stages of development:

1 Where procurement is essentially reactive and fragmented, performance criteria are few or even non-existent. The main objective for the activity is to convert requisitions into orders and get the supplies in.

2 As the function develops, it is likely to be given the responsibility for handling the paperwork involved in the buying system. At this point, in judging the function's contribution, clerical efficiency is probably the main criterion.

3 In the third stage of development, the role is being viewed more in respect of its commercial usefulness to the organisation. At this stage a chief buyer or a procurement manager might be appointed. While clerical and systems efficiency are being measured, the function would also be expected to begin to show savings against budgets or costs. At this stage savings or cost reductions are likely to be measured.

4 At the next important stage of development, procurement is seen as being of more strategic importance. At this point measurement criteria are established to assess key supplier developments through vendor rating schemes. As the profile of procurement becomes higher, its interface with other functions becomes more significant and this may also be measured. At this stage the procurement manager is reporting to the chief executive of the organisation. Almost certainly concern will be shown for total acquisition costs and there will be less emphasis on lowest price.

5 Finally, at the fifth stage procurement is recognised as being of strategic importance, with the head of the function probably at director level. Here measurement is centred around strategic effectiveness. Procurement's ability to make world-class concepts work would be measured, and thus there would be considerable interest in, for example, the following matters:

   (a) moves towards co-makership and strategic supplier alliances;
   (b) education of the supply base;
   (c) improving the strategic profile of suppliers;
   (d) improvements in the supply chain; and
   (e) each supplier's adoption of EDI, JIT, TQM and zero defects philosophies.

Measurement criteria are dynamic and must develop as the organisation develops. Clerical efficiency gives way to cost effectiveness and eventually strategic effectiveness. Figure 19.1 illustrates how measurement criteria change as the function develops.

As one might imagine, the move from one level of development into another is probably accompanied by a range of other changes. Often the transition is far from smooth.

■ Why measure performance?

The main benefits commonly considered to result from performance measurement are as follows.

Figure 19.1
**Purchasing
performance
development**

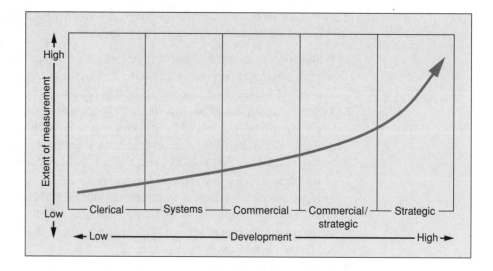

Almost 75 per cent of the respondents to a survey believed that inability to measure procurement performance had hindered management recognition of the function. If a general manager has no means of measuring the effect of a function on its overall performance, they are unlikely to regard it as of great importance. If only crude ways to measure performance are available then these are what will be used, in the absence of more sophisticated means. Crude performance measures of procurement performance tend to be negative, indicators of failure rather than success (e.g. when production supplies fail to arrive or fail to pass inspection).

Improved performance ought to be encouraged by reports of actual performance measured against some kind of standard. Such data should be invaluable in the organisation of the function and relationships with the wider organisation. In the event of a reorganisation, the data on the various jobs involved will be available.

Finally, if staff believe that their efforts will be recognised, they are likely to be better motivated with consequent benefits to morale.

Mini case study – Ford

Ford of Europe displays signs in each of its purchasing departments illustrating where the department is on set performance criteria. The signs indicate suppliers (and responsible buyers) who are performing well. The best are identified as benchmarks for others to aspire to.

■ Measurement areas

What is measured in companies where some form of evaluation is practised? Common areas for the measurement of procurement information are:

Table 19.2
Some commonly used measures of operational procurement performance

Area	Measure
Quality	Percentage of rejects in goods received Percentage of parts rejected in production Percentage of raw materials rejected in production
Quantity	Percentage of stock which has not moved over a specified period Number of production stock-outs Number of small-value orders Number of emergency orders Comparison of stock with target stock
Timing	Supplier's actual delivery performance against promised Time taken to process requisitions Time taken up with remedial action
Price	Prices paid against standard Prices paid for key items compared with market indexes Prices paid against budget Price at the time of use against price at the time of purchase
Operational costs	Cost of processing an order Progressing costs as a percentage of total Communication costs

- operational procurement;
- co-ordination with other functions;
- procurement organisation and system;
- budget performance;
- creative performance;
- policy development; and
- planning and forecasting.

Typical measures which are used in relation to the first of the areas listed above are included in Table 19.2.

Co-ordination with other functions is difficult to measure, important as it is in the overall performance of the procurement function. Measures which have been used include the number of complaints from other department managers regarding procurement performance; the number of complaints to other managers by the head of procurement; and the number of panic purchases. All these are, to say the least, difficult to come to terms with as meaningful measures. One firm uses (i) periodic attitude surveys across departments, and (ii) a sampling method relating to key operational meetings and the content of the minutes.

The system and procedures involved in procurement might reveal lack of control within the department or between departments; they could highlight either staff or system inefficiency and may be indicative of poor management as well as poor liaison.

The aptness of the organisation to its environment and the suitability of the staff who work within it are also important.

Creative performance is difficult to appraise. However, questions which might be asked include: What has been achieved through value analysis?

What has been developed in supplier price/cost analysis? Has the department been successful in locating alternative economic sources, particularly where there was previously a monopoly supplier? Has the department, in conjunction with its suppliers, contributed to productivity and efficiency on the company's production line? What additional services are available to user departments as a result of procurement's initiative which will contribute to their efficiency?

Policy development is another important area which does not lend itself to quantitative measurement; surprisingly few organisations have thought through their policies. Examples of procurement policy areas which might repay study are:

- make or buy;
- the degree of centralisation;
- reciprocity;
- inter-company trading (in groups);
- single or multiple sourcing;
- working with suppliers towards JIT; and
- co-makership arrangements.

Criteria which might be used in judging the quality of the department's efforts include: Is there a clear statement of policy? Is that policy understood and applied by the relevant personnel? Have policies been updated as conditions change?

Planning and forecasting is an increasingly important aspect of procurement work. The basic question is: Is the function involved with long-term and short-term planning within the company at all? If it is, to what extent; what is the quality of the input, and what is the time horizon? How good are the forecasts which underpin the planning input? Perfection in forecasting is not to be expected, but a reasonable improvement both in forecast accuracy and in the quality of the accompanying comment should be achieved over the years. Forecasts may be concerned with: the industrial relations environment; supply and demand; prices; technological development; and legal and social changes which may affect supply markets.

Procurement as the intelligent customer

An alternative to the above approaches to measuring purchasing performance is to ask whether procurement is capable of operating on an 'intelligent customer' basis.

The concept of the intelligent customer is intended to convey the need for organisational expenditure to be made on a professional basis. The term 'intelligent customer' has entered into general procurement language. As a result the specific attributes of an intelligent customer are hard to determine exactly. However, the basis of being an intelligent customer appear to include at least the following:

- *Products.* Do we understand the range of products available in the supply market? Are we aware of the relative advantages and disadvantages of alternative products available in the marketplace? Are we aware of new products which will become available in the marketplace and likely trends in product costs?
- *Suppliers.* Are we aware of the complete range of sources within the supply chain for products or services? Are we aware of the professional reputation of potential suppliers? Do we have market intelligence on the trading circumstances of potential suppliers? Do we understand the organisational and trading culture of potential suppliers within the supply base?
- *Organisational requirement.* Are we capable of identifying the requirements of our internal customers and translating those requirements into specifications which enable suppliers to provide effective solutions? Are we in a position to persuade/require end users to amend their requirements?
- *Procurement.* Are we expert in the processes of procurement, that is, how to buy effectively and efficiently?

The concept of the intelligent customer is often employed in organisations which buy a wide range of products. Where the model identifies weaknesses, the organisation might seek external assistance, or delay buying whilst information on products, markets or organisational requirements is gathered.

Benchmarking in procurement and supply

As we have seen, there are numerous approaches to the assessment of both the performance of the procurement and supply function of an organisation, and the performance of the concern's suppliers. Some have argued that the evaluation of supplier or vendor performance is also an appraisal of procurement's performance, in that it is appropriate that the reputation of procurement should be dependent upon the quality and suitability of the suppliers recruited.

Various monitoring and measurement approaches are employed in the activity of buying. It is sometimes found useful to calculate key ratios, and to watch for changes in the ratios. Examples include purchase expenditure; sales, number of orders placed; expenditure, salary costs; number of transactions, and so on. It is widely argued that if you cannot measure a variable and you cannot control it, then the data which are collected on procurement activity are usually valuable as instruments of control as well as performance indicators.

Benchmarking is more than another name for the kinds of monitoring, assessment and measurement so far mentioned. The idea behind benchmarking is not simply to seek statistics or other evidence as an indication as to whether a new or existing supplier, or the procurement function itself, is meeting specifications or requirements. The idea is to discover 'best practice' wherever it might be found, and to attempt to identify and isolate the variables that accompany or are part of this best practice. The thinking is that once this has been done, the variables can be transported as leading indicators (benchmarks) back to the researching organisation with a view to focusing attention on how the performance might be matched (or bettered). Note that benchmarking is not concerned with copying the methods and systems of other organisations; the attention is given mainly to the factors which are identifiable as demonstrating that an organisation is successful. The term 'best practice benchmarking' occasionally confuses; it is the benchmark which is seen as most readily transferable, and hence most valuable, not the practice.

Given then that benchmarking is not simply attempting to replicate other successful organisations, it should also be clear that it is nothing to do with industrial espionage. The primary concern is with measurement and assessment, not for its own sake, but to keep in touch with current best practice achievements, with a view to matching or exceeding that performance in your own organisation.

There are five basic steps in benchmarking, as follows:

1 What are we going to benchmark? Almost anything that can be measured in procurement might be benchmarked. Outstanding deliveries, rejection rates, production interruptions or price-paid indices are some examples.

2 Who are we going to benchmark against? We first need to identify best practice. An obvious way to do this is to seek advice from our suppliers as to whom they regard as good trading partners. We might also look at organisations which are successful by the accepted measures of market share or profitability, and consider their procurement operations. Industry observers or professional bodies might give us the right kinds of leads.

3 How will we get the information? Much useful information is in the public domain. Much is published in the management journals and trade press, and many successful managers and organisations are very happy to share information. Personal contacts can help, and of course if a competitor is interested in benchmarking, and the leading ones are likely to be, there is mutual benefit in exchanging information.

4 How will we analyse the information? Benchmarking is not concerned with information for the sake of information. Collect only the data you need, and attempt, as far as is possible, to compare like with like. Statistics, ratios and other 'hard' information are usually more valuable than opinion or anecdote.

5 How will we use the information? Basically, if you discover that somebody is doing better than you are in a particular area of activity, set out to catch or overtake them. Set new standards for your own performance, and devise

an appropriate methodology for meeting those standards. This of course means that adequate resources need to be deployed, which in turn requires that top management is enthusiastic about benchmarking. We cannot, unfortunately, simply adopt benchmarking as another valuable procurement management technique. It is unlikely to achieve its potential unless undertaken as a matter of organisational policy.

In an age when EDI and e-procurement are fundamental, measures regarding the development and implementation of information systems may well be benchmarked and measured regularly. For example, one UK retailer targeted its buying staff to have their top 20 suppliers EDI-connected within 20 months.

Finally, it is worth registering the point that one measure of the effectiveness of a procurement function can be its own measurement systems. For example, does it measure the performance of key suppliers? Is this information used for control and management purposes? Does the data obtained from this process influence source decision making?

Reporting to management

Whatever system is used in the evaluation of procurement effort, some kind of report indicating the scope of activity of the department, its objectives and its performance in meeting the requirements of the organisation needs to be produced. It will include exception reports on current and projected market conditions and other pertinent information for top management, for example, data on new products; new materials and processes; information on the development of supply sources; and market intelligence on key raw materials, together with pertinent recommendations for related company policy and strategy. More than one chief executive has told the authors that they regarded such procurement reports as key indicators of the level of performance of the function.

■ Information

Does procurement have access to key data early enough? Does procurement contribute key data on a proactive basis? Does procurement have up-to-date key data available to it on an as-needed basis (e.g. point-of-sale data in retailing; immediate inventory position in manufacturing)? Has procurement promoted the use of EDI with its key suppliers? Are procurement systems up to date? Is it regarded as the source of key data on supply matters?

■ Suppliers

What supplier relationship policies are in being? What programmes are in place to improve supplier performance? What supplier visit programme is in place? Which functions accompany procurement in these visits? Are longer-term considerations taken into account in measuring suppliers/potential suppliers? Are co-makership programmes in place?

Best practice – contractual management of risk

The questions that have to be asked by any buyer in preparing a contract include:

- Who does what?
- For whom?
- When and where?
- At what cost and for what price?
- To what quality?
- For how long?
- Against what performance measures?
- Under what monitoring arrangements?

Also

- How do I know whether the service has been provided?
- How do I prove it?
- How do I judge if it is of acceptable quality?
- How much should I pay for it?

Without performance measurement the buyer cannot manage the contract to optimise value for money and maximise risk control.

■ Risk management

Both parties must understand their responsibilities. A weak contract could leave the client exposed to claims. Tests for the contract include:

- changes in service needs;
- problems in service delivery;
- claims avoidance;
- cost of any variation.

Having to address issues at the time of the event should encourage co-operation and assist in sustaining a partnering relationship.

Administration instructions

The use of an administration instructions section should be one of the key elements in claims avoidance strategy. The contract should require the contractors to provide a monthly report that addresses predetermined issues including:

- highlights – problems, solutions, key events;
- volumes to date and forecast;
- financial information – variations priced and agreed, the estimated value of variations issued but not agreed and, crucially, the estimated value of requested variations considered to be outstanding;
- performance – in line with the basis of reporting stated in the contract;
- resource information;
- health and safety information.

It is difficult for the contractor to make a claim at the end of the contract if no relevant mention has been made in the monthly report during the contract. However, if concerns are raised and the client has not taken appropriate action, the monthly report will be used in support of the claim.

When the preliminary programme of purchases is constructed, the procurement manager has to take into consideration:

- current material/component stocks;
- outstanding orders for relevant production materials;
- agreed stock levels and current lead times;
- the production schedule for the period in question;
- price trends of key materials and components in the long term; and
- unit prices in the short term.

The task of estimating prices and price trends requires the consideration of many things including:

- political or economic factors, world or domestic, which may affect prices;
- labour relations and availability of labour to major suppliers;
- comparative currency changes and levels of inflation in pertinent countries;
- possible changes in import duties, transit and insurance charges, dock charges, etc., as they affect goods from overseas;
- indirect effects on component prices due to fluctuations in prices of raw materials to suppliers;
- the position of long-term contracts as regards fixed prices or escalation clauses;
- the supply position of materials and components in relation to overall demand; and
- lead times and the potential effects of having to buy from more expensive alternative sources in the event of a failure.

Disposing of redundant stock, scrap or waste

Despite the considerable efforts which have been made to improve the management of materials in many organisations some redundant material has to be disposed of. The same thing can be said of scrap or waste and, frequently, the task of disposal is vested in the procurement department. The following short section is designed to suggest something of the role which an effective procurement department might play in the process.

One important point is to consider why the redundant or scrap materials have arisen. Some waste is inevitable, but careful consideration of the reasons behind the surplus, such as a result of poor storage, damage while in stock, the materials/components being faulty on arrival, the product becoming obsolescent or production, can have a profound effect on the economies of an operation. Again, in many cases of these and other types, prevention is always better than disposal.

■ Managing disposal

Space does not permit full treatment of this subject for the variety of types of material which need to be disposed of is extremely wide. However, there are some useful points which apply in many cases and which should be noted.

When considering how to dispose of scrap materials, questions to be considered might be:

- Can we dispose of material within the business (or group)?
- Can the item be cannibalised for useful parts prior to scrapping?
- Can we sell the items in the marketplace rather than scrap (e.g. back to supplier if redundant stock)?
- If we are to sell material as scrap, can we get a better price if we segregate by type or size or by bailing into cube form or cutting to smaller sizes?
- Can we come to an agreement with a merchant whereby they provide skips/containers for housing the scrap prior to collection?

Clearly the costs associated with disposing of materials need to be kept in mind when examining the issues involved. It makes no sense to install some sophisticated scrap system if the cost of doing so is greater than the money received. Usually effective negotiation with a bona fide scrap dealer can provide the buyer with useful guidelines within which to operate.

It is extremely important to ensure that the control systems associated with scrap disposal are clear and watertight. As a principle it is far better not to become involved in ready cash transactions. While converting the scrap into cash in the business as quickly as possible is a sensible requirement, scrap disposal services are not always offered by bona fide businesses. Where cash payment is an acceptable alternative for some reason, it is important that the system ensures that checks on what passes to the merchant and what cash is paid in return are properly documented. Where valuable scrap (e.g. gold, silver, platinum) is involved, security arrangements have to be made to a higher degree than would be the case with other materials.

Finally, it is essential that buyers who are concerned with the disposal of significant amounts of scrap or waste material should keep in touch with market trends. Scrap prices fluctuate as do the prices of materials from which the waste arises.

Mini case study – Cummins Engines

Cummins Engines agrees targets with suppliers in the areas of quality, component cost and administration. Annually, each supplier makes a formal presentation to Cummins indicating its progress towards, or achievement of, the targets.

Summary

1 The chapter discusses the relative importance of post-contract, contract management, service level agreements and key performance indicators.

2 At the lowest level of development, purchasing is often a clerical function, using an adversarial approach to sourcing. Price is the major decision factor between competitors, which are changed regularly. At the highest level, procurement is recognised as a strategic business function, playing a vital part in the adoption of world-class concepts.

3 The higher the degree of procurement development, the greater the extent of measuring performance. Measurement leads to recognition of the function; sets targets and establishes ground rules from which policies can be formed.

4 The role of procurement may be seen as that of the intelligent customer.

5 Benchmarking aims to discover 'best practice' wherever it might be found. The idea is to identify key characteristics of best practice and adopt them.

6 Budgets are derived from objectives such as required return on investment (ROI). A figure is given which is the estimated expenditure required to meet the desired ROI. This budget figure is then used as a control comparing actual expenditure with projected. If necessary, corrective action can be taken.

7 Redundant stock, scrap or waste is a cost to an organisation. The most effective way to reduce it is to avoid the production of waste. Waste occurs through obsolescence, theft, poor storage conditions, damage in transit. With careful management, it can be disposed of profitably!

References and further reading

Anderson, G (1992), *The Handbook of Human Resource Management*, Oxford: Blackwell.

Belbin, R M (1997), *Team Roles at Work*, Oxford: Butterworth-Heinemann.

Bradley, A (2006), 'Clause and effect', *Supply Management*.

Chartered Institute of Purchasing and Supply (1995), Education Scheme.

'Contract Management – Positions on Practice' (2003), CIPS Professional Resources, CIPS website.

Desai, J (2004), 'Performance tests', *Supply Management*, September.

Drake, M (1999), 'Signed and Sealed', 'Supply Management, March.

Finn, W (2000), 'A fresh approach', Supply Management, May.

Gelderman, C J and Van Weel, A J (2003), 'Handling measurement issues and strategic directions in Kraljic Purchasing Portfolio model', Journal of Purchasing and Supply Management, 9(5–6).

Griffin, N S (2003), 'Personalize your management development', Harvard Business Review, March.

Gunasekara, A, Patel, C and Tirtiroglu, E (2001), 'Performance measures and metrics in a supply chain environment', International Journal of Operations and Production Management, 21.

Harrison, N (2001), Improving Employee Performance, London: Kogan Page.

Holmberg, S (2000), 'A systems perspective on supply chain measurements', International Journal of Physical Distribution and Logistics Management, 30 (10).

Landsberg, M (2000), The Tools of Leadership – Vision, Inspiration, London: HarperCollins Business.

Likierman, A (2005), 'Performance measurement: measurably better', Supply Management, July.

Milward, A (2002), 'The talent trap', Supply Management, October.

Pearson, D (1995), 'Contractual management of risk', Purchasing and Supply Management, November.

Purchasing and Supply Lead Body (1997), NVQ and SVQ Qualifications framework, Stamford.

Rana, E (2003), 'Up close and personnel', Supply Management, January.

Simon, H A (1996), The Sciences of the Artificial, Cambridge, MA: MIT Press.

Smith, D (1992), 'Purchasing's contribution to company environmental performance', Purchasing and Supply Management, July.

Whitehead, M (2003), 'Killer solutions – fact or fiction?' Supply Management, February.

Van Weel, A J (1985), 'New concepts in measuring purchasing performances', Journal of Purchasing and Materials Management.

Index

@UK PLC 400, 406–7, 410

80/20 relationship 62
90/10 relationship 62

ABC analysis 356
accelerated
    negotiated procedure 104–5
    restricted procedure 104
Accenture 125
acceptability 50
accountability 85–6, 92
accreditation 149, 152
acquisition cost, total 17–22, 238–9
acquisitions, complexity of 367–8
activities, problems associated with 37–8
actual cost of work performed (ACWP) 279
add ons 262
administration instructions 280–4, 434–5
advertisements 102
advertising services, buying 369
Africa 325
agency selection 369
agents 205
aggregation rules 101–2
agile supply 76
agreement stage 263
aircraft 22, 23
Alcan 295
Alcoa 295
alternatives 194
aluminium 295
analysis 236–9
    stock and sales 355–7
Ansoff Matrix 48, 49
Antill, P.D. 90
appraisal 46, 150–1, 204, 107
    costs 154
approved lists 204
arbitrage 308
arbitration 322–3
Ariba Study 8
arrow diagram 287–8, 289
Asda 350 319, 352, 381
asset specificity 215
assortment 355
attributes 132–4
    of good supplier 199–200
auctions 234
    electronic 109, 407
    reverse 398–9
authority 262
award recognition levels 152, 153

BAA 282–3
backwardation 308
BAE 13
balanced scorecard approach 419
balancing 163, 173–4, 180
bar charts 288, 290, 291
bar-coding 352
Barclays Bank 22, 380
bargaining 262, 266–7

barter trade 327
basis 308
batch
    producers 171
    and queue 187
Baxi 13
bear 308
bear market 308
Behan, P. 86
benchmarking 9, 431–3
Benetton 183
Benmaridja, A. 127
Benmaridja, M. 127
Berger, A.J. 395
best alternative to a negotiated agreement (BATNA)
        258–60
best practice
    drivers 118
    outsourcing 121
    in strategic supply management 32
    team approach 117–18
BHS 357
bills of material 172
blanket orders 163
BMW 14–15
BOC Group 11, 380, 385
body language 267–8
Body Shop, The 212
booking orders 163
Boots 119
Boston Consulting Group 46–7
Boyce, E. 92–6
BP 409
brands 357–8, 359
break-even chart 231
British Aerospace 326
British Airways 140, 371, 379, 420
British Electrical and Allied Manufacturers Association 241,
        242–3, 339
    CPA Advisory Service 242
British Standard
    BS 5750 146–7
    BS 6000 151
    BS 6001 151
    BS 7750 79
    BS EN ISO 9000 147–9, 151
    BS EN ISO 9001 147
    BS EN ISO 9002 147
    BS EN ISO 9003 147
British Standards Institution 132, 146, 147, 149
broker 308
BSkyB 379
BT 374, 380
budgeted cost of work performed (BCWP) 279
budgeted cost of work scheduled (BCWS) 270
bull 308
bull market 308
bundled bid 408
Burt, D. 127
business strategy 40
buy-back, compensation with 328
buy-in 424

buyers 205, 228
  hedge 301
  obtaining prices 233–4
  power 45–6
buying
  price 17
  responsible 383
  techniques 302–4

CADMID cycle 96
call option 307, 308
Canada 320
capacity booking orders 163
capital equipment, acquisition of 331–3
capital items, definition of 333–4
capital procurement 331–48
  capital equipment, acquisition of 331–3
  capital items, definition of 333–4
  decisions 335
  investment appraisal 341–2
  investment appraisal criteria 342–7
  leasing and hiring 334–5
  lifetime costs 340
  project approach 338–40
  requisitions 335–6
  specification 336–8
captive supplier 213
car industry 20, 57
  see also under names of manufacturers
Cardiff Business School 181
Carlisle, J. 251, 252, 253–4, 260, 263
carriage insurance paid (to named place) (CIP) 322, 380–1, 419
carriage paid to (named place) (CPT) 321
cartels 219
cash
  cow 47
  drain 47
  flow 187
  net cash 30 days 316
  provider 47
  see also discounted cash flow
cash-to-cash cycle time (C2C) 190
catalogue library 204
category management 41, 61
central customer 94
central purchasing bodies (CPB) 109
centralisation 58–61
Centre for Effective Dispute Resolution 424
Centre for Procurement Performance (CPP) 409–10
Centrica 13
certification 150
Chartered Institute of Purchasing and Supply 10, 37, 66, 233
  Ethical Code 77–9
  Supply Management 296
charts 105, 106, 231, 277, 288, 290, 291
cherry picking 408
China 302
Christopher, M. 186
citibank 119
Civil Service departments 115–16, 375
co-makership 202
co-operation 264–7
Co-operative Group 350, 383
coal industry 57
cocoa 295
Code of Conduct 78
coercion 249
coffee 295
collaboration 181
colleagues 205
collective approaches 425
Colombia 295
commercial focus 26, 28
commission 308
commodities procurement 294–309
  buying techniques 302–4
  hedging with futures contracts 300–2
  indifference prices 304–7
  price fluctuations 296–8

price stabilisation schemes 298–9
principal commodities 295–6
speculator, role of 299–300
traded options 307–8
Commodity Exchange (COMEX) 295, 296
communication problems 315
company buy-in 424
compensation
  with buy-back 328
  full 328
competition 92, 186–7, 226–8, 264–7
  procurement cycle for goods and services 97
  within the industry 47–8
Competition Act (1980) 227
competitive dialogue 108–9
competitor activity 9
compliance, corporate social responsibility and 382–3
computer aided design 404
concentration in supply markets 204
concept of strategy 38–9
concurrent engineering 145
Confederation of British Industry 220
conferring 265–6
confirmed irrevocable credit 317
conformance
  quality 132
  specifications 140–1
consecutive engineering 145
contango 308
Continuous Replenishment (CRP) 360
contract 163, 215–16
  arrangements 366–7
  award 107
  award notices 102
  branch 93
  futures 163, 300–2
  incentive 241
  issues 257
  major 239–43
  negotiation 369
  notices, individual 102
  period 163
  price adjustment clauses 242, 243
  pricing mechanisms 107–8
  public supply 100
  public works 100
  spot 163
  subsidised works 100
  work 100
  work concessions 100
contract management
  benefits 420
  definition 419
  responsibility for 420–1
contractual relationships 119
contribution of purchasing 332
control 354
convergence 71–3
copper 295
Cores 148
corporate citizenship 380
corporate social responsibility (CSR) 378–89
  best practice 382
  business drivers 384–6
  CIPS and 380–1
  compliance 382–3
  corporations' meaning 379–80
  definition 379
  hierarchy of responsibilities 379
  public accountability 381–4
  responsible buying 383
Corporate Social Responsibility Academy 385
corporate strategy 40
cost
  acquisition 17–22, 239
  analysis 236–9
  appraisal 154
  expected 278
  external failure 154

cost (*continued*)
  and freight 320, 321, 323
  insurance and freight 320, 321, 323
  least cost algorithm 180
  lifetime 340
  minimal 181
  operational 429
  of ownership, total 17–22
  prevention 154
  procurement-acquisition 239
  production 228–32
  reductions analysis 52
  strategic acquisition 239
  variance 279
  see also price
cotton 295
counter purchase and offset 329
countertrade 326–9
Courts UK plc 319
Cox, A. 122
credit, letters of 317–18
credits 424
critical path analysis 277, 286–90
criticality 190, 194
Crosby, P.B. 136, 137
cultural fit 211
culture change, professional 95–6
Cummins Engines 437
currency differences 316
current agreement 256
Currys 357
customer
  central 94
  demands 9
  second 95
customisation 182–4
customs 325–6
cycle time 187

DaimlerChrysler 234
damages 195–6
deadlines 262
decentralisation 58–61
decision-making *see* source decision-making
Declaration on Fundamental Principles and Rights at Work
  (ILO) 381
defects 156
defence acquisition environment 91–2
Defence Logistics Organisation 91
Defence Procurement Agency 91
delivered
  at frontier (named place) 322
  duty paid (named place) 320, 322
  duty unpaid (named place) 320, 322
  ex quay 322
  ex ship 322
delivery
  issues 256
  on-time 187–90
  performance 189
Dell 388
demand 226
Deming, W.E. 132, 136, 137
Department for Employment and Skills 206
Department of Trade and Industry 149, 220, 385, 415
department structure
  medium-sized 63
  small 62
departmental organisation 62–3
design contests 100
design failure mode and effect analysis 139
design innovation 213
Deutsche Telekom 13
development of strategy 38–9
  see also scope and development
devolution 7, 65–6
DHL 88
Diageo 312–13, 381
Direct Marketing Association 373

discount 234–6
  factors 343
  rate 346–7
  special 236
  supplier 235
discounted cash flow 341, 346, 347
discussion stage 261–3
disposal of redundant goods 435–7
distribution 354
  resource planning 176–7
distributive industry 57
distributor 213–14
divergence 71–3
Dixons 119
do-or-buy option 366
documentary letters of credit 317–18
documents
  against acceptance 317
  against payment 317
dogs 47
DRP 36
dynamic purchasing systems (DPS) 109, 397

E.ON UK 17
e-analysis 395
e-auctions 407–15
  awareness of 410–11
  benefits to buyers 410–11, 412
  enablers and inhibitors 412–13
  motivation 411
  success criteria 411–12, 414
  supplier adoption 413
  supplier management initiatives 412
  types 407–9
e-commerce 11, 359
e-communications 109
e-intelligence 395, 401
e-ordering 395
e-payment 394
e-procurement 393–416
  application 399
  benefits 396–7, 400, 405
  business case for 404
  complex 398
  cost 404
  current spend metric 405
  current state 401–2
  definition 393–5
  measuring benefits 405–6
  obstacles to 403, 404–5
  reverse auctions 398–9
  tools 104
e-requisitioning 395
e-sourcing 394–5
earned value 278–80
economic order quantities 163, 165–9, 173, 180
  formulae 166–7
  price breaks and quantity discounts 168–9
  stock-turn rate 167–8
economy 90, 108
education sector 22
Edwards, J.D. 177
effectiveness 90, 108
efficiency 90, 108
efficient consumer response (ECR) 359–62
  barriers to implementation 360
  definition 359–60
  grocery supply chain 361
  implementation issues 360–1
  key requisites 361
  savings 362
electricity 22
electronic auctions 109, 407
electronic data interchange 210, 353, 433, 360
electronic point of sale 352–3, 359, 360
electronic reverse auctions (ERAs) 407–9
emergent approach 42
EMI 312–13
empowerment 397

empty larder 262
end product 61
engineering 145
enterprise resource planning 36–7, 177
enterprise resource systems 404
environment/environmental
    awareness 9
    defence acquisition 91–2
    procurement 79–80
environmental awareness 9
eRFX 401
escalation 242–3
ethical behaviour 78–9
ethical investment 384
Ethical Trading Initiative (ETI) 380, 381, 383, 387, 389
Europe 21
    international purchasing 326
    price and cost 234
    quantity 180
    scope and development 21
    source decision-making 217, 219
    see also European Union
European Commission 99
European Committee for Standardization 146
European Court of Justice 99
European Directives 214
    92/50/EEC 374
    Community Public Contracts 374–5
    Electronic Commerce Regulations 2002 415
    procurement 98–100, 107
    public sector 2004/18/EC 108
    utilities 2004/17/EC 108
European Standard EN 29000 147
European Union
    competition procurement cycle for goods and services 97, 98
    international purchasing 316, 325
    Official Publications Office 102
    price and cost 227
    procurement directives 98–100
    procurement law, origins of 98–9
    quality 146
    source decision-making 215
Eutilia 234
evaluation, agency 369
evaluation criteria 107
Evans, E. 127
evolution 7
Ex Works 320, 323
exchanging 15
exhibitions 205
expected costs 278
expediting 193–5
expenditure 10
experience curves 46, 244–6
external advice 424
extractive industries 57
eyeballing 356

failure
    costs, external 154
    costs, internal 154
    mode and effect analysis 139–40
Fair Trading Act (1973) 227
Fairtrade 387, 388, 389
feasibility 50
feedback loops 135
Feedwater 14
Feigenbaum, A.V. 136
final stage 250
financial presentations 372–3
financial issues 257
    see also cash; cost; payment; price
finite resources 10
Fire Service 22
Fisher, R. 157, 259, 266–7
five forces model 44–5, 48
Flextronics 117
flow 69, 187
    chart 105, 106

of goods 38
principal 69, 70
production 57
focus area 26, 28
force majeure 196
Ford 5, 8, 13, 58, 148, 428
forecasting 170–1
forwardation 308
framework agreements 109
frameworks 181
    evolution 25–6
France 295, 302, 322
free
    alongside ship 321
    on board 320, 321, 323
    carrier (named place) 321
    into store 320
FTSE4GOOD 382
Fujitsu 13
full compensation 328
futures contracts 163, 300–2

Galetto, F.F. 124
Gantt chart 277, 288, 291
Gap 381
gas oil 295
Gattorna, J. 395
General Agreement on Tariffs and Trade see World Trade Organization
general issues 257–8
General Motors 58, 154, 179, 234
General Procurement Agreement 99
generic brands 358
generic strategies 48–9
geographical location 214–15
George, Dudley 410
Germany 316
Gershon, Peter 85
Ghana 295
giving in 249
GlaxoSmithKline 8
global sourcing (procurement) 310–30
    definition 310–11, 312
Global Spend Agenda 2006 8
gold 296
goods
    competition procurement cycle for 97–8
    flow 38
Goods and Services Act (1982) 376
Goodyear 124
grains 296
Guide to Good Practice 78

Hahn, C.K. 178, 180
Hamel, G. 116
hedging with futures contracts 300–2
Hertz 4
Hewlett Packard 13, 79
hierarchy 51
higher authority, approval from 262
hiring 334–5
HMPS 421
Hong Kong 295
Hotpoint 357
House, M. 136
Hughes, J. 73, 75
hygiene factors 421

IBM 8, 11, 13, 21–2, 40, 51, 79, 239, 414
IKEA 204
implementation 157
    plan 51
importing 323
improvement, continuous 181
in-house journals, leaflets and literature 372
incentive contracts 241
Incorporated Society of British Advertisers 371, 373
Incoterms 2000 320–2
indifference prices 304–7
individual contract notices 102

information 433
  collection 255–8
  stage 157
innovation 11, 213
inspectability 366
Institute of Business Ethics 385
Institute of Development Studies (IDS) 381
Institute of Practitioners in Advertising 373
integrated project team 94, 95, 96–7
internal rate of return 346
International Chamber of Commerce 320, 322
International Labour Organization 380, 387, 388, 389
International Organization for Standardization 146, 147
  ISO 9000 204
  ISO 14001/2 79
  see also under British Standard
International Petroleum Exchange (IPE) 295
international procurement 310–30
  arbitration 322–3
  changing 323–5
  communication problems 315
  countertrade 326–9
  currency differences 316
  customs 325–6
  definition 311–12
  importing 323
  Incoterms 2000 320–2
  legal systems, differing 318–19
  payment 316–17
  reasons to source internationally 313–14
  transport 325
International Purchasing and Supply Education and
    Research Association 127
intra-company purchases 218
intra-group buying 77
introductory stage 260–1
inventory
  levels 19
  management 162–84
  unnecessary 155
  as waste 164–5
investigation phase 157
investment
  appraisal 243–4, 341–2
  criteria 342–7
irrevocable letter 317
ISO14000 387
ISO14001 388
Ivory Coast 295

Japan 20, 84, 316
  quality 137, 154
  source decision-making 217, 220
job shops 171
Jones, D. 71
Jones, D.M. 25, 29, 31, 71
Jones, D.T. 132
Jones, M. 127
Juran, J-M. 132
just-in-time 73, 76, 84, 177–80, 210, 357, 360

Kaiser 295
kaizen 20
kanban system 178
Karrass, C.L. 254, 258
Kearney, A T 402
Kellogg's 119, 358
Kennedy, G. 248, 253, 263
key performance indicators (KPIs) 117, 126, 424
Keynes, J.M. 347
Kincaid 90
Kodak 152, 153
Kotler, P. 9
Kraljic, P. 16
Kraljic Procurement Targeting Tool 398
Kyoryoku Kai 217

labour 10
Laing Construction Group 220
Laing Homes 220

large single-factory enterprise 64
late customisation 182–4
lead 296
lead time 188, 190–3
  examination 192
  supply 191
  variability 192–3
leading-edge concepts 9
lean supply 360
lean thinking 155
learning curves 244–6
leasing 334–5
least acceptable agreement 260
least cost algorithm 180
Leeds Teaching Hospital 402
legal services, buying 373–4
legal systems, differing 318–19
letters of credit 317
levels of strategy 40
Levene, Sir Peter 92
Lexcel mark 373
lifetime costs 340
liquidated damages 195–6
lists 204
logistics 355
  management 65, 425
  resources planning 177
London Borough of Lewisham 403–4
London Chamber of Commerce and Industry 323
London Court of Arbitration 322
London Heathrow Airport 282–3
London Metal Exchange 295, 296, 301
Long, B. 26, 27
Lonsdale, C. 122
Lucas Engineering and Systems 160
Lynch, R. 38, 41, 42, 51

maintenance, repair and operations (MRO) goods 214, 233,
    401
make-or-buy decisions 158–60
Malaysia 302, 319
  Rubber Exchange 296
management
  level 36
  reporting 433–4
  in service provision 375–6
manipulative techniques and ploys 263
manufacturing
  company 65
  major 57
manufacturing resource planning 65, 175–6, 177, 178, 360
market
  considerations 20
  structure 213, 218–19
market testing 119
Marketing Communications Consultants Association 373
marketing literature 372–3
marketing services, buying 369
Marks, S. 357
Marks & Spencer 148, 349, 350, 355, 357, 358, 359, 381,
    383, 387
Marsh, P.D.V. 196
master production schedule 171, 172
material/materials
  administration 65, 425
  classification 61
  management 65, 425
  requirement planning 36, 171–5
matrix analysis 46
McIvor, R. 122, 123
measurement criteria 426–7
medium-sized
  department structure 63
  manufacturing company 65
meeting phase 250
merchandise planning 354–5
Mexico 302
Michels, B. 73
Middle East 325
milk round principle 179, 180

minimal cost 181
Ministry of Defence 90–7, 204, 219
mission statement 38, 39, 40–1
Mitel 158
model stock plans 355
Monopolies and Restrictive Practices Acts (1948, 1956
    and 1964) 227
monopoly 219
monopsony 219
Moore, D.M. 90
Moore, N. 336
most desired outcome 260
most favoured position 260
motions, unnecessary 155
multi-meeting 251
multidimensional quality analysis 133
multinational organisations 58
mutual relationship 16

NASA 157
National Accreditation Council for Certification Bodies 149
National Accreditation Mark of Certification Bodies 148
National Audit Office 85, 92
National eProcurement Project (NEPP) 406
National Health Service 22, 85, 88–9, 227, 395, 396
NatWest 13
Negotiate plc 262
negotiated agreement, best alternative to 258–60
negotiated procedure 103, 104
    accelerated 104
    with prior publication of procedure notice 106
    without prior publication of procedure notice 106
    without prior publication of tender notice 105
negotiations 248–70
    agreement stage 263
    alternatives to 249–50
    body language 267–8
    competition and co-operation 264–7
    contract 369
    discussion stage 261–3
    introductory stage 260–1
    mix 268–9
    post-negotiation stage 263–4
    preparation 252–60
        features of 253–5
        information collection 255–8
        issues 260
    skills 251–2
    strategies 268
    three phases 250–1
Nestlé Research Centre 302
net cash 30 days 316
net monthly account terms 316
net present value 341, 346
Netherlands 51, 201, 202, 234
    Eindhoven University 127
network analysis 286–91
network planning 277
network sourcing 69
New York Mineral Exchange (NYMEX) 295
nice guy/hard guy 262
nickel 296
Nielsen Media Research 144
Nielsen, P. 351
Nike 56
Nissan 13, 20
Nokia 4, 8
non-governmental organisations (NGOs) 381
non-manufacturing organisations 22
notices 102
Nuffield, Lord 219

O₂ 385–6, 421
objectives for purchasing 51
off-line control of quality 136–9
Office of Fair Trading 219, 415
Office of Government Commerce 85
Office of Official Publications of the European Communities 375
Official Journal of the European Comm unities 100, 102, 104, 105

Official Journal of the Economic Union (OJEU) 397, 398
Official Publications Office 102
offset, counter purchase and 329
Ohno, T. 155–6
oil industry 57
oligopoly 219
on-time delivery 187–90
open procedure 103
open-to-buy 163
opening statements 261
Operation Requirements branch 93
operational performance metrics 422
operational costs 429
operational decisions 158–60
operational level 36
operational strategy 40
Oracle 177, 402
Orbys 118
order quantities and stock control 163–71
    control, approaches to 165
    economic order quantities 165–9
    forecasting 170–1
    inventory (STOCK) as waste 164–5
    other methods 169–70
order quantities for production 171
    manufacturing resource planning 175–6
    materials requirements planning 171–5
orders 163
order-up-to systems 163
organisation
    expediting work 194
    function 61
    promoting trade 205
    structure 38
organisational expenditure 10
organisational factors
    external 9–11
    internal 11–12
organisational requirement 367, 431
original equipment maker 222
outsourcing 115–29
    contract management skills 118–19
    contractual relationships 119
    contributors to success 118
    key contractual elements 121–2
    methodologies 122–4
    pitfalls 125–8
    process 122
    procurement as candidate for 127–8
    purchasing activity 30–1
    reason for 118–19
Outsourcing Institute 115
overheads 10
overproduction 155
ownership, total cost of 238–9

Palaneeswaran 87
Palgrave Brown 220
paradigm change 39
Pareto analysis 356
Pareto Principle 62
part-periods balancing 163, 173–4, 180
partnership 219–21
    sourcing 220
passing off 359
past performance 150
payment 316–17
    prompt 234–5
Peoplesoft 177
perceived value 232–3
performance
    quality 132
    specifications 140
performance metrics/measurement 12
    administration instructions 434–5
    benchmarking in procurement and supply 431–3
    effectiveness 423–5
    examples of 421–2
    management, reporting to 433–4

performance metrics/measurement (*continued*)
 measurement areas 428–30
 measurement criteria 426–7
 pitfalls 422–3
 procurement as intelligent customer 430–1
 procurement measurement 425–30
 reason for 427–8
 redundant stock, scrap or waste, disposal of 435–7
 reporting to management 433–4
period contracts 163
personnel factors 256, 257
persuasion 249
PERT/COST 291
PERT/TIME 291
PEST analysis 43–4
Pfizer 8
Philippines 302
Philips 202
physical distribution management 65, 425
Pignatelli, A. 124
pipeline management 69
pitch 371
ploys 262
police procurement 400–1
Porter, M. 44–5, 48
portfolio analysis 46–7
positional bargaining 266–7
positive emphasis 261
positive sum 265–6
possibility, ranges of 254
post-negotiation phase 250, 251, 263–4
postures, interpretation of 268
potential suppliers, information sources on 204–5
power 45–6
Powerlink 415
Prahalad, C.K. 116
pre-information notices 102
pre-negotiation phase 250
premium 308
preparatory stage 250
present value 341, 343–6
prevention costs 154
price 429
 adjustment calculation 244
 analysis 236–9
 breaks 168–9
 buying 17
 and cost 225–46
  analysis 236–9
  auctions 234
  buyers obtaining prices 233–4
  competition 226–8
  contracts, major 239–43
  discounts 234–6
  investigation tools 238
  investment appraisal 243–4
  learning curves and experience curves 244–6
  perceived value 232–3
  product life cycle 228
  production cost 228–32
  supply and demand 226
 /cost iceberg 18
 effect 212–13
 fluctuations 296–8
 indifferent 304–7
 mechanism 226
 rings 219
 stabilisation schemes 298–9
Primark 381
primary supply chain 66
principal flows 69, 70
principled bargaining 266–7
Prison Service 22
proactive purchasing 12–15
proactivity focus 26, 28
problem solving 249
procedure notice 106
process failure mode and effects analysis 139–40
process industry 57

processing, inappropriate 155
procurement-acquisition cost 239
procurement cycle 97–8
procurement element 91
procurement positioning 16–17
product 141, 431
 development 20–2
 evaluation 151–2
 life cycle 44, 228, 229
 portfolio matrix 47
product data management (PDM) software 404
production
 continuous 171
 cost 228–32
productivity 384
professionalism 87–8
profit centre 61
project
 administration instructions 280–4
 approach 338–40
 common elements 276–7
 control 277–84
 definition 275
 management via earned value 278–80
 organisation 171
 planning 277–8
 procurement 275–93
 team, integrated 94, 95, 96–7
prompt date 308
provider appraisal 107
provision 367
provisioning systems 162–3
public accountability 85–6, 92, 381–4
public procurement 397–8
Public Relations Consultants Association (PRCA) 373
public relations procurement 371–3
public sector procurement 58, 84–110
 accelerated negotiated procedure 104–5
 accelerated restricted procedure 104
 advertisements 102
 aggregation rules 101–2
 context 84
 contract award 107
 contract pricing mechanisms 107–8
 defence acquisition environment 91–2
 emphasis and approach 92
 European Union 97
 European Union competition procurement cycle for goods
   and services 97–8
 European Union procurement directives 98–100
 evaluation criteria 107
 general principles 86
 historic background 84–8
 integrated project team 96–7
 Ministry of Defence 90–7
 negotiated procedure 104
 negotiated procedure without prior publication of tender
   notice 105
 new approach 93–4
 new developments 108–9
 'old' approach, failures of 92–3
 open procedure 103
 professional culture change 95–6
 professionalism 87–8
 public accountability 85–6
 public supply, services and works contracts, definitions of 100
 restricted procedure 104
 smart procurement/acquisition 94–5
 technical standards and specifications 105–7
 tensions 87
 thresholds 101
 value for money 87
Public Sector Procurement Regulations 98
public supply 100
 contracts 100
public works contracts 100
Public Works Regulations 100
pull 187
punctuality 261

purchase function 36
purchased goods, level and percentages of 12
purchasing
   changing role 8–12
   cycle 6–7
   development 24–32
      focus, area of 26, 28
      frameworks, evolution of 25–6
      matrix 29
      measurement 25
      outsourcing purchasing activity 30–1
      purchasing profile analysis 26–30
      stages 31
   devolution 7, 65–6
   evolution 7
   organisation structure 63–5
   profile analysis 26–30
   and supply chain process model 67–8
   within a group 77
purchasing, scope of 4–8
put option 307, 308

quadratic loss function 137, 138
'Quality First' supplier programme 153
quality improvements 384
quality management 131–61, 429
   assurance 134
   circles 154–5
   concurrent engineering 145
   conformance 132
   control 134
   cost changes over time 153
   definition 132–4
   early supplier involvement 143–4
   economics 153–4
   failure mode and effect analysis 139–40
   multidimensional quality analysis 133
   performance 132
   seven wastes 155–6
   specification 140–3
   standardisation 145–9
   statistical process control 134–6
   supplier assessment 150–2
   Taguchi methods for off-line control of quality 136–9
   value analysis/value engineering 156–7
   see also total quality management
quantity 19–20, 162–84, 235, 429
   discounts 168–9
   distribution resource planning 175–6
   enterprise resource planning 177
   just-in-time 177–80
   late customisation 182–4
   order quantities for production 171
   order quantities and stock control 163–71
   provisioning systems 162–3
   vendor managed inventory 180–2
   see also economic order quantities; order quantities
      for production; order quantities and stock
      control
question mark 47
quick response 360
Quinn, I.E. 38

Rackham, N. 251, 252, 253–4, 260, 263
Railtrack 219
railways 22
Ralf, M. 73
Rank Xerox 51, 201
rate of return 346
recipe change 39
reciprocity 216–17
Reck, R.F. 26, 27
Reckitt and Colman 176
recorded performance 204
relationships
   changing nature 14–15
   right 210–12
representatives 204
reputation 150, 204

reputational management 384
requirement profiles 167
requisitions 335–6
resources
   appraisal 46
   finite 10
responsibility buying 383
responsiveness 214
restricted procedure 104
restrictive practices 219
retail outlets 359
retail procurement 57, 349–62, 368
   brands 357–8
   developments 359
   efficient consumer response (ECR) 359–62
   electronic point of sale 352–3, 359, 360
   merchandise planning 354–5
   research 351
   stock analysis and sales analysis 355–7
   supply chains and 351–2
   supply chains in retailing 351–2
reverse auctions 398–9
   electronic 407
revocable letter of credit 317
Reynolds 295
Rio principles on Environment and Development 381
risk 384
risk management 434
risk priority number 139
RMC 116
Roadchef Motorway Services 128
role of purchasing 332
Rover 148
RS Components 214
rubber 296
Russell, T. 144
Russia 157
Russian front 262

SA8000 389
Sainsbury's 350, 352, 355
Samuelson, P. 347
SAP 177
schedule variance 279
Scheuing, E. 6
scope and development 3–32
   best practice in strategic supply management 32
   external organisational factors 9–11
   internal organisational factors 11–12
   non-manufacturing organisations 22
   proactive purchasing 12–16
   procurement positioning 16–17
   purchasing cycle 6–7
   purchasing development 24–32
   service activity 7
   supply chain concept 23–4
   total acquisition cost and total cost of ownership 17–22
scorecard auction 408
Scottish Parliament 281
Scottish Power 234
screening options 50
Second Party Certification 148
Secretary of State 149
security of supply 213
selection, agency 369
self-help 217
Selfridges 119
service
   cycle 370
   industries 57–8
   provider's bid 107
   provision, management in 375–6
   requirements 424
Service Level Agreement (SLA) 117, 120, 423, 424
services
   competition procurement cycle for 97–8
   definition 100
   level and percentages 12
   see also services procurement

services procurement 364–77
  acquisitions, complexity of 367–8
  contractual arrangements 366–7
  definition 365
  do or buy 366
  European Community Public Contracts Directive 374–5
  inspectability 366
  service provision 368–9
  prerequisites for success 370
  provision 367
  resale 368
  storage, impracticability of 365–6
  variability 368
Setting New Standards: A Strategy for Government Procurement (White Paper) 84
seven wastes 155–6
shareholder pressure 384
sharing 15
Shell 58, 79, 413
short 308
silver 296
Simon, Herb 424
Singapore 319
single-factory enterprise 64
single meeting 251
single-product organisations, small 56
Sitar, C.P. 85
skills 251–2
small and medium enterprises 413
Smart Acquisition 94–5
Smart Procurement Initiative *see* Smart Acquisition
Social Accounting 8000 (SA8000) 386–7
socially responsible procurement, business drivers for 384–5
soft drink can 71, 72
Sony 58
source decision-making 198–224
  attributes of good supplier 199–200
  captive supplier 213
  contract 215–16
  decisions 200–3
  distributor 213–14
  geographical location 214–15
  information sources on potential suppliers 204–5
  intra-company purchases 218
  market structure 218–19
  nature of 198–9
  one or more suppliers 210–12
  price rings, cartels and restrictive practices 219
  reciprocity 216–17
  right relationship 210–12
  source location 203–4
  sourcing, different types of 200
  sourcing process 203
  supplier associations 217
  supplier evaluation 205–10
  tiering of suppliers 221–3
sourcing services 204
South America 326
soya beans 296
Spar 350
specialisation 204
specification 19, 140–1, 336–8
  element 91
  issues 256
  performance 140
  production 141–3
  quality 140–1
Spector, B.I. 252
speculation phase 157
speculator, role of 299–300
spot contracts 163
squirrel stores 183
standardisation 145–9
Stannack, P. 127
star 46–7
statistical process control 134–6
status 235–6
Stevens, John 311

stock
  analysis 355–7
  control *see* order quantities and stock control
  -turn rate 168, 169
stockholder 214
stockist 214
storage, impracticability of 365–6
strategic
  acquisition cost 239
  analysis 42–8
    competition within the industry 47–8
    Porter's five forces 44–5
    portfolio analysis 46–7
    product life cycle analysis 44
    resource appraisal 46
    substitutes, threat of 46
    suppliers and buyers, power of 45–6
  choice 42
  development 48–50, 73–80
  evaluation 50
  implementation 50
  input management 74–7
  level 36
  management 42
  procurement 36–66
    category management 41
    concept of strategy 38–9
    growth in strategic role 36–7
    levels of strategy 40
    mission statement 39
    objectives for purchasing 51
    problems associated with activities and value 37–8
    strategic analysis 42–8
    strategic development 48–50
    strategic management 42
    strategies and their scope 51–2
    strategy implementation 50
    strategy selection 52–4
    supply-market strategies, effective 54–6
  selection 50
  Strategic Defence Review 90, 92
  supply management 32
strategic performance metrics 421
strategy
  decisions 55
  development framework 53
  implementation 50–1
  negotiations 268
  required 41
  and scope 51–2
  selection 52–4
structural change 12
subcontracting 284–6
  see also make-or-buy decisions
subcontractor selection 284–6
subsidised works contracts 100
substitutes, threat of 46
success, prerequisites for 370
suitability 50
supplier management initiatives 412
suppliers 189, 228, 431
  assessment 150–2
  associations 217
  attributes 199–200
  captive 213
  discounts 234–6
  evaluation 205–10
  expediting 194
  involvement, early 143–4
  motivation 213
  potential 204–5
  power 45–6
  relationships 78–9
  reporting to management 433–4
  right 201–2
  or service provider appraisal 107
  or service provider's bid 107
  tiering 221–3
suppliers, larger 9

supply 226
  agile 76
  benchmarking 431–3
  changing role 8–12
  continuity 20
  markets, concentration in 204
  public 100
  security 213
  see also supply chain; supply-market strategies
supply chain 66–71
  concept 23–4
  concept in action 69–71
  efficiency 71–3
  primary and support 66
  in retailing 351–2
  strategic development of purchasing 73–80
    environmental procurement 79–80
    internal purchasing involvement 73
    intra-group buying 77
    strategic input management 74–7
  types 73, 75
  and value added ideas 66–9
supply lead time 191
Supply Management 233, 296
supply-market strategies, effective 54–6
support
  element 91
  supply chain 66
switchtrading 328
SWOT analysis 43, 47–8, 49
symbiosis 200
synergy 200
Syson, R.26, 28, 31

tactical level 36
tactical performance metrics 421–2
Taguchi, G. 136–9
target cost incentive contract arrangement 108
Taylor, Ina 409
technical/technology/technological
  advances 10, 203
  fit 212
  standards and specifications 105–7
telecom 22
Telgen, J. 85
Tenders Electronic Daily database 102
tensions 87
Tesco 349, 350, 352, 355, 357, 380, 381, 384
Texas Instruments 220
Thailand 302
Thames Valley police (TVP) 400–1
third party certification 150
thresholds 101
tiering of suppliers 221–3
Timber Research and Development Association 220
time 186–96
  competitive advantage 186–7
  liquidated damages 195–6
  on-time delivery 187–90
timing 19–20, 429
tools of analysis 43
Top Shop 381
total acquisition cost 238–9
total cost of ownership 238–9
total quality management 73, 76, 84, 134
Toyota 154, 178–9
TR Fastenings 386
trade directories 204
traded options 307–8
Trading Standards Department 415
Traidcraft 380
transactional relationship 17
transactions focus 26, 28
Transfer of Undertakings (Protection of Employment) Regulations 1981 (TUPE) 126–7
transformation reverse auction 408
transport 325

transportation, unnecessary 155
Treaty of Rome 98–9, 105p
two-bin systems 356

Union Coffee Roasters 385
Unisys 13
United Kingdom 21, 22
  Accreditation Service 148–9
  car industry 20
  commodities purchasing 296
  public sector procurement 99, 104
  international purchasing 315, 316, 318, 323, 326
  London Chamber of Commerce and Industry 323
  London Court of Arbitration 322–3
  London Metal Exchange 295, 296, 301
  Metropolitan Police 89–90
  negotiations 262
  price and cost 242
  Procurement Executive 22
  quality 146–9, 152–3, 154
  resale 351, 352
  source decision-making 214, 219, 220
  structure and organisation 62
United Nations
  Convention on the Rights of the Child 386
  Global Compact 380
  Universal Declaration of Human Rights 380–1, 385, 386
United States
  commodities purchasing 295, 296
  international purchasing 316, 318
  New York Mineral Exchange (NYMEX) 295
  quality 154, 157
  quantity 180
  retailing 351
  source decision-making 217, 220
United Utilities 234
Ury,W. 259, 266–7

value 41, 232–3, 341, 343–6
  added ideas 66–9
  analysis/value engineering 156–7
  classification 61
  may be created 265
  for money 85, 87, 90
  problems associated with 37–8
  stream 70, 71, 72
  will be shared 265
Van Weel, AJ. 427
Varetto, M. 124
variability 368
variables 132–4
variety 355
Vauxhall 234, 236
vendor
  accreditation 152
  managed inventory 180–2
virtual organisations 55–6, 127
vision statement 40
visit 150–1
Vita 117

waiting 155
Wal-Mart 382
waste 155–6, 164–5
Webb, R. 262
Wembley Stadium 282
Westfield Medical 402
willingness to oblige 213
Womack, J.P. 71, 132
work breakdown structure (WBS) 279
work concessions contracts 100
works contracts 100
World Trade Organization 99, 314

zero defects approach 137
zero sum 265–6